The Brief American Pageant

The Brief American Pageant

A HISTORY OF THE REPUBLIC

Second Edition

VOLUME I

David M. Kennedy
Stanford University

Thomas A. Bailey

Mel Piehl
Valparaiso University

D. C. Heath and Company
Lexington, Massachusetts   Toronto

Cover: Unidentified artist, *Sun River, Montana,* c. 1885, watercolor on paperboard, 6″ × 9½″. National Museum of American Art, Smithsonian Institution, gift of Herbert Waide Hemphill, Jr., and Museum Purchase, made possible by Ralph Cross Johnson.

Published simultaneously in Canada.

Printed in the United States of America.

International Standard Book Number: 0–669–17840–3

Library of Congress Catalog Card Number: 88–81497

0 9 8 7 6 5 4 3 2 1

PREFACE

The American Pageant has long enjoyed a deserved reputation as one of the most accessible, popular, and effective textbooks in the field of American history. Thomas A. Bailey gave to the book a distinctive personality that mirrored his vast learning and the sparkling classroom style that he had cultivated during his nearly four decades of teaching at Stanford University. Every page of the text captures the charm of his inventive prose, his passion for clarity, his disdain for clutter, and his mastery of the narrative form.

The Brief American Pageant, Second Edition, seeks to preserve the outstanding attributes of the parent text in a format suitable for one-semester courses in American history, as well as for courses that rely heavily on readings in primary sources or specialized monographs. Like the longer Eighth Edition from which it is drawn, it preserves the basic features that have made *The American Pageant* unique, while incorporating the rich, new scholarship in social, economic, cultural, and intellectual history that has appeared in the last generation. This edition of the text reflects the new historical emphasis on the experience of people—including women, the poor, blacks, Hispanics, and certain religious groups—who until recently were often neglected by historians. It is also shaped by the belief that the main drama and the urgent interest of American history reside in the public arena in which these and other groups contend and cooperate with one another. Public affairs, in short, form the spine of the text's account of American history.

This edition includes much new material on the history of the family from colonial times to the twentieth century; on the influence of religion in American life; on the role of ideas in the making of the Revolution, the Constitution, and the two-party system, and in the struggle for women's rights; on the effects of urbanization and suburbanization; and on the causes and consequences of immigration, old and new.

Readers will also find completely new or substantially revised chapters on seventeenth-century American society, the Jacksonian period, the growth of the market economy, slavery and abolitionism, Reconstruction, and the rise of the city in post–Civil War America. The coverage of twentieth-century American history includes a fresh discussion of the domestic and diplomatic dimensions of World War I; new material on the home front during World War II; an updated account of the origins of the Cold War; and a substantial reworking of the entire post-1945 portion of the text.

Most of the "Varying Viewpoints" essays have been substantially revised to reflect recent scholarship and to better stimulate classroom discussion. The end-of-chapter bibliographies include an added subsection recommending primary-source documents for further study. An expanded appendix features tables and graphs with valuable information on American social and economic history.

This *Brief American Pageant,* Second Edition, presents the subject of American history in an engaging and lively way, without distorting the sober reality of the past. Brevity, Shakespeare noted, is the soul of wit. Though condensed, this edition seeks to preserve the bright personality that has led generations of students to discover in *The American Pageant* what Thomas A. Bailey so exuberantly taught—that the pages of history need not be dull. We hope that readers of this book will enjoy learning from it, and that they will come to savor the pleasures and rewards of historical study.

D. M. K.

M. P.

CONTENTS

Appendix

Index   XXXV

MAPS, GRAPHS, and TABLES

Sail, sail thy best, ship of Democracy,
Of value is thy freight, 'tis not the Present only,
The Past is also stored in thee,
Thou holdest not the venture of thyself alone, not of
*   the Western continent alone,*
Earth's résumé entire floats on thy keel, O ship, is
*   steadied by thy spars,*
With thee Time voyages in trust, the antecedent
*   nations sink or swim with thee,*
With all their ancient struggles, martyrs, heroes, epics,
*   wars, thou bear'st the other continents,*
Theirs, theirs as much as thine, the destination-port
*   triumphant. . . .*

WALT WHITMAN
Thou Mother with Thy Equal Brood, 1872

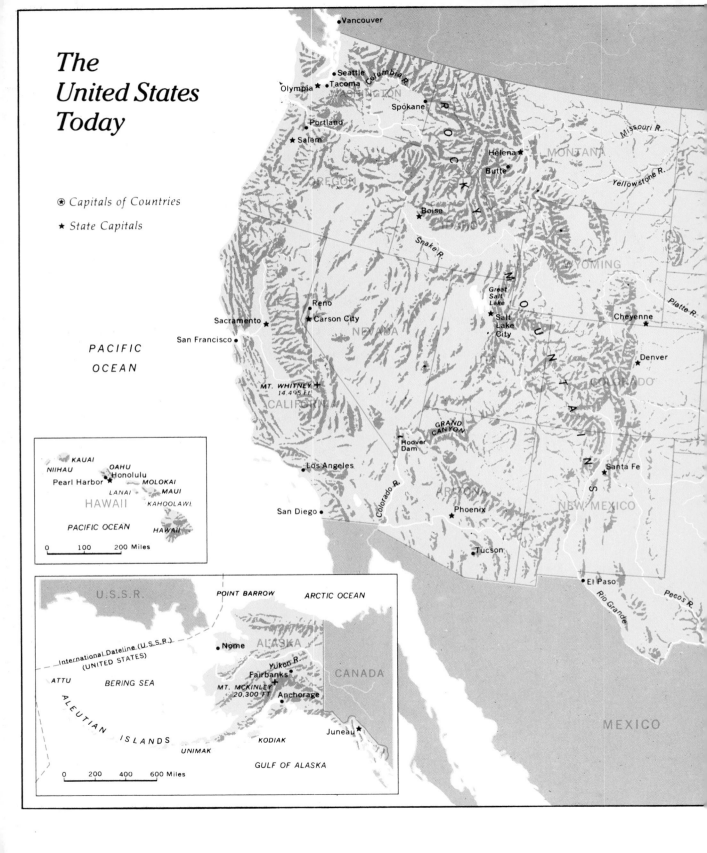

The United States Today

⊛ Capitals of Countries

★ State Capitals

PACIFIC OCEAN

Vancouver
Seattle
★ Olympia ● Tacoma
WASHINGTON
Spokane
Portland
★ Salem
OREGON

Columbia R.

R O C K Y

MONTANA
Missouri R.
Helena ★
Butte ●
Yellowstone R.

★ Boise
IDAHO

Snake R.

WYOMING

Reno
★ Carson City
NEVADA
Sacramento ★
San Francisco ●

M O U N T A I N S

Great Salt Lake
★ Salt Lake City
UTAH

Cheyenne ★

Denver ●

COLORADO

MT. WHITNEY
14,495 ft.
CALIFORNIA

GRAND CANYON

Hoover Dam

Colorado R.

Los Angeles ●

San Diego ●

ARIZONA

Phoenix ●

Tucson ●

El Paso ●

NEW MEXICO

Santa Fe ★

Rio Grande

Pecos R.

Platte R.

HAWAII

KAUAI
NIIHAU
OAHU
Honolulu ★
Pearl Harbor
LANAI
MOLOKAI
MAUI
KAHOOLAWE
HAWAII

PACIFIC OCEAN

0 100 200 Miles

ALASKA

U.S.S.R.

POINT BARROW
ARCTIC OCEAN

International Dateline (U.S.S.R.)
(UNITED STATES)

ATTU

BERING SEA

● Nome
ALASKA

Yukon R.
Fairbanks ●
MT. McKINLEY
20,300 FT.
Anchorage ●

CANADA

A L E U T I A N   I S L A N D S

UNIMAK

KODIAK

Juneau ★

GULF OF ALASKA

MEXICO

0 200 400 600 Miles

The Brief American Pageant

1

New World Beginnings

... For I shall yet live to see it [Virginia] an Inglishe nation.

Sir Walter Raleigh, 1602

Before Columbus

Nearly five hundred years ago, the first Europeans stumbled on the American continents. This dramatic achievement opened breathtaking new vistas and forever altered the future of both the Old World and the New.

Of the numerous new republics that eventually appeared in the Americas, the most influential has been the United States. Born a pygmy, it grew to be a giant whose liberal democratic ideals, robust economy, and achievements in science, technology, and culture have left a deep imprint upon the rest of the world.

The American continents were slow to yield their virginity to intruders from the Old World. Expansive though it was, the ancient Roman Empire extended only as far northwestward as Britain. Except for a brief and soon-forgotten Scandinavian visitation about 1000 A.D., the New World remained unknown and unsuspected to Europeans for fifteen hundred years after the birth of Christ.

First in the chain of events that led to the accidental discovery of the New World were the Christian Crusades of the eleventh to the fourteenth centuries. Although their avowed aim was to wrest the Holy Land from the Moslems, the armored Crusaders were more successful in enhancing "barbarian" European tastes for the exotic delights of Asia: spices for spoiled and monotonous food; silk for rough skins; drugs for aching flesh; perfumes for unbathed bodies; colorful draperies for gloomy castles.

But the distance and difficulties of transportation, for which Moslem and Italian middlemen charged dearly, made these products expensive luxuries in Europe. The consumers and distributors of Western Europe were eager to find a less costly shortcut waterway to Eastern Asia, but made little headway

1

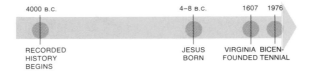

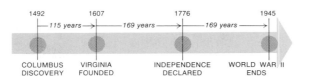

before the Renaissance of the fourteenth century. Then technical innovations, such as better maps, the mariner's compass, and the printing press, improved the science of navigation, while the Renaissance itself created a spirit of optimism, self-reliance, and venturesomeness.

Columbus Comes upon a New World

The spirit of the Renaissance also stimulated the ambition of several European monarchs. As these kings gradually subordinated the nobles, the modern national state emerged in Europe from the feudalism of the Middle Ages. This new type of government alone had the unity, power, and resources to shoulder the formidable tasks of discovery, conquest, and colonization. The first nations to unite—Portugal, Spain, England, France, and the Netherlands—were also the first to flourish as colonial empires.

Little Portugal took the lead in discovering what came to be the coveted water route to the Indies. In the fifteenth century, Portuguese navigators edged cautiously down the coast of Africa. In 1488 Bartholomeu Diaz finally rounded the continent's southern tip, and in 1498 Vasco da Gama successfully crowned Portuguese efforts by reaching India. Portuguese merchants soon established flourishing trading stations in India, Africa, China, and the East Indies. Immense wealth flowed into their coffers from these ventures, as the monopolistic grip of the Italian commercial cities was broken. Although the India-bound navigator Pedro Cabral accidentally discovered Brazil in 1500, and the Portuguese subsequently erected a huge empire there, the return from this New World outpost was only a small fraction of the lush profits that the Portuguese garnered from their rich Asian trade.

The Kingdom of Spain became united—an event pregnant with destiny—late in the fifteenth century. This new unity resulted primarily from the marriage of two sovereigns, Ferdinand and Isabella, and from the brutal expulsion of the "infidel" Moslem Moors. Glorying in their new strength, the Spaniards were eager to outstrip their Portuguese rivals in the race for the fabled Indies.

Christopher Columbus, a skilled Italian seaman, now stepped upon the stage of history. A man of vision, energy, resourcefulness, and courage, he finally managed, after heartbreaking delays, to gain the ear of the Spanish rulers. Like all of his informed contemporaries, he was convinced that the world was round. Then why not find the way to East Asia by sailing directly westward into the darkness of the Atlantic, instead of eastward for unnecessary miles around Africa?

The Spanish monarchs at last decided to gamble on the persistent mariner. They helped outfit him with three tiny but seaworthy ships, manned by a motley crew. Daringly, he spread the sails of his cockleshell craft. Winds were friendly and progress was rapid, but the superstitious sailors, fearful of sailing over the edge of the world, grew increasingly mutinous. Nearly six long weeks passed and failure loomed ahead when, on October 12, 1492, land was sighted—an island in the Bahamas. A new world thus swam within the vision of Europeans.

Although Columbus and other explorers at first simply tried to get through the land barriers that blocked the ocean pathway to Asia, the truth gradually dawned that sprawling new continents had been discovered. Yet Columbus stubbornly maintained until his death in 1506 that he had skirted the rim of the "Indies." So certain was he that he called the near-naked natives "Indians," a gross geographical misnomer that somehow stuck.

The Earliest Americans

Ironically, the remote ancestors of these native Americans were the true discoverers of America. Some twenty thousand years earlier, they had begun to venture from Asia across the land bridge that then connected Siberia and Alaska. Roaming slowly southward through the wilderness, they eventually reached the far tip of South America. They continued to trek across the Asian-American isthmus for thousands of years, until rising seas submerged it and left this far-flung part of the family of man marooned for millennia on the now-isolated American continents.

Time did not stand still for these aboriginal Americans. Over the centuries they split into hundreds of tribes, with different languages, religions, and cultures. Some of them evolved stunning civilizations. Incas in Peru, Aztecs in Mexico, and Mayans in Central America developed advanced agricultural techniques, based primarily on the cultivation of corn. Numbering their population in the millions, these sophisticated societies erected bustling, elaborately carved stone cities, rivaling in size those of Columbus's Europe. They carried on commerce, studied mathematics, and made strikingly accurate astronomical observations.

Indian life in North America was cruder, though some groups reached high levels of development. The Mound Builders of the lower Mississippi Valley built large permanent settlements and radiated their influence as far as the Great Lakes area until—around the time of Columbus's discovery—powerful enemies virtually destroyed their culture. The Pueblos in the Rio Grande Valley constructed elaborate irrigation systems and multistoried terraced buildings. The Creeks in the Southeast practiced a democratic style of government that led Europeans later to include them among the "civilized tribes." The Iroquois in the Northeast developed the political skills to sustain a robust military confederacy.

These exceptions aside, most native peoples lived in small, scattered, and impermanent settlements. So thinly spread across the land was the population of perhaps ten million Native Americans that vast areas were virtually uninhabited, with whispering, primeval forests and sparkling, virgin waters.

Two ecosystems—the fragile, naturally evolved networks of relations among organisms in a stable environment—commingled and clashed when Columbus waded ashore. European explorers marveled at the strange sights that greeted them—buffalo, iguanas, and "snakes with castanets" (rattlesnakes). Native New World plants like tobacco,

corn (maize), beans, tomatoes, and especially the lowly potato revolutionized the international economy and fed the rapid population growth of Europe. These were among the most important Indian gifts to the Europeans.

In exchange, the Europeans introduced cattle, swine, and horses to the New World. Indian tribes like the Blackfoot, the Sioux, and the Apaches swiftly adopted the horse, and were soon roaming the grassy great plains in pursuit of the buffalo. The Europeans also brought the germs that caused smallpox, yellow fever, and malaria—Old World diseases that devastated the Native Americans. Devoid of the antibodies necessary to resist the European sicknesses, Indians died in droves. In the century after Columbus's landfall, nearly 90 percent of the Native American population perished. Perhaps it was poetic justice that the Indians took a kind of revenge by infecting the early explorers with syphilis, injecting that noxious disease for the first time into Europe.

The Spanish Conquistadores

Gradually the realization sank in that the American continents held rich prizes of their own—especially the glittering gold of the advanced Indian civilizations in the southern continent. Spain secured its claim to Columbus's discoveries in the Treaty of Tordesillas (1494), dividing with Portugal the "heathen lands" of the New World. The lion's share went to Spain.

Spain now became the dominant exploring and colonizing power in the 1500s. Love of God joined with the lure of gold in spurring the Spaniards on, as zealous priests sought to convert the pagan natives to Catholic Christianity.

Some early explorers, such as Ponce de León, Coronado, and de Soto ventured into territory that eventually became part of the United States, but the permanent Spanish conquests of the great civilizations of Mexico and Peru had far more impact on subsequent American developments. Hernando Cortés, with seven hundred men and eighteen horses (which awed the horseless natives), tore open the treasure coffers of the Mexican Aztecs in 1519–1521. Francisco Pizarro, an iron-fisted conqueror, crushed the Peruvian Incas in 1532, and added another incredible hoard of gold and silver to the loot from

North American Indian Tribes at the Time of European Colonization. *This map illustrates the great diversity of the Indian population—and suggests the inappropriateness of identifying all the Native American peoples with the single label* Indian. *The more than two hundred tribes were deeply divided by geography, language, and life-style. The map also identifies geographical areas that are similar in climate and terrain.*

Mexico. The Spanish invaders not only robbed the Indians, but subsequently enslaved them and put them to work digging up precious metals. By 1600, Spain was swimming in New World silver, mostly from the fabulously rich mines at Potosi, Bolivia.

The Spanish *conquistadores* (conquerors), curiously enough, were indirect founding fathers of the United States. Their phenomenal success excited the envy of Englishmen, and helped spur some of the early attempts at colonization. Moreover, the dumping of the enormous Indian treasure chests upon Europe inflated the currency and drove prices upward. The pinch further distressed underpaid English toilers, many of whom in turn were later driven to the New World. There, ironically, they challenged Spanish supremacy.

These plunderings by the Spaniards unfortunately obscured their substantial colonial achievements, and helped give birth to the "Black Legend." This false concept implied that the conquerors merely tortured and butchered the Indians ("killing for Christ"), stole their gold, infected them with smallpox, and left little but misery behind. The Spanish invader did kill thousands of natives and exploit the rest, but he intermarried with them as well, creating a distinctive South American culture of *mestizos*—people of mixed Indian and European heritage. He erected a colossal empire, sprawling from California and the Floridas to Tierra del Fuego. He transplanted and engrafted his culture, laws, religion, and language, and laid the foundations for a score of modern-day Spanish-speaking nations.

The bare statistics of Spain's colonial empire are alone impressive. By 1574, thirty-three years before the first primitive English shelters in Virginia, there were about two hundred Spanish cities and towns in North and South America. A total of 160,000 Spanish inhabitants, mostly men, had subjugated some 5 million Indians—all in the name of the gentle Jesus. Majestic cathedrals dotted the land, printing presses were turning out books, and literary prizes were being awarded. Two distinguished universities were chartered in 1551, one at Mexico City and the other at Lima, Peru. Both of them antedated Harvard, the first college established in the English colonies, by eighty-five years.

It is clear that the Spaniards, who had more than a century's head start over the English, were genuine empire builders in the New World. As compared with their Anglo-Saxon rivals, their colonial establishment was larger and richer, and it lasted more than a quarter of a century longer.

England Turns to Empire

Feeble indeed were the efforts of England in the 1500s to compete with the sprawling Spanish Empire. At first England took little interest in establishing her own overseas colonies, but after the Protestant Queen Elizabeth mounted the English throne in 1558, rivalry with Catholic Spain intensified.

The earliest English explorers were semipiratical "sea dogs" like Sir Francis Drake, who swarmed out upon the shipping lanes to plunder Spanish treasure ships and raid Spanish settlements. The first English attempt at colonization occurred in bleak Newfoundland, but it collapsed when its promoter, Sir Humphrey Gilbert, lost his life at sea in 1583. Gilbert's gallant half-brother, Sir Walter Raleigh, then organized a group of settlers who landed in 1585 on North Carolina's Roanoke Island. But with Raleigh busy at home, the hapless Roanoke colony mysteriously disappeared, swallowed up by the wilderness.

These pathetic English failures at colonization contrasted embarrassingly with the glories of the Spanish Empire, whose profits were enriching Spain beyond its most ambitious dreams of avarice. Philip II of Spain, self-anointed foe of the Protestant Reformation, used part of his imperial gains to amass an "Invincible Armada" of ships for an invasion of England in 1588. But the skillful English sea dogs and a devastating storm (the "Protestant wind") destroyed or scattered the cumbersome Spanish ships.

The defeat of the Spanish Armada was a red-letter day in American history. It weakened Spanish power and, important for subsequent American history, ensured England's naval dominance of the North Atlantic. The English victory over the Armada also produced a vibrant national pride that blossomed in a golden age of culture and politics. Shakespeare, who made occasional poetic references to England's

Sir Walter Raleigh (c. 1552–1618). *Here he is shown "drinking tobacco," as smoking was first called. He is credited with introducing both tobacco and the potato into England. A dashing courtier, he launched important colonizing failures in the New World. After seducing (and marrying) one of Queen Elizabeth's maids of honor, he fell out of favor and was ultimately beheaded for treason.*

American colonies, was only one of many contemporary patriots who expressed boundless faith in the future of the English nation.

England's scepter'd isle, as Shakespeare called it, throbbed with social and economic change as the seventeenth century opened. Her population was mushrooming, from some 3 million people in 1550 to about 4 million in 1600. In the evergreen English countryside, landlords were "enclosing" croplands for sheep grazing, forcing many small farmers ("yeomen") into precarious tenancy or off the land altogether. It was no accident that the woolen districts of eastern and western England—where Puritanism had taken strong root—supplied many of the earliest immigrants to America. When economic depression hit the woolen trade in the late 1500s, thousands of unemployed yeomen took to the roads, often ending up as beggars and paupers in cities like Bristol and London.

At the same time, laws of primogeniture decreed that only eldest sons were eligible to inherit landed estates. The landholders' ambitious younger sons—like Gilbert, Raleigh, and Drake—were forced to seek their fortunes elsewhere. By the early 1600s their unsuccessful lone-wolf ventures were replaced by the joint-stock company, which enabled a considerable number of investors to pool their capital.

Peace with a chastened Spain provided the opportunity for English colonization. Population growth provided the workers. Unemployment, as well as a thirst for adventure, for markets, and for religious freedom, provided the motives. Joint-stock companies provided the financial means. The stage was now set for a historic effort to establish an English beachhead in the uncharted American wilderness.

England Plants the Jamestown Seedling

In 1606, two years after peace with Spain, the hand of destiny beckoned toward Virginia. A joint-stock company, known as The Virginia Company of London, received a charter from King James I of England for a settlement in the New World. The main attraction was the promise of gold, although there was also a strong desire to convert the Indians to Christianity and to find a passage through America to the Indies. Like most joint-stock companies of the day, the Virginia Company was intended to endure for only a few years, after which its stockholders hoped to liquidate it for a profit. This arrangement put severe pressure on the luckless colonists, who were threatened with abandonment in the wilderness if they did not quickly strike it rich on the company's behalf. Few of the investors thought in terms of long-term colonization. Apparently no one even faintly suspected that the seeds of a mighty nation were being planted.

The charter of the Virginia Company is a significant document in American history. It guaranteed to the overseas settlers the same rights of Englishmen that they would have enjoyed if they had stayed at home. This precious boon was gradually extended to the other English colonies, and became a foundation stone of American liberties.

Unluckily, the site selected in 1607 for the tiny colony was Jamestown, on the wooded and malarial banks of the James River, named in honor of King James I. Although mosquito-infested and unhealthful, the spot was easy to defend.

Pocahontas (c. 1595–1617) (Detail). *Taken to England by her husband, she was received as a princess. She died when preparing to return, and her infant son ultimately reached Virginia, where hundreds of his descendants have lived, including the second Mrs. Woodrow Wilson. (National Portrait Gallery, Smithsonian Institution, Washington, D.C.)*

The early years at Jamestown proved to be a nightmare for all concerned—except the buzzards. Forty would-be colonists perished during the initial voyage in 1606–1607. Another expedition in 1609 lost its leaders and many of its precious supplies in a shipwreck in Bermuda. Of the 400 settlers who managed to make it to Virginia, only 60 survived the "starving time" winter of 1609–10. Ironically, the woods rustled with game and the rivers flopped with fish, but the greenhorn settlers wasted valuable time grubbing for nonexistent gold when they should have been gathering provisions. Diseased and despairing, the colonists dragged themselves aboard homeward-bound ships in the spring of 1610—only to be met at the mouth of the James River by a relief party, which ordered them back to Jamestown.

Disease continued to reap a gruesome harvest among the Virginians, and Indian raids added to the death toll. By 1625, Virginia contained only some 1200 hard-bitten survivors of the nearly 8000 adventurers who had tried to start life anew in the ill-fated colony.

Virginia was saved from collapse at the start largely by the leadership and resourcefulness of an intrepid young adventurer, Captain John Smith. Tak-ing over in 1608, he whipped the gold-hungry colonists into line with the rule, "He who will not work shall not eat." At times of scarcity the settlers were forced to eat "dogges, Catts, Ratts, and Myce." One man killed, salted, and ate his wife, for which misbehavior he was executed.

Virginia: Child of Tobacco

John Rolfe, who became father of the tobacco industry, was also an economic savior of the Virginia colony. By 1616 he perfected methods of raising and curing the pungent weed (another Indian gift to Europe) which eliminated much of the bitter tang. Tobacco-rush days began, as crops were planted even in the streets of Jamestown and between the numerous graves. So heavy was the concentration on the yellow leaf that some foodstuffs had to be imported.

Virginia's prosperity was finally built on tobacco smoke. This "bewitching weed" played a vital role in putting the colony on firm foundations, and in setting an example for other successful colonizing experiments. But tobacco—King Nicotine—was something of a tyrant. It was ruinous to the soil when greedily planted in successive years, and it also enchained the prosperity of Virginia to the fluctuating price of a single crop. Tobacco also promoted the broad-acred plantation system, and with it a brisk demand for slave labor.

In 1619, the year before the Plymouth Pilgrims landed in New England, what was described as a Dutch warship appeared off Jamestown and sold some twenty black Africans. (The scanty record does not reveal whether they were purchased as lifelong slaves or as servants committed to limited years of servitude.) Yet black slaves were too costly for most of the hard-pinched white colonists to acquire, and for decades they were imported only in driblets. Virginia counted but 300 blacks in 1650, although by the end of the century blacks made up approximately 14 percent of the colony's population.

Representative self-government was also born in primitive Virginia, in the same cradle with slavery and in the same year—1619. The London Company authorized the settlers to summon an assembly, known as the House of Burgesses. A momentous precedent was thus feebly established, for this

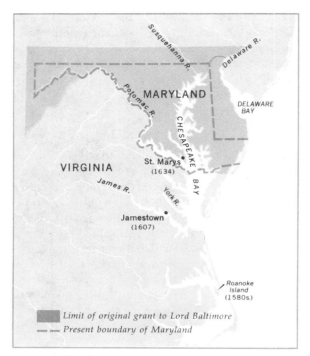

Limit of original grant to Lord Baltimore
— — Present boundary of Maryland

Early Maryland and Virginia.

assemblage was the first of many miniature parliaments to mushroom from the soil of America.

As time passed, James I grew increasingly hostile to Virginia. He detested tobacco and he distrusted the representative House of Burgesses, which he branded a "seminary of sedition." In 1624 he revoked the charter of the bankrupt Virginia Company, thus making Virginia a royal colony directly under his control.

Maryland: Catholic Haven

Maryland—the second plantation colony but the fourth English colony to be planted—was founded in 1634 by Lord Baltimore, of a prominent English Catholic family. He embarked upon the venture partly to reap financial profits and partly to create a refuge for his co-religionists.

Absentee proprietor Lord Baltimore hoped that the 200 settlers who founded Maryland at St. Mary's, on Chesapeake Bay, would be the vanguard of a vast

new feudal domain. Huge estates were to be awarded to his largely Catholic relatives, and gracious manor houses, modeled on those of England's aristocracy, were intended to sprout from the fertile forests. But colonists proved willing to come only if offered the right to acquire land of their own. Soon they were dispersed around the Chesapeake region on modest farms, and the haughty land barons, mostly Catholic, were surrounded by resentful backcountry planters, mostly Protestant. Resentment flared into open rebellion near the end of the century, and the Baltimore family for a time lost its proprietary rights.

Despite these tensions, Maryland prospered. Like Virginia, it blossomed forth in acres of tobacco. Like Virginia, it depended for labor in its early years mainly on white indentured servants—penniless persons who bound themselves to work for a number of years to pay their passage. In both colonies it was only in the later years of the seventeenth century that black slaves began to be imported in large numbers.

Lord Baltimore at first permitted unusual freedom of worship. But when the heavy tide of Protestants threatened to submerge the Catholics, the Catholic settlers threw their support behind the famed Act of Toleration, passed by the local assembly in 1649. This statute guaranteed toleration to all Christians but decreed the death penalty for those, like Jews and atheists, who denied the divinity of Jesus.

Colonizing the Carolinas

Civil wars convulsed England in the 1640s. King Charles I had dismissed Parliament in 1629, and when he eventually recalled it in 1640, the members were mutinous. Finding their great champion in the Puritan-soldier Oliver Cromwell, they ultimately beheaded Charles in 1649, and Cromwell ruled England for nearly a decade. Finally, Charles II, son of the decapitated king, was restored to the throne in 1660.

Colonization had been interrupted during this period of bloody unrest. Now, in the so-called Restoration period, empire building resumed with even greater intensity—and royal involvement. The Carolinas were formally created in 1670 after Charles II granted to eight of his court favorites—Lords Pro-

North Carolina Indians Sitting at Meate. *Painted by John White, a member of Sir Walter Raleigh's second expedition, 1585. Indians such as these may have absorbed the more than one hundred "lost colonists" from Raleigh's ill-starred venture on Roanoke Island. In one nearby county of present-day North Carolina, blue-eyed and fair-haired characteristics have persisted among the Indians, along with Elizabethan words and the family names of forty-one Roanoke colonists. (Library of Congress)*

prietors—an expanse of wilderness ribboning across the continent to the Pacific. These aristocratic founders hoped to grow foodstuffs to provision the sugar plantations in Barbados and to export non-English products like wine, silk, and olive oil.

South Carolina prospered by developing close economic ties with the flourishing British West Indies. In a broad sense, the mainland colony was but the most northwesterly of those islands. Indian slaves were sent from the colony to the West Indies and New England. After much experimentation, rice emerged as the principal export crop in South Carolina. Since rice was grown in Africa, Carolinians were soon paying premium prices for west African slaves experienced in rice cultivation. The Africans' agricultural skill and their relative immunity to malaria made them ideal laborers on the hot and swampy rice plantations. By 1710 they constituted a majority of Carolinians.

Moss-festooned Charles Town—named after King Charles II—rapidly became the most important seaport of the South. Many high-spirited younger sons of English landed families, deprived of an inheritance, came to the Charleston area and lent it a rich aristocratic flavor. The village also became a melting-pot community, to which French Protestant refugees and others were attracted by religious toleration.

Nearby, in Florida, the Catholic Spaniards bitterly resented the intrusion of these English heretics. South Carolina's frontier was often aflame. Spanish-incited Indians brandished their tomahawks, and armor-clad warriors of Spain frequently unsheathed their swords during the successive Anglo-Spanish wars. But by 1700 South Carolina was too strong to be wiped out.

The wild northern expanse of the huge Carolina grant bordered on Virginia. From that older colony there drifted down a motley group of poverty-stricken outcasts and religious dissidents repelled by the rich Anglican planter establishment of Virginia. These small farmers, who were often illegal "squatters" on the land, raised their tobacco and other crops mostly without slaves. Regarded as riff-raff by their snobbish neighbors, the North Carolinians earned a reputation for being irreligious and hospitable to pirates. Located between aristocratic Virginia and aristocratic South Carolina, the area was dubbed "a vale of humility between two mountains of conceit."

North Carolina was officially separated from South Carolina in 1712, and each segment became a royal colony.

Late-Coming Georgia: The Buffer Colony

Pine-forested Georgia, with the harbor of Savannah nourishing its chief settlement, was formally founded in 1733. It proved to be the last of the thirteen colonies to be planted—fifty-two years after Pennsylvania. Chronologically it belongs elsewhere, but geographically it may be grouped with the other Southern colonies.

Georgia was valued by the English crown chiefly as a buffer. It would serve to protect the more valuable Carolinas from inroads by vengeful Spaniards from Florida and by the hostile French from Louisiana. Georgia in truth suffered much buffeting, especially when wars broke out between Spain and England in the European cockpit.

Named in honor of George II of England, Georgia was launched by a high-minded group of philanthropists. Aside from producing silk and wine, and strengthening the empire, they were determined to create a haven for wretched souls imprisoned for debt. The ablest of the founders was the dynamic soldier-statesman James Oglethorpe, who became keenly interested in prison reform after one of his friends had died in a debtors' jail. As an able military leader, Oglethorpe repelled savage Spanish attacks. As an imperialist and a philanthropist, he saved "the Charity Colony" by his energetic leadership and by mortgaging heavily his own personal fortunes.

The hamlet of Savannah, like Charleston, was a melting-pot community that included German Lutherans and Scots Highlanders, among others. All Christian worshipers except Catholics enjoyed religious toleration. Many Bible-toting missionaries arrived to work among debtors and Indians, including young John Wesley, who later founded the Methodist Church in England.

Georgia grew with painful slowness and at the end of the colonial era was perhaps the least populous of the colonies. Prosperity through a large-plantation economy was thwarted by an unhealthful climate, by early restrictions on black slavery, and by demoralizing Spanish attacks.

The Plantation Colonies

Certain distinctive features were shared by all of England's Southern mainland colonies: Maryland, Virginia, North Carolina, South Carolina, and Georgia.

Broad-acred, these outposts of empire were all in some degree dominated by a plantation economy. All, with the partial exception of Georgia, relied heavily on slave labor. Profitable staple crops were the rule, notably tobacco, rice, and indigo, though to a lesser extent in small-farm North Carolina. Immense acreage in the hands of a favored few fostered a strong aristocratic atmosphere, except in North Carolina and to some extent in debtor-tinged Georgia. The wide scattering of plantations and farms, often along stately rivers, made the establishment of churches and schools both difficult and expensive.

Although the tax-supported Church of England became the dominant faith, all the plantation colonies permitted some religious toleration. The plantation colonies were also all in some degree expansionary, as "soil butchery" by excessive tobacco growing and long, lazy rivers encouraged penetration of the continent.

VARYING VIEWPOINTS

The history of discovery and the earliest colonization raises perhaps the single most fundamental question about all American history. Should it be understood as the extension of European civilization into the New World, or as the gradual development of a uniquely "American" culture? An older school of thought tended to emphasize the Europeanization of America. Historians of that persuasion thus paid close attention to the situation in Europe, particularly in England and

Spain, in the fifteenth and sixteenth centuries. They also focused on the various means by which the values and institutions of the mother continent were exported to the new lands in the western sea. Some European writers have varied this general question by asking what transforming effect the discovery of America had on Europe itself. Both of these approaches are Eurocentric.

More recently, historians have concentrated on the distinctive aspects of America, especially the interactions among the various races in the Western Hemisphere. This approach stresses the adaptations of native, African, and European cultures to the challenges of life in a strange new environment and emphasizes the creation of a uniquely *American* society and culture.

SELECT READINGS

Primary Source Documents

Richard Hakluyt, *Divers Voyages Touching the Discovery of America and the Islands Adjacent,** edited by J. W. Jones (1850), supplied the rationale for the establishment of English colonies in North America. John Smith, "Generall Historie of Virginia," in *Travels and Works of Captain John Smith,** edited by Edward Arber (1910), is the account of the amazing, vain man who steered Jamestown through its first few years.

Secondary Sources

The international economic background to colonization is sketched in Ralph Davis, *The Rise of the Atlantic Economies* (1973). More theoretical is Immanuel Wallerstein, *The Modern World-System: Capitalist Agriculture and the Origins of the European World in the Sixteenth Century* (1974). The

immediate English backdrop is colorfully presented in Peter Laslett, *The World We Have Lost* (1965) and in Carl Bridenbaugh, *Vexed and Troubled Englishmen, 1590–1642* (1968). Samuel E. Morison has written several masterful accounts of the discoveries; among the best are *Admiral of the Ocean Sea* (2 vols., 1942; condensed as *Christopher Columbus, Mariner,* 1956), *The European Discovery of America: The Northern Voyages,* A.D. *500–1600* (1971), and *The European Discovery of America: The Southern Voyages,* A.D. *1492–1616* (1974). A modern classic is Wallace Notestein, *The English People on the Eve of Colonization, 1603–1630* (1954). The ablest summary of the Spanish experience is Charles Gibson, *Spain in America* (1966). Contact between Indian and European cultures is handled in Wilcomb E. Washburn, *The Indian in America* (1975) and in Francis Jennings, *The Invasion of America* (1975). The role of slavery in early colonial society gets perceptive treatment in Edmund S. Morgan, *American Slavery, American Freedom* (1975). Gary Nash analyzes relations among the three races of America in *Red, White, and Black: The Peoples of Early America* (1974).

---

*An asterisk indicates that the document, or an excerpt from it, can be found in Thomas A. Bailey and David M. Kennedy, eds., *The American Spirit: United States History as Seen by Contemporaries,* 6th ed. (Lexington, Mass.: D. C. Heath and Company, 1987).

2

Completing the Thirteen Colonies

**God hath sifted a Nation
that he might send Choice Grain into this Wilderness.**

William Stoughton [of Massachusetts Bay], 1669

The Protestant Reformation Produces Puritanism

Little did the German monk Martin Luther know, when he nailed his protests against Catholic doctrines to the door of Wittenberg's cathedral in 1517, that he was shaping the destiny of a yet unheralded nation. Denouncing the authority of priests and popes, Luther declared that the Bible alone was the source of God's word. He ignited a fire of religious reform (the "Protestant Reformation") that licked its way across Europe for more than a century, dividing peoples, toppling sovereigns, and kindling the spiritual fervor of millions of men and women—some of whom helped to found America.

The reforming flame burned especially brightly in the bosom of John Calvin of Geneva. This somber and severe religious radical elaborated Luther's ideas in ways that profoundly affected the thought and character of generations of Americans yet unborn.

Calvinism became the dominant theological credo not only of the New England Puritans but of other American settlers as well.

According to Calvin, God was all-powerful and all-good, while sinful humans were weak and wicked. God was also all-knowing, and since the first moment of creation had destined some souls—the *elect*—for eternal bliss and others for eternal torment. Good works could not save those whom *predestination* had marked for the infernal fires.

But neither could the elect count on their determined salvation and lead lives of wild, immoral abandon. For one thing, no one could be certain of his or her status in the heavenly ledger. Gnawing doubts about their eternal fate caused Calvinists to seek signs of *conversion,* or the receipt of God's free gift of saving grace. Those who had the intense personal experience of conversion were expected to lead "sanctified" lives, demonstrating by their holy behavior that they were among the "visible saints."

These doctrines swept into England just as King Henry VIII was breaking his ties with the Roman Catholic church in the 1530s, making himself the head of the Church of England. Henry would have been content to retain Roman rituals and creeds, but some English religious reformers sought a total purification of English Christianity. Many of these *Puritans,* as it happened, came from commercially depressed woolen districts. Calvinism fed on this social unrest and provided spiritual comfort to the economically afflicted. Increasingly unhappy with the snail-like progress of the Protestant Reformation in England, Puritans burned with pious zeal to see the Church of England wholly de-Catholicized.

One problem was that the Church of England was open to all comers. All Puritans agreed that only "visible saints" should be admitted to church membership, but a group of extreme reformers, known as Separatists, vowed to break away entirely from the Church of England. King James I, who was head of both the church and the state in England, threatened to harass the defiant Separatists out of the land.

The Pilgrims End Their Pilgrimage at Plymouth

The most famous congregation of Separatists, fleeing royal wrath, departed for Holland in 1608. During the ensuing twelve years of toil and poverty, they became increasingly distressed at the growing "Dutchification" of their children. They longed to find a haven where they could live and die as Englishmen. America was the logical refuge.

A group of the Separatists in Holland, after negotiating with the Virginia Company, at length secured rights to settle under its jurisdiction. But their crowded *Mayflower,* sixty-five days at sea, missed its destination and arrived off the rocky coast of New England in 1620, with a total of 102 persons.

The Pilgrims did not make their initial landing at Plymouth Rock, as commonly supposed, but undertook a number of preliminary surveys. They finally chose for their site the shore of inhospitable Plymouth Bay. This area was outside the domain of the Virginia Company, and consequently the settlers became squatters. They were without legal right to the land, and without specific authority to establish a government.

Before disembarking, the Pilgrim Fathers drew up and signed the brief Mayflower Compact. Though setting an invaluable precedent for later written constitutions, this document was not a constitution at all. It was a simple agreement to form a body politic, and to submit to the will of the majority under the regulations agreed upon. The Compact was signed by forty-one adult males, eleven of them with the exalted rank of "mister," though not by the servants and two seamen. The pact was a promising step toward genuine self-government, for soon the adult male settlers were assembling to make their own laws in open-discussion town meetings—a laboratory of liberty.

The Pilgrims' first winter of 1620–1621 took a grisly toll. Only 44 out of 102 survived. Yet when the *Mayflower* sailed back to England in the spring, not a single one of the courageous band of Separatists left. As one of them wrote, "It is not with us as with other men, whom small things can discourage."

God made his children prosperous, so the Pilgrims believed. The next autumn, that of 1621, brought bountiful harvests and with them the first Thanksgiving Day in New England. In time the frail colony found sound economic legs in fur, fish, and lumber. The beaver and the Bible were the early mainstays: the one for the sustenance of the body, the other for the sustenance of the soul.

Quiet and quaint, the little colony of Plymouth was never important economically or numerically. It claimed only seven thousand souls by 1691, when, still charterless, it merged with its giant neighbor, the Massachusetts Bay Colony. But the tiny settlement of Pilgrims was big both morally and spiritually.

The Bay Colony Bible Commonwealth

The Separatist Pilgrims were dedicated extremists—the purest Puritans. More moderate Puritans sought to reform the Church of England by boring from within. But their efforts faced disaster when Charles I dismissed Parliament in 1629 and sanctioned the anti-Puritan persecutions of the reactionary Archbishop William Laud.

In 1629, an energetic group of non-Separatist Puritans, fearing for their faith and for England's future, secured a royal charter to form the Massachusetts Bay Company. Stealing a march on both king and church, the newcomers brought their charter with them when they emigrated to the Massachusetts area. For many years they used it as a kind of constitution, out of easy reach of royal authority.

The Massachusetts Bay enterprise was singularly blessed. The well-equipped expedition of 1630, with eleven vessels carrying nearly a thousand immigrants, started the colony off on a larger scale than any of the other English settlements. Continuing turmoil in England tossed up additional enriching waves of Puritans on the shores of Massachusetts in the following decade. During the "Great Migration" of the 1630s, about seventy-five thousand refugees left mother England, although about sixty thousand of these went to the fertile West Indies rather than to Massachusetts.

Many fairly prosperous, educated persons emigrated to the Bay Colony, including Governor John Winthrop, a well-to-do pillar of English society. A successful attorney and manor lord in England, Winthrop eagerly accepted the offer to become governor of the Massachusetts Bay Colony, believing that he had a *calling* from God to lead the new religious experiment. He served as governor or deputy governor for nineteen years. The resources and skills of talented settlers like Winthrop helped Massachusetts to prosper, and the Bay Colony rapidly shot to the fore as the biggest and the most influential of the New England outposts.

Massachusetts also benefited from a shared sense of purpose among most of the first settlers. "We shall be as a city upon a hill," a beacon to humanity, declared Governor Winthrop. The Puritan bay colonists believed that they had a *covenant* with God, an agreement to build a holy society that would be a model for humankind.

Building the Bay Colony

These common convictions deeply shaped the infant colony's life. Soon after arrival, the franchise was extended to all "freemen"—adult males who belonged to the Puritan congregations, which in time came to be called collectively the Congregational church. On this basis, about two-fifths of adult males enjoyed the franchise in provincial affairs, a far larger proportion than in contemporary England. Town governments, which conducted much important business, were even more inclusive. There all male property holders, and in some cases other residents as well, discussed and voted on public issues.

Yet the provincial government, liberal by the standards of the time, was not a democracy. "If the people be governors," asked one Puritan clergyman, "who shall be the governed?" True, the freemen annually elected the governor and his assistants, as well as a representative assembly called the General Court. But only Puritans—the "visible saints" who were alone eligible for church membership—could be freemen. And according to the doctrine of the covenant, the whole purpose of government was to enforce God's laws—which applied to believers and unbelievers alike. Moreover, unbelievers as well as believers paid taxes for the government-supported church.

Religious leaders thus wielded enormous influence in the Massachusetts "Bible Commonwealth." They powerfully influenced admission to church membership, by conducting public interrogations of persons claiming to have experienced conversions. But the power of the preachers was not absolute. Because Puritans had suffered so much at the hands of a "political" Anglican clergy, they barred clergymen from holding formal political office. In a limited way, the bay colonists thus endorsed the idea of the separation of church and state.

The Puritans were a worldly lot, despite—or even because of—their spiritual intensity. Like John Winthrop, they believed in the doctrine of a "calling" to do God's work on this earth. They shared in what was later called the "Protestant ethic," involving serious commitment to work and to engagement in the world of affairs. Legend to the contrary, they also enjoyed simple pleasures: they ate plentifully, drank heartily, sang songs occasionally, and made love discreetly.

Yet life was serious business, and hellfire was real—a hell where sinners shriveled and shrieked for divine mercy. Puritan clergyman Michael Wigglesworth's poem "Day of Doom" (1662) described the horrifying fate of the damned:

> They cry, they roar for anguish sore,
>   and gnaw their tongues for horrour.
> But get away without delay,
>   Christ pitties not your cry:
> Depart to hell, there may you yell,
>   and roar Eternally.

Trouble in the Bay Commonwealth

The Bay Colony enjoyed a high degree of social harmony, stemming from common beliefs, in its early years. But even in this tightly knit community, dissension soon appeared. Quakers, who flouted the authority of the Puritan clergy, were persecuted with fines, floggings, banishment, and on one occasion, hanging.

A sharp challenge to Puritan orthodoxy came from Mistress Anne Hutchinson. An unusually intelligent, strong-willed, and talkative woman, she claimed that the truly saved need not bother to obey the law of either God or man. This assertion, known as *antinomianism,* was high heresy. At her trial in 1638, the quick-witted Hutchinson bamboozled her clerical inquisitors for days, until she eventually boasted that she had come by her beliefs through a direct revelation from God. This was even higher heresy. After the Puritan magistrates banished her, she moved to Rhode Island and eventually to New York, where she and all but one of her household were killed by Indians.

More threatening to the Puritan leaders was a personable and popular Salem minister, Roger Williams. An extreme Separatist with an unrestrained tongue, Williams demanded a clean break with the corrupt Church of England and challenged the legality of the Bay Colony's charter, which he condemned for its unfairness to the Indians. As if all this were not enough, he went on to deny the authority of civil government to regulate religious behavior—a seditious blow at the Puritan idea of government's very purpose. Their patience exhausted by 1635, the Bay Colony authorities found Williams guilty of dis-

Anne Hutchinson, Dissenter. *Mistress Hutchinson (1591–1643) held unorthodox views that challenged the authority of the clergy and the very integrity of the Puritan experiment in Massachusetts Bay Colony. (Mike Mazzaschi/Stock, Boston)*

seminating "newe & dangerous opinions" and ordered him banished.

New England Spreads Out

Aided by friendly Indians, Williams fled in 1636 to the Rhode Island area, where he built a Baptist church. He established complete freedom of religion, even for Jews and Catholics, a degree of toleration that existed in none of the other English settlements in the New World. He demanded no oaths regarding one's religious beliefs, no compulsory attendance at worship, and no taxes to support a state church.

Those outcasts who clustered about Roger Williams also managed to achieve remarkable freedom of opportunity. They exercised simple manhood suffrage from the start, though this boon was later modified by a property qualification. Opposed to special privilege of any sort, the malcontents and exiles who largely populated "Rogues' Island" had little in common with Roger Williams—except banishment. The Puritan clergy back in Boston sneered at Rhode Island as "that sewer" in which the "Lord's debris" had collected and rotted. Stubbornly individualistic, the squatters in "Little Rhody" finally established rights to the soil when they secured a charter from Parliament in 1644. A huge bronze statue of the "Independent Man" appropriately stands today on the dome of the state house in Providence.

The fertile valley of the Connecticut River had meanwhile attracted a sprinkling of Dutch and English settlers. Hartford was founded in 1635, and the next year an energetic group of Boston Puritans, led by the Reverend Thomas Hooker, swarmed into the area. In 1639, the settlers of the new Connecticut River colony drafted a trailblazing document known as the Fundamental Orders, which established a regime democratically controlled by the "substantial" citizens.

Another flourishing Connecticut settlement sprang up in New Haven in 1638. Hostile to the overbearing Puritan rulers of the Bay Colony, these settlers were equally overbearing themselves. They set up an ironclad regime even more autocratic than the one they had left behind. Dreaming of making New Haven a flourishing seaport, the colonists tried to obtain a charter, but they fell into disfavor with Charles II because they sheltered two of the judges who had condemned his father, Charles I, to death. In 1662 the Crown granted a charter that merged New Haven with the more democratic outposts in the Connecticut Valley.

Two smaller settlements grew up north of Massachusetts Bay. The fishermen and fur traders along the coast of Maine were absorbed by Massachusetts Bay in 1677. The Maine territory remained part of Massachusetts for nearly a century and a half and then became a separate state. In 1641 the Bay Colony also annexed her immediate northern neighbor, New Hampshire, under a strained interpretation of the

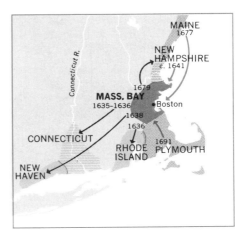

Massachusetts Bay, the Hub of New England. *All earlier colonies grew into it; all later colonies grew out of it.*

Massachusetts charter. The King, annoyed by this display of greed, separated New Hampshire from Massachusetts in 1679, and made her a royal colony.

Seeds of Colonial Unity and Independence

A path-breaking experiment in union was launched in 1643, when four colonies banded together to form the New England Confederation. The primary purpose of the confederation was defense against foes or potential foes, notably the Indians, the French, and the Dutch. Purely intercolonial problems, such as runaway servants and criminals who had fled from one colony to another, also came within the jurisdiction of the Confederation. Each member, regardless of size, wielded two votes—an arrangement that was highly displeasing to the most populous one, Massachusetts Bay.

The confederation was essentially an exclusive Puritan club. It consisted of the two Massachusetts colonies (the Bay Colony and bantam-sized Plymouth) and the two Connecticut colonies (New Haven and the scattered Valley settlements). The Puritan leaders blackballed Rhode Island, as well as the Maine outposts. Weak though it was, the confederation was the first notable milestone on the long and rocky road toward colonial unity.

The New England Confederation functioned

usefully during the bloody war in 1675–1676 with the Indian chieftain King Philip, whose followers struck back at encroachments by whites on their lands. Several hundred settlers were killed and dozens of towns were burned, but the whites finally emerged victorious.

Back home in England, the king paid little attention to the American colonies during the early years of their planting. They were allowed, in effect, to become semi-autonomous commonwealths. This period of benign neglect was further prolonged when the crown, struggling to retain its power, became involved during the 1640s in civil wars with the parliamentarians. A climax came in 1649 when Charles I was beheaded. Meanwhile the American colonists, like children neglected by their parents, became increasingly impatient of overseas restraints.

But when Charles II was restored to the English throne in 1660, the royalists and their Church of England allies were once more firmly in the saddle. Puritan hopes of eventually purifying the old English church withered. Worse, Charles II was determined to take an active, aggressive hand in the management of the colonies. His plans ran headlong against the habits that decades of relative independence had bred in the colonists.

Deepening colonial defiance was nowhere more glaringly revealed than in Massachusetts. As punishment, the king gave new charters to Massachusetts' colonial rivals, Connecticut and Rhode Island. A final and crushing blow fell on the stiff-necked Bay Colony in 1684, when her precious charter was revoked by the London authorities.

Andros Promotes the First American Revolution

Massachusetts suffered further humiliation in 1686, when the Dominion of New England was created by royal authority. Unlike the homegrown New England Confederation, it was imposed from London. Embracing at first all New England, it was expanded two years later to include New York and East and West Jersey. The Dominion also aimed at bolstering colonial defense in the event of war with the Indians.

More importantly, the Dominion of New England was designed to promote urgently needed efficiency in the administration of the English Navigation Laws. Those laws reflected the intensifying colonial rivalries of the seventeenth century. They sought to stitch England's overseas possessions more tightly to the motherland, by restricting American trade with countries not ruled by the English crown. Like colonial peoples everywhere, the Americans chafed at such confinements, and smuggling became an increasingly common and honorable occupation.

At the head of the new Dominion stood autocratic Sir Edmund Andros, an able English military man, conscientious but tactless. Establishing headquarters in Puritanical Boston, he generated much hostility by his open affiliation with the despised Church of England. The colonials were also outraged by his noisy and Sabbath-profaning soldiers, who were accused of teaching the people "to drink, blaspheme, curse, and damn."

Andros was prompt to use the mailed fist. He ruthlessly curbed the cherished town meetings, and laid heavy restrictions on the courts, the press, and the schools. Dispensing with the popular assemblies, he taxed the people without the consent of their duly elected representatives. He also strove to enforce the unpopular Navigation Laws and suppress smuggling. Liberty-loving colonials, accustomed to unusual privileges during long decades of neglect, were goaded to the verge of revolt.

The people of old England, likewise resisting oppression, stole a march on the people of New England. In 1688–1689 they engineered the memorable Glorious (or Bloodless) Revolution. Dethroning the despotic and unpopular Catholic James II, they enthroned the Protestant rulers of the Netherlands, the Dutch-born William III and his English wife, Mary, daughter of James II.

When the news of the Glorious Revolution reached America, the ramshackle Dominion of New England collapsed like a house of cards. A Boston mob, catching the fever, rose against the existing regime. Sir Edmund Andros attempted to flee in woman's clothing, but was betrayed by boots protruding beneath his dress. He was then shipped off to England.

Massachusetts, though rid of the despotic Andros, did not gain as much from the upheaval as she had hoped. In 1691 she was arbitrarily made a royal colony, with a new charter and a new royal governor. The permanent loss of the ancient charter was a staggering blow to the proud Puritans, who never fully recovered. Worst of all, the privilege of voting, which had been a monopoly of church members, was now to be enjoyed by all qualified male property holders.

England's Glorious Revolution had a far-flung impact, for unrest erupted from New England to the Carolinas. The upheaval resulted in a permanent abandonment of many of the objectionable features of the Andros system, as well as a temporary breakdown of the new imperial policy of enforcing the Navigation Laws.

Yet residues remained of Charles II's effort to assert tighter administrative control over his empire. More British officials—judges, clerks, customs officials—were now staffing the courts and strolling the wharves of British America. Many were incompetent, corrupt hacks who knew little and cared less about American affairs. Appointed by influential patrons in far-off England, they blocked by their presence the rise of local leaders to positions of political power. Aggrieved Americans viewed them with mounting contempt and resentment as the eighteenth century wore on.

New Netherland Becomes New York

Late in the sixteenth century, the oppressed people of the Netherlands unfurled the standard of rebellion against Catholic Spain. After bloody and protracted fighting, they finally succeeded, with the aid of Protestant England, in winning their independence. This vigorous little lowland nation quickly emerged as a major commercial and naval power that ungratefully challenged the supremacy of her former benefactor, England.

Holland also became a leading colonial power through the activities of the enterprising Dutch East India Company. The Company's vast riches came mostly from the East Indies, where it maintained an enormous and profitable empire for three centuries. In 1609 it employed an English explorer, Henry Hudson, who ventured into what is now New York Bay and up the river that now bears his name, hoping that he had at last chanced upon the coveted shortcut through the continent. But, as the event proved, he merely filed a Dutch claim to the magnificently watered and wooded area.

New Netherland was permanently planted in 1623–24 by the Dutch West India Company, the less wealthy counterpart of the East India Company. Never more than a secondary interest of the founders, the colony was exploited for its quick-profit fur trade. The company's most brilliant stroke was to buy Manhattan Island from the Indians (who did not actually "own" it) for trinkets worth about $24: 22,000 acres of what is now perhaps the most valuable real estate in the world for one-tenth of a cent an acre.

A threat to New Netherland came from the Swedes, who trespassed on Dutch preserves by planting the colony of New Sweden on the Delaware River from 1638 to 1655. Resenting the Swedish intrusion, the Dutch dispatched a small military expedition in 1655, led by the energetic and hot-headed director-general Peter Stuyvesant, who was dubbed "Father Wooden Leg" by the Indians. The Swedish fort fell easily and the Swedish colony came to an abrupt end, leaving behind only a sprinkling of Swedish place names, log cabins (the first in America), and an admixture of Swedish blood in the area.

New Netherland absorbed New Sweden, but it was soon the turn of the Dutch to be swallowed up by the English. In 1664, after Charles II had granted the area to his brother, the duke of York, a strong English squadron appeared off the decrepit defenses of New Amsterdam. A fuming Peter Stuyvesant, short of all munitions except courage, was forced to surrender without firing a shot. New Amsterdam was thereupon renamed New York, in honor of the Duke of York. England won a splendid harbor, strategically located in the middle of the mainland colonies, and a stately Hudson River penetrating the interior. The English banner now waved triumphantly, with the removal of this foreign wedge, over a solid stretch of territory from Maine to the Carolinas.

The conquered Dutch province tenaciously retained many of the illiberal features of earlier days. An autocratic spirit survived, and the aristocratic element gained strength when certain corrupt English governors granted immense acreage to their favorites. Influential landowning families—such as the Livingstons and the De Lanceys—wielded disproportionate power in the affairs of colonial New York. These monopolistic land policies, combined

New Amsterdam, c. 1653. *The site of latter-day New York, this colonial village was still in Dutch hands in 1653, as shown by the Dutch-style windmill. (Museum of the City of New York)*

with the lordly atmosphere, discouraged many European immigrants from coming. The physical growth of New York was correspondingly retarded.

Penn's Holy Experiment in Pennsylvania

A remarkable group of dissenters, commonly known as Quakers, arose in England during the mid-1600s. Their name derived from the report that they "quaked" when under deep religious emotion. Officially they were known as the Religious Society of Friends.

Quakers were especially offensive to the authorities, both religious and civil. They refused to support the established Church of England with taxes. They built simple meetinghouses, without a paid clergy, and "spoke up" in meetings themselves when moved. Believing that they were all children in the sight of God, they kept their broad-brimmed hats on in the presence of their "betters," and addressed others with simple "thees" and "thous," rather than with conventional titles. They would take no oaths, because Jesus had said, "Swear not at all." This peculiarity often embroiled them with government officials, for "test oaths" were still required to establish the fact that a person was not a Roman Catholic.

The Quakers, beyond a doubt, were a people of deep conviction. They abhorred strife and warfare, and refused military service. As advocates of passive resistance, they would turn the other cheek and rebuild their meetinghouse on the site where their

enemies had torn it down. Their courage and devotion to principle finally triumphed. Though at times they seemed stubborn and unreasonable, they were a simple, devoted, democratic people, contending in their own way for both religious and civic freedom.

William Penn, a well-born and athletic young Englishman, was attracted to the Quaker faith in 1660, when only sixteen years old. His father, disapproving, administered a sound flogging. After various adventures in the army (the best portrait of the peaceful Quaker has him in armor), the youth firmly embraced the despised faith and suffered much persecution. The courts branded him a "saucy" and "impertinent" fellow. Several hundred of his less fortunate co-religionists died of cruel treatment, and thousands more were fined, flogged, or cast into "nasty stinking prisons."

Penn's thoughts naturally turned to the New World, where a sprinkling of Quakers had already fled, notably to Rhode Island, North Carolina, and New Jersey. Eager to establish an asylum for his people, he also hoped to experiment with liberal ideas in government, and at the same time make a profit. Finally, in 1681, he managed to secure from the king an immense grant of fertile land, in consideration of a monetary debt owed to his deceased father by the crown. The king officially named the area Pennsylvania ("Penn's Woodland"), in honor of the father.

Pennsylvania was by far the best advertised of the colonies. Its founder sent out paid agents and distributed countless pamphlets printed in English,

Dutch, French, and German. Unlike the lures of many another American real estate promoter, then and later, Penn's inducements were generally truthful. He especially welcomed forward-looking spirits and substantial citizens, including industrious carpenters, masons, shoemakers, and other manual workers. His liberal land policy, which encouraged substantial holdings of land, was instrumental in attracting a heavy inflow of immigrants.

Quaker Pennsylvania and Her Neighbors

Penn formally launched his colony in 1681. His task was simplified by the presence of several thousand "squatters"—Dutch, Swedes, English, Welsh—who were already scattered along the banks of the Delaware River. Philadelphia, meaning "brotherly love" in Greek, was more carefully planned than most colonial cities, and consequently enjoyed wide and attractive streets. Penn farsightedly bought land from the Indians, including Chief Tammany, later patron saint of New York's political Tammany Hall. His treatment of the red men was so fair that the Quaker "Broad Brims" went among them unarmed, and even employed them as baby tenders.

Penn's new proprietary regime was unusually liberal, and included a representative assembly elected by the landowners. There was no tax-supported state church. Freedom of worship was guaranteed to all residents, although Penn, under pressure from London, was forced to deny Catholics and Jews the privilege of voting or holding office. The death penalty was imposed only for treason and murder, as compared with some two hundred capital crimes in England.

Among other noteworthy features, no provision was made by the peace-loving Quakers of Pennsylvania for a military defense. No restrictions were placed on immigration, and naturalization was made easy. The humane Quakers early developed a strong dislike of black slavery, and in the genial glow of Pennsylvania some progress was made toward social reform.

Because of its many liberal attractions, Pennsylvania attracted a rich mix of ethnic groups. They included numerous religious misfits who were repelled by the harsh practices of neighboring colonies. This Quaker haven boasted a surprisingly modern atmosphere in an unmodern age, and to an unusual degree afforded economic opportunity, civil liberty, and religious freedom. Even so, there were some "blue laws" aimed at "ungodly revelers," stage plays, playing cards, dice, May games, and excessive hilarity.

Under such generally happy auspices, Penn's brainchild grew lustily. The Quakers were shrewd businessmen, and in a short time the settlers were exporting grain and other foodstuffs. Within two years Philadelphia claimed 300 houses and 2,500 people. Modern-minded Benjamin Franklin, entering Philadelphia as a seventeen-year-old youth with a roll of bread under each arm, found a congenial home in the urbane atmosphere of the city. Within nineteen years—by 1700—the colony was surpassed in population and wealth only by long-established Virginia and Massachusetts.

William Penn, who altogether spent about four years in Pennsylvania, was never fully appreciated by his colonists. His governors, some of them incompetent and tactless, quarreled bitterly with the people, who were constantly demanding greater political control. Penn himself became too friendly with James II, the deposed Catholic king. Thrice arrested for treason, thrust for a time into a debtors' prison, and racked by apoplectic seizures, he died full of sorrows. His enduring monument was not only a noble experiment in government but also a new commonwealth. Based on civil and religious liberty, and dedicated to freedom of conscience and worship, it held aloft a hopeful torch in a world of semidarkness.

Small Quaker settlements flourished next door to Pennsylvania. New Jersey was started in 1664, when two noble proprietors received the area from the Duke of York. One of the proprietors sold West New Jersey in 1674 to a group of Quakers, and East New Jersey was also acquired by Quakers a few years later. In 1702 the crown combined the two Jerseys in a royal colony.

Swedish-tinged Delaware consisted of only three counties—two at high tide, the witticism goes—and was named after Lord de la Warr. It harbored some Quakers, and was closely associated with Penn's flourishing colony, Delaware was granted its own

William Penn Signs a Treaty with the Indians. *The peace-loving Quaker founder of Pennsylvania made a serious effort to live in harmony with the Indians, but the westward thrust of white settlement eventually caused friction, as in other colonies. (The Thomas Gilcrease Institute of American History and Art, Tulsa, Oklahoma)*

assembly in 1703. But until the American Revolution it remained under the governor of Pennsylvania.

The Middle Way in the Middle Colonies

The middle colonies—New York, New Jersey, Delaware, and Pennsylvania—enjoyed certain features in common.

In general, the soil was fertile and the expanse of land was broad, unlike rock-bestrewn New England. Pennsylvania, New York, and New Jersey came to be known as the "bread colonies," by virtue of their heavy exports of grain.

Rivers also played a vital role. Broad, languid streams—notably the Susquehanna, the Delaware, and the Hudson—tapped the fur trade of the interior and beckoned adventuresome spirits into the backcountry. The rivers had few cascading waterfalls, unlike New England's, and hence presented little

inducement to manufacturing with water-wheel power.

A surprising amount of industry nonetheless flourished in the middle colonies. Virginal forests abounded for lumbering and shipbuilding. The presence of deep river estuaries and landlocked harbors stimulated both commerce and the growth of seaports, such as New York and Philadelphia. Even Albany, more than a hundred miles up the Hudson, was a port of some consequence in colonial days.

The middle colonies were in many respects midway between New England and the southern plantation group. Except in aristocratic New York, the land holdings were generally intermediate in size—smaller than in the big-acreage South but larger than in small-farm New England. Local government lay somewhere between the personalized town meeting of New England and the diffused county government of the South. There were fewer industries in the middle

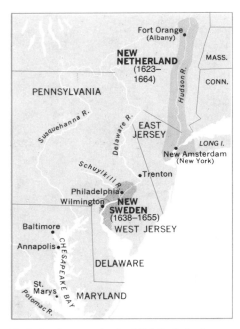

Early Settlements in the Middle Colonies.

the most American part of America, could claim certain distinctions in their own right. Generally speaking, the population was more ethnically mixed than that of other settlements. The people were blessed with an unusual degree of religious toleration and democratic control. Earnest and devout Quakers, in particular, made a contribution to human freedom out of all proportion to their numbers. Desirable land was more easily acquired in the middle colonies than in New England or in the tidewater South. One result was that a considerable amount of economic and social democracy prevailed, though less so in aristocratic New York.

By the mid-eighteenth century, the thirteen colonies as a group revealed striking similarities, even though they had developed wide differences. They were all basically English. They all exercised certain priceless Anglo-Saxon freedoms. They all possessed some measure of self-government, though by no means complete democracy. They all enjoyed some degree of religious toleration and educational opportunity. They all afforded unusual advantages for economic and social self-development. Finally—and perhaps most significantly—they were all separated from home authority by a billowing ocean moat 3,000 miles (4,800 kilometers) wide.

colonies than in New England, more than in the South.

Yet the middle colonies, which in some ways were

VARYING VIEWPOINTS

For many years, historians of the first century of colonial life in British North America focused on the efforts of the colonists to stake out a social order free of the constraints of the mother country. The struggle of the Massachusetts Bay Puritans to escape the regimentation of English society and to seize the religious freedom and economic equality preferred by the American wilderness formed the centerpiece of this interpretation, which was conspicuous in the work of Perry Miller, among others. Similarly, the founding of Quaker settlements in New Jersey and Pennsylvania, and the attempt of Dutch New Yorkers to maintain their cultural heritage, revealed the discord between the colonies and the mother country.

Recent studies, including those by Gary Nash and Patricia Bonomi, have shifted the drama of early American history from the transatlantic to the domestic stage. This perspective emphasizes the contests for economic and political supremacy within the colonies, such as the efforts of the Massachusetts Bay elite to ward off the challenges of religious "heretics" and an increasingly restless lower class. Nowhere was such internal conflict so prevalent as in the ethnically diverse middle colonies, where factional conflict became the distinguishing feature of public life. Some historians even find, in the turbulent middle colonies, the seeds of the later competitive American political system.

SELECT READINGS

Primary Source Documents

John Winthrop, "A Modell of Christian Charity" (1630), in *The American Primer,* edited by Daniel Boorstin, outlines the goals of the Puritan errand into the wilderness. Winthrop's "Speech on Liberty"* (1645), in his *History of New England* (1853), established the colony's fundamental political principles. William Bradford, *Of Plymouth Plantation,** edited by Samuel E. Morison (1952), is a rich contemporary account.

Secondary Sources

New England has received more scholarly attention than any other colonial region. An incisive short account is Edmund S. Morgan's *The Puritan Dilemma: The Story of John Winthrop* (1958). A brilliant and complex intellectual history is Perry Miller's *The New England Mind* (2 vols., 1939, 1953), a work that has long been a landmark for other scholars. Sacvan Bercovitch traces the heritage of the New England temperament in *The Puritan Origins of the American Self* (1975). Edmund S. Morgan describes the crisis that beset the original Puritans when their children displayed a lesser degree of religiosity in *Visible Saints* (1963). Economic questions receive critical attention from Bernard Bailyn in *The New England Merchants in the Seventeenth Century* (1955). Sidney Ahlstrom's *Religious History of the American People* (1972) is comprehensive. Areas outside New England are dealt with in Gary Nash, *Quakers and Politics: Pennsylvania, 1681–1726* (1971); Patricia Bonomi, *A Factious People: Politics and Society in Colonial New York* (1971); and Frederick Tolles, *Meetinghouse and Countinghouse* (1948). Timothy H. Breen, *Puritans and Adventurers* (1980), draws contrasts between Virginia and New England.

3

American Life in the Seventeenth Century

**Being thus passed the vast ocean,
and a sea of troubles before in their preparation . . .,
they had now no friends to wellcome them,
nor inns to entertaine or refresh their weatherbeaten bodys,
no houses or much less towns to repaire too, to seeke for succore.**

William Bradford, Of Plymouth Plantation

The Unhealthy Chesapeake

Life in the American wilderness was nasty, brutish, and short for the earliest Chesapeake settlers. Malaria, dysentery, and typhoid took a cruel toll, cutting ten years off the life expectancy of newcomers from England. Half the people born in early Virginia and Maryland did not survive to celebrate their twentieth birthdays. Few of the remaining half lived to see their fiftieth—or even their fortieth, if they were women.

The disease-ravaged settlements of the Chesapeake grew only slowly in the seventeenth century, mostly through fresh immigration from the mother country. The great majority of immigrants were single men in their late teens and early twenties, and most perished soon after their arrival. Surviving males competed for the affections of the extremely scarce women, whom they outnumbered nearly six to

one in 1650. Eligible women did not remain single for long.

Families were both few and fragile in this ferocious environment. Most men could not find mates, and most marriages were destroyed by the death of a partner within seven years. Weak family ties were reflected in the many pregnancies among unmarried young girls. In one Maryland county, more than a third of all brides were already pregnant when they spoke their marriage vows.

Yet despite these hardships, the Chesapeake colonies struggled on. The native-born adult inhabitants eventually acquired immunity to the killer diseases that had ravaged the original immigrants. The presence of more women allowed more families to form, and by the end of the seventeenth century the white population of the Chesapeake was growing on the basis of its own birthrate. As the eighteenth century opened, Virginia, with some fifty-nine thousand souls, was the most populous colony. Maryland, with about thirty thousand, was the third largest (after Massachusetts).

The Tobacco Economy

Though unhealthy for human life, the Chesapeake was immensely hospitable to tobacco cultivation. Profit-hungry settlers often planted tobacco before they planted corn. Seeking fresh fields to plant tobacco, these new immigrants plunged ever farther up the river valleys. The result was continually rising tobacco production, which reached 40 million pounds (18 million kilograms) a year by the end of the century. This expansion depressed prices for the crop, but tobacco growers continued to plant still more acres to tobacco and bring still more product to market.

More tobacco meant more labor, but where was it to come from? The white population was too small and slow-growing, Indians died too quickly on contact with whites, and African slaves cost too much money. But England still had a "surplus" of displaced yeoman farmers desperate for employment. Many of them, as "indentured servants," voluntarily mortgaged the sweat of their bodies for several years to Chesapeake masters. In exchange they received transatlantic passage and eventual "freedom dues," including a few barrels of corn, a suit of clothes—and perhaps a small parcel of land.

Both Virginia and Maryland employed the "headright" system to encourage the importation of servant workers. Under its terms, the master who paid the passage of a laborer received the right to acquire fifty acres of land. Taking advantage of this system, some masters soon parlayed their investments in servants into huge fortunes in real estate. They became the great merchant-planters who came to dominate the agriculture and commerce of the southern colonies. Chesapeake planters brought some 100,000 indentured servants to the region by 1700. These "white slaves" represented more than three-quarters of all European immigrants to Virginia and Maryland in the seventeenth century.

Indentured servants led a hard but hopeful life in the early days of the Chesapeake settlements, as they looked forward to becoming free and acquiring land of their own after completing their terms of servitude. But as the seventeenth century wore on, prime land became scarcer and the servants' lot grew harsher. Even when formal freedom was granted, penniless freed workers often had little choice but to hire themselves out for pitifully low wages to their former masters.

Frustrated Freedmen and Bacon's Rebellion

An accumulating mass of footloose, impoverished freemen was drifting discontentedly about the Chesapeake region by the late seventeenth century. Mostly single young men, they were frustrated by their broken hopes of acquiring land, as well as by their gnawing failure to find single women.

The swelling number of these wretched bachelors rattled the established planters. Led by Governor Berkeley, the Virginia assembly in 1670 disenfranchised most of the landless knockabouts. About a thousand Virginians then broke out of control in 1676, under the leadership of a twenty-nine-year-old planter, Nathaniel Bacon. Angered by Berkeley's mild Indian policies as well as economic grievances, Bacon and his followers first attacked Indians on the frontier. They then chased Berkeley from Jamestown and put the torch to the capital. Chaos swept the raw colony, as frustrated freedmen and resentful servants—described as "a rabble of the basest sort of people"—went on a rampage of plundering and pilfering.

In the midst of this civil war, Bacon suddenly died of disease. Berkeley thereupon crushed the uprising with brutal cruelty, hanging more than twenty rebels. Back in England Charles II complained, "That old fool has put to death more people in that naked country than I did here for the murder of my father."

The distant English king could scarcely imagine the depths of passion and fear that Bacon's rebellion excited in Virginia. Bacon had ignited the smoldering unhappiness of landless former servants, and he had pitted the hardscrabble backcountry frontiersmen against the haughty gentry of the tidewater plantations. The rebellion was now suppressed, but these tensions remained. Lordly planters, surrounded by a still-seething sea of malcontents, anxiously looked about for less-troublesome laborers to toil in the restless tobacco kingdom. Their eyes soon lit on Africa.

Perhaps 10 million Africans were carried in chains to the New World in the three centuries or so following Columbus's discovery. Only about 400,000 of them ended up in North America. Africans had been brought to Jamestown as early as 1619, but as late as 1670 they numbered only about 7 percent of the 50,000 people in the southern plantation colonies as a whole. For hard-pinched white colonists, white servants were less costly than high-priced slaves.

Drastic change came in the 1680s. The pool of penniless indentured servants from England declined, while large planters increasingly feared the potentially mutinous former servants in their midst. By the mid-1680s, for the first time, black slaves outnumbered white servants among the plantation colonies' new arrivals. In 1698 the Royal African Company lost its crown-granted monopoly on carrying slaves to the colonies. Enterprising Americans, especially Rhode Islanders, rushed to cash in on the lucrative slave trade, and the supply of slaves increased steeply. By 1750 blacks accounted for nearly half the population of Virginia, and in South Carolina they outnumbered whites two to one.

Most of the slaves who reached North America came from the west coast of Africa. Originally captured by African coastal tribes, they were traded in crude markets to itinerant European—and American—flesh merchants. Usually branded and bound, the captives were herded aboard sweltering ships for the gruesome "middle passage," on which death rates ran as high as 20 percent. The terrified survivors were then sold in the slave markets of the New World.

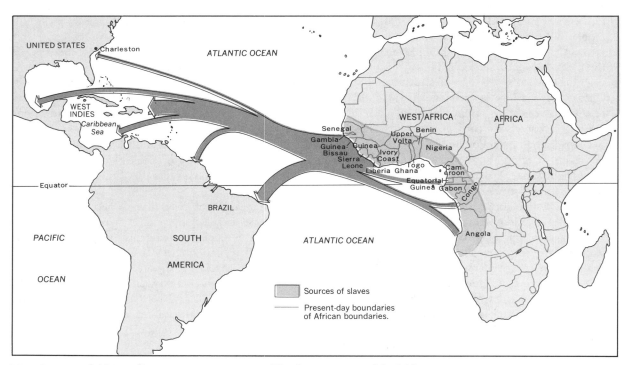

Main Sources of African Slaves, c. 1500 to c. 1800. *The three centuries of the "African Diaspora" scattered blacks all over the New World; about 400,000 came to the English colonies.*

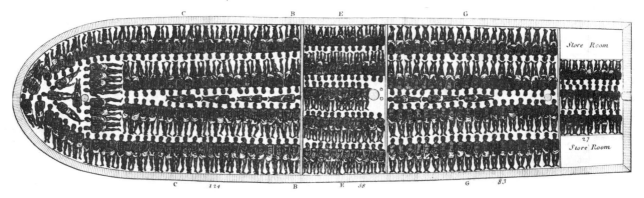

The "Middle Passage."   *Human cargo in the hold of a slave ship. (The Mariners Museum)*

A few of the earliest African immigrants gained their freedom, and some even became slaveowners themselves. But as the number of Africans in their midst increased dramatically toward the end of the seventeenth century, white colonists reacted remorselessly to this supposed racial threat. The iron conditions of black bondage were spelled out in "slave codes" that made blacks and their children the property for life of their white masters. Not even conversion to Christianity entitled a slave to freedom.

Africans in America

In the deepest South, slave life was especially harsh. The climate was hostile to health, and the labor was life-draining. The widely scattered South Carolina rice and indigo plantations were lonely hells on earth where gangs of mostly male Africans toiled and perished. Only fresh imports could sustain the slave population under these cruel conditions.

Blacks in the tobacco-growing Chesapeake region had a somewhat easier lot. Tobacco-growing was less physically demanding, and tobacco plantations were larger and closer to one another than rice plantations. By about 1720 the proportion of females in the Chesapeake slave population had begun to rise, making family life possible. The captive black population of the Chesapeake area soon began to grow not only through new imports but also through its own fertility—making it one of the few slave societies in history to perpetuate itself by natural reproduction.

Native-born Afro-Americans contributed to the growth of a stable and distinctive slave culture, a mixture of African and American elements of speech, religion, and folkways. On the sea islands off South Carolina's coast, blacks evolved a unique language, *Gullah,* that blended English and several African tongues. The ringshout, a West African religious dance performed by shuffling in a circle while answering a preacher's shouts, was brought to colonial America by slaves and eventually contributed to the development of jazz.

Slaves also helped powerfully to build the country with their labor. A few became skilled artisans—carpenters, bricklayers, and tanners. But chiefly they performed the sweaty toil of clearing swamps, grubbing out trees, and other menial tasks. Condemned to life under the lash, slaves naturally pined for freedom. Slave revolts erupted in New York City in 1712, and again in South Carolina in 1739. But in the end slaves proved to be a more reliable labor force than the white indentured servants they gradually replaced. No slave rebellion in American history matched the scale of Bacon's Rebellion.

Southern Society

As slavery spread, the gaps in the South's social structure widened. The rough equality of poverty and disease of the early days was giving way to a defined hierarchy of wealth and status in the early eighteenth century. At the top of the social ladder perched a small but powerful covey of great planters. Owning gangs of slaves and vast domains of land, they ruled the region's economy and virtually monopolized political power. Yet, legend to the contrary, these great seventeenth-century merchant planters were not silk-swathed cavaliers gallantly imitating the ways of English country gentlemen. For the most part they were a hardworking, businesslike lot, laboring long hours over the problems of plantation management.

Far beneath the planters in wealth, prestige, and political power were the small farmers, the largest social group. They lived a ragged, hand-to-mouth existence on their modest plots. Still lower on the social scale were landless whites, and below them indentured servants still serving out their terms. The oppressed black slaves, of course, remained enchained in society's basement.

Few cities sprouted in the colonial South, and consequently an urban professional class, including lawyers and financiers, was slow to emerge. Southern life revolved around the great plantations, distantly isolated from one another. Waterways, rather than the wretched roads, provided the principal means of transportation from one plantation to another.

The New England Family

Nature smiled more benignly on pioneer New Englanders than on their disease-plagued fellow colonists to the south. Healthier living conditions enabled settlers in seventeenth-century New England to *add* ten years to their life spans by migrating from the Old World. The first generations of Puritan colonists enjoyed, on the average, about seventy years on this earth—not very different from the life expectancy of present-day Americans.

In contrast with the Chesapeake, New Englanders tended to migrate not as single individuals but as families, and the family remained at the center of New England life. Early marriage and fertile childbearing enabled New England's population to grow from natural reproductive increase. Women typically wed by their early twenties and produced babies about every two years thereafter until menopause. A married woman could thus expect to experience up to ten exhausting pregnancies, and to rear as many as eight surviving children. A New England woman might well have dependent children in her household from the earliest days of her marriage until the day of her death, and child raising became virtually her full-time occupation.

The longevity of the New Englanders contributed to family stability. Children received nurturing love and guidance not only from their parents but from their grandparents as well. Family stability was reflected in low premarital pregnancy rates, and in the generally strong, tranquil social structure characteristic of colonial New England.

Life in the New England Towns

Sturdy New Englanders evolved a tightly knit society, the basis of which was small villages and farms. Puritanism especially made for unity of purpose— and for concern about the moral health of the whole community.

Even the expansion of New England occurred in orderly, communal fashion. New towns were legally chartered by the colonial authorities, and the distribution of land was entrusted to the steady hands of sober-minded town fathers, or "proprietors." The proprietors usually laid out their town around a meetinghouse, which served as both the place of worship and the town hall, and a village green, where the militia could drill. Each family received several parcels of land.

Towns of more than fifty families were required to provide elementary education, and a majority of adults knew how to read and write. As early as 1636, the Massachusetts Puritans established Harvard College to train local boys for the ministry. Only in 1693, eighty-six years after the founding of Jamestown, did the Virginians establish their first college, William and Mary.

The Changing New England Way of Life

Worries nevertheless plagued the God-fearing pioneers of these tidy New England settlements. The pressure of a growing population was gradually dispersing the Puritans onto outlying farms, far from the control of church and neighbors. And while the core of Puritan belief still burned brightly, the passage of time was dampening the first generation's religious zeal. Alarmed Puritan preachers began scolding their parishioners in a new form of doom-saying sermon— the "jeremiad." In response to the apparent decline in

Graveyard Art. *These New England colonists evidently died in the prime of life. Carving likenesses on grave markers was a common way of commemorating the dead. (American Antiquarian Society)*

conversions, troubled ministers in 1662 announced a new formula for church membership, the "Half-Way Covenant." It offered partial membership rights to persons not yet converted. This widening of church membership gradually erased the distinction between the "elect" and other members of society. In effect, strict religious purity was somewhat sacrificed to the cause of wider religious participation. Interestingly, from about this time onward women made up a larger proportion of Puritan congregations.

Women also played a prominent role in one of New England's most frightening religious episodes. A group of adolescent girls in Salem, Massachusetts, claimed to have been bewitched by certain older women. A hysterical "witch-hunt" ensued, leading to the execution in 1692 of twenty persons. Witchcraft persecutions had occurred before in Europe and America, but the reign of horror in Salem grew not only from the superstitions of the age but also from the unsettled social and religious conditions of the rapidly evolving Massachusetts village. The Salem witchcraft delusion marked an all-time high in the American experience of popular passions run wild and seriously weakened the prestige of the Puritan clergy, some of whom had supported it.

New England soil, like New England religion, was hard and unyielding. Scratching a living from the rock-strewn land put a premium on sharp trading and penny-pinching frugality, for which New Englanders became famous. The grudging earth also left colonial New England less ethnically mixed than its southern neighbors. European immigrants were not attracted in great numbers to a site where the soil was so stony—and the religion so sulfurous.

Yet the harsh climate and unproductive soil eventually encouraged New England to develop a diversified agriculture and industry. Turning away from the land, hardy New Englanders looked to the sea for a living. Hacking timber from their dense forests, they became experts in shipbuilding and commerce. They also ceaselessly exploited the self-perpetuating codfish lode off the coast of Newfoundland—the fishy "gold mines of New England." As a reminder of the importance of fishing, a handsome replica of the "sacred cod" is proudly displayed to this day in the Massachusetts State House in Boston.

The combination of Calvinism, soil, and climate in New England made for energy, purposefulness, sternness, stubbornness, self-reliance, and resourcefulness. Righteous New Englanders prided themselves on being God's chosen people. They long boasted that Boston was "the hub of the universe"— at least spiritually. A famous jingle of later days ran:

> I come from the city of Boston
> The home of the bean and the cod
> Where the Cabots speak only to Lowells
> And the Lowells speak only to God.

As flinty as their stones, as stiff as their cuffs and collars, New Englanders later cross-fertilized innumerable other communities across America with their ideals and democratic practices. The New England conscience inspired many later reformers and added something indispensable to the fiber and backbone of the American people.

The Early Settlers' Days and Ways

The cycles of the seasons and the sun set the schedules of all the earliest American colonists. The overwhelming majority of colonists were farmers whose lives were governed by the natural calendar of the seasons and the natural clock of the sun. They usually rose at dawn and went to bed at dusk. Chores might be performed after nightfall only if they were "worth the candle," a phrase that has persisted in American speech.

Women everywhere wove, cooked, cleaned, and cared for children. Men worked the land, cut firewood, and butchered livestock as needed. Children helped with all these tasks, while picking up such schooling as they could.

Life was humble but comfortable by contemporary standards. Compared to most seventeenth-century Europeans, Americans lived in affluent abundance. Land was relatively cheap, though somewhat less available in the planter-dominated South than elsewhere.

"Dukes don't emigrate," the saying goes, for if people enjoy wealth and security, they are not likely to risk exposing their lives in the wilderness. Similarly, the very poorest members of a society may not possess even the modest means needed to pull up stakes and seek a fresh start in life. Accordingly, most white migrants to early colonial America came neither from the aristocracy nor from the dregs of European society.

In any case, seventeenth-century society in all the colonies had a certain simple sameness to it, especially in the more egalitarian New England and middle colonies. Yet many settlers, who considered themselves to be of the "better sort," tried to recreate on a modified scale the social structure they had known in the Old World. Resentment against such upper-class pretensions helped to spark outbursts such as Bacon's Rebellion in Virginia, the uprising of Maryland's Protestants toward the end of the seventeenth century, and Leisler's Rebellion in New York between 1689 and 1691.

For their part, would-be American bluebloods resented the pretensions of the "meaner sort" and passed laws to try to keep them in their place. Massachusetts in 1651 prohibited poorer folk from "wearing gold or silver lace," and in eighteenth-century Virginia a tailor was fined and jailed for arranging to race his horse—"a sport only for gentlemen." But these efforts to reproduce the finely stratified societies of Europe proved feeble in the early American wilderness, where equality and democracy found fertile soil—at least for white people.

VARYING VIEWPOINTS

The simultaneous evolution of a rigid racial caste system and democratic political traditions in the British colonies has long perplexed students of early America. For many generations historians, most of them of Yankee stock, resolved the apparent paradox by locating the seeds of democracy in New England. The aggressive independence of the people, best expressed by the boisterous town meetings, spawned the American obsession with freedom. On the other hand, this view holds, the slave societies of the South were hierarchical, aristocratic communities under the sway of a few powerful planters.

Recent studies have questioned this interpretation. First, they point out the many undemocratic features of colonial New England. Second, they note that Washington, Jefferson, and Madison—the architects of American government and its commitment to liberty—all hailed from slaveholding Virginia. In fact, nowhere were republican principles stronger than in Virginia. This realization has sparked new speculation about the relationship between American slavery and American freedom. Some scholars, notably Edmund S. Morgan, see the willingness of wealthy planters to concede the equality and freedom of all white males as a device to ensure racial solidarity and mute class conflict. In this view, the concurrent emergence of slavery and democracy poses no paradox. Racism muffled animosity between rich and poor and fostered the devotion to equality (for whites) that became the hallmark of American democracy.

SELECT READINGS

Primary Source Documents

Adolph B. Benson, ed., *The America of 1750; Petar Kalm's Travels in North America* (1937), records the observations of a visiting Swedish naturalist with a keen eye for the behavior of human fauna. The first slave laws of Virginia are collected in Warren M. Billings, ed., *The Old Dominion in the Seventeenth Century** (1975), as are firsthand accounts of Bacon's Rebellion. See also George L. Burr, ed., *Narratives of the Witchcraft Cases, 1648–1706* (1914).*

Secondary Sources

A general survey is Clarence Ver Steeg, *The Formative Years* (1964). On life and labor in the Chesapeake, consult Thad W. Tate and David L. Ammerman, eds., *The Chesapeake in the Seventeenth Century* (1979); Wesley F. Craven, *The Southern Colonies in the Seventeenth Century* (1949); and Edmund S. Morgan, *American Slavery, American Freedom* (1975), which concentrates on race and class relations. Winthrop Jordan's magnificent *White Over Black: American Attitudes Toward the Negro, 1550–1812* (1968) discusses the evolution of racial attitudes. Among the many works that scrutinize life in New England's towns and homes are Edmund S. Morgan, *Puritan Family* (1944); Bernard Bailyn, *Education in the Forming of American Society* (1960); John Demos, *A Little Commonwealth: Family Life in Plymouth Colony* (1970); Philip Greven, *Four Generations: Population, Land, and Family in Colonial Andover, Massachusetts* (1970); Kenneth Lockridge, *New England Town: Dedham* (1970); Lyle Koehler, *A Search for Power: The "Weaker Sex" in Seventeenth-Century New England* (1980); Laurel T. Ulrich, *Good Wives: Image and Reality in the Lives of Women in Northern New England, 1650–1750* (1982); and Philip Greven, *The Protestant Temperament* (1977), which analyzes child-rearing practices. Robert Pope examines *The Half-Way Covenant: Church Membership in Puritan New England* (1969). Witchcraft is the subject of Paul Boyer and Stephen Nissenbaum's *Salem Possessed* (1974) and John Demos's massive *Entertaining Satan* (1982).

4

Colonial Society on the Eve of Revolution

**Driven from every other corner of the earth,
freedom of thought and the right of private judgment in matters of conscience
direct their course to this happy country as their last asylum.**

Samuel Adams, 1776

Conquest by the Cradle

The thirteen colonies on the North American mainland that rebelled against British rule in 1776 differed considerably in economic organization, social structure, and ways of life. Yet all of them had one outstanding feature in common: their population was growing by leaps and bounds. In 1700 they contained fewer than 300,000 souls, about 20,000 of whom were black. By 1775, 2.5 million persons inhabited the thirteen colonies, of whom about half a million were black. Some of this increase came from white immigration and the black "forced immigration." But most of the spurt stemmed from the remarkable natural fertility of all Americans, white and black. The youthful Americans, whose average age in 1775 was about sixteen, were doubling their numbers every twenty-five years. Unfriendly Dr. Samuel Johnson, back in England, growled that the Americans were multiplying like their own rattlesnakes.

This population boom had political consequences. In 1700 there were twenty English inhabitants for each American colonist. By 1775 the English advantage in numbers had fallen to three to one—setting the stage for a momentous shift in the balance of power between the colonies and the mother country.

The bulk of the population was cooped up east of the Alleghenies. The most populous colonies in 1775 were Virginia, Massachusetts, Pennsylvania, North Carolina, and Maryland—in that order. There were only four substantial cities: Philadelphia, including suburbs, was first with about 34,000, while New York, Boston, and Charleston were strung out behind. About 90 percent of the people lived in rural areas.

A Potpourri of Peoples

Colonial America was a melting pot, and had been from the outset. The population, although basically English in stock and language, was picturesquely mottled with numerous foreign groups.

Heavy-accented Germans constituted about 6 percent of the total population, or 150,000, by 1775. Fleeing religious persecution, economic oppression, and the ravages of war, they had flocked to America in the early 1700s, and had settled chiefly in Pennsylvania. Known popularly but erroneously as the Pennsylvania Dutch (a corruption of the German word *Deutsch*), they totaled about one-third of the colony's population. In Philadelphia, where street signs were in both German and English, and in the Pennsylvania back country, where many of them had moved, German immigrants clung tenaciously to their language and customs.

The Scotch-Irish, who in 1775 numbered about 175,000, or 7 percent of the population, were an important non-English group, although English-speaking. They were not Irish at all, but turbulent Scots Lowlanders. Over a period of many decades, they had first been transplanted to Northern Ireland, where they had not prospered under oppressive English rule. The Irish Catholics already there, hating Scotch Presbyterianism, resented the intruders, and still do.

Early in the 1700s tens of thousands of embittered Scotch-Irish finally pulled up stakes and came to America, chiefly to tolerant and deep-soiled Pennsylvania. Finding the best acres already taken by Germans and Quakers, they pushed out onto the frontier. There many of them illegally but defiantly squatted on the unoccupied lands, and quarreled with both red and white owners. It was said, somewhat unfairly, that the Scotch-Irish kept the Sabbath—and all else they could lay their hands on. Pugnacious, lawless, and individualistic, they brought with them the Scottish secrets of whiskey distilling and proceeded to set up their own stills. They cherished no love for the British

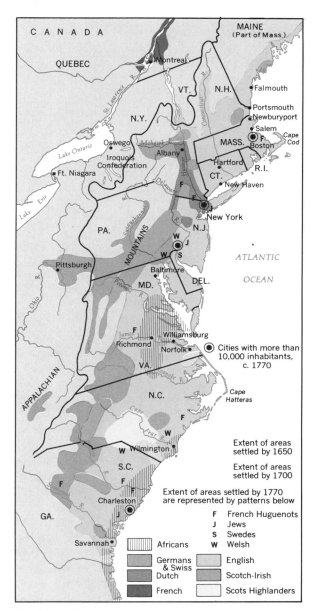

Immigrant Groups in 1775.
America was already a nation of diverse nationalities in the colonial period. This map shows the great variety of immigrant groups, especially in Pennsylvania and New York. It also illustrates the tendency of later arrivals, particularly the Scotch-Irish, to push into the backcountry. The basic ethnic makeup of many of these colonial settlements persists even today, each with distinct cultural patterns and attitudes.

Estimated Population Elements, 1790* (based on family names)

Ethnic Groups	Number	Percentage
English and Welsh	2,605,699	66.3%
Scotch (including Scotch-Irish)	221,562	5.6
German	176,407	4.5
Dutch	78,959	2.0
Irish	61,534	1.6
French	17,619	0.4
All other whites	10,664	0.3
Africans	757,181	19.3
Grand Total	3,929,625	100.0

*Rossiter, *A Century of Population Growth* (1909). Later estimates by Barker and Hansen (1931) are not used here because they are confused by the inclusion of Spanish and French elements *later* a part of the United States.

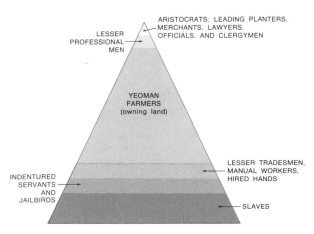

The Colonial Social Pyramid, 1775. *(an approximation)*

government which had uprooted them, and many of them—including the youthful Andrew Jackson—joined the embattled American Revolutionists.

Approximately 5 percent of the colonial population consisted of other ethnic groups, including French, Welsh, Dutch, Swedes, Jews, Irish, Swiss, and Scots Highlanders. Few members of these groups felt much loyalty to the British crown.

The population of the thirteen colonies, though mainly Anglo-Saxon, was perhaps the most mixed to be found anywhere in the world. The South, holding about 90 percent of the slaves, already displayed its historic black-and-white racial composition. New England, mostly staked out by the original Puritan migrants, showed the least ethnic diversity. The middle colonies, especially Pennsylvania, received the bulk of later white immigrants, and boasted an astonishing variety of peoples. Of the fifty-six signers of the Declaration of Independence in 1776, eighteen were non-English, and eight had been born outside the colonies.

The Structure of Colonial Society

In contrast with contemporary Europe, eighteenth-century America was a shining land of equality and opportunity—with the notorious exception of slavery. No titled nobility dominated society from on high, and no pauperized underclass threatened it from below. Most white Americans, and even some free blacks, were small farmers. The cities contained a small class of skilled artisans, as well as a few shopkeepers, tradespeople, and unskilled casual laborers. The most remarkable feature of the social ladder was the rags-to-riches ease with which an ambitious colonial might rise from a lower rung to a higher one.

Yet in contrast with seventeenth-century America, colonial society on the eve of the Revolution was beginning to show signs of stratifications and barriers to mobility that raised worries about the "Europeanization" of America. A new class of merchant princes in New England and the middle colonies, many of whom had made their fortunes as military suppliers in the colonial wars, roosted regally atop the social ladder. They sported imported clothing and dined at tables laid with English china and gleaming silverware. Prominent persons came to be seated in churches and schools according to their social rank.

Poverty and diminished opportunity also began to appear at the bottom of society. Both Philadelphia and New York built almshouses in the 1730s to care for the destitute, although the numbers of poor people remained tiny compared to the numbers in England. In the New England countryside, the rising population meant that existing landholdings were subdivided and the average size of farms shrank drastically. Younger sons were increasingly forced to hire out as wage laborers—or eventually to seek virgin tracts of land beyond the Appalachians.

In the South the power of the great planters continued to be bolstered by their disproportionate ownership of slaves. Wealth was concentrated in the hands of the largest slaveowners, widening the gap between the prosperous gentry and the "poor whites." In all the colonies the ranks of the lower classes were further swelled by the continuing stream of indentured servants. Far less fortunate than the voluntary indentured servants were the paupers and convicts involuntarily shipped to America. Altogether, about fifty thousand "jayle birds"— including robbers, rapists, and murderers—were dumped on the colonies by the London authorities.

Least fortunate of all, of course, were the black slaves. Oppressed and degraded, the slaves were America's closest approximation to Europe's volatile lower classes, and fears of black rebellion plagued the white colonists. Attempts by some colonial legislatures, notably South Carolina's in 1760, to restrict the importation of slaves were vetoed by British authorities. Thomas Jefferson, himself a slaveholder, assailed such vetoes in an early draft of the Declaration of Independence, but his proposed clause was finally dropped, largely out of regard for southern sensibilities.

Clerics, Physicians, and Jurists

Most honored of the professions was the Christian ministry. In 1775 clergymen wielded less influence than in the early days of Massachusetts, when religious fervor had burned more fiercely. But they still occupied a position of high prestige.

Most physicians, on the other hand, were poorly trained and not highly esteemed. Not until 1765 was the first medical school established, although European centers attracted some students. Aspiring young doctors served for a while as apprentices to older practitioners, and were then turned loose on their "victims." Bleeding was a favorite and often fatal remedy; when the physician was not available, a barber was often summoned.

A Pennsylvania Advertisement for Slaves in the 1760s. *Note that the slaves are said to have had smallpox and to be able to speak English. (Rare Book Division, The New York Public Library, Astor, Lenox and Tilden Foundations)*

Plagues were a constant nightmare. Especially dreaded was smallpox (one of Europe's "gifts" to the New World), which afflicted one out of five persons, including the heavily pockmarked George Washington. A crude form of inoculation was introduced in 1721, despite the objections of many physicians and some of the clergy, who opposed tampering with the will of God. Powdered dried toad was a favorite prescription for smallpox. Diphtheria was also a deadly killer, especially of young people. One epidemic in the 1730s took the lives of thousands. This grim reminder of their mortality may have helped to prepare many colonists in their hearts and minds for the religious revival that was soon to sweep them up.

At first the law profession was not favorably regarded. In this pioneering society, which required much honest manual labor, the parties to a dispute often presented their own cases in court. Lawyers were commonly regarded as noisy windbags or troublemaking rogues; an early Connecticut law classed them with drunkards and brothel keepers.

By about 1750, seaboard society had passed the pioneering stage, and trained attorneys were generally recognized as useful. Able to defend colonial rights against the Crown on legal grounds, lawyers like the eloquent James Otis and the flaming Patrick Henry took the lead in the agitation that led to revolt.

Workaday America

Agriculture was the leading industry, involving about 90 percent of the people. Cheap land continued to attract farmers. An acre of virgin soil cost about what an American carpenter could earn in one day as wages, which were roughly three times those of his European counterpart. Tobacco continued to be the staple crop in Maryland and Virginia. The fertile middle ("bread") colonies produced large quantities of grain, and by 1759 New York alone was exporting 80,000 barrels of flour a year. Seemingly the farmer had only to tickle the soil with a hoe and it would laugh with a harvest.

Fishing (including whaling), though ranking far below agriculture, was rewarding. Pursued in all the colonies, this harvesting of the sea was a major industry in New England, which exported smelly shiploads of dried cod to the Catholic countries of Europe. The fishing fleet also stimulated shipbuilding and served as a nursery for the seamen who manned the navy and merchant marine.

Yankee seamen were famous in many climes not only as skilled mariners but as tight-fisted traders. They provisioned the Caribbean sugar islands with food and forest products. They hauled Spanish and Portuguese gold, wine, and oranges to London, to be exchanged for industrial goods, which were then sold for a juicy profit in America.

The so-called triangular trade was infamously profitable, though small in relation to total colonial commerce. A skipper, for example, would leave a New England port with a cargo of rum and sail to the Gold Coast of Africa. Bartering the fiery liquor with African chiefs for captured African slaves, he would proceed to the West Indies with his screaming and suffocating cargo sardined below deck. There he would exchange the survivors for molasses, which he would then carry to New England, where it would be distilled into rum. He would then repeat the trip, making a handsome profit on each leg of the triangle.

Manufacturing in the colonies was of only secondary importance. Huge quantities of "kill devil"

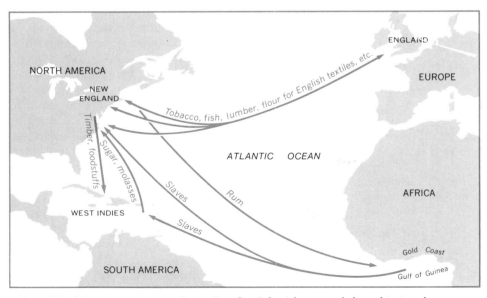

Colonial Trade Patterns, c. 1770. *Future President John Adams noted about this time that "the commerce of the West Indies is a part of the American system of commerce. They can neither do without us, nor we without them. The Creator has placed us upon the globe in such a situation that we have occasion for each other."*

rum were distilled in Rhode Island and Massachusetts, and even some of the "elect of the Lord" developed an overfondness for it. Beaver hats, iron forges, and household spinning and weaving by womenfolk constituted other colonial manufactures. As in all colonial countries, strong-backed laborers and skilled craftsmen were scarce and highly prized.

Lumbering was perhaps the most important single manufacturing activity. Countless cartloads of virgin timber were consumed by shipbuilders, who by 1770 were sending four hundred vessels splashing down the ways each year. Colonial naval stores—such as tar, pitch, resin, and turpentine—were highly valued. Towering trees, ideal as masts for His Majesty's Navy, were marked with the King's broad arrow for future use. The luckless colonial caught cutting down this reserved timber was fined heavily.

Americans held an important flank of a thriving, many-sided Atlantic economy by the dawn of the eighteenth century. Yet strains appeared in this complex network as early as the 1730s. Fastbreeding Americans demanded more and more English products—yet the slow-growing English population early reached the saturation point for absorbing imports from America. How, then, could the colonists sell the goods to make the money to buy what they wanted in the mother country? The answer was obvious: by seeking foreign (non-English) markets.

By the eve of the Revolution the bulk of Chesapeake tobacco was filling pipes in France and other continental countries, though it passed through the hands of English reexporters, who took a slice of the profits. More important was the trade with the West Indies, especially the French islands. West Indian purchases of North American timber and foodstuffs provided the crucial cash for the colonists to continue to make their own purchases in England. In 1733, bowing to pressure from influential British West Indian planters, Parliament passed the Molasses Act, aimed at squelching North American trade with the *French* West Indies. If successful, this scheme would have struck a crippling blow to American international trade, and to the colonists' standard of living. American merchants responded by bribing and smuggling their way around the law. This action foreshadowed the impending imperial crisis, when

headstrong Americans would revolt rather than submit to the dictates of a far-off Parliament apparently bent on destroying their very livelihood.

Horsepower and Sailpower

As a sprawling and sparsely populated pioneer territory, America was cursed with serious transportation problems. Not until the 1700s were there roads connecting even the major cities, and these dirt thoroughfares were treacherously poor.

Roads were often clouds of dust in summer and quagmires of mud in winter. Stagecoach travelers braved such additional dangers as tree-strewn roads, rickety brides, carriage overturns, and runaway horses. Travel was so slow that it actually took twenty-nine days for the news of the Declaration of Independence to reach Charleston from Philadelphia.

Where man-made roads were wretched, heavy reliance was placed on God-grooved waterways. Population tended to cluster along the banks of navigable rivers. There was also much coastwise traffic, which was cheap and pleasant but slow and undependable.

Taverns sprang up along the main routes of travel. Along with such attractions as bowling alleys, pool tables, and gambling equipment, taverns provided plentiful information, rumors, and gossip— frequently stimulated by alcoholic refreshment and impassioned political talk. Taverns were important in crystallizing public opinion, and alehouses like Boston's Green Dragon became hotbeds of agitation as the Revolutionary movement gathered momentum.

The Great Awakening

In all the colonial churches, religion was less fervid in the early eighteenth century than it had been a century earlier, when the colonies were first planted. The Puritan churches in particular sagged under the weight of two burdens: their elaborate theological doctrines and their compromising efforts to liberalize membership requirements. Churchgoers increasingly complained about the "dead dogs" who droned out tedious, overerudite sermons from the pulpit, while many ministers worried that their parishioners had gone soft by embracing liberal ideas about conversion and salvation. Together, these twin trends toward clerical intellectualism and lay liberalism were sapping the spiritual vitality of many denominations.

The stage was thus set for a rousing religious revival. Known as the Great Awakening, it exploded in the 1730s and 1740s and swept through the colonies like a fire through prairie grass. The Awakening was first ignited in Northampton, Massachusetts, by a tall, delicate, and intellectual pastor, Jonathan Edwards. Perhaps the deepest theological mind ever nurtured in America, Edwards proclaimed with burning righteousness the need for complete dependence on God's grace. His preaching style was learned and closely reasoned, but it sparked a warmly sympathetic reaction among his parishioners in 1734.

Four years later, the itinerant English parson George Whitefield loosed a different style of evangelical preaching on America and touched off a conflagration of religious ardor that revolutionized the spiritual life of the colonies. A former alehouse attendant, Whitehead was a magnificent orator whose voice boomed sonorously over thousands of enthralled listeners in an open field. Triumphantly touring the colonies, Whitefield displayed an eloquence that reduced Jonathan Edwards to tears and even caused the skeptical and thrifty Benjamin Franklin to empty his pockets into the collection plate. During Whitefield's roaring revival meetings, countless sinners professed conversion, while hundreds of the "saved" groaned, shrieked, or rolled in the snow from religious excitement. Soon, American imitators took up Whitefield's electrifying style of preaching, and shook enormous audiences with their emotional appeals.

The Awakening left many lasting effects. Orthodox clergymen, known as "old lights," were deeply skeptical of the emotionalism and the theatrical antics of the revivalists. "New light" ministers, on the other hand, defended the Awakening for its role in revitalizing American religion. Several denominations split over the issue, and the resulting schisms greatly increased the numbers and the competitiveness of American churches. The Awakening's emphasis on direct, emotive spirituality seriously undermined the older clergy whose authority had derived from their education and erudition. It also

George Whitefield Preaching. *Americans of both sexes and all races and sections were spellbound by Whitefield's emotive oratory. (National Portrait Gallery, London)*

encouraged a fresh wave of missionary work among the Indians and black slaves. It led to the founding of such "new light" centers of higher learning as Dartmouth, Brown, Rutgers, and Princeton. Perhaps most significant, the Great Awakening was the first spontaneous mass movement of the American people. By breaking down sectional boundaries and denominational lines, it contributed to the growing sense that Americans had of themselves as a single people, united by a shared history and experience.

Schools and Colleges

Only slowly and painfully did American colonials break away from the English ideal that education was a boon reserved for the aristocratic few. In Puritan New England, education was dominated by the Congregational church, which stressed the need for Bible reading by the individual worshiper. Education flourished almost from the outset in these colonies, which boasted an impressive number of graduates from the English universities, especially Cambridge, the intellectual center of England's Puritanism. College education was regarded as important to the training of new ministers for the church. But New Englanders also established primary and secondary schools, which varied widely in the quality of instruction and in the length of time that their doors remained open each year.

Fairly adequate primary and secondary schools were also hammering knowledge into the heads of reluctant "scholars" in the middle colonies and the South. Some of these institutions were tax-supported; others were privately operated. Especially in the South, wealthy families leaned heavily on private tutors, and sometimes sent their boys abroad to English institutions for further learning.

The general atmosphere in the colonial schools and colleges continued grim and gloomy. The emphasis was on rote learning of religious dogma and the classical languages, Latin and Greek. Independent thinking was discouraged, and severe discipline was often administered with a switch cut from a birch tree. Instruction was poor by present-day standards. By 1750, however, there was a distinct trend toward "live" languages and other modern subjects in the colonial colleges. A significant contribution was made by Benjamin Franklin, who had a large hand in launching what became the University of Pennsylvania, the first American college free from denominational control.

Culture in the Backwoods

The dawn-to-dusk toil of pioneer life left little vitality or aptitude for artistic effort. Americans were too busy chopping down trees to sit around painting landscapes, especially when a hostile Indian might burst from a nearby bush. There was no strong esthetic tradition; many clergymen, in fact, regarded art as an invention of the Devil.

As the colonists gradually acquired some wealth and leisure, their surplus energy went into religion and politics, not art. The materialistic atmosphere was not favorable to artistic endeavor. One famous painter, the noted John Trumbull of Connecticut

(1756–1843), was discouraged in his youth by his father's chilling remark, "Connecticut is not Athens." Charles W. Peale (1741–1827), Benjamin West (1738–1820), and John Copley (1738–1815) all succeeded in their ambition to become famous painters, but they had to go to England to complete their training and find patrons for their art.

Colonial architecture, too, was largely imported from the Old World. Best known is the red-bricked Georgian style, exemplified by the beauty of now-restored Williamsburg, Virginia.

Colonial literature, like art, was generally undistinguished, but a few outstanding individuals produced original and enduring work. Precocious black poetess Phillis Wheatley (c. 1753–1784) was an uneducated slave girl who went to Boston and then to England. Remarkably, she overcame her handicaps and produced polished poems that revealed the influence of Alexander Pope.

The greatest "Great Awakener," Jonathan Edwards, customarily arose at four o'clock to begin a day's work on the subtle religious writings that established him as one of the finest theological minds ever produced in America. Some of his treatises on Calvinism, such as *On the Freedom of the Will,* rivaled those of John Calvin himself, and were widely read in Europe.

Many-sided Benjamin Franklin, often called "the first civilized American," lit up both literature and science in America. His classic autobiography was his greatest literary achievement, but he was best known to contemporaries for *Poor Richard's Almanack,* which he edited from 1732 to 1758. Emphasizing the homespun virtues of thrift, industry, and common sense, "Poor Richard" was most famous for his pithy sayings: "Plough deep while sluggards sleep"; "Fish and visitors stink in three days." *Poor Richard's* was well known in Europe and was more widely read in America than anything else except the Bible. As a teacher of both old and young, Franklin had an incalculable influence in shaping the American character.

Franklin's scientific efforts, including his spectacular kite-flying experiments with electricity, made him the colonies' only first-rate scientist, and won him numerous honors in Europe. Among the inventions produced by his practical mind were bifocal spectacles, the Franklin stove, and the lightning rod.

Pioneer Presses

Stump-grubbing Americans were too poor to buy quantities of books and too busy to read them. A few fine private libraries, like that of the Byrd family in Virginia, could be found. Bustling Benjamin Franklin established the first privately supported circulating library, and by 1776 there were about fifty subscription-supported public libraries.

On the eve of the Revolution there were about forty colonial newspapers, chiefly weeklies consisting of a single large sheet folded once. The "news," especially from overseas, often lagged many weeks behind the event, and the papers' columns were filled with dull essays. Nevertheless, newspapers proved to be a powerful agency for airing colonial grievances and building up opposition to British control.

A celebrated legal case, in 1734–1735, involved John Peter Zenger, a newspaper printer. Significantly, the case arose in New York, reflecting the tumultuous give-and-take of politics in the middle colonies, where so many different ethnic groups jostled against one another. Zenger's newspaper had assailed the corrupt royal governor. Charged with seditious libel, the accused was haled into court, where he was defended by a distinguished Philadelphia lawyer, Andrew Hamilton, then nearly eighty. Zenger argued that he had printed the truth, while the bewigged royal chief justice ruled that the mere fact of printing, irrespective of the truth, was enough to convict. Yet the jury, swayed by the eloquence of Hamilton, defied the red-robed judges and daringly returned a verdict of "not guilty." Cheers burst from the spectators.

The Zenger decision was epochal. It pointed the way to the kind of freedom of expression required by the diverse society that was colonial New York, and that all America was to become. Though contrary to existing law and not accepted by other royal judges, in time it helped set a precedent against judicial tyranny in libel suits. Newspaper editors had something of a burden lifted from their backs, even though complete freedom of the press was unknown during the pre-Revolutionary era.

The Great Game of Politics

American colonials may have been backward in natural or physical science, but they were making noteworthy contributions to political science.

The thirteen colonial governments presented a varied structure. By 1775, eight of the colonies had royal governors, who were appointed by the king. Three were under proprietors who themselves chose the governors—Maryland, Pennsylvania, and Delaware. And two—Connecticut and Rhode Island—elected their own governors under self-governing charters.

Practically every colony utilized a two-house legislative body. The upper house, or council, was normally appointed by the Crown in the royal colonies, and by the proprietor in the proprietary colonies. It was chosen by the voters in the self-governing colonies. The lower house, as the popular branch, was elected by the people—or rather by those persons who owned enough property to qualify as voters. In several of the colonies, the backcountry elements were seriously underrepresented, and they hated the ruling colonial clique perhaps more than they did kingly authority. Legislatures, in which the people enjoyed direct representation, voted such taxes as they chose for the necessary expenses of colonial government. Self-taxation through representation was a precious privilege that Americans had come to cherish above most others.

Governors appointed by the king were generally able men. But the appointees were sometimes incompetent or corrupt, and included broken-down politicians badly in need of jobs. The worst of the group was impoverished Lord Cornbury, first cousin of Queen Anne, who was made governor of New York and New Jersey in 1702. He proved to be a drunkard, a spendthrift, a grafter, an embezzler, a religious bigot, and a vain fool, especially when he appeared in public dressed like a woman. Even the best of the king's appointees had trouble with the colonial legislatures, basically because the royal governor embodied a bothersome transatlantic authority some 3,000 miles (4,800 kilometers) away.

But the colonial assemblies were by no means defenseless. Some of them employed the trick of withholding the governor's salary unless he yielded to their wishes. Because he was normally in need of money, the power of the purse usually forced him to terms.

Administration at the local level was also varied. County government remained the rule in the plantation South; town-meeting government predominated in New England; and a modification of the two

Heated Public Gathering. *The spirit of the New England town meeting. (Library of Congress)*

developed in the middle colonies. In the town meeting, with its open discussion and open voting, direct democracy functioned at its best. In this unrivaled cradle of self-government, Americans learned to cherish their privileges and exercise their duties as citizens of the New World commonwealths.

Yet the ballot was by no means a birthright. Religious or property qualifications for voting, with even stiffer qualifications for office holding, existed in all the colonies in 1775. The privileged upper classes, fearful of democratic excesses, were unwilling to grant the ballot to every "biped of the forest." Perhaps half of the adult white males were thus disfranchised. But because of the ease of acquiring land and thus satisfying property requirements, the right to vote was not beyond the reach of most industrious and enterprising colonials.

By 1775 America was not yet a true democracy—socially, economically, or politically. But it was far more democratic than England and Europe. Colonial institutions were giving freer rein to the democratic ideals of tolerance, educational advantages, equality of economic opportunity, freedom of speech, freedom of the press, freedom of assembly, and representative government. And these democratic seeds, planted in rich soil, were to bring forth a lush harvest in later years.

Colonial Folkways

Everyday life in the colonies may now seem glamorous, especially as reflected in antique shops. But judged by modern standards it was drab and tedious. For the mass of the people, the labor was heavy and constant—from daybreak to backbreak.

Basic commodities and comforts now taken for granted were lacking. Food was plentiful, though the diet could be coarse and monotonous. Churches were unheated except for charcoal foot-warmers, so the preaching of hellfire may not have seemed altogether unattractive. There was no running water in the houses, no plumbing, and probably not a single bathtub in all colonial America. Flickering lights were inadequate, for illumination was provided by candles and whale-oil lamps. Garbage disposal was primitive. Long-snouted hogs customarily ranged the streets to consume refuse, while buzzards, protected by law, flapped greedily over tidbits of waste.

Amusement was eagerly pursued where time and custom permitted. Militia "musters," house-raisings, quilting bees, funerals, and weddings all provided opportunities for social gatherings, which customarily involved the swilling of much strong liquor. Winter sports were common in the North, while the non-Puritanical South favored hunting, horse racing, dancing, stage plays, card-playing, and cock-fighting.

Lotteries were universally approved, even by clergy, and were used to raise money for churches and schools, including Harvard. Holidays were celebrated everywhere, but Christmas was frowned upon in New England as an offensive reminder of "Popery." Thanksgiving Day came to be a truly American festival, for it combined thanks to God with an opportunity for jollification, gorging, and guzzling.

England's American colonists in 1775 were a remarkable people: restless, energetic, ambitious, resourceful, ingenious, and independent-minded.

With every passing year they were less willing to bow their necks to the yoke of overseas authority. With a boundless continent before them, with impressive pioneer accomplishments behind them, and with an astonishing fertility within them, they had caught a vision of their destiny and were preparing to grasp it. Woe unto anyone—whether king, governor, or native inhabitant—who tried to thwart them!

VARYING VIEWPOINTS

Many historians, notably Richard Bushman, see pre-Revolutionary America as an expanding, opening society. In this view, colonial society was losing the religious discipline and social hierarchy of the founding generations, as Americans poured out onto the frontier or sailed the commercial seaways in search of fortune and adventure. These scholars portray the Great Awakening as further evidence of the erosion of social constraints. They argue that unbridled religious enthusiasm, directed by itinerant preachers, displayed the kind of questing for personal autonomy that eventually led to demands for national independence.

The opposing view, shown by Gary Nash and Kenneth Lockridge, emphasizes declining opportunities in colonial society. Pressure on land and the continued dominance of church and parental authority gave rise to a landless class, forced to till tenant plots in the countryside or find manual labor in the cities. The simmering discontent of this growing lower class, according to this interpretation, exploded first in the Great Awakening and again some forty years later in the American Revolution.

SELECT READINGS

Primary Source Documents

Noting the ethnic diversity of colonial American society, Michel Guillaume Jean de Crèvecoeur's *Letters from an American Farmer* (1904)* and Benjamin Franklin's "Observations on the Increase of Mankind,"* in Jared Sparks, ed., *The Works of Benjamin Franklin* (1840), respectively celebrate and express unease at that diversity. Franklin's entertaining *Autobiography** (1868) is an indispensable guide to the values and preoccupations of his time. It includes an account of George Whitefield's visit to Philadelphia during the Great Awakening.

Secondary Sources

Social history is painted with broad strokes in James Henretta, *The Evolution of America Society, 1700–1815* (1973), and Daniel Boorstin, *The Americans: The Colonial Experience* (1958). Richard Hofstadter takes a suggestive snapshot in *America in 1750* (1971). Immigration is discussed in Bernard Bailyn, *Voyagers to the West: A Passage in the Peopling of America on the Eve of Revolution* (1987).

Black "immigrants" are studied in Philip D. Curtin, *The Atlantic Slave Trade: A Census* (1969), and indentured servants in Abbot E. Smith, *Colonists in Bondage* (1947). Jackson T. Main astutely analyzes *The Social Structure of Revolutionary America, 1763–1788* (1965). Large-scale economic patterns are traced in Edwin J. Perkins, *The Economy of Colonial America* (1980) and in Alice H. Jones, *The Wealth of a Nation to Be: The American Colonies on the Eve of the Revolution* (1980). Gary B. Nash, *The Urban Crucible: Social Change, Political Consciousness, and the Origins of the American Revolution* (1979) and Rhys Isaac, *The Transformation of Virginia, 1740–1790* (1982) both link social conflict to the Great Awakening, as does Richard L. Bushman, *From Puritan to Yankee: Character and Social Order in Connecticut, 1690–1765* (1967). Cultural history is imaginatively presented in Howard M. Jones, *O Strange New World: American Culture in the Formative Years* (1964). Comprehensive is Henry May, *The Enlightenment in America* (1976). Colonial politics are interpreted in a most suggestive way in Bernard Bailyn, *The Origins of American Politics* (1965).

5

The Duel for North America

A torch lighted in the forests of America set all Europe in conflagration.

François Voltaire, c. 1756

France Finds a Foothold in Canada

France was another latecomer in the scramble for New World real estate, like England and Holland, and for basically the same reasons. She was convulsed during the 1500s by foreign wars and domestic strife, including the frightful clashes between the Roman Catholics and the Protestant Huguenots.

A new era dawned in 1598 when the Edict of Nantes, issued by the Crown, granted limited toleration to the French Protestants. Religious wars ceased, and in the 1600s France blossomed into the mightiest and most-feared nation in Europe.

Success finally crowned the exertions of France in the New World. In 1608, the year after Jamestown, the permanent beginnings of a vast empire were established at Quebec, a rocky sentinel commanding the St. Lawrence River. The leading figure was Samuel de Champlain, an intrepid soldier and explorer whose energy and leadership fairly earned for him the title "Father of New France."

Champlain entered into friendly relations—a fateful friendship—with the nearby Huron Indian tribes. Yielding to their entreaties, he joined them in battle against their feathered foes, the federated Iroquois tribes of the upper New York area.

Two shots from the "lightning sticks" of the whites routed the terrified Indians, who left behind three dead and one wounded. France, to its sorrow, thus earned the lasting enmity of the Iroquois tribes. They thereafter hampered French penetration of the Ohio Valley, ravaged French settlements, and served as allies of the British in the prolonged struggle for supremacy on the continent.

The government of New France (Canada) finally fell under the direct control of the king, after various commercial companies had faltered or failed. This royal regime was almost completely autocratic. There were no popularly elected assemblies, as in the English colonies; there was no trial by jury—merely the decision of the magistrate.

Population in Catholic New France grew with painful slowness: as late as 1750 there were only sixty thousand or so whites. Land-owning French peasants, unlike the dispossessed English tenant farmers who embarked for the British colonies, had little economic incentive to move. Protestant Huguenots, who might have had a religious motive to migrate, were denied a refuge in this raw colony. The French government, in any case, favored its Caribbean island colonies, rich in sugar and rum, over the snow-cloaked wilderness of Canada.

New France Fans Out

New France did contain one valuable resource: the beaver. To adorn the heads of fashionable Europeans, French fur-trappers ranged over the woods and waterways of North America in pursuit of the fur-bearing creature. These colorful *coureurs de bois* (runners of the woods) were also runners of risks—two-fisted drinkers, free spenders, free livers and lovers. They littered the land with scores of place names, including Baton Rouge (red stick), Terre Haute (high land), Des Moines (some monks), and Grand Teton (big breast).

Singing, paddle-swinging French *voyageurs* also recruited Indians into the fur business. But the Indians were unfortunately decimated by the white man's diseases and debauched by his alcohol—"firewater." Slaughtering beaver by the boatload violated many Indian religious beliefs and sadly demonstrated the shattering effect that contact with Europeans wreaked on traditional Indian ways of life.

Pursuing the sharp-toothed beaver ever deeper into the heart of the continent, French trappers and their Indian partners covered amazing distances. They trekked in a huge arc across the Great Lakes, into present-day Saskatchewan and Manitoba, along the valleys of the Platte, the Arkansas, and the Mis-

Chief of the Taensa Indians Receiving LaSalle, March, 1682. *Driven by the dream of a vast North American empire for France, LaSalle spent years exploring the Great Lakes region and the valleys of the Illinois and Mississippi Rivers. This scene of his encounter with an Indian chieftain is imaginatively recreated by the nineteenth-century artist George Catlin. (A Detail. The National Gallery of Art, Washington, D.C., The Paul Mellon Collection)*

souri, west to the Rockies, and south to the border of Texas. In the process, they extinguished the beaver population in many areas, inflicting incalculable ecological damage.

French Catholic missionaries, notably the Jesuits, labored zealously to save the Indians for Christ and from the fur-trappers. Though they made few permanent converts, the Jesuits played a vital role as explorers and geographers.

Other explorers sought neither souls nor beaver, but empire. To check Spanish penetration into the region of the Gulf of Mexico, haughty and ambitious Robert de La Salle floated down the mighty Mississippi in 1682 to the point where it mingles with the gulf. Three years later he tried to return to the territory he had named "Louisiana," but he failed to find the Mississippi delta. He landed instead in Spanish Texas, where he was murdered by his mutinous men. Undismayed, French officials planted several fortified posts in what is now Mississippi and Louisiana, the most important of which was New Orleans (1718). Commanding the mouth of the Mississippi River, this strategic semitropical outpost tapped the fur and grain trade of the huge interior valley, especially the fertile Illinois country.

The Clash of Empires

As the seventeenth century neared its sunset, a titanic struggle was shaping up for mastery of the North American continent. It involved three civilizations: English, French, and Spanish. From 1688 to 1763, four bitter wars among the great powers convulsed Europe. All four of these conflicts were world wars, in which the rival nations struggled for domination in the New World as well as Europe. As British subjects, the American colonists were inevitably caught up in each of these great imperial struggles. Isolation from the broils of Europe was a hope rather than a reality.

The first two wars, known in America as King William's War and Queen Anne's War, pitted British colonials against the French *coureurs de bois* and their Indian allies. Neither France nor England considered America worth the commitment of regular troops, so a kind of primitive guerrilla warfare prevailed. French-inspired Indians ravaged with torch and tomahawk the British colonial frontiers from New York to Massachusetts, while France's Spanish allies

probed at outlying South Carolina settlements. For their part, the English colonials failed miserably in attempts to capture Quebec and Montreal, but did temporarily seize the stronghold of Port Royal in Acadia.

In the Peace of Utrecht (1713), victorious England acquired the French-populated colony of Acadia (renamed Nova Scotia) and the wintry wastes of Newfoundland and Hudson's Bay, thus applying a pincers to the St. Lawrence settlements of France. The British also won limited trading rights in Spanish America, but these later involved much friction over smuggling. Ill-feeling finally led to war when the English Captain Jenkins, whose ear had been sliced off by a Spanish sword, returned to England with his tale of woe on his tongue and the shriveled ear in his hand. The War of Jenkins' Ear was confined to the Caribbean and to the much-buffeted buffer colony of Georgia.

This small-scale scuffle with Spain in America soon merged with the large-scale War of Austrian Succession in Europe. Once again, France allied itself with Spain. Once again a force of rustic New Englanders, with the help of the British fleet, captured a reputedly impregnable French fortress, Louisbourg, on Cape Breton Island, commanding the approaches to the St. Lawrence River. When the peace treaty of 1748 handed Louisbourg back to their French foe, the victorious New Englanders were outraged. Wily Old World diplomats, they believed, had cheated them of their prize. Worse, Louisbourg was still a cocked pistol pointed at the heart of the American continent. France, powerful and unappeased, still clung to its vast holdings in North America.

George Washington Inaugurates War with France

As the drama unfolded in the New World, the Ohio Valley became the chief bone of contention between the French and British. The Ohio country was the critical area into which the westward-pushing English would inevitably penetrate. It was the key to the continent which the French had to retain, particularly if they were going to link their Canadian holdings with those of the lower Mississippi Valley. By the mid-1700s the English colonials, painfully aware of these basic truths, were no longer so reluctant to bear the burdens of empire. Alarmed by French land-grabbing and cutthroat fur-trade competition in the Ohio Valley, they were determined to fight for their economic security and for the supremacy of their way of life in North America.

Rivalry for the lush lands of the upper Ohio Valley brought tensions to the snapping point. In 1749 a group of English colonial speculators, chiefly influential Virginians including the Washington family, had secured rights to some 500,000 acres in this region. In the same disputed wilderness the French were in the process of erecting a chain of forts commanding the strategic Ohio River.

In 1754 the governor of Virginia ushered George Washington, a twenty-one-year-old surveyor and fellow Virginian, onto the stage of history. Washington was sent to the Ohio country as a lieutenant colonel in command of about 150 Virginia militiamen. Encountering a small detachment of French troops in the forest about forty miles from Fort Duquesne, the Virginians opened fire—the first shots of the globe-girdling new war. The French leader was killed, and his men retreated. An exultant Washington wrote: "I heard the bullets whistle, and believe me, there is something charming in the sound." It soon lost its charm.

The French promptly returned with reinforcements, which surrounded Washington back of his hastily constructed breastworks, Fort Necessity. After a ten-hour siege he was forced to surrender his entire command in July 1754—ironically the Fourth of July.

With the shooting already started and in danger of spreading, the British authorities in Nova Scotia took vigorous action. Understandably fearing a stab in the back from the French Acadians, whom England had acquired in 1713, the British brutally uprooted some 4,000 of them in 1755. These unhappy French deportees were scattered as far south as Louisiana, where the descendants of the French-speaking Acadians are now called "Cajuns" and number nearly a million.

Global War and Colonial Disunity

The first three Anglo-French colonial wars had all started in Europe, but the tables were now reversed. A fourth struggle, known as the French and Indian War, began in America. Touched off by George Wash-

ington in the wilds of the Ohio Valley in 1754, it rocked along on an undeclared basis for two years and then widened into the most far-flung conflict the world had yet seen—the Seven Years' War. It was fought not only in America but in Europe, in the West Indies, in the Philippines, in Africa, and on the ocean. The Seven Years' War was a seven-seas war.

In Europe, England weakened France by liberally subsidizing Prussia. The French wasted so much strength in their bloodbath with Frederick the Great of Prussia that they were unable to throw adequate force into the New World. "America was conquered in Germany," declared British statesman William Pitt.

In previous colonial clashes the Americans had revealed an astonishing lack of unity. Colonists near the shooting had responded more generously with volunteers and money than those safely remote from danger. With musketballs already whining in the Ohio country, the crisis called for concerted action.

In 1754 the British government summoned an intercolonial Congress to Albany, New York, near the Iroquois Indian country. Travel-weary delegates from only seven of the thirteen colonies showed up. The immediate purpose was to keep the Iroquois chiefs loyal to the British in the spreading war.

The longer-range purpose at Albany was to bolster the common defense against France by achieving greater colonial unity. The leading spirit in this endeavor was wise and witty Benjamin Franklin.

Famous Cartoon by Benjamin Franklin. *Delaware and Georgia were omitted.*

Before the Albany Congress, Franklin had published his famous cartoon showing the separate colonies as parts of a disjointed snake, with the slogan, "Join, or Die." Franklin gained the Congress's approval for his well-devised scheme of colonial home rule, but it was spurned by the individual colonies and the London regime. To the colonies, it did not seem to give enough independence; to the British officials, it seemed to give too much.

Braddock's Blundering

Led by bull-headed General Braddock, the English stumbled badly in their opening clashes with the French and Indians. Braddock was sent to Virginia in 1755, and set out with a mixed force of 2,000 British regulars and ill-disciplined colonial militiamen to capture Fort Duquesne. Experienced in European warfare, "Bulldog" Braddock was professionally contemptuous of the behind-the-tree Indian-fighting methods of the colonial "buckskins."

Dragging heavy artillery and laboriously hacking a path through the dense forest, Braddock's expedition slowly crept to within a few miles of Fort Duquesne. There it encountered a much smaller French and Indian army, which quickly melted into the thickets and poured murderous fire into the ranks of the Redcoats. Braddock's energetic and fearless aide George Washington had two horses shot from under him and four bullet holes in his coat, and Braddock himself was mortally wounded. The entire force was routed with appalling losses.

Inflamed by this easy victory, the Indians took to a wider warpath. The whole frontier from Pennsylvania to North Carolina, left virtually naked by Braddock's bloody defeat, felt their fury. Scalping forays occurred within eighty miles of Philadelphia, and in desperation the local authorities offered bounties for Indian scalps: $50 for a female's and $130 for a male's. Unwisely trying to attack the widespread French wilderness posts simultaneously, the British paid the price for their lack of sound strategy. Defeat after defeat tarnished their arms.

Pitt's Palms of Victory

In the hour of crisis, Britain brought forth, as she repeatedly has, a superlative leader—William Pitt. A tall and imposing figure, with flashing eyes set in a hawk-like face, Pitt was known as the "Great Commoner." He drew much of his strength from the common people, who admired him so greatly that on occasion they kissed his horses.

In 1757 Pitt became a foremost leader in the London government. He wisely decided to concentrate the war effort on the vitals of Canada—the Quebec-Montreal area.

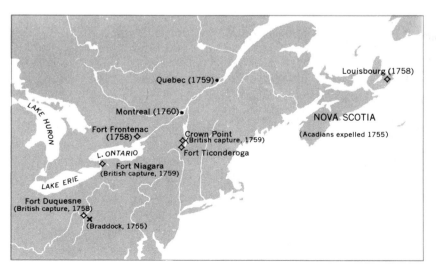

Events of 1755–1760.

Pitt first dispatched a powerful expedition in 1758 against Louisbourg. The frowning fortress, though it had been greatly strengthened, fell after a blistering siege. Wild rejoicing swept England, for this was the first major British victory of the entire war.

Quebec was next on Pitt's list. For this crucial expedition he chose the thirty-two-year-old James Wolfe, who had been an officer since the age of fourteen. In a daring move, Wolfe sent a detachment up a poorly guarded part of the rocky eminence protecting Quebec. This vanguard scaled the cliff, pulling itself upward by the bushes and showing the way for the others. In the morning the two armies faced each other on the Plains of Abraham on the outskirts of Quebec, the British under Wolfe, the French under Montcalm. Both commanders fell fatally wounded, but the French were defeated and the city surrendered.

The battle of Quebec ranks as one of the most significant engagements in British and American history. After Montreal fell in 1760, the French flag waved no more in Canada. By the peace settlement at Paris (1763), French power was thrown completely off the continent of North America, leaving behind only a fertile French population that is to this day a strong minority in Canada. Great Britain thus emerged as the dominant power in North America, and took her place as the leading naval power of the world.

Mother-and-Daughter Friction

England's colonials, baptized by fire, emerged with increased confidence in their military strength. They had borne the brunt of battle at first; they had fought bravely beside the crack British regulars; and they had gained valuable experience, officers and men alike. In the closing days of the conflict some 20,000 American recruits were under arms.

The French and Indian War, while bolstering colonial self-esteem, simultaneously shattered the myth of British invincibility. On Braddock's bloody field the "buckskin" militia had seen the demoralized regulars huddling helplessly together or fleeing their unseen enemy.

Ominously, friction had developed during the war between arrogant English officers and the raw

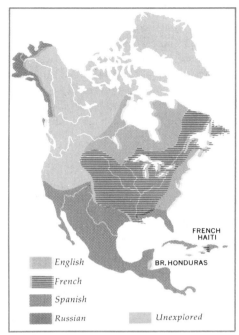

North America Before 1754.

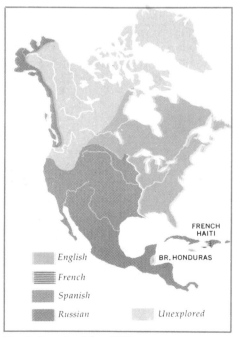

North America After 1763.

colonial "boors." Displaying the contempt of the professional soldier for amateurs, the British refused to recognize any American militia commission above the rank of captain—a demotion humiliating to "Colonel" George Washington. They also showed the usual condescension of snobs from the civilized Old Country toward the "scum" who had confessed failure by fleeing to the "outhouses of civilization." Energetic and hard-working American settlers, on the other hand, sensed that they were the cutting edge of British civilization. They believed that they deserved credit rather than contempt for risking their lives to erect a New World empire.

British officials were further distressed by some colonials' half-hearted support for the common cause. American shippers developed a treasonable but lucrative trade with the Spanish and French West Indian islands at the very time the British navy was trying to subdue them. Other colonials, self-centered and regarding the war as remote, refused to provide men and money for the conflict until Pitt offered to reimburse the colonies for their expenditures. In effect, the colonists demanded the rights and privileges of Englishmen without the duties and responsibilities of Englishmen. If Americans had to be bribed to defend themselves against a relentless foe, would they ever unite to strike the mother country?

The curse of intercolonial disunity, present from early days, had continued throughout the recent hostilities. It had been caused mainly by enormous distances; by geographical barriers like rivers; by conflicting religions, from Catholic to Quaker; by varied national backgrounds, from German to Irish; by differing types of colonial governments; by numerous boundary disputes; and by the resentment that the crude back-country felt toward the aristocratic seaboard bigwigs.

Yet unity received some encouragement during the French and Indian War. When soldiers and statesmen from widely separated colonies met around common campfires and council tables, they were often agreeably surprised by what they found. Despite deep-seated jealousy and suspicion, they discovered that they were all fellow Americans who generally spoke the same language and shared common ideals. Barriers of disunity began to melt, although a long and rugged road lay ahead before a nation could emerge.

Americans: A People of Destiny

The removal of the French menace in Canada profoundly affected American attitudes. While the French hawk had been hovering in the North and West, the colonial chicks had been forced to cling close to the wings of the mother hen. Now that the hawk was killed, they could range far afield with a new spirit of independence.

Frenchmen, humiliated by the British and saddened by the fate of Canada, consoled themselves with one wishful thought. Perhaps the loss of their American empire would one day result in Britain's loss of her American empire. In a sense the history of the United States began with the fall of Quebec and Montreal; the infant republic was cradled on the Plains of Abraham.

The Spanish and Indian menaces, in like manner, were removed by the recent war. Spain was eliminated from Florida, although now entrenched in Louisiana and New Orleans. And the Indian allies of France were left in the lurch. A violent postwar flare-up against the white men occurred in the Ohio Valley and Great Lakes region in 1763, with the vengeful chieftain Pontiac as the principal leader. Catching the British napping, the Indians wiped out a number of their posts. But the whites, rallying in superior numbers, crushed the uprising and pacified the frontier, temporarily.

Land-hungry American colonials were now free to burst over the dam of the Appalachian Mountains, and flood out over the grassy Western lands. A tiny rivulet of pioneers, such as Daniel Boone, had already trickled into Tennessee and Kentucky; other courageous pioneers were preparing for the long trek over the mountains.

Then, out of a clear sky, the London government issued its Proclamation of 1763. It flatly prohibited settlement in the area beyond the Appalachian Mountains, pending further adjustments. The truth is that this hastily drawn document was not designed to oppress the colonials at all, but to work out the Indian problem fairly in the interests of the fur traders and the other groups concerned.

But countless Americans, especially land speculators, were dismayed and angered. Was not the land beyond the mountains their birthright? Had they not, in addition, bought it with their blood in the recent war? In complete defiance of the paper Proclamation, they clogged the westward trails. In 1765 an estimated 1,000 wagons rolled through the town of Salisbury, North Carolina, on their way "up west." This wholesale flouting of royal authority boded ill for continued British rule in America.

The French and Indian War also caused the colonials to develop a new vision of their ultimate destiny. With the path cleared for the conquest of a continent, with their birthrate high and their energy boundless, they sensed that they were a potent people on the march. And they were in no mood to be restrained.

Lordly Britons, whose suddenly swollen empire had tended to produce swollen heads, were in no mood for back talk. Puffed up over their recent victories, they were already annoyed with their unruly colonials. The stage was thus set for a violent family quarrel.

VARYING VIEWPOINTS

The duel for North America was but one episode in the epochal story of the worldwide expansion of European commerce and culture after 1500. Dominated by the "imperial school," a group of historians who see transatlantic economic stresses as leading to revolution, scholarly inquiry has revolved around four principal questions: How did New World developments fit into the overall pattern of rivalries among the great European powers? What were the relative strengths and weaknesses of the British and French imperial systems that spelled the final triumph of the British and the defeat of the French? How well or poorly did the British Empire function? Finally, were the

Americans well or badly treated in the British imperial system? In short, how economically justifiable was the eventual American Revolution?

Social historians have recently looked at the colonial rivalries in a different light. They view the social and economic dislocations wrought by war as a stimulus to class conflict and revolutionary ferment. Some scholars have also asked whether the Revolution would have occurred at all without the British victory over the French in North America. If a powerful, Catholic, hostile France had retained its foothold in Canada, the British colonials might have thought twice about challenging their mother country.

SELECT READINGS

Primary Source Documents

"The Albany Plan of the Union" was the first great statement of colonial unity; "The Proclamation of 1763" forbade settlement west of the Appalachians. Both are collected in Henry Steele Commager, *Documents of American History.*

Secondary Sources

The workings of the British mercantile system are detailed in Charles M. Andrews' vast *Colonial Period of American*

History (4 vols., 1935–1938) and in Lawrence H. Gipson's still more ambitious *British Empire before the American Revolution* (15 vols., 1936–1970). Recent efforts to analyze the colonial empire are James Henretta, *"Salutary Neglect": Colonial Administration under the Duke of Newcastle* (1972) and Michael Kammen's especially interesting *Empire and Interest* (1970). The French colonial effort is described in George M. Wrong, *The Rise and Fall of New France* (2 vols.,

1928). The Anglo-French struggle is recounted in Howard H. Peckham, *The Colonial Wars, 1689–1762* (1964). Alan Rogers, *Empire and Liberty: American Resistance to British Authority, 1755–1763* (1974) investigates American participation in the Seven Years' War. Classic accounts are Francis Parkman's several volumes, including *Count Frontenac and New France under Louis XIV* (1877), *Montcalm and Wolfe* (2 vols., 1884), and *A Half-Century of Conflict* (1892). Parkman's tomes are condensed in *The Battle for North America*, edited by John Tebbel (1948), and *The Parkman Reader*, edited by Samuel E. Morison (1955). An impressive biography is Douglas S. Freeman, *Young Washington* (2 vols., 1948).

6

The Road to Revolution

**The Revolution was effected before the war commenced.
The Revolution was in the minds and hearts of the people.**

John Adams, 1818

The Deep Roots of Revolution

In a broad sense, the American Revolution was not the same thing as the American War of Independence. The war itself lasted only eight years. But the revolution lasted over a century and a half, and began when the first permanent English settlers set foot on the new continent. Insurrection of thought usually precedes insurrection of deed. And over the years such a ferment occurred in the thinking of the colonists that the revolution was partially completed in their minds before the musket balls began to fly. America was a revolutionary force from the day of its discovery.

England's colonies were settled largely by emigrants who were discontented or rebellious in spirit—by people who had failed to adjust themselves to their harsh lot in the Old World. Most of them had not been able to get along, whether socially, politically, economically, or religiously. Some of them were tired of taking off their hats and standing bareheaded in the presence of their "betters." Others wanted a larger share in government, or a richer portion of this world's goods, or an opportunity to worship God in their own peculiar way.

The long and perilous Atlantic crossing was the first big step in the emigrants' emotional and spiritual isolation from the faraway Old World. Food shortages, epidemics, and even occasional cannibalism turned ships into "floating coffins." A sailor's song ran:

> We ate the mice, we ate the rats,
> And through the hold we ran like cats.

Survivors who staggered ashore were ever aware that the long arm of the London government, enfeebled by 3,000 miles (4,800 kilometers) of ocean, could not reach them nearly so effectively as at home. Distance

52

weakens authority; great distance weakens authority greatly.

America's lonely wilderness likewise stimulated ideas of independence. Back in England some villagers had lived near graveyards that contained the bones of their ancestors for a thousand years past. Born into such conservative surroundings, the poor peasants did not question the social rut in which they found themselves. But in the New World they were not held down by the scowl of their overlords.

Rugged pioneering conditions changed patterns of living and consequently habits of thought. Before long, Americans were eating Indian corn, wearing Indian moccasins and buckskin, and in extreme instances on the frontier uttering the war whoop as they scalped their fallen Indian foe. Hacking a home out of the wildwood with an ax developed self-confidence, individualism, and a spirit of independence.

As the Americans matured, they acquired privileges of self-government enjoyed by no other colonial peoples. They set up thirteen parliaments of their own and aped the parliamentary methods of the mother country. Ultimately they came to regard their own legislative bodies as more or less on a footing with the great mother of parliaments in London.

The Mercantile Theory

Britain's empire was acquired in a "fit of absent-mindedness," as the old saying goes, and there is much truth in it. Only one of the original thirteen colonies, Georgia, was formally planted by the British government. The others were founded haphazardly by trading companies, religious groups, land speculators, and others.

Britain controlled the colonies through simple machinery. The principal agency, the Board of Trade, made recommendations that were often enacted into law by Parliament or the Privy Council (the King's advisers).

The theory that shaped and justified English exploitation of the American colonies was mercantilism. According to this doctrine the colonies existed for the benefit of the mother country; they should add to its wealth, prosperity, and self-sufficiency. Otherwise, why go to all the trouble and expense of governing and protecting them? The settlers were regarded more or less as tenants. They were expected to produce tobacco and other products needed in England, and not to bother their heads with dangerous experiments in agriculture or self-government.

Specifically, how were the American colonies to benefit the mother country? First of all, they were to ensure Britain's naval supremacy by furnishing ships, ships' stores, sailors, and trade. In addition, they were to provide a profitable consumer's market for the goods manufactured in England. Finally, they were to keep gold and silver money within the empire by growing products, such as sugar, that otherwise would have to be bought from foreigners. The idea of "Buy British" would thus be promoted in a manner that foreshadowed later protective tariffs.

Mercantilist Trammels on Trade

Parliament passed numerous measures to enforce the mercantile system. The first of these, the Navigation Laws of 1650, were aimed at rival Dutch shippers. As finally perfected, these Navigation Laws allowed only English ships to trade with the colonies. Such regulation kept money within the empire and bolstered the British—and colonial—merchant marine.

An alert Parliament from time to time enacted additional laws favorable to the motherland. European goods consigned to America had to be landed first in England, where customs duties could be collected and the British middleman could get his cut of the profit. Still other curbs required certain "enumerated" products, notably tobacco, to be shipped to England and not to foreign markets, though prices in Europe might be higher. Settlers were also forbidden to manufacture for export such products as woolen cloth and beaver hats, because the colonies were supposed to complement, and not compete with, British industry.

Americans also felt the pinch in the area of currency. No banks existed in the colonies, and the money problem on the eve of the Revolution was acute. Industrious colonials were now busily buying more goods from England than they were selling to her, so the difference had to be made up in hard cash. Every year gold and silver money, much of it in quaint Spanish coins from the West Indies, was drained out of the colonies. The colonials simply did not have

The Female Combatants. *Britain is symbolized as a lady of fashion, and her rebellious daughter as an Indian princess. (Lewis Walpole Library, Farmington)*

enough left for the convenience of everyday purchases. Barter became necessary, and even butter, nails, pitch, and feathers were used for purposes of exchange.

Currency problems came to a boil when dire need finally forced many of the colonies to issue paper money, which unfortunately depreciated. British merchants and creditors, understandably worried, squawked so loudly that Parliament was compelled to act. It restrained the colonial legislatures from printing paper currency and from passing lax bankruptcy laws—practices that might result in defrauding British merchants. The Americans, who felt that their welfare was again being sacrificed, reacted angrily. Another burning grievance was thus heaped upon the pile of combustibles already smoldering.

London officialdom kept a watchful eye on legislation passed by colonial assemblies, and the Privy Council vetoed any laws that conflicted with British regulations or policy. This "royal veto" was used sparingly—only 469 times in connection with 8,563 laws.

But the colonists were nevertheless aggrieved when they were forbidden to make reforms they deemed desirable, such as curbing the degrading trade in African slaves.

The Menace of Mercantilism

Red-blooded Americans have long regarded the British mercantile system as thoroughly selfish and deliberately oppressive. The truth is that until 1763 the Navigation Laws imposed no intolerable burden, partly because they were laxly enforced. Ingenious colonial merchants early learned how to evade restrictions they found vexatious. Some of the early American fortunes were amassed through smuggling, like that of vain John Hancock, known as the "King of Smugglers."

Americans, in addition, were fortunate to reap direct benefits from the mercantile system. London paid liberal bounties to colonial producers of ships' parts and ships' stores, even though London competitors complained heatedly. Virginia tobacco planters enjoyed the valuable privilege of a monopoly in the British market for their pungent yellow leaf, and tobacco growing was outlawed in England and Ireland.

American colonials also enjoyed the rights of Englishmen and the protection of the British government at little cost. A strong army of British redcoats and the mightiest navy in the world sheltered them against foreign powers, Indians, and pirates—without a penny of tax on themselves.

"Prosperity trickles down" is a common saying; and in truth the Americans enjoyed a generous share of Britain's profits under the time-honored mercantile system. The average American was probably better off economically than the average Englishman at home. If the colonies existed for the benefit of the mother country, it was hardly less true that the mother country existed for the benefit of the colonies. The well-meaning officials in London were working for the welfare of the empire as a whole, and they gave overall unity to its policies. A wise man does not disembowel or starve the goose that lays the golden eggs. Mistakes were made by the British authorities, but they were not, until revolt had erupted, the mistakes of malice.

The Merits of Mercantilism

Even when painted in its rosiest colors, the mercantile system burdened the colonials with annoying liabilities. Economic initiative was stifled because Americans were not at complete liberty to buy, sell, ship, or manufacture under conditions that they found most profitable. The Southern colonies, as "pets," were generally favored over the Northern ones, chiefly because they grew non-English products like tobacco, sugar, and rice. Revolution was one seed that sprouted vigorously from the stony soil of New England, for the proud children of the Puritans resented being treated like unwanted relatives.

One-crop Virginians also nursed rankling grievances. Forced to sell their tobacco in England, they were at the mercy of British merchants, who often gouged them. Many of the fashionable Virginia planters were plunged into debt by the falling price of tobacco and were forced to buy their necessities in England by mortgaging future crops. Countless Virginians welcomed the opportunity to end their economic bondage to the mother country.

Finally—and of supreme importance—mercantilism was debasing to the Americans. They were to be kept in a state of perpetual economic adolescence and never allowed to come of age. As Benjamin Franklin wrote in 1775:

> We have an old mother that peevish is grown;
> She snubs us like children that scarce walk
>   alone;
> She forgets we're grown up and have sense of
>   our own.

Revolution broke out, as Theodore Roosevelt later remarked, because England failed to recognize an emerging nation when it saw one.

The Stamp Tax Uproar

The costly Seven Years' War, which ended in 1763, marked a new relationship between Britain and her transatlantic colonies. A revolution in British colonial policy precipitated the American Revolution.

Victory-flushed Britain emerged from the conflict possessing one of the biggest empires in the world—and also, less happily, the biggest debt. It amounted to £140 million, about half of which had been incurred in defending the American colonies. British officials wisely had no intention of asking the colonials to help pay off this crushing burden. But London felt that the Americans should be asked to defray one-third the cost of maintaining a garrison of some 10,000 redcoats, presumably for the colonies' own protection.

Prime Minister George Grenville aroused the resentment of the colonials in 1763 by ordering the British navy to enforce the Navigation Laws. He also secured from Parliament the so-called Sugar Act of 1764, the first law ever passed by that body for raising revenue in the colonies for the crown. Among various provisions, it increased the duty on foreign sugar imported from the West Indies. After bitter protests from the colonials, the duties were lowered substantially, and the agitation died down. But resentment was kept burning by the Quartering Act of 1765. It required certain colonies to provide food and quarters for British troops.

Then in the same year, 1765, Grenville proposed the most ominous measure of all: a stamp tax, to raise revenues to support the new military force. The Stamp Act required the use of stamped paper or the affixing of stamps, certifying payment of tax. Involved were about fifty trade items and certain types of commercial and legal documents, including playing cards, pamphlets, newspapers, diplomas, bills of lading, and marriage licenses.

Grenville regarded all these measures as reasonable and just. He was simply asking the Americans to pay their fair share for colonial defense, through taxes that were already familiar in England. In fact, Englishmen for two generations had endured a stamp tax far heavier than that passed for the colonies.

Yet the Americans were angrily aroused at what they regarded as Grenville's fiscal aggression. The new laws pinched their pocketbooks and, even more ominously, menaced the local liberties they had come to assume as a matter of right. Thus, some colonial assemblies defiantly refused to comply with the Quartering Act or voted only a fraction of the supplies that it called for.

Worse still, Grenville's noxious legislation seemed to menace the basic rights of the colonists as

Englishmen. Both the Sugar Act and the Stamp Act provided for trying offenders in the hated admiralty courts, where juries were not allowed. The burden of proof was on the defendant, who was assumed to be guilty unless he could prove himself innocent. Trial by jury and the doctrine of "innocent until proved guilty" were ancient privileges that Englishmen everywhere, including American colonials, held most dear. And why was a British army needed at all in the colonies, now that the French were vanquished and Pontiac's warriors crushed? Could its real purpose be to whip rebellious colonials themselves into line? Many Americans began to sniff the strong scent of a conspiracy to strip them of all their historic liberties. They lashed back violently, and the Stamp Act soon became a target that drew their most ferocious fire.

Angry throats raised the cry, "No taxation without representation." Taking the high ground of principle, the agitated colonials vividly recollected the theories of popular government developed during England's own Puritan revolution a century earlier. American firebrands hurled these doctrines back at their English masters, who were stunned at the keenness of the colonials' historical memory.

The Americans made a distinction between "legislation" and "taxation." They conceded the right of Parliament to legislate about matters that affected the entire empire, including the regulation of trade. But they steadfastly denied the right of Parliament, in which no Americans were seated, to impose taxes on Americans. Only their own elected colonial legislatures, the Americans insisted, could legally tax them.

Grenville dismissed these American protests as hairsplitting absurdities. The power of Parliament was supreme and undivided, he asserted, and in any case the Americans *were* represented in Parliament. Elaborating the theory of "virtual representation," Grenville claimed that every member of Parliament represented all British subjects, even those Americans in Boston or Charleston who had never voted for a member of the London Parliament. The Americans scoffed at the notion of virtual representation.

Thus the principle of no taxation without representation was supremely important, and the colonials clung to it with tenacious consistency. When the English replied that the sovereign power of government could not be divided between "legislative" authority in London and "taxing" authority in the colonies, they forced the Americans to deny the authority of Parliament altogether and to begin to consider their own political independence. This chain of logic eventually led to revolutionary consequences.

Parliament Forced to Repeal the Stamp Act

Among colonial outcries against the hated stamp tax, the most conspicuous was the Stamp Act Congress, held in New York City in 1765. Twenty-seven distinguished delegates from nine colonies petitioned the king and Parliament to repeal the odious legislation. The congress made little splash in England or America at the time, but it was one more halting but significant step toward intercolonial unity.

More effective than the congress was the widespread adoption of nonimportation agreements against British goods. Woolen garments of homespun became fashionable, and the eating of lamb chops was discouraged so that the wool-bearing sheep would be allowed to mature. Nonimportation agreements were in fact a promising stride toward union; they spontaneously united the American people for the first time in common action.

Violence also attended colonial protests. Crying "Liberty, Property, and No Stamps," ardent Sons and Daughters of Liberty enforced the nonimportation agreements against violators, often with a generous coat of tar and feathers. They ransacked the houses of unpopular officials and hanged stamp agents on liberty poles, albeit in effigy.

Shaken by violence, the machinery for collecting the tax broke down. On that dismal day in 1765 when the new act was to go into effect, the stamp agents had all been forced to resign, and there was no one to sell the stamps. While flags flapped at half-mast, the law was openly and flagrantly defied—or rather, nullified.

England was hard hit. Merchants and manufacturers greatly suffered from the colonial nonimportation agreements, and hundreds of laborers were thrown out of work. Loud demands converged on

Parliament for repeal of the Stamp Act. But many of the members could not understand why 7.5 million Britons had to pay heavy taxes to protect the colonies, while some 2 million colonials refused to pay for only one-third of the cost of their own defense.

After a stormy debate, and as a matter of expedience and not of right, Parliament in 1766 reluctantly repealed the Stamp Act. At the same time, and by an overwhelming vote, it saved face by passing the Declaratory Act. This futile measure proclaimed that Parliament had the right "to bind" the colonies "in all cases whatsoever." A bare assertion of this right was but a feeble victory for parental authority, for the unruly colonials had proved that the London government could be forced to yield to boycotts and mob action.

The Townshend Tea Tax and the Boston "Massacre"

Control of the British ministry was now seized by the gifted but erratic "Champagne Charley" Townshend, who could deliver brilliant speeches in Parliament while drunk. Rashly promising to pluck feathers from the colonial goose with a minimum of squawking, he persuaded Parliament in 1767 to pass the Townshend Acts. The most important of these new regulations was a light import duty on glass, white lead, paper, and tea. Townshend deferred to the sensitive colonials by making this tax, unlike the Stamp Act, an indirect customs duty payable at American ports.

Flushed with their recent victory over the stamp tax, the colonists were in a rebellious mood. The impost on tea was especially irksome, for an estimated 1 million Americans regularly sipped the brew.

Worse yet, the new Townshend revenues would be used to pay the salaries of the royal governors and judges in America. The ultrasuspicious Americans, who had beaten the royal governors into line by controlling the purse, regarded Townshend's tax as another attempt to enchain them. Their worst fears took on a greater reality when the London government, after passing the Townshend taxes, suspended the New York legislature for failure to comply with the Quartering Act of 1767.

Nonimportation agreements, previously potent, were quickly revived against the Townshend Acts. But they proved less effective than those devised against the Stamp Act. The colonials, again enjoying prosperity, took the new tax less seriously than might have been expected, largely because it was light and indirect. They found, moreover, that they could secure smuggled tea at a cheap price, and consequently smugglers increased their activities, especially in Massachusetts.

British officials, faced with a breakdown of law and order, landed two regiments of troops in Boston in 1768. A clash between citizens and soldiers was inevitable. On the evening of March 5, 1770, a crowd of some sixty townspeople set upon a squad of about ten "bloody backs," one of whom was hit by a club and another of whom was knocked down. Acting apparently without orders but under extreme provocation, the troops opened fire and killed or wounded eleven "innocent" citizens. One of the first to die was Crispus Attucks, described by contemporaries as a "mulatto" and a leader of the mob. Both sides were in some degree to blame, and in the subsequent trial only two of the soldiers could be found guilty of manslaughter.

The so-called Boston Massacre further inflamed the colonials against the British. Massacre Day was observed in Boston as a patriotic holiday until 1776, when the more glorious Fourth of July eclipsed it.

The Seditious Committees of Correspondence

By 1770 King George III was strenuously attempting to restore the declining power of the British monarchy. Earnest, industrious, stubborn, lustful for power, and later plagued with periodic fits of supposed madness, he surrounded himself with cooperative "yes men," notably his corpulent prime minister, Lord North.

The ill-timed Townshend Acts had failed to produce revenue, though producing near rebellion. Net proceeds from the tax in one year were £295, and during that time the annual military costs to Britain in the colonies had mounted to £170,000. Nonimportation agreements, though feebly enforced, were pinching British manufacturers. The government of Lord

The Boston Massacre, 1770. *This widely reprinted engraving by Paul Revere was both art and propaganda. (Library of Congress)*

North, bowing to various pressures, finally persuaded Parliament to repeal the Townshend revenue duties. But the three-pence tax on tea was retained to keep alive the principle of parliamentary taxation.

Flames of discontent, stirred by periodic incidents involving British officials, were continually fanned by a master propagandist and engineer of rebellion, Samuel Adams. An unimpressive-looking cousin of John Adams, he had failed miserably in private life. His friends had to buy him a presentable suit of clothes when he left Massachusetts on intercolonial business. Nevertheless, he was zealous and courageous in defense of colonial rights and the common man. His skillful pamphleteering won him the title "Penman of the Revolution."

Samuel Adams's signal contribution was to organize in Massachusetts the local committees of correspondence. After he had formed the first one in Boston during 1772, some eighty towns in the colony speedily set up similar organizations. Their chief function was to spread propaganda and information by interchanging letters, and thus keep alive opposition to British policy.

Intercolonial committees of correspondence were the next logical step. Virginia led the way in 1773 by creating such a body as a standing committee of the House of Burgesses. Within a short time every colony had established a central committee through which it could exchange ideas and information with other colonies. These intercolonial groups, which were supremely significant in stimulating and disseminating sentiment in favor of united action, evolved directly into the first American congresses.

Tea Parties at Boston and Elsewhere

Thus far—that is, by 1773—nothing had happened to make rebellion inevitable. Nonimportation was weakening. Increasing numbers of colonials were reluctantly paying the tea tax, because the legal tea was now cheaper than the smuggled tea, and cheaper than tea in England.

A new ogre entered the picture in 1773. The powerful British East India Company, overburdened with 17 million pounds of unsold tea, was facing bankruptcy. If it collapsed, the London government would lose heavily in tax revenue. The ministry therefore decided to assist the company by awarding it a complete monopoly of the American tea business. The terms thus granted would enable the giant corporation to sell the coveted leaves more cheaply than ever before, even with the threepence tax added. But to many American consumers, principle was more important than price.

The new tea monopoly seemed to the Americans like a shabby attempt to trick them into acceptance of the detested tax with the bait of cheaper tea. Once more the colonials rose in wrath. Not a single one of the several thousand chests of tea shipped by the company reached the consignees.

Boston was host to the most famous tea party of all. A band of white townfolk, disguised as Indians, boarded three tea ships on December 16, 1773. They smashed open 342 chests and dumped the "cursed weed" into the harbor, while a silent crowd watched approvingly from the wharves as salty tea was brewed for the fish.

Parliament Passes the "Intolerable Acts"

An outraged Parliament responded speedily to the Boston Tea Party with measures that brewed a revolution. By huge majorities in 1774 it passed a series of "Repressive Acts," which were designed to chastise Boston in particular, Massachusetts in general.

Most drastic of all was the Boston Port Act. It closed the tea-stained harbor until damages were paid and order could be assured. By other "Intolerable Acts"—as they were called in America—many of the chartered rights of colonial Massachusetts were swept away. Restrictions were likewise placed on the precious town meetings. Contrary to previous practice, enforcing officials who killed colonials in line of duty could now be sent to England for trial. There, suspicious Americans assumed, they would be likely to get off scot-free.

By a fateful coincidence, the "Intolerable Acts" were accompanied in 1774 by the Quebec Act. Passed at the same time, it was erroneously regarded in English-speaking America as one of the "repressive" measures. Actually, the Quebec Act was a good law in bad company. For many years the British government had debated how it should administer the 60,000 or so conquered French subjects in Canada, and it had finally framed this farsighted and statesmanlike measure. The French were guaranteed their Catholic religion. They were also permitted to retain many of their old customs and institutions, which did not include a representative assembly or trial by jury in civil cases. In addition, the old boundaries of the Province of Quebec were now extended southward all the way to the Ohio River.

The Quebec Act, from the viewpoint of the French Canadians, was a shrewd and conciliatory measure. If England had only shown as much foresight in dealing with her English-speaking colonies, she might not have lost them.

But from the viewpoint of the American colonials as a whole, the Quebec Act was especially noxious. All the other "repressive" laws slapped directly at Massachusetts, but this one had a much wider range. It seemed to set a dangerous precedent in America against jury trials and popular assemblies. It alarmed land speculators, who were distressed to see the huge trans-Allegheny area snatched from their grasp. It aroused the host of anti-Catholics, who were shocked by the extension of Roman Catholic jurisdiction southward into a huge region that had once been earmarked for Protestantism—a region about as large as the thirteen original colonies.

The Continental Congress and Bloodshed

American dissenters, outraged by the Quebec Act, responded sympathetically to the plight of Massachusetts. Their most significant action was the summoning of a Continental Congress, which met in Philadelphia from September 5 to October 26, 1774. John Adams played a stellar role at the Congress. Eloquently swaying his colleagues to a revolutionary course, he helped defeat by the narrowest of margins a

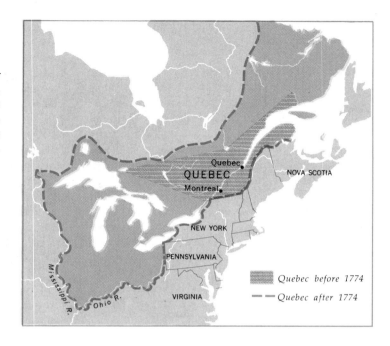

Quebec Before and After 1774. *Young Alexander Hamilton voiced the fears of many colonists when he warned that the Quebec Act of 1774 would introduce "priestly tyranny" into Canada, making that country another Spain or Portugal. "Does not your blood run cold," he asked, "to think that an English Parliament should pass an act for the establishment of arbitrary power and Popery in such a country?"*

a proposal by moderates for a species of American home rule under British direction.

The most significant action of the Congress was the creation of The Association. Unlike previous nonimportation agreements, this one called for a *complete* boycott of British goods. Still, there was no genuine drive toward independence—merely an effort to bring about a repeal of the offensive legislation and a return to the happy days before parliamentary taxation.

But the deadly drift toward war continued. The petitions of the Continental Congress were rejected, after considerable debate, by strong majorities in Parliament. In America, chickens squawked and tar kettles bubbled as violators of The Association were tarred and feathered. Muskets were being collected, men were openly drilling, and a confrontation seemed imminent.

In April 1775, the British commander in Boston sent a detachment of troops to nearby Lexington and Concord. They were to seize stores of colonial gunpowder, and also to bag the "rebel" ringleaders, Samuel Adams and John Hancock. At Lexington, the colonial "Minute Men" refused to disperse rapidly enough, and shots were fired which killed eight Amer-

icans and wounded several more. The redcoats pushed on to Concord, whence they were forced to retreat by the homespun Americans, whom Emerson immortalized:

> By the rude bridge that arched the flood,
> Their flag to April's breeze unfurled,
> Here once the embattled farmers stood,
> And fired the shot heard round the world.*

The bewildered British, fighting off murderous fire from militiamen crouched behind thick stone walls, finally regained the sanctuary of Boston. Licking their wounds, they could count about 300 casualties, including some 70 killed. England now had a war on her hands.

Imperial and Colonial Pluses and Minuses

Aroused Americans had brashly rebelled against a mighty empire. The population odds were about three to one against the rebels—some 7.5 million Britons to 2.5 million colonials. The odds in monetary

---

*Ralph Waldo Emerson, "Concord Hymn."

Abigail Adams. *The wife of Revolutionary leader and future president John Adams, she was a prominent Patriot in her own right. She was also among the first Americans to see, however faintly, the implications of Revolutionary ideas for changing the status of women. (New York State Historical Association, Cooperstown, New York)*

wealth and naval power were overwhelmingly in favor of the mother country.

Black people were only a partial asset to the American cause, for they could hardly be expected to fight for a society that had enslaved them. Still, about 5,000 saw military service, whether as freemen or as slaves promised freedom, and in a number of engagements fought bravely. Even larger numbers, often guaranteed freedom with no strings attached, fled to enemy lines and left the country when the British departed.

Britain boasted a trained professional army of 50,000 men. In addition, George III employed some 30,000 German soldiers—so-called Hessians. The British also enlisted the services of about 50,000 American loyalists and many Indians, who ravaged long stretches of the frontier.

Yet the mother country was weaker than she seemed at first glance. British troops had to be detached to watch the latent volcano of oppressed Ireland. Recently defeated France was bitterly awaiting an opportunity to stab Britain in the back. Other handicaps loomed. The redcoats had to conquer the Americans; a draw would be a victory for the colonials. Britain was operating some 3,000 miles (4,800 kilometers) from her home base, and distance added greatly to the delays and uncertainties arising from storms and other mishaps.

To conquer and control the vast North American territories would be a tremendous task. America's geographical expanse was enormous: roughly 1,000 by 600 miles (1,600 by 970 kilometers). The united colonies had no urban nerve center like Paris or London. British armies captured every city of any size, yet like a boxer punching a feather pillow, they made little more than a dent in the entire country. The Americans wisely traded space for time.

In addition to geographical advantages, the revolutionists were also blessed with outstanding leadership. George Washington was a giant among men. Master diplomat Benjamin Franklin eventually secured open foreign aid from France. Glory-loving Marquis de Lafayette, a young French noble fleeing boredom, became a major general in the colonial army at age nineteen. The services of the teenage "French gamecock" secured further invaluable aid from France.

Other conditions aided the Americans. They were fighting defensively on their own terrain. Agriculturally, the colonies were almost totally self-sufficient. The colonial "buckskins" were a tough, self-reliant people. Their marksmen, far superior to the British, could hit a man's head at 200 yards (183 meters). Americans also enjoyed the moral advantage that came from belief in a just cause.

Yet the American rebels were badly organized for war. Almost fatally lacking in unity, the new nation lurched forward uncertainly like an uncoordinated centipede. Even the Continental Congress, which was supposedly directing the conflict, was hardly more than a debating society that grew feebler as the struggle dragged on. Disorganized colonials fought almost the entire war before adopting a written constitution—the Articles of Confederation—in 1781.

Economic difficulties were well-nigh insuperable. With metal money drained away and taxation an explosive issue, a cautious Continental Congress financed the war with "Continental" paper money. As this currency poured from the presses, it depreciated until it became "not worth a Continental," as the saying went. Prices inevitably skyrocketed, hitting especially hard the families of soldiers at the front and creditors, who were often paid off with handfuls of the semiworthless money.

A Thin Line of Heroes

Basic military supplies in the colonies were dangerously scanty, especially firearms and powder. Benjamin Franklin seriously proposed going back to the bow and arrow. Even where food was accumulated, wagons were often not available to haul it. At Valley Forge, in the winter of 1777–1778, the shivering American soldiers were without bread for three successive days.

Manufactured goods were generally in short supply in agricultural America, and clothing and shoes were appallingly scarce. The path of the patriot fighting men was often marked by bloody snow. At frigid Valley Forge, during one anxious period, 2,800 men were barefooted or nearly naked.

American militiamen were numerous but highly unreliable. Able-bodied American males—perhaps several hundred thousand of them—had received rudimentary training, and many of these recruits served for short terms in the rebel armies. But poorly trained plowboys, though better shots, could not stand up in the open field against professional British troops advancing with bare bayonets. Many of these undisciplined warriors would, in the words of Washington, "fly from their own shadows."

A few thousand regulars—perhaps 7,000 or 8,000 at war's end—were finally whipped into shape by stern drillmasters. Notable among these officers was an organizational genius, the salty German Baron von Steuben. He spoke no English when he reached America, but he soon taught his men that bayonets were not for broiling beefsteaks over open fires. As they gained experience, these soldiers of the Continental line could hold their own in open battle against crack British troops.

Morale in the Revolutionary army was badly undermined by American profiteers. These grasping gentry, putting profits before patriotism, sold to the British because the invader could pay in gold. Speculators forced prices sky-high, and some Bostonians made profits of 50 percent to 200 percent on army clothing while the American army was freezing at Valley Forge. Washington never had as many as 20,000 effective troops in one place at one time, despite bounties of land and other inducements. Yet if the rebels had thrown themselves into the struggle with Revolutionary zeal, they could easily have raised many times that number.

The brutal truth is that only a select minority of the American colonials attached themselves to the cause of independence with a spirit of selfless devotion. These were the dedicated souls who bore the burden of battle and the risks of defeat; these were the freedom-loving patriots who deserved the gratitude and esteem of generations yet unborn. Seldom have so few done so much for so many.

VARYING VIEWPOINTS

Historians once assumed that the Revolution was just another chapter in the unfolding story of human liberty—a kind of divinely ordained progress toward perfection in human affairs. This approach is often called the Whig view of history. Around the beginning of this century, the concept was sharply challenged by the so-called progressive historians, who argued that not God but a sharp struggle among different social groups brought about change. "Progressives" thus saw the Revolution as stemming from class conflict and ending in a truly transformed social order. As one of them put it, the Revolution was not only about home rule, but about "who should rule at home."

Since World War II, scholars have questioned this interpretation. They have uncovered evidence that the British imperial system really was not unduly burdensome to the colonists, and more important, that colonial society was *already* fairly democratic before 1776 (at least as regards white people).

Two questions naturally arise: What really caused the divorce of mother country and colo-

nists, and precisely how "revolutionary" was the Revolution? Interestingly, recent scholarship has tended to emphasize not economic or political friction, but rather ideological and even psychological factors. The root causes of the Revolution may well have been the felt need to defend existing political liberties, combined with an exaggerated fear of conspiracy against them.

SELECT READINGS

Primary Source Documents

Adam Smith's *An Inquiry into the Nature and Causes of the Wealth of Nations** (1776) is a penetrating analysis of British mercantilism. Patrick Henry's "Speech before the Virginia House of Burgesses against the Stamp Act"* (1765) was an influential statement of colonial opposition to British policy, as was John Dickinson's response to the Townshend Acts, *Letters from a Farmer in Pennsylvania* (1768). For contemporary accounts of the beginning of hostilities, see Peter Force, ed., *American Archives,* Fourth Series, Vol. 2 (1839).*

Secondary Sources

Edmund S. Morgan, *The Birth of the Republic, 1763–1789* (1959) is among the best brief accounts of the Revolutionary era. It stresses the happy coincidence of the revolutionaries' principles and their interests. Lawrence Gipson, *The Coming of the Revolution, 1763–1775* (1954), summarizes his 15-volume masterwork (cited in Chapter 5). Merrill Jensen, *The Founding of a Nation* (1968) is a more recent attempt at synthesis, as is Robert Middlekauff's *The Glorious Cause:*

The American Revolution, 1763–1789 (1982). Bernhard Knollenberg examines the effects of the British tightening of the imperial system in the 1760s in *Origin of the American Revolution, 1759–1766* (1960), as does Michael Kammen in *Empire and Interest* (1970). John Shy imaginatively explores an important aspect of the imperial system's effect on America in *Toward Lexington: The Role of the British Army in the Coming of the American Revolution* (1965). Clinton Rossiter, *Seedtime of the Republic* (1953), stresses the importance of ideas in pushing the Revolution forward, as does Bernard Bailyn's seminal *Ideological Origins of the American Revolution* (1967), which also emphasizes the colonists' fears of a conspiracy against their liberties. Edward A. Countryman emphasizes class conflict in *A People in Revolution: The American Revolution and Political Society in New York, 1760–1790* (1981). Two recent books take a psychological approach to the problem of the Revolutionary generation's assault on established authority: Kenneth S. Lynn, *A Divided People* (1977), and Jay Fliegelman, *Prodigals and Pilgrims: The American Revolution against Patriarchal Authority, 1750–1800* (1982).

7

America Secedes from the Empire

**These are the times that try men's souls.
The summer soldier and the sunshine patriot will, in this crisis,
shrink from the service of their country; but he that stands it *now*,
deserves the love and thanks of man and woman.**

Thomas Paine, December 1776

Congress Drafts George Washington

Bloodshed at Lexington and Concord, in April 1775, was a clarion call to arms. About 20,000 musket-bearing "Minute Men" swarmed around Boston, there to coop up the outnumbered British.

The Second Continental Congress met in Philadelphia the next month, on May 10, 1775; and this time the full slate of thirteen colonies was represented. The conservative element in Congress was still strong, despite the shooting in Massachusetts. There was no real sentiment for independence—merely a desire to continue fighting in the hope that king and Parliament would consent to a redress of grievances. Congress hopefully drafted new appeals to the British people and king—appeals that were spurned. Anticipating a possible rebuff, the delegates also adopted measures to raise money and to create an army and a navy.

Perhaps the most important single action of the Congress was to select George Washington, one of its members already in officer's uniform, to head the hastily improvised army besieging Boston. This choice was made with considerable misgivings. The tall, powerfully built, dignified, blue-eyed Virginia planter, then forty-three, had never risen above the rank of a colonel in the militia. His largest command had numbered only twelve hundred men, and that had been some twenty years earlier. Falling short of true military genius, he was actually destined to lose more pitched battles than he won.

But the distinguished Virginian was gifted with outstanding powers of leadership and immense strength of character. He radiated patience, courage, self-discipline, and a sense of justice. He was a great moral force rather than a great military mind—a symbol and a rallying point. People instinctively trusted him. As a man of wealth, both by inheritance and by marriage, Washington could not be accused of being a fortune seeker. He insisted on serving without pay, though he kept a careful expense account amounting to more than $100,000.

The Continental Congress initially selected Washington more for political reasons than for his leadership qualities. Other sections distrusted the large New England army gathering around Boston, and prudence suggested a commander from Virginia.

Bunker Hill and Hessian Hirelings

The clash of arms continued on a strangely contradictory basis. On the one hand, the Americans were emphatically affirming their loyalty to the king and earnestly voicing their desire to patch up existing difficulties. On the other hand, they were raising armies and shooting down His Majesty's soldiers. This curious war of inconsistency was fought for fourteen long months—from April 1775 to July 1776—before the fateful plunge into independence was taken.

Gradually the tempo of warfare increased. In May 1775, a tiny American force, under Ethan Allen and Benedict Arnold, surprised and captured the British garrisons at Ticonderoga and Crown Point, on the scenic lakes of upper New York. A priceless store of powder and artillery for the siege of Boston was thus secured.

In June 1775, the colonials seized a hill, now known as Bunker Hill (actually Breed's Hill), from which they menaced the enemy in Boston. The British blundered bloodily when they launched a frontal attack with 3,000 men. Sharp-shooting Americans, numbering 1,500 and strongly entrenched, mowed down the advancing foe with frightful slaughter. But their scanty store of powder finally gave out, and they were forced to abandon the hill in disorder. With two more such victories, remarked the French foreign minister, the British government would have no army left in America.

Following Bunker Hill, the king slammed the door on all hope of reconciliation. In August 1775 he formally proclaimed the colonies in rebellion. The next month he further widened the chasm by hiring thousands of German troops, shocking colonials who feared the so-called Hessians' exaggerated reputation for butchery and bestiality. In fact, the Hessians turned out to be more interested in booty than duty. Hundreds of them deserted and remained in the United States as respected citizens.

The Abortive Conquest of Canada

The unsheathed sword continued to take its toll. In October 1775, on the eve of a cruel winter, the British burned Falmouth (Portland), Maine. In that same autumn the rebels daringly undertook a two-pronged invasion of Canada. American leaders believed, erroneously, that the conquered French were explosively restive under the British yoke. A successful assault on Canada would add a fourteenth colony, while depriving Britain of a valuable base for striking at the colonies in revolt. But this large-scale attack, involving some two thousand American troops, contradicted the claim of the colonials that they were merely fighting defensively for a redress of grievances. Invasion northward was undisguised offensive warfare.

This bold stroke for Canada narrowly missed success. One invading column under the Irish-born General Richard Montgomery, formerly of the British army, pushed up the Lake Champlain route and captured Montreal. He was joined at Quebec by the bedraggled army of General Benedict Arnold, whose men had been reduced to eating dogs and shoe leather during their grueling march through the Maine woods. An assault on Quebec, launched on the last day of 1775, was beaten off. The able Montgomery was killed; the dashing Arnold was wounded in one leg. Scattered remnants under his command retreated up the St. Lawrence River, reversing the way Montgomery had come. French-Canadian leaders, who had been generously treated by the British in the Quebec Act of 1774, showed no real desire to welcome the plundering anti-Catholic invaders.

Bitter fighting continued in the colonies, though the Americans still disclaimed all desire for independence. In January 1776 the British set fire to the Virginia town of Norfolk. In March they were finally forced to evacuate Boston, taking with them the leading friends of the king. (Evacuation Day is still celebrated annually in Boston.) In the South the

Revolution in the North, 1775–1776.
Benedict Arnold's troops were described as "pretty young men" when they sailed from Massachusetts. They were considerably less pretty on their arrival in Quebec, after eight weeks of struggling through wet and frigid forests, often without food. "No one can imagine," one of them wrote, "the sweetness of a roasted shotpouch (ammunition bag) to the famished appetite."

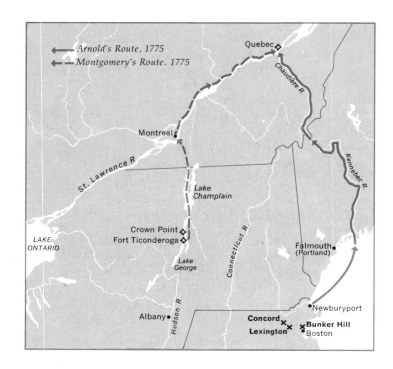

rebellious colonials won two victories in 1776; one in February against some 1,500 Loyalists at Moore's Creek Bridge, in North Carolina; and the other in June against an invading British fleet at Charleston harbor.

Thomas Paine Preaches Common Sense

Why did Americans continue to deny any intention of independence? Loyalty to the empire was deeply ingrained; colonial unity was poor; and open rebellion was dangerous, especially against a formidable Britain. Irish rebels of that day were customarily hanged, drawn, and quartered. American rebels might have fared no better. As late as January 1776—five months before independence was declared—the king's health was being toasted by the officers of Washington's mess near Boston. "God save the king" had not yet been replaced by "God save the Congress."

Gradually the Americans were shocked into an awareness of their inconsistency. Their eyes were opened by harsh British acts like the burning of

Falmouth and Norfolk, and especially by the hiring of the Hessians. Early in 1776 came the publication of *Common Sense,* one of the most potent pamphlets ever written. Its author was the radical Thomas Paine, once an impoverished corset-maker's apprentice, who had come over from England a year earlier. His tract became a whirlwind best seller, and within a few months reached the astonishing total of 120,000 copies in circulation.

Paine flatly branded the shilly-shallying of the colonials as contrary to "common sense." Why not throw off the cloak of inconsistency? Nowhere in the physical universe did the smaller heavenly body control the larger one. Then why should the tiny island of England control the vast continent of America? As for the king, whom the Americans professed to revere, he was nothing but "the Royal Brute of Great Britain." America had a sacred mission—a moral obligation to the world—to set herself up as an independent, democratic republic, untainted by association with corrupt and monarchical Britain.

Paine's passionate protest was simple and somewhat shallow, but it was direct and persuasive. Thousands of American waverers, their eyes jolted open, were prodded into going the whole way. They not only perceived the folly of their position, but—perhaps most important—they realized that they could not hope for open aid from France as long as they swore allegiance to the king. The French Crown was interested in the destruction of the British Empire, not in its reconstruction under a plan of reconciliation.

Jefferson's Justification of Independence

Members of the Philadelphia Congress, instructed by their respective colonies, gradually edged toward a clean break. On June 7, 1776, fiery Richard Henry Lee of Virginia moved that "These United Colonies are, and of right ought to be, free and independent states. . . ." After considerable debate, the motion was adopted nearly a month later, on July 2, 1776.

The passing of Lee's resolution was the formal "declaration" of independence by the American colonies, and technically this was all that was needed to cut the British tie. John Adams wrote confidently that ever thereafter July 2 would be celebrated annually with fireworks. But something more was required. An epochal rupture of this kind called for some formal explanation to "a candid world." An inspirational appeal was also needed to enlist other English colonies in the Americas, to invite assistance from foreign nations, and to rally resistance at home.

Shortly after Lee made his memorable motion on June 7, Congress appointed a committee to prepare an appropriate statement. The task of drafting it fell to Thomas Jefferson, a tall, freckled, sandy-haired Virginia lawyer of thirty-three. Despite his youth, he was already recognized as a brilliant writer, and he measured up splendidly to his opportunity. After some debate and amendment, the Declaration of Independence was formally approved by the Congress on July 4, 1776.

Jefferson's pronouncement, couched in a lofty style, was magnificent. He gave his appeal universality by invoking the "natural rights" of mankind—not just British rights. He argued persuasively that because the king had flouted these rights, the colonials were justified in cutting their connection. He then set forth a long list of the presumably tyrannous misdeeds of George III. The overdrawn bill of indict-

ment included imposing taxes without consent, dispensing with trial by jury, abolishing valued laws, establishing a military dictatorship, maintaining standing armies in peacetime, cutting off trade, burning towns, hiring mercenaries, and inciting savage Indians.*

Jefferson's withering blast was admittedly one-sided. He owned many slaves, and his affirmation that "all men are created equal" was to haunt him and his countrymen for generations.

The formal declaration of independence cleared the air as a thundershower does on a muggy day. Foreign aid could be solicited with greater hope of success. Those patriots who defied the king were now rebels, not loving subjects shooting their way into reconciliation. They must all hang together, Franklin is said to have grimly remarked, or they would all hang separately. Or, in the eloquent language of the great declaration, "We mutually pledge to each other our lives, our fortunes and our sacred honor."

Loyalists Stick with Mother England

The War of Independence was a civil war between two factions of Americans as well as a war between Americans and British. Besides battling the British redcoats, the American rebels, called Patriots or Whigs, fought Americans loyal to the king, called Loyalists or Tories.

Like many revolutions, the American Revolution was a minority movement. Many colonists were apathetic or neutral, including those Byrds of Virginia who sat on the fence. The opposing forces contended not only against each other but also for the allegiance and support of the civilian population. In this struggle for the hearts and minds of the people, the Patriot militia proved to be far more successful than the inept British. The British military were able to control only those areas where it could maintain a massive military presence. Elsewhere, as soon as the redcoats had marched on, the rebel militiamen appeared and took up the task of "political education"—sometimes by coercive means. Often lacking bayonets but always

---

*For an annotated text of the Declaration of Independence, see the Appendix.

Tory Suspended, While Goose Is Plucked for Coat of Feathers. *(The Bettmann Archive, Inc)*

loaded with political zeal, the ragtag militia units convinced many colonists, even those indifferent to independence, that the British army was an unreliable friend and that they had better throw in their lot with the Patriot cause.

Loyalists, numbering perhaps 20 percent of the American people, remained true to their king. Some fifty thousand Loyalist volunteers at one time or another bore arms for the British. They also helped the king's cause by serving as spies, by inciting the Indians, and by keeping Patriot soldiers at home to protect their families.

Who were the Loyalists? Conservative Americans generally remained loyal—the people of education and wealth, of culture and caution. Loyalists were also more numerous among the older generation, for young people make revolutions. Loyalists included the king's officers and other beneficiaries of the crown—people who knew which side their daily bread came from. Loyalists were most numerous

where the Anglican church was strongest, except in Virginia, where debt-burdened Anglican aristocrats flocked into the rebel camp. The king's followers were well entrenched in aristocratic New York City and Charleston, and also in Quaker Pennsylvania and New Jersey, where General Washington felt that he was fighting in "the enemy's country." Loyalists were least numerous in New England, where flourishing Presbyterianism and Congregationalism produced strong support for rebellion.

Before independence was declared in 1776, persecution of the Loyalists was relatively mild. But after the Declaration of Independence, Loyalists were more roughly handled. A Patriot definition of a Tory betrayed the bitterness many felt: "A Tory is a thing whose head is in England, and its body in America, and its neck ought to be stretched." A few noncombatant Loyalists were in fact hanged, and others were imprisoned. About eighty thousand loyal supporters of George III were driven out or fled, and their estates were confiscated to finance the war. But no reign of terror comparable to that of the later French and Russian Revolutions occurred.

The Loyalists were tragic figures. Loyalty is ordinarily a major virtue, and for generations the English in the New World had been taught fidelity to their king. If the king had triumphed, as he seemed likely to do, the Loyalists would have been acclaimed patriots, and defeated rebels like Washington would have been disgraced, severely punished, and probably forgotten.

General Washington at Bay

With Boston evacuated in March 1776, the British concentrated on New York as a base of operations. Here was a splendid seaport, centrally located, where the king could count on cooperation from the numerous Loyalists. An awe-inspiring British fleet appeared off New York in July 1776. It consisted of some 500 ships and 35,000 men—the largest armed force to be seen in America until the Civil War. General Washington, dangerously outnumbered, could muster only 18,000 ill-trained troops with which to meet the crack army of the invader.

Disaster befell the Americans in the summer and fall of 1776. Outgeneraled and outmaneuvered, they

New York and New Jersey, 1776–1777.

were routed at the Battle of Long Island, where panic seized the raw recruits. By the narrowest of margins, and thanks to a favoring wind and fog, Washington escaped to Manhattan Island. Retreating northward, he crossed the Hudson River to New Jersey, and finally reached the Delaware River with the British close at his heels. Tauntingly, enemy buglers sounded the fox-hunting call, so familiar to Virginians of Washington's day. The Patriot cause was at low ebb when the rebel remnants fled across the river, after collecting all available boats to forestall pursuit.

The wonder is that Washington's adversary, General William Howe, did not speedily crush the demoralized American forces. But he was no military genius, and he well remembered the horrible slaughter at Bunker Hill, where he had commanded. The country was rough, supplies were slow in coming, and as a professional soldier Howe did not relish the rigors of winter campaigning.

Washington, now almost counted out, stealthily recrossed the ice-clogged Delaware River. At Trenton, on December 26, 1776, he surprised and captured a thousand Hessians who were sleeping off the effects of their Christmas celebration. A week later, leaving his campfires burning as a ruse, he slipped away and inflicted a sharp defeat on a smaller British detachment at Princeton.

Burgoyne's Blundering Invasion

London officials adopted an intricate scheme for capturing the vital Hudson River Valley in 1777. If successful, the British would sever New England from the rest of the states and paralyze the American cause. The main invading force, under an actor-playwright-soldier, General ("Gentleman Johnny") Burgoyne, would push down the Lake Champlain route from Canada. General Howe's troops in New York, if needed, could advance up the Hudson River to meet Burgoyne near Albany. A third and much smaller British force, commanded by Colonel St. Leger, would come in from the west by way of Lake Ontario and the Mohawk Valley.

British planners did not reckon with General Benedict Arnold. Retreating slowly from Quebec, Arnold had heroically kept his army in the field and assembled a small fleet on Lake Champlain, an essential supply route. The British finally constructed a fleet that defeated Arnold's tiny flotilla, but winter was descending and the British were compelled to retire to Canada.

Forced to start over from Canada rather than farther south, General Burgoyne began his fateful invasion in the spring of 1777 with 7,000 regular troops, a heavy baggage train, and many officers' wives. Progress was painfully slow, for sweaty men had to chop a path through the forest, while American militiamen began to gather like hornets on Burgoyne's flanks.

Meanwhile, astonished eyebrows rose at General Howe, who took the main British army toward Philadelphia at a time when it seemed obvious he should be starting up the Hudson to join Burgoyne. Scholars now know that Howe wanted to engage and destroy Washington's army, apparently assuming he had ample time to assist Burgoyne directly should he be needed.

General Washington, keeping a wary eye on the British in New York, hastily transferred his army to the vicinity of Philadelphia. There, late in 1777, he was defeated in two pitched battles, at Brandywine Creek and Germantown. Pleasure-loving General Howe then settled down comfortably in the lively capital, leaving Burgoyne to flounder through the wilds of upper New York. Benjamin Franklin, recently sent to Paris as an envoy, truthfully jested that Howe had not

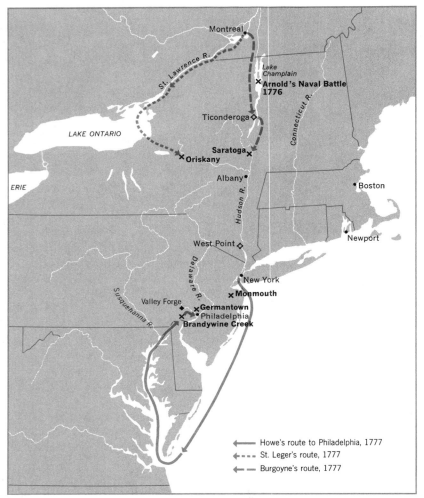

New York–Pennsylvania Theater, 1777–1778. *Distinguished members of the Continental Congress fled from Philadelphia in near-panic as the British army approached. Thomas Paine reported that at three o'clock in the morning the streets were "as full of Men, Women, and Children as on a Market Day." John Adams had anticipated that "I shall run away, I suppose, with the rest," since "we are too brittle ware, you know, to stand the dashing of balls and bombs." Adams got his chance to decamp with the others into the interior of Pennsylvania, and tried to put the best face on things. "This tour," he commented, "has given me an opportunity of seeing many parts of this country which I never saw before."*

captured Philadelphia but that Philadelphia had captured Howe. Washington finally retired to winter quarters at Valley Forge, a strong hilly position some twenty miles northwest of Philadelphia, and there his frost-bitten and hungry men were short of about everything except misery. This rabble was nevertheless whipped into a professional army by the recently arrived Prussian drillmaster, the profane but patient Baron von Steuben.

Burgoyne meanwhile had begun to bog down north of Albany, while a host of American militiamen, scenting the kill, swarmed about him. In a series of sharp engagements, in which General Arnold was

again shot in the leg previously wounded at Quebec, the British army was trapped. Meanwhile the Americans had driven back St. Leger's force at Oriskany. Unable to advance or retreat, Burgoyne was forced to surrender his entire command at Saratoga, on October 17, 1777, to the American General Gates.

Saratoga ranks high among the decisive battles of both American and world history. The victory immensely revived the faltering colonial cause. Even more important, it convinced the French government that the colonies would win the war, which thereupon supplied the urgently needed aid that was instrumental in bringing about that victory.

The Colonial War Becomes a World War

France, thirsting for revenge, was eager to inflame the quarrel that had broken out in America. After the shooting at Lexington in April 1775, French agents undertook to blow on the embers. They secretly provided the Americans with life-saving amounts of powder and other munitions. About 90 percent of all the gunpowder used by the Americans during the first two and a half years of the war came from French arsenals.

Secrecy enshrouded these French schemes. Open aid to the American rebels might provoke England into a declaration of war; and France, still weakened by her recent defeat, was not ready to fight. She feared that the American rebellion might fade out, for the colonies were proclaiming their desire to patch up differences. But the Declaration of Independence in 1776 showed that the Americans really meant business; and the smashing victory at Saratoga seemed to indicate that they had an excellent chance of winning their freedom.

After the humiliation at Saratoga in 1777, the British Parliament belatedly passed a measure which in effect offered the Americans home rule within the empire. This was essentially all that the colonials had ever asked for—except independence. If the French were going to break up the British Empire, they would have to bestir themselves. Wily and bespectacled old Benjamin Franklin, whose simple fur cap and witty sayings had captivated the French public, played skillfully on France's fears of reconciliation.

Seeing an opportunity to undo the victor's peace of 1763, and fearing a reconciliation between Britain and her colonies, France offered the Americans a treaty of alliance in 1778. It was the first entangling military alliance in the experience of the republic, and one that later caused prolonged trouble.

England and France thus came to blows in 1778, and the shot fired at Lexington rapidly widened into a global conflagration. Spain entered the fray against Britain in 1779, as did Holland. Catherine the Great of Russia lined up the remaining European neutrals into what was called the Armed Neutrality, which maintained an attitude of passive hostility toward England.

To the mother country, the struggle with these great powers for her very life made the scuffle in the New World seem secondary. The Americans deserve credit for having kept the war going, with secret French aid, until 1778. But they did not achieve their independence until the conflict erupted into a multi-power world war that was too big for Britain to handle. From 1778 to 1783, France provided the rebels with large sums of money, immense amounts of equipment, about one-half of America's regular armed forces, and practically all of the new nation's naval strength.

France's entrance into the conflict also forced the British to change their basic strategy in America. With powerful French fleets in American waters, Britain was no longer able to count on blockading the colonial coast and commanding the seas. To shorten their lines of supply, the British evacuated Philadelphia in 1778 and concentrated their strength in New York City, where they were followed by Washington's army. Henceforth, except for the Yorktown interlude in 1781, Washington remained in the New York area, hemming in the British.

Blow and Counterblow

In the summer of 1780 a powerful French army of 6,000 regular troops, commanded by the Comte de Rochambeau, arrived in Newport, Rhode Island. Preparations were made for a Franco-American attack on New York.

Improving American morale was staggered later in 1780, when General Benedict Arnold turned traitor. A leader of undoubted dash and brilliance, he was ambitious, greedy, unscrupulous, and suffering from a well-grounded but petulant feeling that his valuable services were not fully appreciated. He plotted with the British to sell out the key stronghold of West Point, which commanded the Hudson River, for £6,300 and an officer's commission. By the sheerest accident the plot was detected in the nick of time, and Arnold fled to the British. "Whom can we trust now?" cried General Washington in anguish.

The British meanwhile had devised a plan to roll up the colonies, beginning with the South, where the Loyalists were numerous. Georgia was ruthlessly overrun in 1778–1779. Charleston, South Carolina, fell in

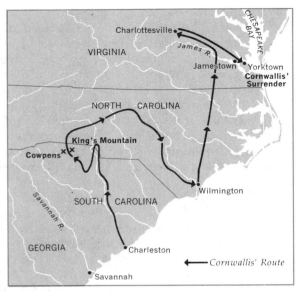

War in the South, 1780–1781.

1780. The surrender of the city to the British involved the capture of five thousand men and four hundred cannon, and was a heavier loss to the Americans, in relation to existing strength, than that of Burgoyne was to the British.

Warfare now intensified in the Carolinas, where Patriots bitterly fought their Loyalist neighbors. It was not uncommon for prisoners on both sides to be butchered in cold blood after they had thrown down their arms. A turn of the tide came late in 1780 and early in 1781, when American riflemen wiped out a British detachment at King's Mountain, and then defeated a smaller force at Cowpens. In the Carolina campaign of 1781, General Nathanael Greene, a Quaker-reared tactician, distinguished himself by his strategy of delay. Standing and then retreating, he exhausted his foe, General Cornwallis, in vain pursuit. By losing battles but winning campaigns, the "Fighting Quaker" finally succeeded in clearing most of Georgia and South Carolina of British troops.

The Land Frontier and the Sea Frontier

The West was ablaze during much of the war. Indian allies of George III, hoping to protect their land, were busy with torch and tomahawk; they were egged on by British agents branded as "hair buyers" because they allegedly paid bounties for American scalps. Yet the human tide of westward-moving pioneers did not halt its flow. Eloquent testimony is provided by place names in Kentucky, such as Lexington (named after the battle) and Louisville (named after America's new ally, Louis XVI).

In the wild Illinois country the British were vulnerable to attack, for they held scattered posts which they had captured from the French. An audacious frontiersman, George Rogers Clark, conceived the idea of seizing these forts by surprise. With the blessing of Virginia and £1,200 in depreciated currency, he floated down the Ohio River with about 175 men and captured in quick succession Kaskaskia, Cahokia, and Vincennes.

America's infant navy, commanded by daring officers like the hard-fighting Scotsman, John Paul Jones, was more successful in destroying British merchant shipping than in engaging Britain's thunderous fleets. Even more damaging to British commerce were the swift privateers—privately owned armed ships authorized by Congress to prey on enemy shipping. Over a thousand of these legalized pirates captured some six hundred British prizes. Although they diverted manpower from the main war effort and involved Americans in speculation and graft, privateers brought in urgently needed gold, harassed the enemy, and raised American morale. Merchant ships were compelled to sail in convoy, and British shippers and manufacturers brought increasing pressure on Parliament to end the war on honorable terms.

Yorktown and the Final Curtain

One of the darkest periods of the war was 1780–1781, before the last decisive victory. Inflation of the currency was continuing at full gallop, and the government was virtually bankrupt. Despair was prevalent; disunion was increasing among the states; and mutiny over back pay was spreading in the army.

Meanwhile the British General Cornwallis was blundering into a trap. After futile operations in Virginia, he had fallen back to Chesapeake Bay at Yorktown, there to await seaborne supplies and reinforcements. He assumed that Britain would continue to control the sea. But these few fateful weeks just happened to be one of the brief periods during the war in America when British naval superiority slipped away.

The French were now prepared to cooperate energetically in a brilliant stroke. Admiral de Grasse, operating with a powerful fleet in the West Indies, advised the Americans that he was free to join with them in an assault on Cornwallis at Yorktown. Quick to seize this opportunity, General Washington made a swift march of more than 300 miles (483 kilometers) to the Chesapeake from the New York area. Accompanied by Rochambeau's French army, he beset the British by land, while De Grasse blockaded them by sea after beating off the British fleet. Completely cornered, Cornwallis surrendered his entire force of seven thousand men, on October 19, 1781, as his band appropriately played "The World Turn'd Upside Down." The triumph was no less French than American: the French provided essentially all the seapower and about half the regular troops in the besieging army of some sixteen thousand men.

Stunned by news of the disaster, Prime Minister Lord North cried, "Oh God! It's all over! It's all over!" But it was not. George III stubbornly planned to continue the struggle, for England was far from being crushed. She still had fifty-four thousand troops in North America, including thirty-two thousand in the United States. Washington returned with his army to New York, there to continue keeping a vigilant eye on the British force of ten thousand men.

Fighting actually continued for more than a year after Yorktown, with Patriot-Loyalist warfare in the South especially savage. "No quarter for Tories" was the common battle cry. One of Washington's most valuable contributions was to keep the languishing cause alive, the army in the field, and the states together during these critical months. Otherwise a satisfactory peace treaty might never have been signed.

Peace at Paris

After Yorktown, the war-weary British were increasingly ready to come to terms. They had suffered heavy reverses in India and in the West Indies. The island of Minorca in the Mediterranean had fallen; the Rock of Gibraltar was tottering. Lord North's ministry collapsed in March 1782, temporarily ending the personal rule of George III. A Whig ministry, rather favorable to the Americans, replaced the Tory regime of Lord North.

Three American peace negotiators had meanwhile gathered at Paris: the aging but astute Benjamin Franklin; the flinty John Adams, vigilant for New England interests; and the impulsive John Jay of New York, deeply suspicious of Old World intrigue. The three envoys had explicit instructions from Congress to make no separate peace, and to consult with their French allies at all stages of the negotiations. But the American representatives chafed under this directive. They well knew that it had been written by a subservient Congress, with the French Foreign Office indirectly guiding the pen.

France was in a painful position. She had induced Spain to enter the war on her side, and Spain also coveted the immense trans-Allegheny area. Wanting an America that would be independent but feeble, the French joined the scheme to keep the new republic cooped up east of the Allegheny Mountains.

But John Jay was unwilling to play France's game. Suspiciously alert, he perceived that the French could not satisfy the conflicting ambitions of both Americans and Spaniards. He saw signs—or thought he did—which indicated that the Paris Foreign Office was about to betray America's trans-Allegheny interests to satisfy those of Spain. He therefore secretly made separate overtures to London, contrary to his instructions from Congress. The hard-pressed British, eager to entice one of their enemies from the alliance, speedily came to terms with the Americans. A preliminary treaty of peace was signed in 1782; the final peace, the next year.

By the Treaty of Paris of 1783, the British formally recognized the independence of the United States. In addition, they granted generous boundaries, stretching majestically to the Mississippi on the west, to the Great Lakes on the north, and to Spanish Florida on the south. (Spain had recently captured Florida from Britain.) The Yankees, though now divorced from the Empire, were to retain a share in the priceless fisheries of Newfoundland. The Canadians, of course, were profoundly displeased.

The Americans, on their part, had to yield important concessions. Loyalists were not to be further persecuted, and Congress was to *recommend* to the state legislatures that confiscated Loyalist property be restored. As for the debts long owed to British creditors, the American states were bound to put no lawful obstacles in the way of their collection. Unhap-

The Reconciliation between Britannia and Her Daughter America. *America (represented by an Indian) is invited to buss (kiss) her mother. (Detail from an English cartoon. New York Public Library)*

pily for future harmony, the assurances regarding both debts and Loyalists were not carried out in the manner hoped for by London.

A New Nation Legitimized

Britain's terms were liberal almost beyond belief. The enormous trans-Allegheny area was thrown in as a virtual gift, for George Rogers Clark had captured only a small segment of it. Why the generosity? Had the United States beaten the mother country to her knees?

The key to the riddle may be found in the Old World. At the time the peace terms were drafted, England was trying to seduce America from her French alliance, so she made the terms as alluring as possible. The shaky Whig ministry, hanging on by its fingernails for only a few months, was more friendly to the Americans than were the Tories. It was determined, by a policy of liberality, to salve recent wounds, reopen old trade channels, and prevent future wars

over the coveted trans-Allegheny region. This far-visioned policy was regrettably not followed by the successors of the Whigs.

In spirit, the Americans made a separate peace—contrary to the French alliance. In fact, they did not. The Paris Foreign Office formally approved the terms of peace, though disturbed by the lone-wolf course of its American ally. France was immensely relieved by the prospect of bringing the costly conflict to an end, and of freeing herself from the embarrassing promises she had made to the Spanish crown.

America alone gained from the world-girdling war. The British, though soon to stage a comeback, were battered and beaten. The French gained sweet revenge, but plunged headlong down the slippery slope to bankruptcy and revolution. In truth, Dame Fortune smiled benignly on the Americans. Snatching their independence from the furnace of world conflict, they began their national career with a splendid territorial birthright and a priceless heritage of freedom. Seldom, if ever, has any people been so favored.

VARYING VIEWPOINTS

As the first colonial struggle for "national liberation," the Revolutionary War has long captured the attention of military historians. Early accounts concentrated on the engagements between British regulars and the Continental army, and the war's place in the context of European rivalries. The French alliance, the dramatic battles at Saratoga and Yorktown, and the terrible winter at Valley Forge receive the greatest emphasis in most of these studies.

During the last thirty years, the proliferation of guerrilla conflicts in the Third World has prompted scholars to emphasize another distinctive feature of the War for American Independence—the "triangularity" of the Revolutionary struggle. Focusing on the efforts of the patriot militia to disrupt British supply lines and win the loyalty of the general public, recent accounts, most notably those of John Shy and Charles Royster, portray the conflict less as a battle between two armies than as a contest between the British and the militia for control of the civilian population. By forcing the apathetic majority to associate actively with the Patriot cause, the militia won this war for the hearts and minds of the people and made it unlikely that the British could have recovered the loyalty of the colonists, even had they achieved a military victory.

SELECT READINGS

Primary Source Documents

Thomas Paine's fiery *Common Sense** (1776) is the manifesto of the Revolution. "The Declaration of Independence"* (1776) is one of the foundations of American political theory. See also the "Treaty of Peace with Great Britain" (1783), in Henry Steele Commager, *Documents of American History*.

Secondary Sources

The war is sketched in John R. Alden, *A History of the American Revolution* (1969), and in Don Higgenbotham's excellent military history, *The War of American Independence: Military Attitudes, Policies, and Practice, 1763–1789* (1971). On the implications of the Revolutionary conflict, see John Shy, *A People Numerous and Armed: Reflections on the Military Struggle for American Independence* (1976) and Charles Royster, *A Revolutionary People at War: The Continental Army and the American Character* (1980). Carl Becker's classic *The Declaration of Independence* (1922) is masterful; on the same subject see also Garry Wills, *Inventing America: Jefferson's Declaration of Independence* (1980).

The role of the Loyalists is treated in William H. Nelson, *The American Tory* (1961); Robert M. Calhoun, *The Loyalists in Revolutionary America* (1973); Mary Beth Norton, *The British-Americans: The Loyalist Exiles in England* (1972); and Bernard Bailyn's unusually sensitive biography of the governor of colonial Massachusetts, *The Ordeal of Thomas Hutchinson* (1974). Attention to the social history of the Revolution has been largely inspired by John F. Jameson's seminal *The American Revolution Considered as a Social Movement* (1926). Jackson T. Main, *The Social Structure of Revolutionary America* (1969) takes the exploration further along the same lines, with conclusions somewhat at variance with Jameson's. Women in the revolutionary era are the subject of Linda K. Kerber, *Women of the Republic: Intellect and Ideology in Revolutionary America* (1980), and Mary Beth Norton, *Liberty's Daughters: The Revolutionary Experience of American Women* (1980). Michael Kammen brilliantly evokes the ways that the Revolution has been enshrined in the national memory in *A Season of Youth: The American Revolution and the Historical Imagination* (1978).

8

The Confederation and the Constitution

This example of changing the constitution
by assembling the wise men of the state, instead of assembling armies,
will be worth as much to the world as the former examples we have given it.

Thomas Jefferson, 1787

A Revolution of Sentiments

The American Revolution was not a revolution in the sense of a radical or total change. It did not suddenly and violently overturn the entire political and social framework, as later occurred in the French and Russian revolutions. What happened was accelerated evolution rather than outright revolution.

Yet some striking changes were ushered in, affecting social customs, political institutions, and ideas about society and government. The exodus of some eighty thousand aristocratic Loyalists paved the way for new Patriot elites to emerge. It also cleared the field for the "leveling" ideas of unbridled democracy to sweep across the land.

Equality was everywhere the watchword. When a group of Continental Army officers in 1783 formed an exclusive military order, the Society of the Cincinnati, they were roundly denounced for their aristocratic pretensions. Most states reduced (but usually did not

eliminate altogether) property-holding requirements for voting. Social democracy was further stimulated by the growth of trade organizations for artisans and laborers.

A protracted fight for separation of church and state resulted in notable gains. The well-entrenched Congregational church continued to be legally established in some New England states, but the Loyalist-tainted Anglican church was humbled. De-Anglicized, it re-formed as the Protestant Episcopal church and was everywhere disestablished. The bitter struggle for divorce between religion and government in Virginia was prolonged to 1786, when free-thinking Thomas Jefferson and his co-reformers, including the lowly Baptists, won a complete victory with the passage of the Virginia Statute for Religious Freedom.

The egalitarian sentiments unleashed by the war likewise challenged the institution of slavery. Phila-

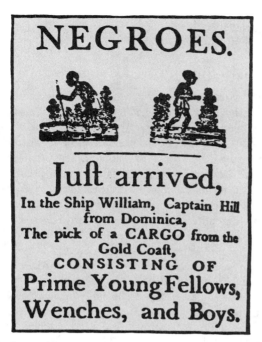

Charleston Slave Advertisement. *(State Gazette of South Carolina, 1787)*

delphia Quakers in 1775 founded the world's first antislavery society. The Continental Congress in 1774 called for complete abolition of the slave trade, a summons to which most of the states responded positively. Several northern states went farther and either abolished slavery outright or provided for the gradual emancipation of blacks. Even in slave-burdened Virginia, a few idealistic masters freed their human chattels. In this still sadly incomplete revolution of sentiments, symbolized and inspired by the Declaration of Independence's concept that "all men are created equal," were to be found the first frail sprouts of the later abolitionist movement.

Likewise incomplete was the extension of the doctrine of equality to women. Some women did serve (disguised as men) in the military. New Jersey's new constitution in 1776 temporarily enabled women to vote. But though Abigail Adams teased her husband John in 1776 that "the ladies" were determined "to foment a rebellion" of their own if they were not given political rights, most of the women in the Revolutionary era were still doing traditional women's work.

Constitution Making in the States

The Continental Congress in 1776 called upon the colonies to draft new constitutions. In effect, the Congress was asking the colonies to summon themselves into being as new states, whose sovereignty, according to the theory of republicanism, would rest on the authority of the people. In most of the states, constitution writers worked feverishly to capture the democratic spirit of the age on black-inked parchment.

Massachusetts contributed one especially noteworthy innovation when it called a special convention to draft its constitution and then submitted the final draft directly to the people for ratification. This procedure for forming the basic charter of government was later imitated in the drafting and ratification of the federal Constitution.

The newly penned state constitutions enjoyed many features in common. As *written* documents, the state constitutions were intended to represent a *fundamental* law, superior to the transient whims of ordinary legislation. Most of these documents included bills of rights, specifically guaranteeing long-prized liberties against later legislative encroachment. All of them deliberately created weak executive and judicial branches. A generation of quarreling with His Majesty's officials had implanted a deep distrust of despotic governors and arbitrary judges. But the legislatures, as presumably the most democratic branch of government, were given sweeping powers.

The democratic character of the new state legislatures was vividly reflected by the presence of many members from the recently enfranchised poorer western districts. Their influence was powerfully felt in their several successful movements to relocate state capitals from the haughty eastern seaports into the less pretentious interior. These geographical shifts portended political shifts with which many of the more conservative Americans grew increasingly uncomfortable.

Economic Crosscurrents

Economic changes begotten by the war were likewise noteworthy, but not overwhelming. States seized control of former crown lands, and although rich speculators had their day, many of the large Loyalist holdings were confiscated and eventually cut up into small farms. Roger Morris' huge estate in New York, for example, was sliced into 250 parcels—thus accelerating the spread of economic democracy. The frightful excesses of the French Revolution were avoided, partly because cheap land was easily available. Men do not chop off heads so readily when they can chop down trees. It is significant that in the United States economic democracy, broadly speaking, preceded political democracy.

A sharp stimulus was given to manufacturing by the prewar nonimportation agreements, and later by the war itself. Goods that had formerly been imported from England were mostly cut off, and the ingenious Yankees were forced to make their own. Ten years after the Revolution the busy Brandywine Creek, south of Philadelphia, was turning the waterwheels of numerous mills along an 8-mile (13-kilometer) stretch. Nevertheless, America remained overwhelmingly a nation of soil-tillers.

Economically speaking, independence had drawbacks. Much of the coveted commerce of the mother country was still reserved for the loyal parts of the empire; and now that the Americans were aliens, they were forced to find new customers. Fisheries were disrupted, and bounties for ships' stores had abruptly ended. In some respects, the hated British Navigation Laws were more disagreeable after independence than before.

New commercial outlets, fortunately, compensated partially for the loss of old ones. Americans could now trade freely with foreign nations, subject to local restrictions—a boon they had not enjoyed in the old days of mercantilism. Enterprising Yankee shippers ventured boldly—and profitably—into the Baltic and China seas.

Yet the general economic picture was far from being rosy. War had spawned demoralizing extravagance, speculation, and profiteering, with profits as indecently high as 300 percent. Runaway inflation had been ruinous to middle-class citizens on fixed incomes, and Congress had failed in its feeble attempts to curb economic laws by fixing prices. The issues leading up to the war had bred a keen distaste for taxes. The average citizen was probably worse off

financially at the end of the shooting than at the beginning.

A Shaky Start Toward Union

What would the Americans do with the independence they had so dearly won? Prospects for erecting a lasting regime were far from bright. It is always difficult to set up a new government, doubly difficult to set up a new type of government. The picture was further confused in America by men preaching "natural rights" and looking suspiciously at all persons clothed with authority. America was more a name than a nation, and unity ran little deeper than the color on the map.

Disruptive forces stalked the land. The stabilizing Tory element had been tossed overboard. Patriots had fought the war with a high degree of disunity, but they had at least enjoyed the unifying cement of a common cause. Now even that was gone. It would have been almost a miracle if any government fashioned in all this confusion had long endured.

Hard times, the bane of all regimes, set in shortly after the war, and hit bottom in 1786. As if other troubles were not enough, British manufacturers, with dammed-up surpluses, began flooding the American market with cut-rate goods. War-baby American industries, in particular, suffered industrial colic from such ruthless competition.

Yet hopeful signs could be discerned. The thirteen sovereign states were basically alike in governmental structure, and functioned under similar constitutions. Americans enjoyed a rich political inheritance, derived partly from England and partly from their own homegrown devices for self-government. Finally, they were blessed with political leaders of a high order in men like George Washington, James Madison, John Adams, Thomas Jefferson, and Alexander Hamilton.

Creating a Confederation

The Second Continental Congress of Revolution days was little more than a conference of ambassadors from the thirteen states. In all respects the states were sovereign, for they coined money, raised armies and navies, and erected tariff barriers.

Western Lands, 1783.

Western Lands, 1802.

Shortly before declaring independence in 1776, the Congress appointed a committee to draft a written constitution for the new nation. The finished product was the Articles of Confederation. Adopted by Congress in 1777, it was translated into French after the battle of Saratoga so as to convince France that America had a genuine government in the making. In due course this new constitution was sent out to the states for their approval. But final action was delayed for four years, until 1781, less than eight months before the decisive victory at Yorktown.

The chief apple of discord was western lands. Six of the jealous states, including Pennsylvania and Maryland, had no holdings beyond the Allegheny Mountains. Seven, notably New York and Virginia, were favored with enormous acreage, on the basis of earlier sea-to-sea charter grants. The six landless states argued that their more fortunate sisters would not have retained possession of this splendid prize if all the other states had not fought for it also. A major complaint was that the land-blessed states could sell their trans-Allegheny tracts, and thus pay off pensions and other debts incurred in the common cause. States without such holdings would have to tax themselves

heavily to defray these obligations. Why not turn the whole western area over to the central government?

Unanimous approval of the Articles of Confederation by the thirteen states was required, and landless Maryland stubbornly held out until March 1, 1781. She at length gave in when New York surrendered her western claims, and Virginia seemed about to do so. To sweeten the pill, Congress pledged itself to dispose of these vast areas for the "common benefit." It further agreed to carve from the new public domain not colonies but a number of "republican" states, which in time would be admitted to the union on terms of complete equality with all the others. This extraordinary commitment faithfully reflected the anti-colonial spirit of the Revolution, and the pledge was later fully redeemed in the famed Northwest Ordinance of 1787.

Fertile public lands thus transferred to the central government proved to be an invaluable bond of union. The states that had thrown their heritage into the common pot had to remain in the Union if they were to reap their share of the advantages from the land sales. An army of westward-moving pioneers purchased their farms from the federal government, directly or indirectly, and they learned to look to the national capital, rather than to the state capitals—with a consequent weakening of local influence. Finally, a uniform national land policy was made possible.

The Articles of Confederation: America's First Constitution

The Articles of Confederation provided for a loose confederation or "firm league of friendship." Thirteen independent states were thus linked together for joint action in dealing with common problems, such as foreign affairs. A clumsy Congress was to be the chief agency of government. There was no executive branch—George III had left a bad taste—and the vital judicial arm was left almost exclusively to the states, which remained sovereign.

Congress, though dominant, was closely hobbled by the suspicious states. All bills dealing with specified subjects of importance required a two-thirds vote; any amendment of the Articles themselves required an almost-impossible unanimous vote. Purposely designed to be weak, the Congress was crippled by its lack of power to regulate commerce, which left the states free to establish conflictingly different laws regarding tariffs and navigation. With no tax-collection power, Congress could only set a tax quota for the individual states and ask them please to contribute their shares voluntarily.

Despite their defects, the Articles of Confederation were a significant steppingstone toward the present Constitution. They clearly outlined the general powers that were to be exercised by the central government, such as making treaties and establishing a postal service. As the first written constitution of the Republic, the Articles kept alive the flickering ideal of union and held the states together—until such time as they were ripe for a strong constitution by peaceful, evolutionary methods. The anemic Articles represented what the states regarded as an alarming surrender of their power. Without this intermediary jump, they probably would never have consented to the breathtaking leap from the old boycott Association of 1774 to the Constitution of the United States.

Landmarks in Land Laws

Handcuffed though the Congress of the Confederation was, it managed to pass two supremely farsighted pieces of legislation. These related to an immense part of the public domain recently acquired from the states, and commonly known as the Old Northwest. This area lay northwest of the Ohio River, east of the Mississippi River, and south of the Great Lakes.

The first of these red-letter laws was the Land Ordinance of 1785. It provided that the acreage of the Old Northwest should be sold, and that the proceeds should be used to help pay off the national debt. The vast area was to be surveyed before sale and settlement, thus forestalling endless confusion and lawsuits. It was to be divided into townships six miles square, each of which in turn was to be split into thirty-six sections of one square mile each. The sixteenth section of each township was set aside to be sold for the benefit of the public schools—a priceless gift to education in the Northwest.

Even more noteworthy was the Northwest Ordinance of 1787, which related to governing of the Old Northwest. This law came to grips with the problem of how a nation should deal with its colonial peoples—the same problem that had bedeviled the king and Parliament in London. The solution provided by the Northwest Ordinance was a judicious compromise: temporary tutelage, then permanent equality. First, there would be two evolutionary territorial stages, during which the area would be subordinate to the federal government. Then, when a territory could boast sixty thousand inhabitants, it might be admitted by Congress as a state, with all the privileges of the thirteen charter members. (This is precisely what the Continental Congress had promised the states when they surrendered their lands in 1781.) The Ordinance also forbade slavery in the Old Northwest—a pathbreaking gain for freedom.

The wisdom of Congress in handling this explosive problem deserves warm praise. If it had attempted to chain the new territories in permanent subordination, a second American Revolution almost certainly would have erupted in later years, fought this time by the West against the East. Congress thus neatly solved the seemingly insoluble problem of

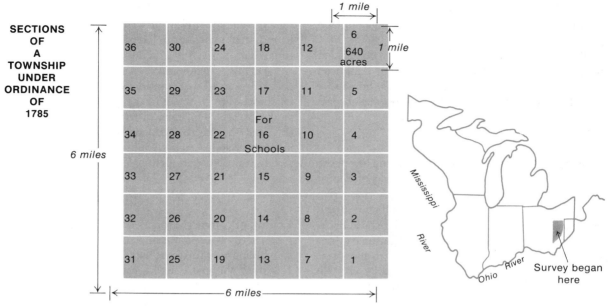

Surveying the Old Northwest.

empire. The scheme worked so well that its basic principles were ultimately carried over from the Old Northwest to other frontier areas.

The World's Ugly Duckling

Foreign relations, especially with London, continued troubled during the anxious years of Confederation. Britain flatly declined to make a commercial treaty or to repeal her ancient Navigation Laws. Lord Sheffield argued that England would win back America's trade anyhow, as commerce naturally returned to old channels. The British also shut off their profitable West Indian trade from the United States.

Along the northern border British agents schemed with the disgruntled Allen brothers to annex Vermont to Canada. Redcoats continued to hold a chain of trading posts on United States soil, maintaining a profitable fur trade and keeping the Indians lined up on the side of the king as a barrier against future American attacks on Canada.

Maddened by these grievances, some patriotic Americans demanded that the United States force the British into line by imposing restrictions on their

imports. But Congress could not control commerce, and the states refused to adopt a uniform tariff policy.

Spain, though recently an enemy of England, was openly unfriendly to the new Republic. She controlled the mouth of the all-important Mississippi, down which the pioneers of Tennessee and Kentucky were forced to float their produce, and in 1784 closed the river to American commerce. The West was thus threatened with strangulation. Spain likewise claimed a large area north of the Gulf of Mexico, including Florida, granted to the United States by the British in 1783. At Natchez, on disputed soil, she held an important fort. She also intrigued with the neighboring Indians to hem the Americans in east of the Alleghenies. Spain and England together, radiating their influence out among warlike Indian tribes, prevented America from exercising effective control over about half of its total territory.

Even America's wartime ally France demanded repayment of money loaned during the war, and restricted trade with her bustling West Indies islands. North African pirates, including the arrogant Dey of Algiers, ravaged America's Mediterranean commerce and enslaved Yankee seamen. The British purchased protection for their subjects, but as an independent nation the United States was too weak to fight and too poor to bribe.

John Jay, secretary for foreign affairs, hoped that these insults would at least humiliate the American people into framing a new government at home that would be strong enough to command respect abroad.

The Horrid Specter of Anarchy

Economic storm clouds continued to hang low in the mid-1780s. A small but alarming tornado of debtor uprising, known as Shays's rebellion, swept across western Massachusetts in 1786 and set off widespread fear of further insurrection. Impoverished back-country farmers, many of them Revolutionary War veterans, were losing their farms through mortgage foreclosures and tax delinquencies. Led by Captain Daniel Shays, a veteran of the Revolution, these desperate debtors demanded cheap paper money, lighter taxes, and a suspension of mortgage foreclosures. Hundreds of angry men, again seizing their muskets, attempted to enforce their demands.

Massachusetts authorities responded with drastic action. Supported partly by contributions from wealthy citizens, they raised a small army under General Lincoln. Several skirmishes occurred—at Springfield three Shaysites were killed and one was wounded—and the movement collapsed. Daniel Shays, who believed that he was fighting anew against tyranny, was condemned to death but was later pardoned.

Shays's followers were crushed—but the nightmarish memory lingered on. The outbursts of these and other distressed debtors struck fear in the hearts of the propertied class, which began to suspect that the Revolution had raised up a Frankenstein's monster of "mobocracy."

How critical were conditions under the Confederation? Conservatives, anxious to safeguard their wealth and position, naturally exaggerated the seriousness of the nation's plight. They were eager to persuade their countrymen to scrap the Articles of Confederation, under which the states were sovereign, in favor of a muscular central government, in which the federal authority would be sovereign. But the poorer states'-rights people, who favored at most a simple amending of the Articles, pooh-poohed the talk of anarchy. Many of them were debtors who feared that a powerful federal government would force them to pay their creditors.

Yet both friends and critics of the Confederation generally agreed that it needed strengthening. Popular toasts were "Cement to the Union" and "A hoop to the barrel." The chief differences arose over how this goal should be attained, and how a maximum amount of states' rights could be reconciled with a strong central government.

A Convention of "Demi-Gods"

Control of commerce touched off the chain reaction that led to a constitutional convention. Interstate squabbling over this issue had become so alarming by 1786 that Virginia issued a call for a convention at Annapolis. When delegates from only five states showed up, nothing could be done about the ticklish commerce question. Classic-featured Alexander Hamilton brilliantly saved the convention from failure by securing adoption of a call for another convention to meet the next year in Philadelphia to bolster the entire fabric of the Articles of Confederation.

Congress was reluctant to take a step that might be the signing of its own death warrant. But after six states appointed delegates anyhow, Congress belatedly issued the call for a convention *"for the sole and express purpose of revising"* the Articles of Confederation.

Every state chose representatives, except independent-minded Rhode Island (still "Rogues' Island"), a stronghold of paper-moneyites. These statesmen were all appointed by the state legislatures, whose members had been elected by voters who could qualify as property holders. This double distillation inevitably brought together a select group of propertied men.

A quorum of the fifty-five emissaries from twelve states finally convened at Philadelphia on May 25, 1787, in the imposing red-brick statehouse. The smallness of the assemblage facilitated intimate acquaintance and hence compromise. Sessions were held in complete secrecy, with armed sentinels posted at the doors. Delegates knew that they would generate heated differences, and they did not want to advertise their own dissensions, or put crippling arguments into the mouths of the opposition.

The caliber of the participants was extraordinarily high—"demi-gods," Jefferson called them. The crisis was such as to induce the ablest men to drop their personal pursuits and come to the aid of their country. Most of the members were lawyers, and most of them fortunately were old hands at constitution-making in their own states.

George Washington, towering austere and aloof among the "demi-gods," was unanimously elected chairman. His enormous prestige, as "the Sword of the Revolution," served to quiet overheated tempers. Benjamin Franklin, then eighty-one, added the urbanity of an elder statesman, though he was inclined to be indiscreetly talkative in his declining years. James Madison, then thirty-six and a profound student of government, made contributions so notable that he has been dubbed "the Father of the Constitution." Alexander Hamilton, then only thirty-two, was present as an advocate of a superpowerful central government. His five-hour speech in behalf of his plan, though the most eloquent of the convention, netted only one favorable vote—his own.

Most of the flaming Revolutionary leaders of 1776 were absent. Thomas Jefferson and Thomas Paine were in Europe; Samuel Adams and John Hancock were not elected by Massachusetts. Patrick Henry, ardent champion of states' rights, was chosen as a delegate from Virginia but declined to serve, declaring that he "smelled a rat." It was perhaps well that these architects of revolution were absent. The time had come to yield the stage to statesmen interested in fashioning solid political systems.

Patriots in Philadelphia

The fifty-five delegates were a conservative, well-to-do body: lawyers, merchants, shippers, land speculators, and moneylenders. Not a single spokesperson was present from the poorer debtor groups. They were young (the average age was about forty-two) but experienced statesmen. Above all, they were nationalists, more interested in preserving and strengthening the young Republic than in further stirring the roiling cauldron of popular democracy.

The delegates hoped to crystallize the evaporating pools of revolutionary idealism into a stable political structure that would endure. They strongly desired a firm, dignified, and respected government. They believed in republicanism but sought to protect the American democratic experiment from its weaknesses abroad and excesses at home. They aimed to clothe the central authority with genuine power, especially in controlling tariffs, so that the United States could wrest satisfactory commercial treaties from foreign nations.

Other motives were present in the stately Philadelphia hall. Delegates were determined to preserve the union, forestall anarchy, and ensure security of life and property against dangerous uprisings by the "mobocracy." Above all, they sought to curb the unrestrained democracy rampant in the various states. The specter of the recent outburst in Massachusetts was especially alarming, and in this sense, Daniel Shays was a Founding Father. Grinding necessity extorted the Constitution from a reluctant nation. There were fifty-five delegates; fear of anarchy occupied the fifty-sixth chair.

Hammering Out a Bundle of Compromises

Some of the travel-stained delegates, when they first reached Philadelphia, decided upon a daring step. They would completely *scrap* the old Articles of Confederation, despite explicit instructions from Congress to *revise*. Technically, these bolder spirits were determined to overthrow the existing government of the United States by peaceful means. The sovereign states were in danger of losing their sovereignty.

A scheme proposed by populous Virginia, and known as "the large-state plan," was first pushed forward as the framework of the Constitution. Its essence was that representation in Congress should be based on population—an arrangement that would naturally give the larger states an advantage. Tiny New Jersey, suspicious of Virginia, countered with "the small-state plan." This provided for equal representation in Congress by states, regardless of size and population.

After bitter and prolonged debate, the "Great Compromise" of the convention was hammered out and agreed upon. The larger states were conceded representation by population in the House of Representatives (Art. I, Sec. II, para. 3; see the Appendix at end of this book), and their smaller sisters were appeased by equal representation in the Senate (see Art. I, Sec. III, para. 1). Each state, no matter how poor or small, would have two senators. The big states, which would have to bear the major burden of taxation, obviously yielded more. As a sop to them, the delegates agreed that every tax bill or revenue measure must originate in the House, where population counted the more heavily (see Art. I, Sec. VII, para. 1). This critical compromise broke the logjam, and from then on success seemed within reach.

The Constitution as drafted was a bundle of compromises; they stand out in every section. A vital compromise was the method of electing the President indirectly by the Electoral College, rather than by direct means (see Art. II, Sec. I, para. 2).

Sectional jealousy also intruded. Should the voteless slave of the Southern states count as a person in apportioning direct taxes and also representation in the House of Representatives? The South, not wishing to be deprived of influence, answered "yes." The North replied "no," arguing that the North might as logically have additional representation based on its horses. As a compromise between total representation and none at all, it was decided that a slave might count as three-fifths of a person. Hence the memorable, if somewhat illogical, "three-fifths compromise" (see Art. I, Sec. II, para. 3).

Most of the states wanted to shut off the African slave trade. But South Carolina and Georgia, requiring slave labor in their rice paddies and malarial swamps, raised vehement protests. By way of compromise the convention stipulated that the slave trade might continue until the end of 1807, at which time Congress could turn off the spigot (see Art. I, Sec. IX, para. 1). It did so as soon as the prescribed interval had elapsed. Meanwhile all the new state constitutions except Georgia's forbade overseas slave trade.

Safeguards for Conservatism

Heated clashes among the delegates have been overplayed. The area of agreement was actually large; otherwise the convention would have speedily disbanded. Economically, the members generally saw eye to eye; they demanded sound money and the protection of private property. Politically, they were in basic agreement; they favored a stronger government, with three branches and with checks and balances among

Strengthening the Central Government

Under Articles of Confederation	Under Federal Constitution
A loose confederation of states	A firm union of people
1 vote in Congress for each state	2 votes in Senate for each state; representation by population in House (see Art. I, Secs. II, III)
⅔ vote (9 states) in Congress for all important measures	Simple majority vote in Congress, subject to presidential veto (see Art. I, Sec. VII, para. 2)
Laws executed by committees of Congress	Laws executed by powerful President (see Art. II, Secs. II, III)
No congressional power over commerce	Congress to regulate both foreign and interstate commerce (see Art. I, Sec. VIII, para. 3)
No congressional power to levy taxes	Extensive power in Congress to levy taxes (see Art. I, Sec. VIII, para. 1)
No federal courts	Federal courts, capped by Supreme Court (see Art. III)
Unanimity of states for amendment	Amendment less difficult (see Art. V)
No authority to act directly upon individuals, and no power to coerce states	Ample power to enforce laws by coercion of individuals and to some extent of states.

them—what critics called a "triple-headed monster." Finally, the convention was virtually unanimous in believing that manhood-suffrage democracy—government by "democratick babblers"—was something to be feared and fought.

Daniel Shays, the prime bogeyman, still frightened the conservative-minded delegates. They deliberately erected safeguards against the excesses of the "mob," and they made these barriers as strong as they dared. The awesome federal judges were to be appointed for life. The powerful President was to be elected *indirectly* by the Electoral College; the lordly senators were to be chosen *indirectly* by state legislatures (see Art. I, Sec. III, para. 1). Only in the case of one-half of one of the three great branches—the House of Representatives—were qualified (propertied) citizens permitted to choose their officials by *direct* vote (see Art. I, Sec. II, para. 1).

Yet the new charter also contained democratic elements. Above all, it stood foursquare on the great principle that the only legitimate government was one based on the consent of the governed. "We the people," the Preamble began, in a ringing affirmation of the doctrine of popular sovereignty.

At the end of seventeen muggy weeks—May 25 to September 17, 1787—only forty-two of the original fifty-five members remained to sign the Constitution. Three of the forty-two, refusing to do so, returned to their states to resist ratification. The remainder, adjourning to the City Tavern, appropriately celebrated the occasion.

The Clash of Federalists and Anti-Federalists

The Framing Fathers early foresaw that nationwide acceptance of the Constitution would not be easy to obtain. A formidable barrier was unanimous ratification by all thirteen states, as required for amendment by the still-existent Articles of Confederation. But since absent Rhode Island was certain to veto the Constitution, the delegates boldly adopted a different scheme. They stipulated that when *two-thirds* of the states—that is, nine—had registered their approval through specially elected conventions, the Constitution would become the supreme law of the land in those states ratifying (see Art. VII).

This was extraordinary, even revolutionary. It was in effect an appeal over the heads of the Congress that had called the convention, and over the heads of the legislatures that had chosen its members, to the people—or those of the people who could vote. In this way, the framers could claim greater popular sanction for their handiwork. Congress reluctantly submitted the document to the states on this basis, without recommendation of any kind.

People were somewhat shocked, so well had the secrets of the convention been kept. The public had expected the old Articles of Confederation to be patched up; now it was handed a frightening document in which, many thought, the precious jewel of state sovereignty was swallowed up. One of the hottest debates of American history forthwith erupted. The anti-federalists, who opposed the stronger federal government, were arrayed against the federalists, who naturally favored it.

A motley crowd gathered in the anti-federalist camp. It consisted primarily, though not exclusively, of the states'-rights devotees, the back-country men, the one-horse farmers, the work-grimed artisans, the ill-educated and illiterate—in general, the poorer classes. They were joined by paper-moneyites and debtors, many of whom feared that a potent central government would force them to pay off their debts—and at full value.

Silver-buckled federalists were more respectable; they generally embraced the cultured and propertied groups. Most of them lived in the settled areas along the seaboard, not in the raw back country. They were in outlook rather closely akin to the conservative Loyalist group of Revolutionary days. In fact, many of the remaining former Loyalists gave vigorous support to the Constitution; without them it might have failed of ratification.

Anti-federalists, their worst fears aroused, voiced vehement objections to the "gilded trap" known as the Constitution. They cried with much truth that it had been drawn up by the aristocratic elements, and hence was antidemocratic. They likewise charged that the sovereignty of the states was being swallowed up, and that the freedoms of the individual were jeopardized by the absence of a bill of rights. They decried the dropping of annual elections for congressmen; the setting up of a federal stronghold ten miles square

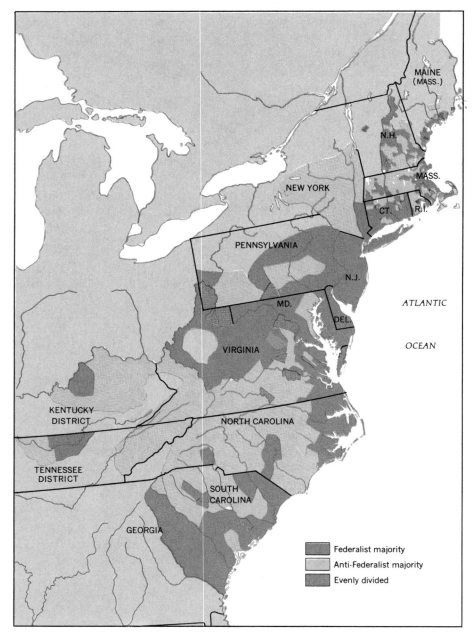

The Struggle over Ratification.   *This mottled map shows that federalist support tended to cluster around the coastal areas, which had enjoyed profitable commerce with the outside world, including the export of grain and tobacco. Impoverished frontiersmen, suspicious of a powerful new central government under the Constitution, were generally anti-federalists.*

(later the District of Columbia); the creation of a standing army; the omission of any reference to God; and the highly questionable procedure of ratifying with only two-thirds of the states.

The Great Debate in the States

Special elections, some apathetic but others hotly contested, were held in the various states for members of the ratifying conventions. Candidates—federalist or anti-federalist—were elected on the basis of their pledges for or against the Constitution.

The newly forged document was quickly accepted by four small states, for they had come off much better than they could have expected. Pennsylvania, number two on the list of ratifiers, was the first large state to act, but not until high-handed irregularities had been employed by the federalist legislature in calling a convention. These included the forcible seating of two anti-federalist members, their clothes torn and their faces red with rage, in order to complete a quorum.

Massachusetts, the second most populous state; provided an acid test. If the Constitution had failed there, the entire movement might easily have bogged down. The Boston ratifying convention at first contained an anti-federalist majority, including weather-beaten Shaysites and suspicious Samuel Adams, who now distrusted change. The absence of a bill of rights

especially alarmed anti-federalists, but federalists solemnly assured them that the first Congress would add such a safeguard by amendment. Massachusetts then ratified by the narrow margin of 187 to 168.

Three more states fell into line. Nine states—all but Virginia, New York, North Carolina, and Rhode Island—had now taken shelter under the "new federal roof," and the document was officially adopted on June 21, 1788. But if the new union was to succeed, the four dissenters—and especially New York and Virginia—had to be brought into the fold.

The Four Laggard States

Proud Virginia, the biggest and most populous state, provided fierce anti-federalist opposition. There the college-bred federalist orators, for once, encountered worthy antagonists, including the fiery Patrick Henry. He professed to see in the fearsome parchment the death warrant of liberty. George Washington, James Madison, and John Marshall, on the federalist side, lent influential support. The new Union was going to be formed anyhow, and Virginia could not very well continue comfortably as an independent state. After a close and exciting debate in the state convention, the ratification carried, 89 to 79.

New York, which also experienced an uphill struggle, was the only state that permitted a manhood-suffrage vote for the members of the ratifying

A Triumphant Cartoon. *It appeared in the* Massachusetts Centinel *on August 2, 1788. Note the two laggards, especially the sorry condition of Rhode Island.*

convention. The result was a heavy anti-federalist majority. Alexander Hamilton at heart favored a much stronger central government than that under debate, but he contributed his sparkling personality and persuasive eloquence to whipping up support. He also joined John Jay and James Madison in penning a masterly series of articles for the New York newspapers. Though designed as propaganda, these essays remain the most penetrating commentary ever written on the Constitution, and are still widely sold in book form as *The Federalist*.

New York finally yielded. Realizing that the state could not prosper apart from the Union, the convention ratified the document by the close count of 30 to 27.

Last-ditch dissent developed in only two states. A hostile convention met in North Carolina, then adjourned without taking a vote. Rhode Island did not even summon a ratifying convention. The two most ruggedly individualist centers of the colonial era—homes of the "otherwise minded"—thus ran true to form. They were to change their course, albeit unwillingly, only after the new government had been in operation for some months.

The battle for ratification, despite much apathy, was close and extremely bitter in some localities. No lives were lost, but riotous disturbances broke out in New York and Pennsylvania, involving bruises and bloodshed. There was much behind-the-scenes pressure on delegates who had solemnly promised their

Hamiltonian Frigate. *A victory parade in New York City honoring Hamilton and the ratification of the Constitution. At the key New York ratifying convention at Poughkeepsie, Hamilton, by sheer eloquence and cogent argument, turned a two-thirds majority against the Constitution into a majority of three in favor of it. (The Granger Collection)*

constituents to vote against the Constitution. The last four states ratified, not because they wanted to, but because they had to. They could not safely exist apart from the Union.

A Conservative Triumph

The minority had triumphed—doubly. A militant minority of American radicals had engineered the military revolution which cast off the unwritten British constitution. A militant minority of conservatives—now embracing many of the earlier radicals—had engineered the peaceful revolution which overthrew the inadequate constitution known as the Articles of Confederation. Eleven states, in effect, had seceded from the Confederation, leaving two out in the cold.

A majority had not spoken. Only about one-fourth of the adult white males in the country, chiefly the propertied people, had voted for delegates to the ratifying conventions. Careful estimates indicate that if the new Constitution had been submitted to a manhood-suffrage vote, as in New York, it would have encountered much more opposition, probably defeat.

Conservatism was victorious. Safeguards had been erected against mob-rule excesses, and the democratic gains of the Revolution were conserved in the face of possible anarchy. Radicals like Patrick Henry, who had overthrown British rule, had in turn been overthrown by American conservatives. The result was a kind of peaceful counter-revolution. It restored the economic and political stability of colonial years, and set the drifting ship of state on a more promising course.

Yet if the architects of the Constitution were conservative, it is worth emphasizing that what they conserved was the principle of popular democratic government, made forever sacred in the fires of the Revolution. By an ingenious system of checks and balances, the Constitution reconciled the potentially conflicting principles of liberty and order. It preserved the ideals of the Revolution while setting limits to them. One of the distinctive—and enduring—paradoxes of American history was thus revealed: in the United States, conservatives and radicals alike have championed the heritage of democratic revolutionism.

VARYING VIEWPOINTS

Charles Beard's book, *An Economic Interpretation of the Constitution of the United States* (1913), has long defined the area around which debate on the constitutional period has revolved. Beard described the Constitution as the "reactionary" phase of the Revolutionary era—a shrewd maneuver by conservative property owners to curtail the democratic excesses let loose in 1776.

Most modern scholars, if they accept Beard's argument at all, accept it only with severe qualifications. The most recent discussions of the Constitution have been cast in terms of reflections on the ancient riddle of republicanism: Does republican self-government rest on the virtue of the people or on the formal political institutions that control human behavior? Writing about the "ideological

origins" of the Revolution, Bernard Bailyn saw disputes over the principles of republicanism—not economic and social conflict—as the force driving the evolution of American institutions. Building on Bailyn's interpretation, scholars such as Gordon Wood have concluded that the Constitution was actually a bold experiment in channeling selfish human instincts toward the common good. By constructing a strong, balanced national government to rule an "extensive republic," the founding fathers challenged the conventional wisdom that a republic could only survive if extended over a small area with a homogeneous population. Therefore it was the federalists, rather than their fearful antifederalist opponents, who carried out the most advanced ideas of the Revolutionary era.

SELECT READINGS

Primary Source Documents

A comparison of the text of the Articles of Confederation (1781), in Henry Steele Commager, *Documents of American History,* with the Constitution* makes an intriguing study. See also Madison, Hamilton, and Jay's explanations of the Constitution in *The Federalist Papers,* especially "Federalist No. 10."*

Secondary Sources

John Fiske, in *The Critical Period of American History* (1888), portrayed America under the Articles of Confederation as a crisis-ridden country. His view has been sharply qualified by Merrill Jensen in *The New Nation* (1950). Jack N. Rakove's *The Beginning of National Politics* (1979) offers a history of the Continental Congress that substantially revises Jensen's work. Especially learned is Gordon S. Wood's massive and brilliant study of the entire period, *The Creation of the American Republic, 1776–1787* (1969). An influential transatlantic perspective on the roots of American republicanism is J.G.A. Pocock, *The Machiavellian Moment: Florentine Political Thought and the Atlantic Republican Tradition* (1975). On the Constitutional Convention, see Clinton Rossiter, *1787: The Grand Convention* (1966). Robert A. Rutland's *The Ordeal of the Constitution* (1966) describes the ratification struggle. Charles A. Beard shocked conservatives with *An Economic Interpretation of the Constitution of the United States* (1913). It has been seriously weakened by two blistering attacks: Robert E. Brown, *Charles Beard and the Constitution* (1956), and Forrest McDonald, *We the People: The Economic Origins of the Constitution* (1958). Michael A. Kammen, *A Machine That Would Go of Itself* (1987) examines the changing attitudes toward the Constitution throughout American history.

9

Launching the
New Ship of State

I shall only say that I hold with Montesquieu, that a government
must be fitted to a nation, as much as a coat to the individual;
and, consequently, that what may be good at Philadelphia
may be bad at Paris, and ridiculous at Petersburg [Russia].

Alexander Hamilton, 1799

A New Ship on an Uncertain Sea

When the Constitution was launched in 1789, the Republic was continuing to grow at an amazing rate. Population was still doubling about every twenty-three years, and the first official census of 1790 recorded almost 4 million souls. Cities had blossomed proportionately: Philadelphia numbered 42,000; New York, 33,000; Boston, 18,000; Charleston, 16,000; and Baltimore, 13,000.

America's population was still about 90 percent rural, despite the flourishing cities; all but 5 percent lived east of the mountains. The trans-Allegheny overflow was concentrated chiefly in Kentucky, Tennessee, and Ohio, all of which were welcomed as states within fourteen years. (Vermont had preceded them, becoming the fourteenth state in 1791.) Foreign travelers everywhere looked down their noses at the roughness and crudity resulting from ax-and-rifle pioneering life. Yet, critical though they might be,

they were impressed by evidences of energy, self-confidence, and material well-being.

The new ship of state, despite these promising signs of fair weather, did not spread its sails to the most favorable breezes. Within twelve troubled years the American people had risen up and thrown overboard their first two constitutions: the British constitution and the Articles of Confederation. A decade of constitution smashing and law breaking was not the best training for government making. Americans had come to regard a central authority, replacing that of George III, as a necessary evil—something to be distrusted, watched, and curbed.

People of the western waters, in the stump-studded clearings of Kentucky, Tennessee, and Ohio, were restive and dubiously loyal. The mouth of the Mississippi, their life-giving outlet, lay in the hands of unfriendly Spaniards. Smooth-tongued Spanish and

British agents, jingling gold, moved freely among the settlers and held out seductive promises of independence.

The finances of the infant government were likewise precarious. The revenue had declined to a trickle, while the public debt, with interest heavily in arrears, was mountainous. Worthless paper money, both state and national, was as plentiful as metallic money was scarce. The Americans, moreover, were brashly attempting to erect a republic on an immense scale, something that no other people had attempted and that traditional political theory held to be impossible. The eyes of a skeptical world were on the upstart United States, and the bejeweled monarchs of Europe in particular feared that the new republic would provide a dangerous example for their long-oppressed subjects.

Washington's Pro-Federalist Regime

General Washington, the esteemed war hero, was unanimously drafted as president by the Electoral College in 1789—the only presidential nominee ever to be honored by unanimity.

His presence was imposing: 6 feet 2 inches, 175 pounds (1.88m, 79.5kg), broad and sloping shoulders, strongly pointed chin, and pockmarks (from smallpox) on nose and cheeks. Much preferring the quiet of Mount Vernon to the turmoil of politics, he was

perhaps the only president who did not in some way angle for this exalted office. Balanced rather than brilliant, he commanded men by strength of character rather than by the arts of the politician.

Washington's long journey from Mount Vernon to New York City, the temporary capital, was a triumphal procession. He was greeted by roaring cannon, pealing bells, flower-carpeted roads, and singing and shouting citizens. With appropriate ceremony, he solemnly and somewhat nervously took the oath of office on April 30, 1789, on a crowded balcony overlooking Wall Street.

The Constitution does not mention a cabinet; it merely provides that the President "may require" written opinions of the heads of his departments (see Art. II, Sec. II, para. 1). But this system proved so cumbersome, and involved so much homework, that cabinet meetings gradually evolved during the Washington administration. At first the cabinet consisted of only three department heads: Secretary of State Thomas Jefferson, Secretary of the Treasury Alexander Hamilton, and Secretary of War Henry Knox.

The Bill of Rights

Drawing up a bill of rights headed the list of tasks facing the new government. Many antifederalists had sharply criticized the Constitution drafted at Philadelphia for its failure to provide guarantees of individ-

Evolution of the Cabinet

Original Members	Added, 1798–1913	Added, 1947–1979
Secy. of state, 1789	Secy. of navy, 1798 (Lost cabinet status, 1947)	Secy. of defense, 1947 (Subordinate to him, without cabinet rank, are secys. of army, navy, air force)
Secy. of treasury, 1789	Postmaster general, 1829 (Lost cabinet status, 1970)	Secy. of health, education, and welfare, 1953 (divided in 1979)
Secy. of war, 1789 (Lost cabinet status, 1947)	Secy. of interior, 1849	Secy. of housing and urban development, 1965
Attorney general, 1789 (Not head of justice dept. until 1870)	Secy. of agriculture, 1889	Secy. of transportation, 1966
	Secy. of commerce and labor, 1903 (Office divided in 1913)	Secy. of energy, 1977
	Secy. of commerce, 1913	Secy. of health and human services, 1979
	Secy. of labor, 1913	Secy. of education, 1979

President-Elect Washington Honored in New Jersey. *Before leaving home he wrote, "My movements to the chair of government will be accompanied by feelings not unlike those of a culprit who is going to the place of his execution." (Lithograph, Library of Congress)*

ual rights such as freedom of religion and trial by jury. Many states had ratified the federal Constitution with the understanding that it would soon be amended to include such guarantees.

The proposed amendments were drafted and submitted to Congress by James Madison, whose scholarly and political skills had made him the leading figure in the new body. Approved by a two-thirds vote of both houses of Congress and ratified by the necessary number of states in 1791, the first ten amendments to the Constitution, popularly known as the Bill of Rights, safeguarded some of the most precious of American principles. Among these are protections for freedom of religion, speech, and the press; the right to bear arms and to be tried by a jury; and the right to assemble and petition the government for redress of grievances. The Bill of Rights also prohibited cruel and unusual punishments, and arbitrary government seizure of private property.

To guard against the danger that enumerating such rights might lead to the conclusion that they were the only ones protected, Madison inserted the crucial Ninth Amendment. It declared that specifying certain rights "shall not be construed to deny or disparage others retained by the people." To reassure states' righters, he included the equally significant Tenth Amendment, which reserved all rights not explicitly delegated or prohibited by the federal Constitution "to the States respectively, or to the people." By preserving a strong central government while specifying protections for minority and individual liberties, Madison's amendments partially swung the federalist pendulum back in an antifederalist direction. (See Amendments I–X, in the Appendix.)

The first Congress also nailed other newly sawed governmental planks into place. It created effective federal courts under the Judiciary Act of 1789. The act organized the Supreme Court, with a chief justice and five associates, as well as federal district and circuit courts, and established the office of attorney general. New Yorker John Jay, Madison's collaborator on *The Federalist Papers,* became the first chief justice of the United States.

Hamilton Revives the Corpse of Public Credit

The key figure in the new government was smooth-faced Treasury Secretary Alexander Hamilton, a thirty-four-year-old native of the British West Indies. Hamilton's genius was unquestioned, but critics claimed he loved his adopted country more than his countrymen. Doubts about his character and his loyalty to the republican experiment always swirled about his head. He was said to have shocked Jefferson by exclaiming, "Your people, sir, are a great beast."

A financial wizard, Hamilton set out immediately to correct the economic vexations that had crippled the Articles of Confederation. His plan was to shape the fiscal policies of the administration in such a way as to favor the wealthier groups. They, in turn, would gratefully lend the government monetary and moral support. The new federal regime would flourish, the propertied classes would grow fat, and prosperity would trickle down to the masses.

The youthful financier's first objective was to bolster the national credit. Without public confidence in the government, Hamilton could not secure the funds with which to float his risky schemes. He therefore boldly urged Congress to "fund" the entire national debt at par, and to assume completely the debts that had been incurred by the states during the recent war.

"Funding at par" meant that the federal government would pay off its debts at face value, plus accumulated interest—a then enormous total of more than $54 million. So many people believed the infant Treasury incapable of meeting those obligations that government bonds had depreciated to ten or fifteen cents on the dollar. Yet speculators held fistfuls of them, and when Congress passed Hamilton's measure in 1790, they grabbed for more. Some of them galloped into rural areas ahead of the news, buying for a song the depreciated paper holdings of farmers, war veterans, and widows. Hamilton was willing, even eager, to have the new government shoulder additional obligations. While pushing the funding scheme, he urged Congress to assume the debts of the states, totaling some $21.5 million.

The secretary made a convincing case for "assumption." The state debts could be regarded as a proper national obligation, for they had been incurred in the war for independence. But foremost in Hamilton's thinking was the belief that assumption would chain the states more tightly to the "federal chariot." Thus, the secretary's maneuver would shift the attachment of wealthy creditors from the states to the federal government. The support of the rich for the national administration was a crucial link in Hamilton's political strategy of strengthening the central government.

States burdened with heavy debts, like Massachusetts, were delighted by Hamilton's proposal. States with small debts, like Virginia, were less happy. The stage was set for some old-fashioned horse trading. Virginia did not want the state debts assumed, but she did want the forthcoming federal district*— now the District of Columbia—to be located on the Potomac River. She would thus gain in commerce and prestige. Hamilton persuaded a reluctant Jefferson, who had recently come home from France, to line up enough votes in Congress for assumption. In return, Virginia would have the federal district on the Potomac. The bargain was carried through in 1790.

Customs Duties and Excise Taxes

The new ship of state thus set sail dangerously overloaded. The national debt had swelled to $75 million owing to Hamilton's insistence on honoring the outstanding federal and state obligations alike. But Hamilton, "Father of the National Debt," was not greatly worried. His objectives were as much political as economic. He believed that, within limits, a national debt was a "national blessing"—a kind of cement of union. The more creditors to whom the government owed money, the more people there would be with a personal stake in the success of his ambitious enterprise.

Where was the money to come from to pay interest on this huge debt and to run the government? Hamilton's first answer was customs duties, derived from a tariff. Tariff revenues, in turn, depended on a vigorous foreign trade, another crucial link in Hamilton's overall economic strategy for the new republic.

The first tariff law, a low one of about 8 percent on the value of dutiable imports, was speedily passed by the first Congress in 1789, even before Hamilton was sworn in. Revenue was by far the main goal, but the measure was also designed to erect a low protective wall around infant industries, which bawled noisily for more shelter than they received. Hamilton had the vision to see that the Industrial Revolution would soon reach America, and he argued strongly in

---

*Authorized by the Constitution, Art. I, Sec. VIII, para. 17.

favor of more protection for the well-to-do manufacturing groups—another vital element in his economic program. But Congress was still dominated by the agricultural and commercial interests, and it voted only two slight increases in the tariff during Washington's presidency.

Hamilton, with characteristic vigor, sought additional internal revenue, and in 1791 secured from Congress an excise tax on a few domestic items, notably whiskey. The new levy of seven cents a gallon was borne chiefly by the distillers who lived in the back country, where the wretched roads forced the farmer to reduce his bulky bushels of grain to horseback proportions. Whiskey flowed so freely on the frontier that it was used for money.

But Hamilton was not unduly bothered by the cries of outrage from the backwoods. The federal regime had to be bolstered, no matter how unpopular his measures. In any case the secretary had little sympathy for Western distillers who had

opposed the new Constitution and Hamilton's centralizing schemes from the outset.

Hamilton Battles Jefferson for a Bank

As the capstone of his financial system, Hamilton proposed a powerful Bank of the United States. Although a private institution, the bank would have the government as its major stockholder, and the federal Treasury would deposit its surplus monies there. The bank would provide a convenient strongbox for federal funds, stimulate business by keeping money in circulation, and print a badly needed sound paper currency.

Jefferson, whose written opinion Washington requested, argued vigorously against the bank. There was, he insisted, no specific authorization in the Constitution for such a financial octopus. He was convinced that all powers not specifically granted to the central government were reserved to the states, as

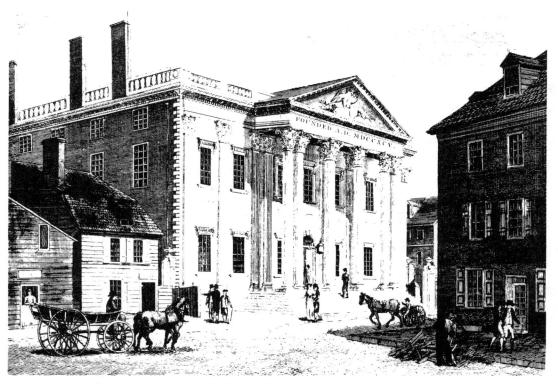

The First Bank of the United States.   *The first Bank of the United States, established in Philadelphia, lasted from 1789 to 1811; the second, from 1816 to 1836. (Library of Congress)*

provided in the about-to-be-ratified Bill of Rights (see Art. X). He therefore concluded that the states, not Congress, had the power to charter banks. Believing that the Constitution should be interpreted "literally" or "strictly," Jefferson and his states'-rights disciples zealously embraced the theory of "strict construction."

Hamilton, also at Washington's request, prepared a brilliantly reasoned reply to Jefferson's arguments. He boldly invoked that clause of the Constitution which stipulates that Congress may pass any laws "necessary and proper" to carry out the powers vested in the various governmental agencies (see Art. I, Sec. VIII, para. 18). The government was explicitly empowered to collect taxes and regulate trade. In carrying out these basic functions, Hamilton argued, a national bank would be not only "proper" but also "necessary." By inference or by implication—that is, by virtue of some "implied powers"—Congress would be fully justified in establishing the Bank of the United States. In short, Hamilton contended for a "loose" or "broad" interpretation of the Constitution. He and his federalist followers thus evolved the theory of "loose construction" by invoking the "elastic clause" of the Constitution—a precedent for enormous federal powers.

Hamilton's financial views prevailed. His eloquent and realistic arguments were accepted by Washington, who reluctantly signed the Bank measure into law. This explosive issue had been debated with much heat in Congress, where the old North-South cleavage again appeared ominously. The most enthusiastic support for the Bank naturally came from the commercial and financial centers of the North, while the strongest opposition arose from the agricultural South.

The Bank of the United States, as created by Congress in 1791, was chartered for twenty years. Located in Philadelphia, it was to have a capital of $10 million, one-fifth of which was to be owned by the federal government.

Mutinous Moonshiners in Pennsylvania

The Whiskey Rebellion, which flared up in southwestern Pennsylvania in 1794, sharply challenged the new national government. Hamilton's excise bore harshly on the homespun pioneer folk. They regarded it not as a tax on a luxury but as a burden on an economic necessity and a medium of exchange. Even preachers of the gospel were paid in "Old Monongahela rye." Defiant distillers finally erected whiskey poles, similar to the liberty poles of anti–stamp tax days in 1765, and raised the cry "Liberty and No Excise." Boldly tarring and feathering revenue officers, they brought collections to a halt.

President Washington, once a revolutionist, was alarmed by what he called these "self-created societies." With the warm encouragement of Hamilton, he summoned the militia of several states. Anxious moments followed the call, for there was much doubt as to whether men in other states would muster to crush a rebellion in a sister state. Despite some opposition, an army of about thirteen thousand rallied to the colors, and two widely separated columns marched briskly forth in a gorgeous, leaf-tinted Indian summer, until knee-deep mud slowed their progress. When the troops reached the hills of western Pennsylvania, they found no insurrection. The "Whiskey Boys" were overawed, dispersed, or captured. Washington, with an eye to healing old sores, pardoned the two small-fry convicted culprits.

The Whiskey Rebellion was small—some three rebels were killed—but its consequences were large. George Washington's government, now substantially strengthened, commanded a new respect. Yet the numerous foes of the federalists condemned the administration for its brutal display of force—for having used a sledge hammer to crush a gnat. The ranks of the Jeffersonians were consequently enlarged. Back-country men, taught a harsh lesson, now saw the wisdom of forsaking the tar kettle for the ballot box—and voting for Jefferson.

Hamiltonian Elitism and the Federalists

Almost overnight Hamilton's fiscal feats had established the public credit. The Treasury was now able to secure needed funds in the Netherlands on terms more favorable than those being extended to any other borrowing nation.

The dynamic secretary, under the leadership of Washington, also strengthened the government politically while bolstering it financially. His major schemes—funding, assumption, the excise, the bank—all encroached sharply upon states' rights. This trend, facilitated by "loose construction," was destined to continue its controversial course to the Civil War and beyond. Hamilton navigated skillfully on the sea of economic policy, but politically he encountered increasingly heavy weather. Out of the resentment against his revenue-raising and centralizing policies an organized opposition began to emerge.

National political parties, in the modern sense, were unknown to America when George Washington took the inaugural oath. There had been Whigs and Tories, federalists and anti-federalists, but these groups were factions rather than parties. They had sprung into existence over hotly contested special issues; they had faded away when their cause had triumphed or had become hopelessly lost.

The Founding Fathers at the Philadelphia Constitutional Convention had not envisioned the existence of political parties. Organized opposition to the government seemed tainted with disloyalty, an affront to the spirit of national unity that the glorious cause of the Revolution had inspired. The notion of a formal and permanent party apparatus was therefore a novelty. American political parties, primitive at first, date their birth from these bitter clashes between Hamilton and Jefferson, chiefly over fiscal policy and foreign affairs. By 1792–1793 two well-defined groupings had crystallized: the Hamiltonian Federalists and the Jeffersonian Republicans. The two-party system has existed in the United States since that time and has provided indispensable machinery for self-government.

As might be expected, most federalists of the pre-Constitution period (1787–1789) became Federalists in the Washington era. By 1793 they were welded into an effective group, largely through the magnetic leadership and organizational genius of Alexander Hamilton.

Federalists openly advocated rule by the "best people." "Those who own the country," remarked Federalist John Jay, "ought to govern it." With their intellectual elitism and Tory tastes, Hamiltonians deplored democratic tendencies and distrusted the common people. The untutored masses would only throw monkey wrenches into the machinery of government. Let the rich rule, insisted many Federalist leaders, for they had the intelligence, education, and leisure to study the problems of government.

Hamiltonian Federalists advocated a potent central government with the power to crush democratic excesses like Shays's Rebellion, protect the lives and estates of the wealthy, and subordinate the sovereignty-loving states. The national government should also foster business, not interfere with it. This attitude was natural because the Federalists were dominated by merchants, manufacturers, and shippers who lived in the urban seaboard areas. If a gunner had fired cannonballs 50 miles (80.5 kilometers) inland, he would have hit few Hamiltonians.

The Federalists, in addition, were at bottom pro-British. Many Hamiltonians were mild Loyalists who retained a sentimental attachment to the mother country. Basically conservative in their outlook, they felt that the nation's foreign policy should be slanted toward friendship and trade with England.

Jeffersonian Idealism and the Republicans

Leading the anti-Federalist forces was Thomas Jefferson. Lanky and relaxed in appearance, lacking personal aggressiveness, weak-voiced, and unable to deliver a rabble-rousing speech, he became a master political organizer through his ability to lead men rather than drive them. His strongest appeal was to the middle class and to the underprivileged—the "dirt" farmers, the laborers, the artisans, and the small shopkeepers.

Liberal-thinking Jefferson, with his aristocratic head set on a farmer's frame, was a bundle of inconsistencies. By one set of tests he should have been a Federalist, for he was a Virginia aristocrat and slaveowner who lived in an imposing hilltop mansion at Monticello. A so-called traitor to his upper class, Jefferson cherished uncommon sympathy for the common man, especially the down-trodden, the oppressed, and the persecuted. As he wrote in 1800, "I have sworn upon the altar of God eternal hostility against every form of tyranny over the mind of man."

Jeffersonian Republicans, or Democratic-Republicans, as they were called, demanded a weak central regime. They believed that the best government was one that governed least, and that the bulk of

Monticello, Jefferson's Self-Designed Architectural Marvel. (Virginia Chamber of Commerce, photo by D'Adamo)

the power should be retained by the states and localities, where the people could keep a vigilant eye on their public servants. The national debt should be paid off, and government should provide no special privileges for any economic interest, especially manufacturing. For Jeffersonians, agriculture was the most ennobling occupation because it kept people away from wicked cities and close to the sod and God.

Most of their following naturally came from the rural South and Southwest.

Above all, Jefferson advocated the rule of the people. He favored government *for* the people, but not *by* all the people. Since the ignorant were incapable of self-government, only those literate enough to inform themselves about citizenship should have the ballot. Universal education would have to precede universal suffrage. Jefferson had a profound faith in the reasonableness of the masses and, once they had been educated, in their collective wisdom. His enduring appeal was to America's better self.

The open-minded Jefferson championed free speech, because without free speech the misdeeds of tyranny could not be exposed. Though he suffered foul abuse from the Federalist press, he said that he would choose "newspapers without a government" rather than "a government without newspapers."

Jeffersonian Republicans, unlike the Federalist "British boot-lickers," were basically pro-French. They earnestly believed that it was to America's advantage to support the liberal ideals of the French Revolution, rather than applaud the reaction of the English Tories. So it was that foreign policy and domestic politics became perilously intermingled, as the fledgling American Republic was caught up in the bloody international conflicts of the French Revolutionary era.

VARYING VIEWPOINTS

The Federalist era witnessed some of the sharpest political conflicts in American history. The first students of the period framed these disputes as a contest between two opposing philosophies—the Jeffersonian demand for small government and strict construction of the Constitution, versus the loose constructionism and belief in active government of Hamilton and his allies.

This view was challenged in the early years of the twentieth century by historians who emphasized the economic rivalries at the root of political debates. They saw the Hamiltonian-Jeffersonian dispute as a smoke screen for battles between

creditors and debtors, commercial interests and agrarian interests, northern merchants and southern planters.

Recently, the pendulum has swung back in the other direction, and ideological issues have regained prominence in the historical literature. The new interpretations, advanced by scholars like Lance Banning and Drew McCoy, see the turmoil of the Federalist era as a continuation of the debate over the proper conduct of a republican government that gave rise to the Revolution and the Constitution.

SELECT READINGS

Primary Source Documents

"The Report on Manufactures" (in Daniel Boorstin, ed., *American Primer*), the last of Alexander Hamilton's messages to Congress, presented the case for the development of American industry. Thomas Jefferson expounded his views in *Notes on the State of Virginia* (1784). For further study of the Hamiltonian-Jeffersonian debate, see Henry Cabot Lodge, ed., *The Works of Alexander Hamilton** (1904), and Paul L. Ford, ed., *The Writings of Thomas Jefferson** (1985).

Secondary Sources

Perceptive introductions are provided by Marcus Cunliffe's succinct *The Nation Takes Shape, 1789–1837* (1959) and John C. Miller's more detailed *The Federalist Era, 1789–1801* (1960). On administration, consult Leonard D. White, *The Federalists* (1948); on the economy, see Curtis P. Nettels, *The Emergence of a National Economy, 1775–1815* (1962). The emergence of party politics is treated in William N. Chambers, *Political Parties in the New Nation* (1963) and Richard Hofstadter's thoughtful *The Idea of a Party System* (1969). Among the new interpretations of that subject, stressing the ideology of republicanism, are Drew McCoy, *The Elusive Republic: Political Economy in Jeffersonian America* (1980) and Lance Banning, *The Jeffersonian Persuasion* (1978). For a trenchant analysis of Jeffersonianism, see Joyce Appleby, *Capitalism and a New Social Order: The Republican Vision* (1984). Also illuminating is Gerald Stourzh, *Alexander Hamilton and the Idea of Republican Government* (1970).

10

Federalists and Foreign Friction

**And ne'er shall the sons of Columbia be slaves,
While the earth bears a plant, or the sea rolls its waves.**

Popular Song by Robert Treat Paine
"Adams and Liberty," 1798

The Impact of the French Revolution

When Washington's first administration ended, early in 1793, domestic controversies had already formed two political camps—Hamiltonian Federalists and Jeffersonian Republicans. As his second term began, issues of foreign policy brought differences between these groups to a fever pitch.

Only a few weeks after Washington's inauguration in 1789, the curtain had risen on the first act of the French Revolution. Twenty-six years were to pass before the seething continent of Europe settled back into a peace of exhaustion. Few non-American events have left a deeper scar on American political and social life.

Most Americans, except a few ultraconservative Federalists, applauded the early, peaceful stages of the French Revolution, which involved a successful attempt to impose constitutional shackles on Louis XVI. The Revolution entered upon a more ominous phase in 1792, when France declared war on hostile Austria. Late in that year the electrifying news reached America that French citizen armies had hurled back the invading foreigners, and that France had proclaimed itself a republic. Americans enthusiastically sang "The Marseillaise" and other rousing French Revolutionary songs and renamed thoroughfares to honor revolutionary principles.

But centuries of pent-up poison could not be purged without baleful results. The guillotine was set up and the king beheaded in 1793. Christianity was abolished, and the head-rolling Reign of Terror was begun. Back in America, God-fearing Federalist aristocrats nervously fingered their tender white necks and eyed the Jeffersonian masses apprehensively. Lukewarm Federalist approval of the early Revolution turned, almost overnight, to heated opposition to "blood-drinking cannibals."

The Contrast. *Adaptation of an English cartoon. C. C. Coffin,* Building a Nation, *1882. (Boston Public Library)*

Sober-minded Jeffersonians regretted the bloodshed. But they felt, with Jefferson, that one could not expect to be carried from "despotism to liberty in a feather bed," and that a few thousand aristocratic heads were a cheap price to pay for human freedom.

America had initially watched the unfolding Revolution as a distant spectacle, but now dire perils loomed. The earlier battles of the French Revolution had not hurt America directly, but soon Britain was sucked into the titanic conflict. The conflagration speedily spread to the New World, where it vitally affected the expanding young American Republic.

Washington's Neutrality Proclamation

Ominously, the Franco-American alliance of 1778 was still on the books, and many Republicans favored honoring it. Aflame with the ideals of the French Revolution, red-blooded Jeffersonians were eager to enter the conflict against Britain, the recent foe, at the side of France, the recent friend.

But level-headed President Washington could not be swayed by the clamor of the crowd. Backed by Hamilton, he sought to avoid war at any cost. Accordingly, Washington boldly issued his Neutrality Proclamation in 1793, shortly after the outbreak of war between Britain and France. This epochal document not only proclaimed the government's official neutrality in the widening conflict, but sternly warned American citizens to be impartial toward both armed camps. It was America's first formal declaration of aloofness from Old World quarrels, and as such proved to be a major prop of the spreading isolationist tradition.

The pro-French Jeffersonians were enraged by the Neutrality Proclamation; the pro-British Federalists were enheartened. A few days earlier an impetuous, thirty-year-old representative of the French Republic, Citizen Genêt, had landed at Charleston, South Carolina. With unrestrained zeal, he undertook to fit out privateers and otherwise take advantage of the existing Franco-American alliance. The giddy-headed envoy—all sail and no anchor— was soon swept away by his enthusiastic reception by the Jeffersonian Republicans. He foolishly came to believe that the Neutrality Proclamation did not reflect the true wishes of the American people, and he consequently embarked upon unneutral activity not authorized by the French alliance. After he had threatened to appeal over the head of "Old Washington" to the sovereign voters, the President demanded Genêt's withdrawal and the Frenchman was replaced by a less impulsive spokesman.

Washington's Neutrality Proclamation clearly illustrates the truism that self-interest is the basic cement of alliances. In 1778, both France and America stood to gain; in 1793, only France. Technically, the Americans did not flout their obligation, because France never officially called upon them to honor it. Her homeland, and especially her blockaded West Indian Islands, were urgently in need of Yankee foodstuffs. If the Americans had entered the war, the

American Posts Held by the British After 1783.

British fleets would have blockaded their coasts and cut off those desperately needed supplies. America was much more useful to France as a prosperous provider than as a prostrate partner.

Jay's Treaty Ends Embroilment with Britain

President Washington's far-visioned policy of neutrality was sorely tried by the British. For ten long years they had been retaining the chain of northern frontier posts on United States soil, all in defiance of the peace treaty of 1783. There they openly sold firearms and firewater to the Indians, who continued to attack pale-faced pioneers invading their lands. When General "Mad Anthony" Wayne crushed the Northwest Indians at the Battle of Fallen Timbers on August 20, 1794, the fleeing foe left on the field British-made arms, as well as the corpses of a few British-Canadians. In the Treaty of Greenville in 1795, the Indians, finally abandoned by their red-coated friends, ceded their claims to a vast virgin tract in the Ohio country.

On the sea frontier, the British were eager to starve out the French West Indies, and naturally expected the United States to defend them under the Franco-American alliance. Hard-boiled commanders of the Royal Navy, acting under instructions from London in 1793, struck savagely. They seized about three hundred American merchant ships in the West Indies, impressed scores of seamen into service on English vessels, and threw hundreds of others into foul dungeons.

A mighty outcry arose, chiefly from Jeffersonians, that America should once again fight George III in defense of her liberties. President Washington, in a last desperate gamble to avert war, decided to send John Jay to London in 1794. The Jeffersonians were acutely unhappy over the choice, partly because they feared that so notorious a Federalist and Britain-lover would sell out his country. Arriving in London, Jay gave the Jeffersonians further cause for alarm when, at the presentation ceremony, he routinely kissed the Queen's hand.

Unhappily, Jay entered the negotiations with weak cards, which were further weakened by Hamilton. The latter, fearful of war with England, secretly supplied the British with the details of America's bargaining strategy. Not surprisingly, Jay won few concessions. The British did promise to evacuate the chain of posts on United States soil—a concession that inspired little confidence, since it had been made before in Paris (to the same John Jay!) in 1783. In addition, Britain consented to pay damages for the recent seizures of American ships. But the British stopped short of pledging anything about *future* maritime seizures and impressments, or about Indian butcheries. And they forced Jay to give ground by binding the United States to pay the debts still owed to British merchants on pre-Revolutionary accounts.

When the Jeffersonians learned of Jay's concessions, their rage was fearful to behold. The treaty seemed like an abject surrender to Britain, as well as a betrayal of the Jeffersonian South. Southern planters would have to pay the major share of the pre-Revolutionary debts, while rich Federalist shippers were collecting damages for recent British seizures. Jeffersonian mobs hanged, burned, and guillotined in effigy that "damn'd archtraitor, Sir John Jay." His unpopular pact, more than any other issue, vitalized the newborn Democratic-Republican party of Thomas Jefferson.

Jay's Treaty had other unforeseen consequences. Fearing that the treaty foreshadowed an Anglo-American alliance, Spain moved hastily to strike a deal with the United States. Pinckney's Treaty of 1795 granted the Americans virtually everything they demanded, including free navigation of the Mississippi and the large disputed territory north of Florida.

Exhausted after the diplomatic and partisan battles of his second term, President Washington decided to retire. His choice contributed powerfully to establishing a two-term tradition for American presidents.* In his farewell address to the nation in 1796, Washington strongly advised the avoidance of "permanent alliances" like the still-vexatious French Treaty of 1778. Contrary to general misunderstanding, Washington did not oppose all alliances, but favored only "temporary alliances" for "extraordinary emergencies."

Washington's contributions as President were enormous, even though the sparkling Hamilton at times seemed to outshine him. The central government, its fiscal feet now under it, was solidly established. The West was expanding. The merchant marine was plowing the seas. Above all, Washington had kept the nation out of both overseas entanglements and foreign wars. The experimental stage had passed, and the presidential chair could now be turned over to a less impressive figure. But republics are notoriously ungrateful. When Washington left office in 1797, he was showered with the brickbats of partisan abuse, quite in contrast with the bouquets that had greeted his coming.

"Bonny Johnny" Adams Becomes President

Who should succeed the exalted "Father of His Country"? Alexander Hamilton was the best-known member of the Federalist party, now that Washington had bowed out. But his financial policies, some of which had fattened the speculators, had made him so unpopular that he could not hope to be elected President. The Federalists were forced to turn to the experienced but ungracious John Adams, a rugged chip off old Plymouth Rock. The Democratic-Republicans rallied behind their master-organizer and leader, Thomas Jefferson.

Political passions ran feverishly high in the presidential canvass of 1796. Cultured Federalists referred to the Jeffersonians as "fire-eating salamanders, poison-sucking toads." Federalists and Democratic-Republicans even drank their liquor in separate taverns. The Jeffersonians again assailed the too-forceful crushing of the Whiskey Rebellion and, above all, the negotiation of Jay's hated treaty.

John Adams, with most of his support in New England, squeezed through by the narrow margin of 71 votes to 68 in the Electoral College. Jefferson, as runner-up, became Vice-President.*

One of the ablest statesmen of his day, Adams at sixty-two was a stuffy figure. Sharp-featured, bald, short (5 feet 7 inches; 1.7 meters) and thickset ("His Rotundity"), he impressed observers as a man of stern principles who did his duty with stubborn devotion. Though learned and upright, he was a tactless and prickly intellectual aristocrat, with no appeal to the masses, and with no desire to cultivate any. Many citizens regarded him with "respectful irritation."

The crusty New Englander suffered from other handicaps. He had stepped into Washington's shoes, which no successor could hope to fill. In addition, Adams was hated by Hamilton, who had resigned from the Treasury in 1795, and who now headed the war faction of the Federalist party. The famed financier even secretly plotted with certain members of the cabinet against the President, who had a conspiracy rather than a cabinet on his hands. Most ominous of all, Adams inherited a violent quarrel with France—a quarrel which foreshadowed blazing gunpowder.

Unofficial Fighting with France

The French were infuriated with Jay's Treaty. They condemned it as the initial step toward an alliance with England, their relentless foe. French warships, in retaliation, began to seize defenseless American merchant vessels, altogether about three hundred by mid-1797.

President Adams kept his head, temporarily, even though the nation was mightily aroused. Trying to

---

*Not broken until 1940 by Franklin D. Roosevelt, and made a part of the Constitution in 1951 by the 22nd Amendment. (See the text of the Constitution in the Appendix.)

*The possibility of such an inharmonious two-party combination in the future was removed by the 12th Amendment to the Constitution in 1804. (See text in Appendix.)

Preparation for War to Defend Commerce. *The building of the frigate* Philadelphia. *In 1803 this frigate ran onto the rocks near Tripoli harbor, and about 300 officers and men were imprisoned by the Tripolitans. The ship was refloated for service against the Americans, but Stephen Decatur led a party of men that set her afire. (Prints Division, The New York Public Library, Astor, Lenox and Tilden Foundations)*

reach an agreement with the French, he appointed a diplomatic commission of three men, including John Marshall, the future chief justice. When they reached Paris in 1797, Adams's envoys were secretly approached by three French go-betweens, later referred to as X, Y, and Z in the published dispatches. The French spokesmen demanded an unneutral loan of 32 million florins, plus what amounted to a bribe of $250,000 for the privilege of merely talking with Talleyrand.

These terms were intolerable. The American trio knew that bribes were standard diplomatic devices in Europe, but they gagged at paying a quarter of a million dollars for mere talk, without any assurance of a settlement. Negotiations quickly broke down.

War hysteria swept the United States, catching up President Adams. The slogan of the hour became "Millions for defense, but not one cent for tribute." Despite considerable Jeffersonian opposition in Congress, war preparations were pushed feverishly. The Navy Department was created; the three-ship navy was expanded; the Marine Corps was established.

Bloodshed was confined to the sea, and principally to the West Indies. In two and one-half years of undeclared hostilities (1798–1800), American privateers and men-of-war of the new navy captured over eighty armed vessels flying the French colors, though several hundred Yankee merchantmen were lost to the enemy. Evidently only a slight push would plunge both nations into a full-dress war.

Adams Puts Patriotism Above Party

Embattled France, her hands full in Europe, wanted no war. An outwitted Talleyrand realized that to fight the United States would merely add one more foe to his enemies. The British, who were lending the Americans cannon and other war supplies, were actually driven closer to their wayward cousins than they were to be again for many years. Talleyrand therefore let it be known, through roundabout channels, that if the Americans would send a new minister, he would be received with proper respect.

Adams unexpectedly exploded a bombshell when, early in 1799, he submitted to the Senate the name of a new minister to France. Hamilton and his war-hawk faction were enraged. But public opinion—Jeffersonian and reasonable Federalist alike—was favorable to one last try for peace.

America's envoys (now three) found the political

skies brightening when they reached Paris early in 1800. The ambitious "Little Corporal," the Corsican Bonaparte, had recently seized dictatorial power. He was eager to free his hands of the American squabble so that he might continue to redraw the map of Europe, and perhaps create a New World empire in Louisiana. The distresses and ambitions of the Old World were again working to America's advantage.

After prolonged haggling, a memorable treaty known as the Convention of 1800 was signed in Paris. France agreed to grant a divorce from the twenty-two-year-old marriage of (in)convenience, but as a kind of alimony the United States itself agreed to pay the damage claims of American shippers. So ended the nation's only peacetime military alliance for a century and a half. Its troubled history does much to explain the traditional antipathy of the American people to foreign entanglements.

Adams, flinty to the end, deserves immense credit for his belated push for peace, even though moved in part by jealousy of Hamilton. He not only avoided the hazards of war, but unwittingly smoothed the path for the peaceful purchase of Louisiana three years later. He should indeed rank high among the forgotten purchasers of this vast domain. If America had drifted into a full-blown war with France in 1800, Napoleon would not have been willing to sell her Louisiana on any terms in 1803.

President Adams, the bubble of his popularity pricked by peace, was aware of his signal contribution to the nation. He later suggested as the epitaph for his tombstone (not used): "Here lies John Adams, who took upon himself the responsibility of peace with France in the year 1800."

The Federalist Witch Hunt

Exulting Federalists had meanwhile capitalized on the anti-French frenzy to drive through Congress in 1798 a sheaf of laws designed to reduce or gag their Jeffersonian foes.

The first of these oppressive laws was aimed at supposedly pro-Jeffersonian "aliens." The Federalist Congress, hoping to discourage the "dregs" of Europe, erected a disheartening barrier. They raised the residence requirements for aliens who desired to become citizens from a tolerable five years to an intolerable fourteen. This drastic new law violated the traditional American policy of open-door hospitality and speedy assimilation.

Two additional Alien Laws struck heavily at undesirable immigrants. The president was empowered to deport dangerous foreigners in time of peace, and to deport or imprison them in time of hostilities. These were arbitrary grants of power contrary to American tradition and to the spirit of the Constitution—though the stringent Alien Laws were never enforced.

The "lockjaw" Sedition Act, the last of the harsh Federalist measures, was a direct slap at two priceless freedoms guaranteed in the Constitution by the Bill of Rights—freedom of speech and freedom of the press (First Amendment). This law provided that anyone who impeded the policies of the government or falsely defamed its officials, including the president, would be liable to a heavy fine and imprisonment. Severe though the measure was, the Federalists believed that it was justified. The verbal violence of the day was unrestrained, and foul-penned editors, some of them exiled aliens, assailed Adams's anti-French policy in vicious terms.

Many outspoken Jeffersonian editors were indicted under the Sedition Act, but only ten were brought to trial. All of them were convicted, often by packed juries swayed by prejudiced Federalist judges.

The Sedition Act, at least in spirit, was in direct conflict with the Constitution. But the Supreme Court, dominated by Federalists, was of no mind to declare this Federalist law unconstitutional. (The law expired, in March 1801, to much rejoicing from Jeffersonians.) This high-handed attempt by the Federalists to crush free speech and silence the opposition party undoubtedly made many converts for the Jeffersonian cause.

Yet the Alien and Sedition Laws, despite pained outcries from the Jeffersonians, commanded widespread popular support. Anti-French hysteria played directly into the hands of witch-hunting conservatives. In the congressional elections of 1798–1799 the Federalists, riding a wave of popularity, scored the most sweeping victory of their entire history.

The Virginia (Madison) and Kentucky (Jefferson) Resolutions

Resentful Jeffersonians naturally refused to take the Alien and Sedition Laws lying down. Jefferson himself feared that if the Federalists managed to choke free speech and free press, they would then wipe out other precious constitutional guarantees. His own political party might even be stamped out of existence.

Fearing prosecution for sedition, Jefferson secretly penned a series of resolutions, which the Kentucky legislature approved in 1798 and 1799. His friend and fellow Virginian James Madison drafted a similar but less extreme statement, which was adopted by the Virginia legislature in 1798.

Both Jefferson and Madison stressed the compact theory—a theory popular among English political philosophers in the seventeenth and eighteenth centuries. As applied to America by the Jeffersonians, this concept meant that the thirteen sovereign states, in creating the federal government, had entered into a "compact" or contract regarding its jurisdiction. The national government was consequently the agent or creation of the states. Because water can rise no higher than its source, the individual states were the final judges of whether their agent had broken the "compact" by overstepping the authority originally granted. Invoking this logic, Jefferson's Kentucky resolutions concluded that the federal regime had exceeded its constitutional powers, and that with regard to the Alien and Sedition Acts "nullification" was the "rightful remedy."

No other state legislatures, despite Jefferson's hopes, fell into line. Some of them flatly refused to endorse the Virginia and Kentucky resolutions. Others, chiefly in Federalist states, added ringing condemnations. Many Federalists argued that the people, not the states, had made the original compact, and that it was up to the Supreme Court—not the states—to nullify unconstitutional legislation passed by Congress. This practice, though not specifically authorized by the Constitution, was finally adopted by the Supreme Court in 1803.

The Virginia and Kentucky resolutions were a brilliant formulation of the extreme states'-rights view regarding the Union. They were later used by Southerners to support nullification—and ultimately secession. Yet neither Jefferson nor Madison, as Founding Fathers of the Union, had any intention of breaking it up: they were groping for ways to preserve it. Their resolutions were basically campaign documents designed to crystallize opposition to the Federalist party, and to unseat it in the upcoming presidential election of 1800. The only real nullification that Jefferson had in view was the nullification of Federalist abuses.

Federalist and Republican Mudslingers

In the heated presidential contest of 1800, Adams and Jefferson were again the standard-bearers of their respective parties. The Federalists labored under heavy handicaps. Their Alien and Sedition Acts had aroused a host of enemies.

The most damaging blow to the Federalists was the refusal of Adams to give them a rousing fight with France. Their feverish war preparations had swelled the public debt and had required disagreeable new taxes, including a stamp tax. After all these unpopular measures, the war scare had petered out, and the country was left with an all-dressed-up-but-no-place-to-go feeling.

Thrown on the defensive, the Federalists concentrated their fire on Jefferson himself, who became the victim of one of the earliest "whispering campaigns." He was accused of having robbed a widow and her children of a trust fund, and of having fathered numerous mulatto children by his own slave women. As a liberal in religion, he had earlier incurred the wrath of the orthodox clergy, largely through his successful struggle to separate church and state in Virginia. From the New England stronghold of Federalism and Congregationalism, the preachers thundered against his atheism, although he did believe in God. Old ladies of Federalist families, fearing Jefferson's election, went so far as to bury their Bibles or hang them in wells.

The Jeffersonian "Revolution of 1800"

Jefferson won by a majority of 73 electoral votes to 65. But the colorless and presumably unpopular Adams polled more electoral strength than he had gained

The Providential Detection (Federalist Propaganda). *The American eagle snatches the Constitution from Jefferson, who is about to burn it (together with the works of Voltaire, Paine, and others) on the altar to French Revolutionary despotism. (Massachusetts Historical Society)*

four years earlier—except for New York. The Empire State fell into the Jeffersonian basket, and with it the election, largely because Aaron Burr, a master wire-puller, turned New York to Jefferson by the narrowest of margins. The Virginian polled the bulk of his strength in the South and West, particularly in those states where universal manhood suffrage (for whites) had been adopted.

But Jeffersonian joy was dampened by an unexpected deadlock. Through a technicality Jefferson, the presidential candidate, and Burr, his vice-presidential running mate, received the same number of electoral votes for the presidency. Under the Constitution the tie could be broken only by the House of Representatives (see Art. II, Sec. I, para. 2). This body was controlled for several more months by the lame-duck Federalists, who had been swept into office

during the French war scare and who were eager to elect Burr.*

Voting in the House moved slowly to a climax. As ballots were taken in wearisome succession, congressmen snored in their seats. The deadlock was broken when a few Federalists, despairing of electing Burr and hoping for moderation from Jefferson, refrained from voting. The election then went to the rightful candidate.

---

*A "lame duck" has been humorously defined as a politician whose political goose has been cooked at the recent elections. The possibility of another such tie was removed by the 12th Amendment in 1804 (for text, see Appendix). Before then, each elector had two votes, with the second-place finisher becoming Vice-President.

Presidential Election of 1800 (with electoral vote by state). *New York was the key state in this election, and Aaron Burr helped swing it away from the Federalists with tactics that anticipated the political "machines" of a later day. Federalists complained that Burr "travels every night from one meeting of Republicans to another, haranguing . . . them to the most zealous exertions. [He] can stoop so low as to visit every low tavern that may happen to be crowded with his dear fellow citizens." But Burr proved that the price was worth it. "We have beat you," Burr told kid-gloved Federalists after the election, "by superior Management."*

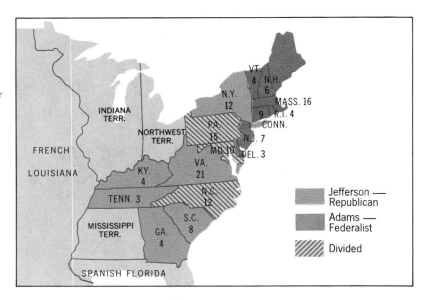

Jefferson later claimed that the election of 1800 was a "revolution" comparable to that of 1776. But it was no revolution in the sense of a massive popular upheaval or an upending of the political system. What *was* revolutionary was the peaceful and orderly transition of power on the basis of an election whose results all parties accepted. This was a remarkable—indeed, even "revolutionary"—achievement for a raw young nation, especially after all the partisan bitterness that had agitated the country during Adams's presidency. Americans could take justifiable pride in the vigor of their experiment in democracy.

The Federalist Finale

John Adams, as fate would have it, was the last Federalist president of the United States. His party sank slowly into the mire of political oblivion and ultimately disappeared completely in the days of Andrew Jackson.

Whatever their shortcomings, the Federalists were a party of the elite. They boasted a much higher concentration of brains, talent, and ability than any other major American political party, past or present. Their political and financial leaders had built enduring foundations for the new government. Their diplomats, with a strong helping hand from Europe's dis-

tresses, had signed advantageous treaties with England, Spain, and France. Their statesmen had kept the peace during a crucial period when peace had to be kept.

After all the turmoil of the American Revolution, a conservative party served a needed function in preserving democratic gains and fending off anarchy. The Federalists provided a welcome breathing spell, a chance for the nation to get its bearings. They served, in the words of historian Henry Adams, great-grandson of John Adams, as the "half-way house between the European past and the American future."

But by 1800 the Federalists, blessed with more talent than wisdom, were out of place. The bustling new republic knew instinctively where it was going. It was eager to take the high road over the mountains that would one day lead to the fulfillment of America's democratic experiment. The Federalists lost out because they were content to mark time, and failed to get in step with the westward march of progress. They were unable or unwilling to unbend and appeal to the common man. They could not adapt—so they died, like the dinosaur. Distinguished though their past service had been, it was no substitute for a capacity to grapple democratically with future problems. The victorious Jeffersonians were prepared to keep the Federalist edifice while ousting its architects.

VARYING VIEWPOINTS

Historians have rightly regarded the Federalist era as the seedtime of the nation's foreign policy. As debate continues over America's role abroad, so does argument still swirl about the diplomacy of the Federalists. Was George Washington the father of unreasoning "isolationism," or did he set forth a realistic policy for the infant nation to follow? Could Washington reasonably expect that "in extending our commercial relations" with foreign nations, the United States could "have with them as little political connection as possible"? Was that policy equally applicable when the infant nation had matured? What was the historical basis of Washington's ideas? Some scholars regard his policies as opportune rationalizations of the country's weak position. Others, especially Felix Gilbert, see them as high expressions of all the best Enlightenment thought about an ideal international order. This question—concerning the degree to which American foreign policy reflects self-interest or idealism—has continued to be argued from Washington's day to the present.

SELECT READINGS

Primary Source Documents

Important salvos in the battle between national power and state sovereignty, and between Federalists and Jeffersonians, were the Virginia and Kentucky resolutions* (1798) and the reply of Rhode Island* (1799). Washington's Farewell Address* (1796) established the foundation for American attitudes about party politics and foreign policy. See also Benjamin Franklin Bache's stinging editorial on Washington's retirement, Philadelphia *Aurora** (1797).

Secondary Sources

See the titles by Marcus Cunliffe and John C. Miller cited in the preceding chapter. On the rise of parties, consult Noble E. Cunningham, *The Jeffersonian Republican* (1958). On aspects of foreign policy, see Alexander De Conde, *Entangling Alliance* (1958) and his *Quasi-War: The Politics and Diplomacy of the Undeclared War with France, 1797–1801* (1966); Gilbert Lycan, *Alexander Hamilton and American Foreign Policy* (1970); Lawrence S. Kaplan, *Colonies into Nation: American Diplomacy, 1763–1801* (1972); Louis M. Sears, *George Washington and the French Revolution* (1960); Paul A. Varg, *Foreign Policies of the Founding Fathers* (1963); Felix Gilbert, *To the Farewell Address* (1961); and Julian N. Boyd, *Number 7* (1964), on Hamilton's devious dealings with the British. On Adams, consult Page Smith, *John Adams* (2 vols., 1962) and Stephen G. Kurtz, *The Presidency of John Adams* (1957). John C. Miller, *Crisis in Freedom* (1951) and James M. Smith, *Freedom's Fetters* (1956) treat the Alien and Sedition Laws, as does Leonard Levy, *Legacy of Suppression* (1960).

11

The Triumph of Jeffersonian Democracy

Timid men ... prefer the calm of despotism to the boisterous sea of liberty.

Thomas Jefferson, 1796

Responsibility Breeds Moderation

"Long Tom" Jefferson was inaugurated President on March 4, 1801, in the swampy village of Washington, the crude new national capital. Tall (6 feet 2.5 inches; 1.89 meters), with large hands and feet, reddish hair ("The Red Fox"), and prominent cheekbones and chin, he was an arresting figure. Believing that the customary pomp did not befit his democratic ideals, he spurned a horse-drawn coach and simply walked over to the Capitol from his boarding house.

The inaugural address, beautifully phrased, was a classic statement of democratic principles. Seeking to allay Federalist fears of a bull-in-the-china-closet overturn, Jefferson blandly stated, "We are all Republicans, we are all Federalists." As for foreign affairs, he pledged "honest friendship with all nations, entangling alliances with none."

With its rustic setting, Washington lent itself admirably to the simplicity and frugality of the Jeffer-sonian Republicans. In this respect, it contrasted sharply with the elegant atmosphere of Federalist Philadelphia, the former temporary capital.

A widower, Jefferson was shockingly unconventional. Having no wife to police his apparel, he would receive callers in sloppy attire—on one occasion in a dressing gown and heelless slippers. He also began the tradition, unbroken for 112 years, of sending messages to Congress to be read by a clerk. Personal appearances, in the Federalist manner, suggested too strongly a monarchical speech from the throne.

As if plagued by an evil spirit, Jefferson was forced to reverse many of the political principles he had so vigorously championed. There were in fact two Thomas Jeffersons. One was the private citizen, who had philosophized in his study. The other was the public official, who made the disturbing discovery that bookish theories worked out differently in the

110

noisy arena of practical politics. The open-minded Virginian was therefore consistently inconsistent; it is easy to quote one Jefferson to refute the other.

In his role as practical politician, Jefferson proved highly skillful. He was especially effective in the informal atmosphere of a dinner, where he wooed congressional representatives while personally pouring imported wine and serving French food.

In part, Jefferson had to rely on his personal charm because his party was so weak-jointed. The president permitted his friends to make few patronage appointments, so the disappointed Democratic-Republicans could not build a political following. Opposition to the Federalists was the chief glue holding them together, and as the Federalists faded, so did Democratic-Republican unity. The era of well-developed, well-disciplined political parties still lay in the future.

At the outset, Jefferson was determined to undo the Federalist abuses begotten by the anti-French hysteria. The hated Alien and Sedition Laws had already expired. The incoming President speedily pardoned the "martyrs" serving sentences under the Sedition Law, and the government returned many fines. Shortly after the Congress met, the Jeffersonians enacted the new naturalization law of 1802. It reduced the unreasonable requirement of fourteen years of residence to the former and more reasonable requirement of five years.

Jefferson actually kicked away only one substantial prop of the Hamiltonian system. He hated the excise tax, which bred bureaucrats and bore heavily on his farmer following, and he early persuaded Congress to repeal it.

Except for excising the excise tax, the Jeffersonians left the Hamiltonian framework essentially intact. They launched no attack on the Bank of the United States, and they did not repeal the mildly protective Federalist tariff.

Paradoxically, Jefferson's moderation thus further cemented the gains of the "Revolution of 1800." That revolution had consisted above all in the peaceful replacement of one governing party by another. By shrewdly absorbing many major Federalist programs, Jefferson showed that a change of regime need not be disastrous for the defeated party. His restraint pointed the way toward the two-party system that was

Mad Tom in a Rage. *A Federalist cartoon shows "Mad Tom" Jefferson, assisted by brandy and the Devil, trying to pull down the federal edifice erected by Washington and Adams. (Houghton Library, Harvard)*

later to become a characteristic feature of American politics.

The "Dead Clutch" of the Judiciary

The "death bed" Judiciary Act of 1801 was one of the last important laws passed by the expiring Federalist Congress. It created sixteen new federal judgeships and other judicial offices. President Adams remained at his desk until nine o'clock in the evening of his last day in office, allegedly signing the commissions of the Federalist "midnight judges." (Actually only three commissions were signed on his last day.)

This Federalist-sponsored Judiciary Act, though a long-overdue reform, aroused bitter resentment. This "packing" of these lifetime posts with anti-

Jeffersonian partisans was, in Republican eyes, a brazen attempt by the defeated party to entrench itself in one of the three powerful branches of government. Jeffersonians condemned the "midnight judges" in violent language.

The newly elected Republican Congress bestirred itself to repeal the Judiciary Act of 1801 in the year after its passage. Jeffersonians thus swept sixteen benches from under the recently appointed "midnight judges."

Jeffersonians likewise had their knives sharpened for the scalp of Chief Justice John Marshall, whom Adams had appointed to the Supreme Court (as a fourth choice) in the dying days of his term. The lanky Marshall, with his rasping voice and steeltrap mind, was a cousin of Thomas Jefferson. As a Virginia Federalist, he was cordially disliked by the states'-rights Jeffersonians. He served for about thirty days under a Federalist administration, and thirty-four years under the administrations of the Jeffersonian Republicans and their successors. The Federalist party died out, but Marshall went on handing down Federalist decisions serenely for many more years. He probably did more than Hamilton himself to engraft the Hamiltonian concept of a powerful central government upon the American political and economic system.

One of the "midnight judges" of 1801 presented John Marshall with a historic opportunity. He was obscure William Marbury, whom President Adams had named a justice of the peace for the District of Columbia. When Marbury learned that his commission was being held up by the new secretary of state, James Madison, he sued for its delivery. Chief Justice John Marshall knew that his Jeffersonian rivals, entrenched in the executive branch, would hardly spring forward to enforce a writ to deliver the commission to his fellow Federalist Marbury. He therefore dismissed Marbury's suit, avoiding a direct political showdown. But the wily Marshall snatched a victory from the jaws of this judicial defeat. In explaining his ruling, Marshall said that the part of the Judiciary Act of 1789 on which Marbury tried to base his appeal was unconstitutional. The Act had attempted to assign to the Supreme Court powers that the Constitution had not foreseen.

In this self-denying opinion, Marshall greatly magnified the authority of the Court—and slapped at the Jeffersonians. Until the case of *Marbury* v. *Madison* (1803), controversy had clouded the question of who had the final authority to determine the meaning of the Constitution. Jefferson in the Kentucky resolutions (1798) had tried to assign that right to the individual states. But now his cousin on the Court had cleverly promoted the contrary principle of "judicial review"—that the black-robed tribunal of the Supreme Court alone had the last word on the question of constitutionality. In this epochal case, Marshall thus neatly inserted the keystone into the arch that supports the tremendous power of the Supreme Court in American life.*

The Pacifist Jefferson Turns Warrior

As a passionate champion of freedom, Jefferson distrusted large standing armies as a standing invitation to dictatorship. Trusting the ill-trained militia, Jefferson reduced the military establishment to a mere police force of 2,500 officers and men. The navy was also reduced to a peacetime level.

But harsh realities forced a penny-pinching Jefferson to change his tune on navies and war. Pirates of the North African states had long made a national industry of blackmailing and plundering merchant ships that ventured into the Mediterranean. Preceding Federalist administrations, in fact, had been forced to buy protection. At the time of the French crisis of 1798, when Americans were shouting, "Millions for defense, but not one cent for tribute," twenty-six barrels of blackmail dollars were being shipped to piratical Algiers.

The showdown came in 1801. The Pasha of Tripoli, dissatisfied with his share of protection money, informally declared war on the United States by cutting down the flagstaff of the American consulate. A challenge was thus thrown squarely into the face of Jefferson—the noninterventionist, the pacifist, the

---

*The next invalidation of a federal law by the Supreme Court came fifty-four years later with the explosive Dred Scott decision (see pp.).

critic of a big-ship navy, and the political foe of Federalist shippers. He reluctantly rose to the occasion by dispatching the infant navy to "the shores of Tripoli," as related in the song of the U.S. Marine Corps. After four years of intermittent fighting, marked by hair-raising exploits, Jefferson succeeded in extorting a treaty of peace from Tripoli in 1805. It was secured at the bargain price of only $60,000—a sum representing ransom payments for captured Americans.

The Louisiana Godsend

A secret pact, fraught with peril for America, was signed in 1800. Napoleon Bonaparte induced the king of Spain to cede to France, for attractive considerations, the immense trans-Mississippi region of Louisiana, which included the New Orleans area.

Rumors of the transfer were partially confirmed in 1802, when the Spaniards at New Orleans withdrew the right of deposit guaranteed America by the treaty of 1795. Deposit privileges were vital to frontier farmers who floated their produce down the Mississippi to its mouth, there to await oceangoing vessels. A roar of anger rolled up the mighty river and into its tributary valleys. American pioneers talked wildly of descending upon New Orleans, rifles in hand, to drive out the haughty Spaniards.

Thomas Jefferson, both pacifistic and antientanglement, was again on the griddle. Louisiana in the senile grip of Spain posed no real threat; America could seize the territory when the time was ripe. But Louisiana in the iron fist of Napoleon, the preeminent military genius of his age, foreshadowed a dark and blood-drenched future.

Hoping to quiet the clamor of the West, Jefferson moved decisively. Early in 1803 he sent James Monroe to Paris to join forces with the regular minister there, Robert R. Livingston. The two envoys were instructed to buy New Orleans and as much land to the east as they could get for a maximum of $10 million.

Napoleon now suddenly decided to sell all Louisiana and abandon his dream of a New World empire. He had failed in his efforts to reconquer the sugar-rich island of Santo Domingo, for which Louisiana was to serve as a granary. Infuriated ex-slaves, ably led by a gifted black, Toussaint L'Ouverture, had put up a stubborn resistance that was ultimately broken. Then the island's second line of defense—mosquitoes carrying yellow fever—had swept away thousands of crack French troops. Santo Domingo could not be reconquered, except perhaps at a staggering cost; hence there was no need for the granary.

Bonaparte was about to end the twenty-month lull in his deadly conflict with Britain. Because the British controlled the seas, he feared that he might be forced to make them a gift of Louisiana. Rather than drive America into the arms of England by attempting to hold the area, he decided to sell the huge wilderness to the Americans and pocket the money for his schemes nearer home. He hoped that the United States, strengthened by Louisiana, would one day grow up to be a military and naval power that would thwart the ambitions of the lordly British in the New World. The distresses of France in Europe were again paving the way for America's diplomatic successes.

Events now moved with dizzying speed. Suddenly, out of a clear sky, the French foreign minister asked the American minister Livingston how much he would give for all Louisiana. Scarcely able to believe his ears (he was partially deaf anyhow), Livingston nervously entered upon the negotiations. After about a week of haggling, the treaties were signed on April 30, 1803, ceding Louisiana to the United States for $15 million.

Out-Federalizing the Federalists in Louisiana

When the news of the bargain reached America, Jefferson was startled. He had authorized his envoys to offer not more than $10 million for New Orleans, and as much to the *east* in the Floridas as they could get. Instead, they had signed three treaties which pledged $15 million for New Orleans and a vast wilderness entirely to the *west*—an area that would more than double the United States. They had bought a wilderness to get a city.

Once again the two Jeffersons wrestled with each other in private: the theorist and the former strict constructionist versus the realist and public official.

Louisiana Purchase, 1803. *Seeking to avert friction with France by purchasing all of Louisiana, Jefferson bought trouble because of the vagueness of the boundaries. Among the disputants were Spain in the Floridas, Spain and Mexico in the Southwest, and Great Britain in Canada.*

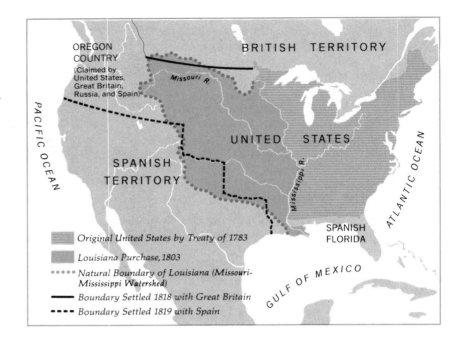

Where in his beloved Constitution was the President authorized to negotiate treaties incorporating a huge new expanse into the union—an expanse containing some 50,000 red, white, and black inhabitants? There was no such clause. So Jefferson shamefacedly submitted the treaties to the Senate, while privately admitting that the purchase was unconstitutional.

The senators were less finicky than Jefferson. Reflecting enthusiastic public support, they registered their prompt approval of the transaction. Land-hungry Americans were not disposed to split constitutional hairs when confronted with perhaps the most magnificent real estate bargain in history—828,000 square miles (2,144,520 square kilometers) at about three cents an acre.

What really worried the Federalists was that the signing of the Louisiana treaties was the signing of their own political death warrant. New states would be carved from the immense area—states that would outvote the thirteen charter members, including Federalist New England. The Jeffersonian agrarians would then become unassailable. At Williams College, in Massachusetts, a debating group voted fifteen to one that the purchase of Louisiana was undesirable.

A few Federalist extremists even threatened to secede from the Union.

The purchase of Louisiana—the most glorious achievement of Jefferson as President—was a triumph for which neither he nor anyone else could claim much direct credit. Napoleon, for reasons purely selfish, dumped this rich prize into the laps of Livingston, Monroe, and Jefferson. Louisiana was so desirable that Jefferson found it less embarrassing to reverse himself on strict construction than to lose the magnificent windfall.

Louisiana in the Long View

Jefferson's bargain with France was epochal. By scooping up Louisiana, America secured at one bloodless stroke the western half of the richest river valley in the world, and further laid the foundations of a future major power. The ideal of a great agrarian democracy, as envisioned by Jefferson, would have elbowroom in the vast "Valley of Democracy." At the same time, the transfer established a precedent that was to be followed repeatedly: namely, the acquisition of foreign territory and peoples by purchase.

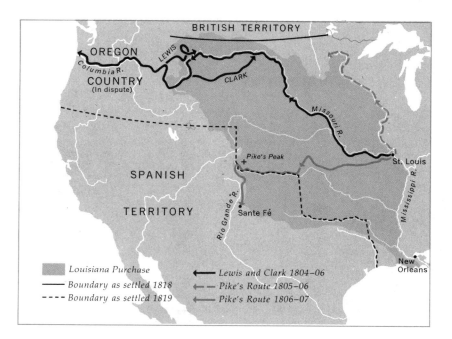

Exploring the Louisiana Purchase. *An amazing Indian woman, Sacagawea, a Shoshone married to a Canadian interpreter, accompanied the Lewis and Clark expedition. She shared the hardships and privations with an infant strapped to her back. Without her assistance and the aid she obtained from the Shoshone Indians, Lewis and Clark might never have reached the Pacific Coast.*

The extent of the huge new area was more fully unveiled by a series of explorations under the direction of Jefferson. He was keenly interested in the natural treasures of his purchase, including an enormous (and non-existent) mountain of salt. The expedition of Meriwether Lewis and William Clark ascended the "Great Muddy" Missouri River and struggled through the Rockies to the mouth of the Columbia River. This hazardous venture into the uncharted Western wilderness, from 1804 to 1806, bolstered America's claim to Oregon, while further opening the West to Indian trade and exploration. Zebulon M. Pike, in 1805–1806, explored the Louisiana territory near the headwaters of the Mississippi River, and in 1806–1807 ventured into Colorado and New Mexico, sighting the peak that bears his name.

Jefferson's reluctant purchase of Louisiana proved to be a landmark in American foreign policy. Overnight he avoided a possible rupture with France, and the consequent entangling alliance with England. The nation was thus able to continue the noninterventionist policies of the Founding Fathers, though it later quarreled with Spain and Britain over the vague boundaries of Louisiana, north, south, and west.

The Louisiana godsend likewise boosted national unity. Once-proud Federalists, now mere sectionalists, sank ever lower in public esteem as they were reduced to whining impotence. A few of their more extreme spokesmen attempted to plot with scheming Aaron Burr for the secession of New England and New York. But the intrigue failed, largely owing to the vigilance of Alexander Hamilton, who subsequently provoked Burr to a duel. The pistol that killed Hamilton in 1804 blew the brightest brain out of the Federalist party—and destroyed its one remaining hope of effective leadership.

A once-restive West, which now toasted the "immortal Jefferson," was more securely riveted to the Union by the purchase. The people of the western waters were grateful to the federal government for having safeguarded their interests, particularly in securing the mouth of the Mississippi. A new spirit of unity surged through the West.

Aaron Burr, turning his disunionist plottings to the trans-Mississippi West, was arrested in 1806 for treason. Tried the next year at Richmond, Virginia, he was freed after the presiding judge, Chief Justice Marshall, had infuriated the Jeffersonians by what

Intercourse or Impartial Dealings. *A cartoon by "Peter Pencil" (1809) shows Jefferson being victimized by both England* (left) *and France* (right). *(Houghton Library, Harvard)*

seemed to be bias in favor of the accused. The government's case collapsed when two witnesses to the same overt act of treason could not be found, as required by the Constitution (see Art. III, Sec. III). Burr's schemes are still somewhat shrouded in mystery, but he apparently planned to separate the western part of the United States from the eastern and unite it with to-be-conquered Spanish territory west of the Louisiana Purchase. The very fact that so dashing a figure as Burr could muster only three-score followers was significant. It indicated, among other things, that the West was developing a deeper sense of loyalty to the Washington government.

America: A Nutcrackered Neutral

Jefferson was triumphantly reelected in 1804, with 162 electoral votes to only 14 for his Federalist opponent. His success was not so much due to Republicanizing the Federalists, as he fondly supposed, as to Federalizing the Republicans. The iron hand of reality gradually forced him, quite unintentionally, to kill off the opposition party by stealing many of its principles and embracing them as his own.

As was said, he caught the Federalists in bathing and made off with their clothes.

But the laurels of Jefferson's first administration soon withered under the blasts of the new storm that broke in Europe. After unloading Louisiana in 1803, Napoleon deliberately provoked a renewal of his war with Britain—a conflict that crashed to an awesome close eleven long years later.

For two years a maritime United States—the number one neutral carrier since 1793—enjoyed juicy commercial pickings. But a setback came in 1805. At the Battle of Trafalgar, one-eyed Lord Nelson achieved immortality by smashing the combined French and Spanish fleets off the coast of Spain, thereby ensuring Britain's supremacy on the seas. At the Battle of Austerlitz in Austria—the Battle of the Three Emperors—Napoleon crushed the combined Austrian and Russian armies, thereby ensuring his mastery of the land. Like the tiger and the shark, France and Britain were supreme in their chosen elements.

Unable to hurt each other directly, the two antagonists were forced to strike indirect blows. England ruled the waves and waived the rules. The London government, beginning in 1806, issued a series of Orders in Council. These edicts closed the ports under French continental control to foreign shipping, including American, unless the vessels first stopped at a British port. There they would pay the necessary fees and, if acceptable, secure clearance papers. Napoleon struck back savagely in a series of decrees. In effect, they ordered the seizure of all merchant ships, including American, that entered British ports.

British Man-Stealing

Even more galling to American pride than the seizure of wooden ships was the seizure of flesh-and-blood American seamen. Impressment—the forcible enlistment of sailors—was a crude form of conscription which the British, among others, had employed for over four centuries. Clubs and stretchers (for men knocked unconscious) were standard equipment of press-gangs from His Majesty's man-hungry ships.

The London authorities themselves set limits to this ugly practice. They claimed the right to impress only British subjects on their own soil, in their own harbors, or on merchant ships on the high seas. But many fair-skinned Americans looked like Englishmen, and the benefit of the doubt was seldom given to an experienced seaman in those short-handed days. The result was that some six thousand bona fide United States citizens, according to the best estimates, were impressed by the "piratical man-stealers" of England from 1808 to 1811 alone.

Britain had her back to the wall, and her desperate plight colored her views. The British feared that they would lose the war if they gave up the hoary method of conscription—and they would fight before they did. Their determination was highlighted in 1807 when a British warship, seeking deserters, fired on the American frigate *Chesapeake,* killing three Americans and wounding eighteen. Infuriated Federalists and Republicans alike joined in an outburst of national wrath. Jefferson could easily have led a united nation into war, but he chose instead to use the *Chesapeake* outrage diplomatically to force the British to renounce impressment altogether, which they refused to do.

Jefferson's Backfiring Embargo

National honor would not permit a slavish submission to British and French mistreatment. Yet a large-scale foreign war was contrary to the settled policy of the new Republic—and in addition it would be futile. The navy was weak, thanks largely to Jefferson's anti-navalism; and the army was even weaker. A disastrous defeat would not improve America's plight.

The warring nations in Europe were heavily dependent upon the United States for raw materials and foodstuffs. In his eager search for an alternative to war, Jefferson seized upon this essential fact. He reasoned that if America voluntarily cut off her exports, the offending powers would be forced to come, hat in hand, and agree to respect her rights.

Responding to the presidential lash, Congress hastily passed the Embargo Act late in 1807. This rigorous law forbade the export of all goods from the United States, whether in American or in foreign ships. It was a compromise between submission and shooting.

Jefferson, the onetime strict constructionist, had once more flip-flopped into the camp of the loose constructionists. In the interests of the Federalist shippers, whom he disliked, he was rereading the Constitution with strange bifocals. To him, it now meant that Congress, under its authority to "regulate" commerce, could go so far as to stop foreign trade altogether. Regulation thus became strangulation.

Federalist New England could well have prayed for relief from its newly found Virginia friend, "Mad Tom" Jefferson. Forests of dead masts gradually filled once-flourishing harbors; docks that had once rumbled were deserted (except for illegal trade); and soup kitchens cared for some of the hungry unemployed. Jeffersonian Republicans probably hurt the commerce of New England, which they avowedly were trying to protect, far more than Old England and France together were doing.

Farmers of the South and West, the strongholds of Jefferson, suffered no less disastrously than New England. They were alarmed by the mounting piles of exportable cotton, grain, and tobacco. Tart-tongued John Randolph of Virginia remarked that enacting the embargo was like cutting off one's toes to cure one's corns. Jefferson in truth seemed to be waging war on

The Embargo (Ograbme). *As a snapping turtle, it halts overseas shipments. (Prints Division, New York Public Library, Astor, Lenox and Tilden Foundations)*

his fellow citizens, rather than on the offending belligerents.

The American people, from the days of the colonial Navigation Acts, have never submitted meekly to unpopular legislation. Though basically law-abiding, they habitually flout laws that are opposed by large numbers of the population. An enormous illicit trade mushroomed in 1808, especially along the Canadian border, where bands of armed Americans on loaded rafts overawed or overpowered federal agents. Irate citizens cynically transposed the letters of "Embargo" to read "O Grab Me," "Go Bar 'Em," and "Mobrage," while they heartily denounced the "Dambargo."

Jefferson nonetheless induced Congress to pass iron-toothed enforcing legislation. It was so inquisitorial and tyrannical as to cause some Americans to think more kindly of George III, whom Jefferson had berated in the Declaration of Independence. One indignant New Hampshire poet burst out in song:

> Our ships all in motion,
> Once whiten'd the ocean;
>   They sail'd and return'd with a Cargo;
> Now doom'd to decay
>   They are fallen a prey,
> To Jefferson, worms, and EMBARGO.

New England seethed with talk of secession; and Jefferson later admitted that he felt the foundations of government tremble under his feet.

An alarmed Congress, bowing to the storm of public anger, finally repealed the embargo, on March 1, 1809, three days before Jefferson's retirement. A half-loaf substitute was provided by the Non-Intercourse Act. This measure formally reopened trade with all the nations of the world, except the two most important, England and France. Though thus watered down, economic coercion continued to be the policy of the Jeffersonians from 1809 to 1812, when the nation finally plunged into war.

The Wooden-Gun Embargo: A Successful Failure

Why did the embargo, Jefferson's most daring act of statesmanship, collapse after fifteen dismal months? First of all, he underestimated the bulldog determination of the British, as others have, and overestimated their dependence on America's trade. Bumper grain crops blessed the British Isles during these years, and the revolutionary Latin American republics unexpectedly threw open their ports for compensating commerce.

The hated embargo was not continued long enough or tightly enough to achieve the desired results. But a statesman must know the temper of his people, and Jefferson should have foreseen that such a self-crucifying weapon could not possibly command public support. The Americans, notoriously people of action, did not take kindly to the passive type of heroism. They much preferred commercial activity, with all its risks, to enforced inactivity, with no chance of profit.

A crestfallen Jefferson himself admitted that the embargo was three times more costly than war. The irony is that with only a fraction of its cost to the country, he could have built a fairly strong navy. Such a fighting force would have won more respect for American rights on the high seas, and might well have prevented the War of 1812.

The embargo further embroiled relations with both Britain and France. It embittered the British, partly because it hit them more forcibly than it did Napoleon. The French despot naturally applauded the embargo, for it was an indirect American blockade of his foe.

A stoppage of exports hurt Federalist shipping, but revived the Federalist party. Gaining new converts, its leaders hurled their nullification of the embargo into the teeth of the "Virginia lordlings" in Washington. In 1804, the discredited Federalists had polled only 14 electoral votes out of 176; in 1808, the embargo year, the figure rose to 47 out of 175.

Curiously enough, New England plucked a new prosperity from the ugly jaws of the embargo. With shipping tied up and imported goods scarce, the resourceful Yankees reopened old factories and erected new ones. The real foundations of modern America's industrial might were laid behind the protective wall of the embargo, followed by non-intercourse and the War of 1812. Jefferson, the avowed critic of factories, may have unwittingly done more for American manufacturing than Alexander Hamilton, the outspoken friend of factories.

Jefferson's embargo, followed in modified form by non-intercourse, undeniably pinched England. Many British importers and manufacturers suffered severe losses, especially those dependent on American cotton. As thousands of factory workers were thrown out of jobs, agitation mounted for a repeal of the restrictions that had brought on the embargo. A petition to Parliament in 1812, from the city of Birmingham alone, bore 20,000 names on a sheet of parchment 150 feet long. So strong was public pressure that two days before Congress declared war in June 1812, the British foreign secretary announced that the offensive Orders in Council would be immediately suspended. The supreme irony is that Jefferson's policy of economic coercion did win in the end, but America was not patient enough to wait for it to work and thus reap the reward of her sacrifices.

The Living Jefferson

Thomas Jefferson retained much of his popularity, even though it was severely tarnished by the embargo. One public toast ran: "May he receive from his fellow citizens the reward of his merit, a halter [hangman's noose]." But his grip on his party was such that he could easily have won a third nomination and election. The international crisis was still acute; and although Jefferson was sixty-five years old, he was mentally alert and physically vigorous. He lived eighteen more years, relieved to have escaped what he called the "splendid misery" of the presidential penitentiary.

Jefferson, rather than Washington, was the real father of the two-term tradition. Unlike the first President, who had no serious constitutional qualms, he feared that more than two terms might open the door to dictatorship. Yet Jefferson strongly favored the nomination and election of a kindred spirit, his friend and fellow Virginian, the quiet, intellectual, and unassuming James Madison.

Though bitterly assailed, Jefferson left office with the consolation that he had remained true to the guiding star of the other Founding Fathers. He had kept the country out of a serious foreign war. Despite numerous reversals of policy under the whiplash of practicality, he never lost his faith in democracy and in the common people. He brought a renovation rather than a revolution; the real revolution that did occur was in his own thinking. If the Federalists were the steppingstone between monarchical Europe and republican America, then the Jeffersonians were the steppingstone between aristocratic Federalism and democratic Jacksonianism.

Thomas Jefferson and John Adams died on the same day—appropriately the Fourth of July, 1826. The last words of Adams, then ninety-one, were: "Thomas Jefferson still survives." He was wrong, for three hours earlier Jefferson had breathed his last. But Thomas Jefferson still survives in the democratic ideals and liberal principles of the great nation which he risked his all to found, and which he served so long and faithfully.

VARYING VIEWPOINTS

The Jeffersonian era has long presented observers with a series of paradoxes, none greater than the question of how the man who proclaimed, "We are all Republicans, we are all Federalists," came to preside over one of the most bitterly partisan periods in American history.

Some scholars play down the importance of party conflict in this era. Stressing the early parties' lack of concern for organizing the electorate, these accounts note that the Jeffersonians and the Federalists distrusted parties; saw them only as temporary, necessary evils; and looked forward to their elimination. Thus, historians like James S. Young argue that the Jeffersonian era possessed no true party system.

Others, among them Noble E. Cunningham, see the organizations of the early national period as the prototypes of the modern American party system. Conceding that the Federalists and Jeffersonians never became mass-based organizations like the later Jacksonian parties, this interpretation emphasizes the innovations of the period. The Jeffersonians created a partisan press, maintained control of Congress by dominating committee chairmanships, and pioneered campaign tactics like stump speaking and door-to-door canvassing. Most important, the experiences of the Federalists and Jeffersonians, in the two decades after the ratification of the Constitution, led both groups to accept, grudgingly, the idea that party competition was inevitable and potentially beneficial in a republican society. This realization paved the way for the evolution of a full-blown two-party system in the 1830s.

SELECT READINGS

Primary Source Documents

Jefferson's "First Inaugural Address" (1801), in Henry Steele Commager, *Documents of American History,* echoed the themes of Washington's Farewell and set the tone for his presidency. Reuben G. Thwaites, ed., *Original Journals of the Lewis and Clark Expedition** (1904), chronicles the explorers' adventures. For the political flavor of the age, see the debate over the Embargo Act* (1807). For Constitutional history, read the decision of John Marshall in *Marbury v. Madison** (1803).

Secondary Sources

A monument of American historical writing is Henry Adams, *History of the United States during the Administrations of Jefferson and Madison* (9 vols., 1889–1891), available in a one-volume abridgement edited by Ernest Samuels. Especially fascinating are Adams' epilogue and prologue on the United States in 1800 and 1817. A brief introduction is given in Marshall Smelser, *The Democratic Republic, 1801–1815* (1968). Problems with the judiciary can be traced in Albert J. Beveridge's still-respected *Life of John Marshall*

(4 vols., 1919). A more recent and succinct analysis is Richard E. Ellis, *The Jeffersonian Crisis: Courts and Politics in the New Republic* (1971). Politics are treated in a broad, imaginative context in James S. Young, *The Washington Community, 1800–1829* (1966) and more traditionally in Noble E. Cunningham's rebuttal, *The Process of Government under Jefferson* (1979). Daniel Boorstin vividly evokes the intellectual climate of the age in *The Lost World of Thomas Jefferson*

(1948). On Jefferson himself, see Dumas Malone's monumental study *Jefferson and His Times* (5 vols., 1948–1981). A briefer standard biography is Merrill D. Peterson, *Thomas Jefferson and the New Nation* (1970). Peterson has also scrutinized *The Jefferson Image in the American Mind* (1960). John C. Miller, *The Wolf by the Ears: Thomas Jefferson and Slavery* (1977) probes the third president's attitudes on an important question.

12

James Madison and the Second War for Independence

The Existing War—the Child of Prostitution.
May no American Acknowledge it Legitimate.
A Federalist Toast During the War of 1812

Madison: Dupe of Napoleon

Scholarly James Madison took the presidential oath on March 4, 1809, as the awesome conflict in Europe was roaring to its climax. Small of stature (5 feet 4 inches; 1.62 meters), light of weight (about 100 pounds; 45 kilograms), bald of head, and weak of voice, he fell tragically short of providing vigorous executive leadership. Crippled also by factions within his cabinet, he was unable to dominate his party, as Jefferson had once done.

The Non-Intercourse Act of 1809—the limited substitute for the embargo aimed solely at Britain and France—would expire in about a year. Congress, desperately attempting to uphold American rights, adopted in 1810 a bargaining measure known as Macon's Bill No. 2. While permitting American trade with all the world, it dangled an attractive lure. If either England or France repealed her commercial restrictions, America would restore nonimportation against the non-repealing nation. In short, the United States would bribe the belligerents into respecting its rights.

This opportunity was made to order for Napoleon, a past master of deceit. He was eager to have nonimportation clamped down once more on the British, because it would serve as a partial blockade which he would not have to raise a finger to enforce. He was hopeful that such a boycott would embroil the Americans in war with Britain, for then they would be serving as his indirect allies to weaken his arch-enemy. Accordingly, he blandly announced, in August 1810, that his objectionable decrees had been repealed.

Responsible Americans, rising above self-delusion, should have examined the hollow-sounding

French announcement with extreme caution. Napoleon, prince of liars, had no intention whatever of repealing his damaging decrees. But Madison, frantically seeking to wrest a recognition of American rights from England, accepted French bad faith as good faith. He formally announced, in November 1810, that France had complied with the terms of Macon's Bill No. 2, and that non-importation would consequently be reestablished against Britain.

Madison's decision was fateful. Britons were angered by America's apparent willingness to be the dupe and partner of Napoleon. Once Madison had aligned his nation against England commercially, he found himself gravitating toward France politically—and edging toward the whirlpool of war.

War Whoops Arouse the War Hawks

The complexion of the Twelfth Congress, which met late in 1811, differed markedly from that of its predecessor. Recent elections had swept away many of the older "submission men" and replaced them with young hotheads, chiefly from the South and West. The youthful newcomers—"the boys," John Randolph sneeringly called them—were on fire for a new war with the old enemy. Not having had a conflict in their own generation, these war hawks were weary of hearing how their fathers had "whipped" the British single-handedly. They won control of the House of Representatives, and elevated to the speakership the tall (6 feet 2 inches; 1.88 meters), eloquent, and magnetic Henry Clay of Kentucky, the gallant "Harry of the West," then only thirty-four years old.

Western war hawks, first of all, were eager to wipe out the renewed Indian resistance against the white settlers streaming steadily into the western wilderness. As this white flood spread through the green forests, more and more Indians were pushed farther and farther toward the setting sun. Two remarkable Shawnee twin brothers, Tecumseh and the Prophet, knew that if this onrushing tide were ever to be stopped, that time had come. They began to weld together a far-flung confederacy of all the tribes east of the Mississippi. Their braves forswore firewater in order to be fit for the last-ditch battle with the "paleface" intruders. To make matters worse, the sturdy pioneers and their war hawk representatives in Congress widely believed that the Indians' firearms and scalping knives were being furnished by British "hair buyers" in Canada.

Only a few days after the war hawk Congress convened in Washington, news of stirring events on the frontier further inflamed anti-Indian and anti-British feeling. General William H. Harrison, advancing with 1,000 men upon the Indian headquarters, repelled a surprise attack at Tippecanoe, in present Indiana, on November 7, 1811. He then put the torch to the settlement.

Harrison's onslaught broke the back of the Indian rebellion. It also made the blood course faster in the veins of the impetuous war hawks. Men like Representative Felix Grundy of Tennessee, three of whose brothers had been murdered, cried that there was only one way to remove the menace of the Indians: wipe out their Canadian base. Southern expansionists, less vocal, cast a covetous eye on Florida, then weakly held by Britain's ally Spain.

The war hawks wanted "Free Trade and Sailors' Rights" as well as free land. It may seem strange that settlers beyond the mountains, many of whom had never seen a body of salt water larger than a salt lick, should want to fight for maritime rights. But the proud, nationalistic westerners were outraged by the manhandling of American sailors, and by the British Orders in Council that dammed up their agricultural products from shipment to Europe. Westerners also joined many of their fellow citizens in believing that only a vigorous assertion of American rights could demonstrate the viability of American nationhood—and of democracy as a form of government. If America could not fight to protect itself, its experiment in republicanism would be discredited in the eyes of a scoffing world.

Militant war hawks, with scattered but essential support from other sections, finally engineered a declaration of war in June 1812. The vote in the House was 79 to 49, in the Senate 19 to 13. The close tally betrayed a dangerous degree of national disunity. Congressmen from the pro-British maritime and commercial centers, as well as from the middle Atlantic states, almost solidly opposed hostilities. Thus the West and Southwest, mostly landlocked, presented the sea-fronting East with a war for a free sea that the East vehemently resented.

Britain or Napoleon: A Choice of Foes

But why fight Britain rather than France, which had committed nearly as many maritime offenses? The traditional Republican attachment to France partly explains the choice of foe, as does the visibility of British impressments and the British arming of the Indians, who were smashing pioneer cabins on the frontier.

The choice prize of Canada also beckoned from the north. Americans fondly (but wrongly) believed that taking Canada would be absurdly simple, a "frontiersman's frolic." If this northern mirage had not been so inviting, the administration would have waited a few more months, and thereby learned of London's intention to repeal the Orders in Council. In fact, the announcement of the intention to repeal was made two days *before* Congress voted for war. Had there been an Atlantic cable, the war hawks probably could not have forced a declaration of hostilities through the Senate.

American Allies of the Napoleonic Anti-Christ

Seafaring New England damned the war for a free sea. The news of the declaration of war was greeted with muffled bells, flags at half-mast, and public fasting.

Why the opposition? To New Englanders, impressment was an old and exaggerated wrong. New England shippers and manufacturers were still raking in money, and profits dull patriotism. Pro-British New England Federalists also sympathized with the mother country, and resented the Virginia dynasty's sympathy with Napoleon, whom they regarded as the "Corsican butcher" and "the anti-Christ of the age."

Federalists also condemned the War of 1812 because they opposed the acquisition of Canada, which would merely add more agrarian states from the wild Northwest. Fearing the New West far more than Old England, New England Federalists were determined, wrote one versifier:

> To rule the nation if they could,
> But see it damned if others should.

The bitterness of New Englanders against "Mr. Madison's War" led them to treason or near-treason.

In a sense America fought two enemies simultaneously: Old England and New England. New England gold holders probably lent more dollars to the British than to the Federal treasury. New England farmers sent huge quantities of supplies and foodstuffs to Canada, enabling British armies to invade New York. New England governors stubbornly refused to permit their militia to serve outside their own states.

Fight Over Canada on Land and Lakes

The War of 1812, largely because of widespread disunity, ranks as one of America's worst-fought wars. There was no burning national anger, as there had been in 1807, following the *Chesapeake* outrage. War hawks in Congress were no more than a zealous minority. President Madison, while supporting their aims, knew that there was serious disunity. The supreme lesson of this conflict was the folly of leading a divided and apathetic people into war.

The Republic was dangerously unprepared, despite warnings going back nineteen years to the outbreak of the European war in 1793. The nation was still suffering from its own embargo and nonintercourse, which it had partially enforced for the better part of four years. Congress had shortsightedly permitted the Bank of the United States to expire in 1811, at a time when a powerful financial institution was needed. It was knifed largely by the jealousies of the competing state banks.

The regular army was scandalously inadequate, for it was ill-trained, ill-disciplined, and widely scattered. It had to be supplemented by the even more poorly trained militia, who were sometimes distinguished by speed of foot in leaving the battlefield. Some of the ranking generals were semi-senile heirlooms from the Revolutionary War, rusting on their laurels and lacking in vigor and vision.

The offensive strategy in Canada was poorly conceived. Had the Americans captured Montreal, the center of population and transportation, everything to the west would have died, just as the leaves of a tree wither when the trunk is girdled. But instead of laying ax to the trunk, the Americans frittered away their strength in the three-pronged invasion of 1812. The trio of invading forces that set out from Detroit,

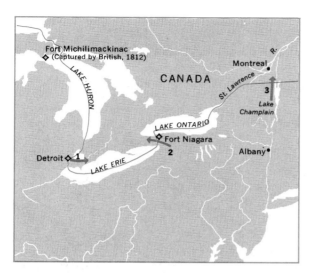

The Three U.S. Thrusts of 1812. *Colored line delineates the Canadian border.*

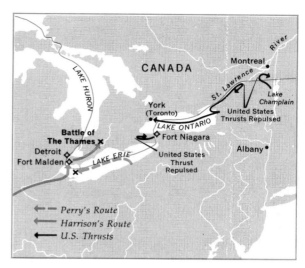

Campaigns of 1813. *Colored line denotes Canadian boundary.*

Niagara, and Lake Champlain were all beaten back shortly after they had crossed the Canadian border.

By contrast, the British and Canadians displayed energy from the outset. Early in the war they captured the American fort of Michilimackinac, which commanded the upper Great Lakes and the Indian-inhabited area to the south and west. Their brilliant defensive operations were led by the inspired British general Isaac Brock, and assisted (in the American camp) by "General Mud" and "General Confusion."

When several American land invasions of Canada were again hurled back in 1813, Americans looked for success on water. Control of the Great Lakes was vital, and an energetic American naval officer, Oliver Hazard Perry, managed to build a fleet of green-timbered ships on the shores of Lake Erie, manned by even greener seamen. When he captured a British fleet in a furious engagement on Lake Erie, he reported to his superior, "We have met the enemy and they are ours." Perry's victory and his slogan infused new life into the drooping American cause. Forced to withdraw from Detroit and Fort Malden, the retreating redcoats were overtaken by General Harrison's army and beaten at the Battle of the Thames in October 1813. The gifted Indian leader Tecumseh, now a brigadier general in the British army, lost his life in that historic battle.

Despite these successes, the Americans by late 1814, far from invading Canada, were grimly defending their own soil against the invading British. In Europe, the diversionary power of Napoleon was destroyed in mid-1814, and the dangerous despot was marooned on the Mediterranean isle of Elba. The United States, which had so brashly provoked war behind the protective skirts of Napoleon, was now left to face the music alone. As thousands of red-coated veterans began to pour into Canada, Europe's distresses, for once, failed the Americans.

Assembling some 10,000 crack troops, the British prepared in 1814 for a crushing blow into New York, along the familiar lake-river route. In the absence of roads, the invader was forced to bring his supplies over the Lake Champlain waterway. A weaker American fleet, commanded by the thirty-year-old Thomas Macdonough, challenged the British. The ensuing battle was desperately fought near Plattsburg, on September 11, 1814, on floating slaughterhouses. The American flagship at one point was in grave trouble. But Macdonough, unexpectedly winching his ship about with cables thrown to shore, confronted the enemy with a fresh broadside, and snatched victory from the jaws of defeat.

The results of this heroic naval battle were momentous. The invading British army was forced to

The Burning of Washington. *America's military fortunes hit rock bottom on August 24, 1814, when British forces, having routed a ragtag American army on the outskirts of the capital, put the torch to Washington, D.C. (Courtesy of the New-York Historical Society, New York City)*

retreat. Macdonough thus saved at least upper New York from conquest, New England from further disaffection, and the Union from possible dissolution. He also profoundly affected the concurrent negotiations of the Anglo-American peace treaty in Europe.

Washington Burned and New Orleans Defended

A second formidable British force, numbering about four thousand, landed in the Chesapeake Bay area in August 1814. Advancing rapidly on Washington, it easily dispersed some six thousand panicky militia at Bladensburg ("the Bladensburg races"). The invaders then entered the capital and set fire to most of the public buildings, including the Capitol and the White House ("the Yankee Palace"). President Madison and his aides, chased into the surrounding hills like frightened rabbits, witnessed from afar the billowing smoke. The British fleet next appeared before Baltimore, a nest for privateers, but was beaten off by the doughty defenders at Fort McHenry, despite "bombs bursting in air." At the same time the American land

defenders, though driven back at first, caused the attacking army to withdraw. The memory of the Chesapeake campaign was further kept alive when Francis Scott Key, a detained American anxiously watching the bombardment at Baltimore from a British ship, was inspired to write the words of "The Star-Spangled Banner."

A third British blow of 1814, aimed at New Orleans, menaced the entire Mississippi Valley. Gaunt and hawk-faced Andrew Jackson, fresh from crushing the southwest Indians at the Battle of Horseshoe Bend in what is now Alabama, was placed in command. His hodgepodge force consisted of seven thousand sailors, regulars, pirates, and Frenchmen, as well as militiamen from Louisiana, Kentucky, and Tennessee. Among the defenders were two Louisiana regiments of free black volunteers, numbering about 400 men. The Americans threw up their entrenchment, and in the words of a popular song:

> Behind it stood our little force—
> None wished it to be greater;
> For ev'ry man was half a horse,
> And half an alligator.

***Constitution* and *Guerrière*, 1812.** *The* Guerrière *was heavily outweighed and outgunned, yet its British captain eagerly—and foolishly—sought combat. His ship was totally destroyed. Historian Henry Adams later concluded that this duel "raised the United States in one half hour to the rank of a first-class Power in the world." (U.S. Naval Academy Museum)*

The overconfident British, numbering some eight thousand battle-seasoned veterans, blundered badly. They made the mistake of launching a frontal assault, on January 8, 1815, on the entrenched American riflemen and cannoneers. The attackers suffered the most devastating defeat of the entire war, losing over two thousand, killed and wounded, in half an hour, as compared with some seventy for the Americans. This slaughter was as useless as it was horrible, for the treaty of peace had been signed at Ghent, in Europe, two weeks earlier. But Jackson became more than ever the hero of the West.

The "glorious news" from New Orleans reached Washington early in February 1815, and about two weeks later came the tidings of the treaty of peace. Naive citizens promptly concluded that the British, beaten to their knees by Jackson, had hastened to make terms.

Ship Duels and Privateer Prizes

Man for man and ship for ship the American navy did much better than the army. But the results of its heroism have been exaggerated.

Britain's navy in 1812 boasted more than 800 men-of-war. Of these oaken craft, 219 were ships-of-the-line of the 74-gun class, and 296 were frigates of roughly the 44-gun class. America, by contrast, had only 16 ships in her entire navy, the largest of which were a few 44-gun frigates, unable to stand up to British ships-of-the-line. There could obviously be no saltwater fleet engagements in the slam-bang Trafalgar tradition; the only fleet battles were fought on the interior lakes.

American frigates and smaller sloops did clash with the enemy in a series of spectacular duels. In the frigate class, the Americans won four out of five of the single-ship contests, and in the sloop class, eight out of nine. American craft on the whole were more skillfully handled, had better gunners, and were manned by non-press-gang crews who were burning to avenge numerous indignities. The American frigates were specially designed super-frigates, notably the *Constitution* ("Old Ironsides"). They had thicker sides, heavier firepower, and larger crews, of which one sailor in six was a free black.

The British were deeply humiliated by their naval defeats, all the more so because they had sneered at America's "few fir-built frigates, manned by a handful of bastards and outlaws." In a few months they lost more warships to the Yankees than the French and Spaniards together had captured in years of fighting.

Swift and annoying American privateers—the "militia of the sea"—numbered about 500. They were in fact much more damaging than the regular navy, and had an important bearing on the coming of peace. Built to fly from stronger ships, rather than fight them, these speedy craft captured or destroyed some 1,350 British merchantmen, even pursuing them into the English Channel and the Irish Sea. Assisted by fast-sailing sloops of the navy, Yankee privateers were so destructive that Lloyd's of London refused to insure unconvoyed British merchantmen crossing the Irish Sea. (At the same time British warships and privateers were capturing hundreds of American merchant ships.)

Yet the American privateers were not an unmixed blessing. They lost scores of their own craft, and diverted valuable manpower from the navy and army. But they brought urgently needed wealth into the country, boosted sagging morale, and slowed up British operations in Canada and elsewhere by capturing arms and supplies. More than that, the privateers brought the war home to British manufacturers, merchants, and shippers, who in turn exerted strong pressure on Parliament to end this costly war.

Its wrath aroused, the Royal Navy finally retaliated by throwing a ruinous naval blockade along America's coast, and by landing raiding parties almost at will. American economic life, including fishing, was crippled. Customs revenues were choked off, and near the end of the war the bankrupt Treasury was unable to meet its maturing obligations.

The Treaty of Ghent

Confident after their military successes, Britain's envoys made sweeping demands for a neutralized Indian buffer state in the Great Lakes region, control of the Great Lakes, and a substantial part of conquered Maine. The Americans flatly rejected these terms, and the talks appeared stalemated. But news of British reverses in upper New York and at Baltimore, and increasing war-weariness in Britain, made London more willing to compromise. Preoccupied with the Congress of Vienna and still-dangerous France, the British lion resigned himself to licking his wounds. Revenge against its upstart American offspring would be sweet—but expensive. Once again European distress brought American diplomatic success, for the War of 1812 was "won" by the United States, so far as it was won at all, in Europe.

Czar Alexander I of Russia, hard-pressed by Napoleon's army and not wanting his British ally to fritter away its strength in America, proposed mediation between the clashing Anglo-Saxon cousins in 1812. The Czar's feeler eventually set in motion the machinery that brought five American peacemakers to the quaint Belgian city of Ghent in 1814. The bickering group was headed by early-rising, puritanical John Quincy Adams, son of John Adams, who deplored the late-hour card playing of his high-living colleague Henry Clay.

The Treaty of Ghent, signed on Christmas Eve in 1814, was essentially an armistice. Both sides simply agreed to stop fighting and to restore conquered territory. No mention was made of those grievances for which America had ostensibly fought: the Indian menace, search and seizure, Orders in Council, impressment, and confiscations. These maritime omissions have often been cited as further evidence of the insincerity of the war hawks. Rather, they are proof that the Americans did not defeat the British decisively. With neither side able to impose its will, the treaty negotiations—like the war itself—ended as a virtual draw.

The news from Ghent triggered an outburst of rejoicing in the United States. Many Americans had rather expected to lose some territory, so dark was the military outlook early in 1815. But when the treaty arrived, the public mood rocketed from gloom to glory. The popularity of the pact was so overwhelming that it was unanimously approved by the Senate. A slogan of the hour became "Not One Inch of Territory Ceded or Lost"—a watchword that contrasted strangely with the "On to Canada" widely heard at the outset of the war.

Federalist Grievances and the Hartford Convention

Defiant New England remained a problem. She was by far the most prosperous section during the conflict, owing largely to illicit trade with the enemy in Canada and to the absence of a British blockade until 1814. But the embittered opposition of the Federalists to the war continued unabated. Late in 1812, when the first wartime presidential election was held, unhappy

"Three Wise Men of Gotham Went to Sea in a Bowl—."
This satirical anti-Federalist cartoon shows three Massachusetts men sailing precariously for Washington in a large chamber pot bearing Hartfordite demands. They are quieting their fears of sinking by exchanging off-color remarks. (Massachusetts Historical Society)

Federalists combined with disaffected Republicans and almost unseated President Madison. If the state of Pennsylvania alone had been transferred to their electoral column, they would have won.

As the war dragged on, New England extremists became more vocal. A small minority of them proposed secession from the Union, or at least a separate peace with England. Ugly rumors were afloat about "Blue Light" Federalists—treacherous New Englanders who supposedly flashed lanterns on the shore so that blockading British cruisers would be alerted to the attempted escape of American ships.

The most spectacular manifestation of Federalist discontent was the ill-omened Hartford Convention. Late in 1814, when the capture of New Orleans seemed imminent, Massachusetts issued a call for a convention at Hartford, Connecticut. The states of Massachusetts, Connecticut, and Rhode Island dispatched full delegations, while New Hampshire and

Vermont sent partial representation. This group of prominent men, twenty-six in all, met in complete secrecy for about three weeks—December 15, 1814, to January 5, 1815—to discuss their grievances and to seek redress for their wrongs.

In truth, the Hartford Convention was less radical than alarmists supposed. Its immediate goal was to secure financial assistance from Washington, because the shores of New England were then being menaced by British blockading squadrons. A minority of the delegates gave vent to much wild talk of secession, but they were outvoted by the moderate Federalists.

Three special envoys from Massachusetts, bearing demands of the Hartford Convention for financial support to promote defense, journeyed to the burned-out capital of Washington. The trio arrived just in time to be overwhelmed by the glorious news from New Orleans, followed by that from Ghent. Pursued by the sneers and jeers of the press, they slunk away into obscurity and disgrace.

The Hartford resolutions, as it turned out, were the death song of the Federalist party. In 1816, the next year, the Federalists nominated their last presidential candidate. He was lopsidedly defeated by James Monroe, yet another Virginian.

Unhappily, the stench of treason has clung to the Hartford Convention. The taint was not justified by its formal resolutions. Yet if the war had not ended when it did, the Convention might well have paved the way for treasonable courses.

Federalist doctrines of disunity, which long survived the party, blazed a fateful trail. Until 1815, there was far more talk of nullification and secession in New England than in any other section, including the South. The outright flouting of the Jeffersonian embargo and the later crippling of the war effort were the two most damaging acts of nullification in America prior to the events leading to the Civil War.

The Second War for American Independence

The War of 1812 was a small war, involving about 6,000 Americans killed or wounded. It was but a footnote to the mighty European conflagration. In 1812, when Napoleon invaded Russia with about

500,000 men, Madison tried to invade Canada with about 5,000 men. But if the American conflict was globally unimportant, its results were highly important to the United States.

Americans wrested no formal recognition of their rights on the high seas, but informally they did. No longer did British aristocrats jeer at the "striped bunting" over "American cockboats." The republic had shown that it would resent, sword in hand, what it regarded as grievous wrongs. Other nations developed a new respect for American fighting men. Naval officers like Perry and Macdonough were the most effective type of negotiators; the hot breath of their broadsides spoke the most eloquent diplomatic language. America's diplomats abroad were henceforth treated with less scorn. In a diplomatic sense, if not in a military sense, the conflict could be called the Second War for American Independence.

A new nation, moreover, was welded in the fiery furnace of armed conflict. Sectionalism, now identified with discredited New England Federalists, was given a black eye. The painful events of the war glaringly revealed, as perhaps nothing else could have done, the folly of sectional disunity. In a sense, the most conspicuous casualty of the war was the Federalist party.

The nation thrilled to the victories of its warriors. A brilliant naval tradition, already well launched, was strengthened by the exploits of the gallant seamen. The ineptitude of insubordinate or fleeing militia was forgotten. The battle-singed regular army, which in the closing months of the war had fought bravely and well, had won its spurs. New war heroes emerged, such as Andrew Jackson and William Henry Harrison, both of whom were to become president.

Hostile Indians in the South had been crushed by Jackson at Horseshoe Bend (1814), and those in the North by Harrison at the Battle of the Thames (1813). Left in the lurch by their British friends at Ghent, the Indians were forced to make such terms as they could. They reluctantly consented, in a series of treaties, to relinquish vast areas of forested land north of the Ohio River.

Manufacturing increased behind the fiery wooden wall of the British blockade. In an economic sense, as well as in a diplomatic sense, the War of 1812 may be regarded as the Second War for American Independence. The industries that were thus stimulated by the fighting rendered America less dependent on the workshops of Europe.

International Legacies

Regrettably, the war revived and intensified bitterness toward the mother country. The uglier incidents of the conflict, notably the burning of Washington, added fuel to a century of Britain-hating and Britain-baiting. Mutual suspicion and hate were perhaps the most enduring heritages of this frustrating little war. Few Americans could have guessed in 1815 that it was to be the nation's last armed conflict with England.

Canadian patriotism and nationalism, no less than American patriotism and nationalism, received a powerful stimulus from the clash. The outnumbered Canadians, fighting bravely in defense of their homeland against the Yankee invader, won their full share of the laurels. Their stirring song, "The Maple Leaf," ringingly recalls these battles, including Chippewa and Lundy's Lane, which Americans regard as their victories.

Many Canadians felt betrayed by the Treaty of Ghent. They were especially aggrieved by the failure to secure an Indian buffer state, or even mastery of the Great Lakes. Canadians fully expected the frustrated Yankees to come again, and for a time the Americans and British engaged in a naval armaments race on the Great Lakes. But in 1817 the Rush-Bagot agreement between Britain and the United States severely limited naval armament on the lakes. Better relations brought the last border fortifications down in the 1870s, with the happy result that the United States and Canada came to share the longest unfortified boundary in the world—5,527 miles (8,899 kilometers) long.

After Napoleon's final defeat at Waterloo in 1815, Europe slumped into a peace of exhaustion. Deposed monarchs returned to battered thrones, as the mother continent took the rutted road back to conservatism, illiberalism, and reaction.

But Americans were largely unaffected by these European developments. Freed from the humiliating side blows of the belligerents, they no longer had to scan the Atlantic horizon for approaching sails—sails that might bring news of impending calamities. Americans thrilled to a new sense of nationality. They were like subject peoples attaining their majority, and for the first time shaking off the shackles of colonialism. Turning their backs on the Old World, they faced resolutely toward the untamed West. Unlike monarchy-cursed Europe, they were ready to take the high road toward democracy, liberalism, and freedom. The steady tramp, tramp, of the westward-moving pioneers became the giant drumbeat of a new destiny.

VARYING VIEWPOINTS

The causes and consequences of the War of 1812 have long sparked spirited debate. Was war the result of western war-hawk expansionism or of British provocations on the high seas? Most recent historians emphasize the naval issue. The young nation's pride and independence, they argue, could not tolerate John Bull's repeated affronts. The Jeffersonian Republicans accepted the need for war because they believed that the future of their party, and indeed of the entire American experiment in republican government, rested on the infant nation's ability to prove that it could meet external challenges.

Perhaps more interestingly, scholars also have seen the first vague outlines of an American identity emerging from the smoke of the War of 1812. Henry Adams's magisterial *History* made this theme a central motif; Adams found evidence of a distinctive American character even in the tactics and techniques of Yankee seamen. The war does appear to have dissolved many localisms and to have begun the forging of a genuine national consciousness—thus paving the way for an upsurge of expansionism and nationalism in the so-called Era of Good Feelings, which is discussed in the next chapter.

SELECT READINGS

Primary Source Documents

See James Madison's "War Message"* (1812), in James D. Richardson, ed., *Messages and Papers of the Presidents* (1896), Vol. I, pp. 500–504; and the protest of thirty-four Federalist congressmen, *Annals of Congress** 12 Cong., I sess., II cols. 2219–2221 (1812). Timothy Dwight offers a participant's view of the opposition to the war in *The History of the Hartford Convention** (1833).

Secondary Sources

An important recent work that sets the War of 1812 in a broad context of early American history is J. C. A. Stagg, *Mr. Madison's War: Politics, Diplomacy and Warfare in the Early American Republic* (1983). On the causes of the war, Julius W. Pratt, *Expansionists of 1812* (1925) stresses western pressures; Bradford Perkins, *Prologue to War: England and the United States, 1805–1812* (1961) and Reginald Horsman, *The Causes of the War of 1812* (1962) discuss free seas; Roger H. Brown, *The Republic in Peril: 1812* (1964) emphasizes the need for saving the republican form of government. The relevant volumes of Henry Adams's nine-volume *History of the United States* (1889–1891) still contain magnificent reading, both on the war and on the peace. Federalist reaction to Republican foreign policy is vividly etched in David H. Fischer, *The Revolution of American Conservatism* (1965) and James M. Banner, *To the Hartford Convention: The Federalists and the Origins of Party Politics in Massachusetts* (1970).

13

The Postwar Upsurge of Nationalism, 1815–1824

> The American continents . . . are henceforth not to be considered as subjects for future colonization by any European powers.
>
> James Monroe, December 2, 1823

Nascent Nationalism

The most impressive by-product of the War of 1812 was a heightened nationalism—the spirit of nation-consciousness or national oneness. America may not have fought the war as one nation, but she emerged one nation.

A weak nationalism had existed since Revolutionary days, but the vibrant new nationalism was composed of many additional ingredients. It sprang partly from pride in recent victories, partly from the setback suffered by Federalist sectionalism and states'-rights-ism, partly from a lessening of economic and political dependence on Europe, and partly from an exulting confidence in the future. Swelling numbers of citizens—although probably not yet a majority—were coming to regard themselves as first of all Americans, and secondarily as citizens of their respective states.

The changed mood even manifested itself in the birth of a distinctively national literature. Washington Irving and James Fenimore Cooper attained international recognition in the 1820s, significantly as the nation's first writers of importance to use American scenes and themes. School textbooks, often British in an earlier era, were now being written by Americans for Americans. In the world of magazines, the highly intellectual *North American Review* saw the light of day in 1815—the year of the triumph at New Orleans. Even American painters increasingly celebrated the glories of American landscapes on their canvases.

A fresh nationalistic spirit could be recognized in many other areas. A more handsome national capital began to rise from the ashes of Washington. The army was expanded to ten thousand men. The navy cov-

132

Washington, D.C., 1824. *This view of the Capitol building, much smaller than it is today, reveals the rustic conditions of the early days in the nation's capital. (Metropolitan Museum of Art, Purchase, 1942, Joseph Pulitzer Bequest)*

ered itself with glory in 1815 when the naval heroes of the late war administered a thorough beating to the piratical plunderers of North Africa. These gratifying victories, inspired by the spirit of nationalism, further inflamed nationalism.

The rising tide of nation-conciousness also touched finance. The War of 1812 demonstrated the folly of permitting the Bank of the United States to expire in 1811, as weak state banks flooded the country with depreciated bank notes. Borrowing Hamiltonian arguments, Republicans in Congress revived the institution in 1816, while the dying Federalist minority denounced it as unconstitutional. The Second Bank of the United States—the "moneyed monster," to its enemies—broadened nationalism as it thrust its numerous branches out across state boundaries.

Tariffs and Internal Improvements

Nationalism likewise manifested itself in manufacturing. Patriotic Americans took pride in the factories that had recently mushroomed forth, largely as a result of the self-imposed embargoes and the war.

When hostilities ended in 1815, British competitors dumped the contents of their bulging warehouses on the United States, often cutting their prices below cost in an effort to strangle the American war-baby factories in the cradle. The infant industries thereupon bawled lustily for protection.

A nationalist Congress, out-Federalizing the old Federalists, responded by passing the pathbreaking Tariff of 1816. The legislators were impressed with the desirability of saving the new industries for the national defense, while at the same time promoting the general welfare. Significantly, the Tariff of 1816 was the first in American history with aims that were primarily protective. Its rates—roughly 20 to 25 percent on the value of dutiable imports—were not high enough to provide completely adequate safeguards, but the law was a bold beginning. A strongly protective trend was started that stimulated the appetites of the protected for more protection.

The battle in Congress over the Tariff of 1816 reflected North-South sectional crosscurrents. Thirty-four-year-old Representative John C. Calhoun of South Carolina—slender, handsome, black-haired, intense, and intellectual—played a stellar role in the debates. A recent war hawk and an ardent nationalist, he supported the tariff bill with all his eloquence and vigor. In 1816 there was some likelihood that the destiny of his native South lay in manufacturing, as well as in the intensive cultivation of cotton. But within a few years Calhoun became a relentless foe of a highly protective tariff. He sadly concluded that it was being used to enrich a few Yankee manufacturers, rather than to build up the economic self-sufficiency and well-being of the entire nation.

Calhoun encountered a worthy adversary in Daniel Webster of New Hampshire, also thirty-four. Stocky, bushy-browed, and dark-haired, "Black Dan" Webster eloquently opposed the highly protective duties of the Tariff of 1816. He took this stand even though he was later to be a zealous nationalist and an ardent champion of high protection. The explanation is simple. Manufacturing in New England had not yet pushed shipping into a back seat, and the shippers of Webster's New Hampshire district feared that a tariff would interfere with their carrying trade. New England, though favoring some protection, was not yet completely willing to exchange the mainsail for the loom—but that day was slowly dawning.

Nationalism was further highlighted by Henry Clay's grandiose plan for developing a profitable home market. Still radiating the nationalism of war hawk days, Clay threw himself behind an elaborate scheme known by 1824 as the American System. This system began with a protective tariff, behind which Eastern manufacturing would flourish. Revenues gushing from the tariff would provide funds for roads and canals, especially in the fast-developing Ohio Valley. Through these new arteries of transportation would flow foodstuffs and raw materials from the South and West to the North and East. In exchange, a stream of manufactured goods would flow in the return direction.

Persistent and eloquent demands by Henry Clay and others for internal improvements struck a responsive chord with the public, especially in the road-poor West. Attempts to invade Canada during the War of 1812 had all failed partly because of oath-provoking roads—or no roads at all.

But attempts to secure federal funding for roads and canals stumbled on Republican constitutional scruples. Congress passed the Bonus Bill in 1817, which would have parceled out $1.5 million from the Second Bank of the United States to the states for internal improvements. But President Madison sternly vetoed the measure as unconstitutional, forcing the individual states to undertake building programs on their own. Jeffersonian Republicans, who had gulped down Hamiltonian loose construction on other important problems, choked on the idea of direct federal support for intrastate internal improvements. They were supported by the turncoat New England Federalists, now strict constructionists, who also opposed federal roads and canals because they would further drain away population to new states beyond the mountains.

The So-Called Era of Good Feelings

James Monroe—6 feet (1.83 meters) tall, somewhat stooped, courtly, and mild-mannered—was nominated for the presidency in 1816 by the Republicans. They thus undertook to continue the so-called Virginia Dynasty of Washington, Jefferson, and Madison. The fading Federalists ran a candidate for the last time in their checkered history, and he was crushed by 183 electoral votes to 34.

The death of the once-proud Federalist party was due to various diseases, shortcomings, and misfortunes. A list would include its disgraceful war record; its inability to choke down the new nationalistic program; and the theft of its tenets by the Jeffersonians. Many Federalists followed their stolen principles into the opposition camp; others gradually crawled away to the political graveyard.

In James Monroe, the man and the times auspiciously met. As the last President to wear an old-style cocked hat, he straddled two generations: the bygone age of the Founding Fathers and the emergent age of nationalism. Never brilliant, and perhaps not great, the serene Virginian with gray-blue eyes was in intellect and personal force among the least distinguished of the first eight Presidents. But the times called for sober administration, not heroics. And Monroe was an experienced, level-headed executive, with an ear-to-the ground talent for interpreting popular rumblings.

President Monroe further cemented emerging nationalism with a goodwill tour in 1817 that took him to New England. The heartwarming welcome he received even in "the enemy's country" ushered in the "Era of Good Feelings," as the Monroe administrations commonly have been called.

The Era of Good Feelings, unfortunately, was something of a misnomer. Considerable tranquility and prosperity did in fact smile upon the early years of Monroe, but the period was a troubled one. The acute issues of the tariff, the Bank, internal improvements, and the sale of public lands were being hotly contested. Sectionalism was crystallizing, and the conflict over slavery was beginning to raise its hideous head.

A vanquished Federalist party was breathing its dying gasps, leaving the field to the triumphant Republicans and one-party rule. But where there is only one party, or where one of the parties enjoys a lopsided majority, the tendency is for factions to develop and fight among themselves. By the early 1820s there was an Era of Inflamed Feelings. Political giants—men like Clay, Calhoun, Jackson, and John Quincy Adams—were elbowing for power and championing the clashing economic interests of their respective sections.

The Panic of 1819 and the Curse of Hard Times

Much of the goodness went out of the good feelings in 1819, when a paralyzing economic panic descended. It brought deflation, depression, bankruptcies, bank failures, unemployment, soup kitchens, and overcrowded pesthouses known as debtors' prisons.

This was the first of the national financial panics since President Washington took office. It was to be followed by a succession of others every twenty or so years, in what seemed an inevitable cycle. Many factors contributed to the catastrophe of 1819, but looming large was overspeculation in frontier lands. The Bank of the United States, through its Western branches, had become deeply involved in this popular type of outdoor gambling.

Financial paralysis from the panic, which lasted in some degree for several years, gave a rude setback to the nationalistic ardor. Various parts of the country tended to drift back toward the old sectionalism, as they concentrated on bailing themselves out. The West was especially hard hit. When the pinch came, the Bank of the United States forced the speculative ("wildcat") western banks to the wall, and foreclosed mortgages on countless farms.

A more welcome child of the panic was fresh legislation for the public domain. The plight of the western farmer, combined with the evils of land speculation, laid bare the defects of the Land Act of 1800, as amended in 1804. By its terms, the pioneer could buy a minimum of 160 acres at $2 an acre over a period of four years, with a down payment of $80. When hard times came, whole communities would default on their installments. An improved Land Act of 1820 lightened the burden somewhat, for it permitted the buyer to secure 80 virgin acres at a minimum of $1.25 an acre in cash—for a total cost of $100. There was less acreage but less outlay.

The Panic of 1819 also created backwashes in the political and social world. It hit especially hard the poorer classes—the one-suspender men—and hence helped cultivate the seedbed of Jacksonian democracy. It also directed attention to the inhumanity of imprisoning debtors. In extreme cases, often overplayed, mothers were torn from their infants for owing a few dollars. Mounting agitation against imprisonment for debt bore fruit in remedial legislation in an increasing number of states.

Growing Pains of the West

Beyond doubt the West, out of which had swooped the war hawks of 1812, was by far the most nationalistic of the sections. Being new, it had no long-established states'-rights tradition. Moreover, it had early learned to lean on the national government, from which it had secured most of its land, directly or indirectly. It was a mixing bowl within the huge American melting pot, for people from all the sections rubbed elbows on the frontier.

Marvelous indeed had been the onward march of the West; nine frontier states had joined the original

Wagons West. *This busy scene on the Frederick Road, leading westward from Baltimore, was typical as pioneers flooded into the newly secured West in the early 1800s. (Maryland Historical Society)*

thirteen between 1791 and 1819. With an eye to preserving the North-South sectional balance, most of these commonwealths had been admitted alternately, free or slave. (See Admission of States, in Appendix.)

Why this explosive expansion? Fundamentally, there was the generations-old westward movement, which had been going on since early colonial days. In addition, the siren call of cheap lands—"the Ohio fever"—had a special appeal to European immigrants. Quaintly garbed newcomers from abroad were beginning to shuffle down the gangplanks in impressive numbers, especially after the war of embargoes and bullets. Land exhaustion in the older tobacco states, where the soil was "mined" rather than cultivated, likewise drove people westward. Glib-tongued speculators, accepting small down payments, made easier the purchase of new holdings.

The western boom was stimulated by additional developments. Acute distress during the embargo years turned many saddened faces toward the setting sun. The crushing of the Indians in the Northwest and South, by Generals Harrison and Jackson, soothed the frontier and opened up vast virgin tracts. The building of highways improved the land routes to

the Ohio Valley. Noteworthy was the Cumberland Road, begun in 1811, which ran ultimately from western Maryland to Illinois. The employment of the first steamboat on western waters, also in 1811, heralded a new era of upstream navigation.

Slavery and Sectional Balance

Sectional tensions were nakedly revealed in 1819, when the territory of Missouri knocked on the doors of Congress for admission as a slave state. This fertile and well-watered area contained sufficient population to warrant statehood. But the House of Representatives threw a monkey wrench into the plans of the Missourians by passing the incendiary Tallmadge amendment. It stipulated that no more slaves should be brought into Missouri, and also provided for the gradual emancipation of children born to slave parents already there. A mounting roar of anger burst from slave-holding Southerners.

Southerners saw in the Tallmadge amendment, which was defeated in the Senate, an ominous threat to the sectional balance. When the Constitution was adopted in 1788, the North and South were running

The Missouri Compromise and Slavery, 1820–1821. *In the 1780s Thomas Jefferson had written of slavery in America: "Indeed I tremble for my country when I reflect that God is just; that his justice cannot sleep forever; that . . . the Almighty has no attribute which can take side with us in such a contest." Now, at the time of the Missouri Compromise, Jefferson feared that his worst forebodings were coming to pass. "I considered it at once," he said of the Missouri question, "as the knell of the Union."*

neck and neck in wealth and population. But with every passing decade the North was becoming wealthier and more thickly settled—an advantage reflected in an increasing Northern majority in the House of Representatives. Yet in the Senate, with eleven states free and eleven slave, the Southerners had maintained equality. They were therefore in a good position to thwart any Northern effort to interfere with the expansion of slavery, and they did not want to lose this veto.

The future of the slave system caused Southerners profound concern. Missouri was the first state entirely west of the Mississippi River to be carved out of the Louisiana Purchase, and the Missouri emancipation amendment might set a damaging precedent for all the rest of the area. Even more disquieting was another possibility. If Congress could abolish the "peculiar institution" in Missouri, might it not attempt to do likewise in the older states of the South? The wounds of the Constitutional Convention of 1787 were once more ripped open.

Burning moral questions also protruded, even though the main issue was political and economic balance. A small but growing group of antislavery agitators in the North seized the occasion to raise an outcry against the evils of slavery. They were determined that the plague of human bondage should not spread further into the virgin territories.

The Uneasy Missouri Compromise

Deadlock in Washington was at length broken in 1820 by the time-honored American solution of compromise—actually a bundle of three compromises. Congress, despite abolitionist pleas, agreed to admit Missouri as a slave state. But at the same time, free-soil Maine, which until then had been a part of Massachusetts, was admitted as a separate state. The balance between North and South was thus kept at twelve states each, and remained there for fifteen years. Although Missouri was permitted to retain slaves, all future bondage was prohibited in the remainder of the Louisiana Purchase north of the line of 36° 30′—the southern boundary of Missouri.

Neither North nor South was acutely displeased, although neither was completely happy. Fortunately, the Missouri Compromise lasted thirty-four years—a vital formative period in the life of the young Republic—and during that time it preserved the shaky unity of the states. Yet the embittered dispute over slavery heralded the future breakup of the Union. Ever after, the morality of the South's "peculiar institution" was an issue that could not be swept under the rug. Sooner or later, Thomas Jefferson predicted, the question of slavery would "burst on us as a tornado."

The Missouri dispute proved to be another serious setback to nationalism and a tremendous stimulus to sectionalism in the North, South, and West. From this time forward the embattled South began to develop a kind of sectional nationalism of its own. Needing sectional reinforcement, it cast flirtatious eyes upon the adolescent West, which was also seeking allies. Meanwhile, with every passing decade, the North was becoming stronger in population, wealth, industry, and transportation—all of which added up to military strength.

Subsequent generations have tended to sneer at the architects of the Missouri solution as weak appeasers. Yet compromise and statesmanship are often Siamese twins. Compromise made the Union in 1789; compromise saved the Union until 1860. When compromise broke down, the Union broke up.

The Missouri Compromise and the Panic of 1819 should have dimmed the political star of President Monroe. But smooth-spoken James Monroe was so popular, and the Federalist opposition so weak, that he received every electoral vote but one in the election of 1820. Unanimity remained an honor reserved for George Washington.

John Marshall and Judicial Nationalism

The upsurging nationalism of the post-Ghent years, despite setbacks, was further reflected and strengthened by the Supreme Court.

The august tribunal was dominated by the tall, thin, and aggressive Chief Justice John Marshall, a "deathbed" Federalist appointee of John Adams's expiring administration. He had served at Valley Forge during the Revolution, and while suffering from cold and hunger, had been painfully impressed with the drawbacks of feeble central authority. Before Marshall mounted the Supreme Court bench in 1801, the judiciary had been the weakest and most timid of the three arms of the federal government. But he boldly asserted the doctrine of judicial review of con-

gressional legislation in the case of *Marbury* v. *Madison* (1803).* And long before the end of his thirty-four years of service, he had made the judiciary, in some respects, the strongest branch of the national government.

Marshall, whose formal legal schooling had lasted only six weeks, was a judicial statesman rather than a strictly impartial judge. He examined a case through the colored lenses of his Federalist philosophy, and undertook to find legal precedents to support his Hamiltonian preconceptions. Sure of his ground, he wrote some of his most important decisions even before the lawyers had concluded their arguments.

For over three decades, the ghost of Alexander Hamilton spoke through the lanky, black-robed judge. As a shaper of the Constitution in the direction of a more potent central government, Marshall ranks as the foremost of the Molding Fathers. As a wealthy businessman and land speculator, he instinctively shared Hamilton's preference for the propertied class. As a Virginia aristocrat, he deplored democratic excesses, and opposed universal manhood suffrage and the rule of the unwashed masses.

The Supreme Court Curbs States' Rights

One group of Marshall's decisions—perhaps the most famous—resulted in bolstering the power of the federal government at the expense of the states. A notable case in this category was *McCulloch* v. *Maryland* (1819). The suit involved an attempt by the state of Maryland to destroy a branch of the Bank of the United States by imposing a tax on its notes. John Marshall, speaking for the Court, declared the Bank constitutional by invoking the Hamiltonian doctrine of implied powers (see pp. 84–85). At the same time, he strengthened federal authority and slapped at state infringements when he denied the right of Maryland to tax the Bank. With ringing emphasis, he affirmed "that the power to tax involves the power to destroy,"

---

*See p. 112.

and "that a power to create implies a power to preserve."

Marshall's ruling on this case gave the doctrine of "loose construction" its most famous formulation. The Constitution, he said, derived from the consent of the people, and thus permitted the government to act for their benefit. He further argued that the Constitution was "intended to endure for ages to come and, consequently, to be adapted to the various crises of human affairs." Finally, he declared: "Let the end be legitimate, let it be within the scope of the Constitution, and all means which are appropriate, which are plainly adapted to that end, which are not prohibited, but consist with the letter and spirit of the Constitution, are constitutional."

Two years later (1821) the case of *Cohens* v. *Virginia* gave Marshall one of his greatest opportunities. The Cohens, found guilty by the Virginia courts of illegally selling lottery tickets, appealed to the highest tribunal. Virginia won, in that the conviction of the Cohens was upheld. But she lost, in that Marshall resoundingly asserted the right of the Supreme Court to review the decisions of the state supreme courts in all questions involving powers of the federal government. The states' rights people were aghast.

Hardly less significant in Marshall's career was the celebrated "steamboat case," *Gibbons* v. *Ogden* (1824). The suit grew out of an attempt by the state of New York to grant to a private concern a monopoly of waterborne commerce between New York and New Jersey. Marshall sternly reminded the upstart state that the Constitution conferred on Congress alone the control of interstate commerce (see Art. I, Sec. VIII, para. 3). He thus struck another blow at states' rights, while upholding the sovereign powers of the federal government. Interstate streams were thus cleared of this judicial snag, while the departed spirit of Hamilton may have applauded.

Judicial Dikes Against Democratic Excesses

Another sheaf of Marshall's decisions bolstered judicial barriers against democratic or demagogic attacks on property rights.

The notorious case of *Fletcher* v. *Peck* (1810) arose when a Georgia legislature, swayed by bribery,

granted 35 million acres in the Yazoo River country (present-day Mississippi) to private speculators. The next legislature, yielding to an angry public outcry, canceled the crooked transaction. But the Supreme Court, with Marshall presiding, decreed that the legislative grant was a contract (even though fraudulently secured), and that the Constitution forbids state laws "impairing" contracts (Art. I, Sec. X, para. 1). The decision is perhaps most noteworthy as further protecting property rights against popular pressures. It is also one of the earliest clear assertions of the right of the Court to invalidate state laws conflicting with the federal Constitution.

A similar principle was upheld in the case of *Dartmouth College* v. *Woodward* (1819), perhaps the best-remembered of Marshall's decisions. The college had been granted a charter by King George III in 1769, but the democratic New Hampshire state legislature had seen fit to change it. Marshall put the states firmly in their place when he ruled that the original charter must stand. It was a contract, and the Constitution protected contracts against state encroachments. The Dartmouth decision had the fortunate effect of safeguarding business enterprise from domination by the states. But it had the unfortunate effect of creating a precedent which enabled chartered corporations, in later years, to escape the handcuffs of needed public control.

Marshall's decisions are felt even today. In this sense his nationalism was the most tenaciously enduring of the era. Even after the masses had won control under President Andrew Jackson, they could not successfully assault the highest towers of the judicial fortress. While buttressing the federal union and nascent nationalism, Marshall checked the excesses of popularly elected state legislatures, and thus stabilized business. Through him the conservative Hamiltonians triumphed from the tomb.

Sharing Oregon and Acquiring Florida

The yeasty nationalism of the years after the War of 1812 was likewise reflected in foreign policy. To this end, the nationalistic President Monroe teamed with his nationalistic secretary of state, John Quincy Adams, the cold and scholarly son of the frosty and bookish ex-President. The younger Adams, a statesman of the first rank, happily rose above the ingrown Federalist sectionalism of his native New England and proved to be one of the great secretaries of state.

To its credit, the Monroe administration negotiated the much-underrated Treaty of 1818 with England. This multisided agreement permitted Americans to share the coveted Newfoundland fisheries with their Canadian cousins. It also fixed the vague northern limits of Louisiana along the forty-ninth parallel from the Lake of the Woods to the Rocky Mountains. The treaty further provided for a ten-year joint occupation of the untamed Oregon country, without a surrender of the rights or claims of either America or Britain.

To the south lay semitropical Spanish Florida, which many Americans believed geography and providence had destined to become part of the United States. Americans already claimed West Florida, where uninvited American settlers had torn down the hated Spanish flag in 1810. Congress ratified this grab in 1812, and during the War of 1812, a small American army seized the Mobile region. But the great bulk of Florida remained, tauntingly, under Spanish rule.

When an epidemic of revolutions broke out in South America, Spain was forced to denude Florida of troops to fight the rebels. With Spanish authority weakened, bands of Indians, runaway slaves, and white outcasts raided across the border into American territory and then fled to safety behind the surveyor's line.

General Andrew Jackson, idol of the West and scourge of the Indians, reappeared in 1817. The Monroe administration formally commissioned him to punish the Indians, and, if necessary, to pursue them into Florida. But he was to respect all posts under the Spanish flag.

Early in 1818 Jackson swept across the Florida border with all the fury of an avenging angel. He hanged two Indian chiefs without ceremony and, after hasty military trials, executed two British subjects for assisting the Indians. He also seized the most important Spanish posts in the area, St. Marks and Pensacola, and deposed the Spanish governor.

Jackson had clearly exceeded his instructions from Washington. Alarmed, President Monroe consulted his cabinet. Its members were for disavowing or disciplining the overzealous Jackson—all except the lone wolf John Quincy Adams, who refused to howl with the pack. An ardent nationalist, the flinty New Englander took the offensive and won the others over to his point of view. He emphatically told the Spanish that their alternatives were to control the area or cede it to the United States.

Distressed in Latin America and at home, and believing that they were going to lose Spanish Florida in any case, the Spanish decided to dispose of the alligator-infested area while they could still get something for it. In the mislabeled Florida Purchase Treaty of 1819, Spain ceded Florida as well as shadowy Spanish claims to Oregon, in exchange for America's abandonment of equally shadowy claims to Texas, soon to become part of independent Mexico. The hitherto vague western boundary of Louisiana was made to run zigzag along the Rockies to the forty-second parallel and then to turn due west to the Pacific, dividing Oregon from Spanish holdings.

The Menace of Monarchy in America

After the Napoleonic nightmare, the rethroned autocrats of Europe banded together in a kind of monarchical protective association. Determined to restore the good old days, they undertook to stamp out the democratic tendencies that had sprouted from soil richly manured by the ideals of the French Revolution. The world must be made safe *from* democracy.

The crowned despots acted promptly. With complete ruthlessness, they smothered the embers of rebellion in Italy (1821) and in Spain (1823). According to the European rumor-factory, they were also gazing across the Atlantic. Russia, Austria, Prussia, and France, acting in partnership, would presumably send powerful fleets and armies to the revolted colonies of Spanish America, and there restore the autocratic Spanish king to his ancestral domains.

Many Americans were alarmed. Sympathetic to democratic revolutions everywhere, they had cheered when the Latin American republics rose from the ruins of monarchy. Americans feared that if the European powers intervened in the New World, the cause of republicanism would suffer irreparable harm. The

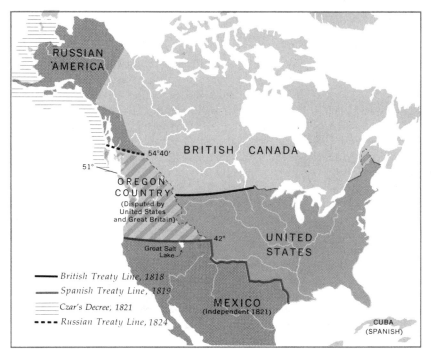

The West and Northwest, 1819–1824. *The British Hudson's Bay Company moved to secure its claim to the Oregon country in 1824, when it sent a heavily armed expedition led by Peter Skene Ogden into the Snake River country. In May, 1825, Ogden's party descended the Weber River, "and found it discharged into a large Lake of 100 miles in length." This was the Great Salt Lake, which had been sighted eight years earlier by American trapper Jim Bridger.*

physical security of the United States—the mother lode of democracy—would be endangered by the proximity of powerful and unfriendly forces.

The southward push of the Russian bear, from the chill region now known as Alaska, had already publicized the menace of monarchy to North America. In 1821 the Czar of Russia issued a decree extending Russian jurisdiction over 100 miles (161 kilometers) of the open sea down to the line of 51°, an area which embraced most of the coast of present-day British Columbia. The energetic Russians had already established trading posts almost as far south as the entrance to San Francisco Bay, and the fear prevailed in the United States that they were planning to cut the republic off from California, its prospective window on the Pacific.

Great Britain, still Mistress of the Seas, was now beginning to play a lone-hand role on the complicated international stage. In particular, it recoiled from joining hands with the continental European powers in crushing the newly won liberties of the Spanish-Americans. These revolutionists had thrown open their monopoly-bound ports to outside trade, and British shippers, as well as Americans, had found the profits sweet.

Accordingly, in August 1823, George Canning, the haughty British foreign secretary, approached the American minister in London with a startling proposition. Would not the United States join with Britain in a joint declaration, specifically warning the European despots to keep their harsh hands off the Latin American republics? The American minister, lacking instructions, referred this fateful scheme to his superiors in Washington.

Mr. Monroe and His Doctrine

Reactions in America to the Canning proposal varied. The intimate advisers of President Monroe, including the aged Jefferson and Madison, recommended that the republic lock arms with the hitherto distrusted mother country. The one notable exception was again the lone-wolf nationalist, Secretary Adams, who was hardheaded enough to beware of Britons bearing gifts. Why should the lordly British, with the mightiest navy afloat, need America as an ally—an America which had neither naval nor military strength? Such a union, argued Adams, was undignified—like a tiny American "cockboat" sailing "in the wake of the British man-of-war."

The ever-alert Adams thought he detected a joker in the Canning proposal. If Canning could seduce the United States into supporting existing territorial arrangements in the New World, America's hands would be morally tied against expansion into Cuba or Britain's Caribbean possessions. Suspecting that European powers had no definite plans for invading the Americas, and knowing that the British navy would not permit hostile fleets to interfere with South American markets, Adams decided it was safe for Uncle Sam to blow a defiant nationalistic blast at all Europe.

The Monroe Doctrine was born late in 1823, when the nationalistic Adams won the nationalistic Monroe over to his way of thinking. The President, in his regular annual message to Congress of December 2, 1823, incorporated a stern warning to the European powers. Its two basic features were (1) noncolonization and (2) nonintervention.

Monroe first directed his verbal blast primarily at the lumbering Russian bear in the Northwest. With emphatic tones he proclaimed, in effect, that the era of colonization in the Americas had ended, and that henceforth there would be a permanently closed season. What the great powers had they might keep, but neither they nor any other Old World powers could seize or otherwise acquire more.

At the same time Monroe sounded a trumpet blast against foreign intervention. He was clearly concerned with regions to the south, where fears were felt for the newly fledged Spanish-American republics. He bluntly warned the crowned heads of Europe to keep their hated monarchical systems out of this hemisphere. For its part, the United States would not intervene in the war that the Greeks were then fighting against the Turks for their independence.

Monroe's Dictum Appraised

Monroe's ringing declaration quickened the patriotic pulse of nationalistic young America. The American people were thrilled, even though they had no effective army or navy, to shake their collective fists at all the European despots and loudly warn them to stay away. While gratifying national pride and striking a blow for democratic rule, Monroe was also striking a blow for the "Almighty Dollar," as represented by the freshly opened Latin American markets.

Reactions in England were mixed. The British press, likewise savoring the juicy Latin American markets, was generally favorable to Monroe's forceful warning. But Canning was irked, for he perceived that the Monroe Doctrine was aimed at possible land-grabbing by Britain, as well as by Europe. "Hands off" applied to all outside powers, including proud Britain.

The ermined monarchs of Europe were angered. Having resented the incendiary American experiment from the beginning, they were now deeply offended by Monroe's high-flown pronouncement—all the more so because of the gulf between America's loud pretensions and her weak military strength. But though offended by the upstart Yankee, the European powers found their hands tied, and their frustration increased their annoyance. Even if they had worked out plans for invading the Americas, they would have been helpless before the booming broadsides of the British navy.

Monroe's solemn warning, when issued, made little splash in the newly hatched republics to the south. Anyone could see that Uncle Sam was only secondarily concerned about his neighbors, because he was primarily concerned about defending himself against future invasion. Only a relatively few upper-class Latin Americans knew of the message, and they generally recognized that the British navy—not the paper pronouncement of James Monroe—stood between them and a hostile Europe.

In truth, Monroe's message actually did not have very much contemporary significance. Americans applauded it, and then forgot it as they turned back to such activities as felling trees and fighting Indians. Not until 1845 did President Polk revive it, and not until midcentury did it become an important national dogma.

The Monroe Doctrine might more accurately have been called the Self-Defense Doctrine. President Monroe was concerned basically with the security of his own country—not of Latin America. The United States has never willingly permitted a powerful foreign nation to secure a foothold near its strategic Caribbean vitals. Yet in the absence of the British navy or other allies, the strength of the Monroe Doctrine has never been greater than America's power to eject the trespasser. The doctrine, as often noted, was only as strong as the nation's armed forces—and no stronger. But attaching Monroe's name to the Self-Defense Doctrine has given it the prestige that comes from a distinguished personage.

The Monroe Doctrine has had a long career of ups and downs. It was never law—domestic or international. It was not, technically speaking, a pledge or an agreement. It was merely a simple, personalized statement of the policy of President Monroe.

But the Monroe Doctrine in 1823 was largely an expression of the post-1812 nationalism energizing the United States. Although directed at a specific menace in 1823, and hence a kind of period piece, the doctrine proved to be the most famous of all the long-lived offspring of that nationalism. While giving vent to a spirit of patriotism, it simultaneously deepened the illusion of isolationism. Many Americans falsely concluded, then and later, that the republic was in fact isolated from European dangers simply because it wanted to be, and because, in a nationalistic outburst, Monroe had publicly warned the Old World powers to stay out of what America was coming to regard as her New World domain.

VARYING VIEWPOINTS

The Era of Good Feelings, at first, generated little ill feeling among historians. They generally agreed in seeing the period in terms not of conflict but of consolidation. There were then few irreconcilable controversies, but rather a remarkable consensus on laying the new nation's institutional base. In effect, the era set up a political program for the future; defined the power of the Supreme Court and its relation to the other branches of government; stabilized national boundaries; and established basic elements of foreign policy in the Monroe Doctrine.

Recently, historians have uncovered the smoldering tensions seething under the calm surface of the period. One-party rule masked deep divisions over economic and sectional issues that would soon erupt into bitter struggles over the tariff, expansion, and especially, slavery. The tenuous Missouri Compromise revealed the fragility of the era's buoyant nationalism.

SELECT READINGS

Primary Source Documents

See James Madison's "War Message"* (1812), in James D. Richardson, ed., *Messages and Papers of the Presidents* (1896), Vol. I, pp. 500–504; and the protest of thirty-four Federalist congressmen, *Annals of Congress** 12 Cong., I sess., II cols. 2219–2221 (1812). Timothy Dwight offers a participant's view of the opposition to the war in *The History of the Hartford Convention** (1833).

Secondary Sources

An excellent introduction is George Dangerfield, *The Awakening of American Nationalism, 1815–1828* (1965), which supplements his *Era of Good Feelings* (1952). Perry

Miller, *The Life of the Mind in America* (1965) contains suggestive insights on legal thought and the role of the legal profession in the Marshall era. This and other topics are astutely placed in context by Lawrence Friedman in *A History of American Law* (1973). George R. Taylor's classic *Transportation Revolution* (1955) remains a valuable source on that subject. Glover Moore, *The Missouri Controversy, 1819–1821* (1953) and Charles S. Sydnor, *The Development of Southern Sectionalism, 1819–1848* (1948) place the Missouri Compromise in a broader context. On the Monroe Doctrine, the best single volume is Dexter Perkins, *A History of the Monroe Doctrine* (1955).

14

The Rise of
Jacksonian Democracy

**The most disagreeable duty I have to perform is the removals, and appointments
to office. . . . You will see from the public journals we have begun reform,
and that we are trying to cleans[e] the Augean stables, and expose to view
the corruption of some of the agents of the late administration.**

Andrew Jackson, 1829

Politics for the People

Democracy was something of a taint in the days of the lordly Federalists. But by the 1820s, if not before, aristocracy was becoming a taint, and democracy was becoming respectable. Politicians were now forced to unbend and curry favor with the voting masses. Lucky indeed was the aspiring office seeker who could boast of birth in a log cabin. A semiliterate frontiersman like Tennesseean Davy Crockett could be elected to Congress mainly on the basis of his bear-hunting prowess. Even the wealthy and prominent citizens who continued to fill most high offices had to forsake all social pretensions and cultivate the common touch if they hoped to win elections.

Jeffersonian democracy had proclaimed that the people should be governed as little as possible; Jacksonian democracy now added that whatever govern-ing was to be done should be done directly by the people. The common man was at last moving to the center of the national political stage. Instead of the old divine right of kings, America was now witnessing the divine right of the people.

The New Democracy, so called, was based on universal white manhood suffrage rather than the old property qualifications. The frontier state of Vermont, admitted to the Union in 1791, was the first to allow all adult white males to vote. This trend continued, notably in the West, where land was so easily obtained as to render almost meaningless the old property qualifications. Property tests for officehold-ing were also widely abolished, and even judges were now being popularly elected. The South trailed other regions in giving up property requirements, but it,

The New Politics. *Politicians in the Jacksonian era had to take their message to the common man, as shown in this painting by George Caleb Bingham. (Nelson-Atkins Museum of Art, Kansas City, Missouri, Nelson Fund)*

too, eventually extended suffrage and the right to hold office to all white men.

Nourishing the New Democracy

What caused this lush flowering of political democracy? In part it was simply the logical outgrowth of the egalitarian ideas that had taken root in colonial days and been lavishly fertilized during the Revolutionary era. More immediately, the panic of 1819 and the Missouri Compromise of 1820 rank high on the list of the New Democracy's nutrients.

The economic downturn was blamed by many workers and farmers on banking irregularities and speculation. In particular, the panic nurtured burning resentment at the government-granted privileges of the banks. While debt-ridden farmers often lost their farms to foreclosure, overextended bankers protected their property by simply suspending payment on their bank notes and leaving their customers holding worthless paper. Such practices reeked of favor-

itism and seemed to mock the democratic principles of equality and fair play. The desire to purge the land of this sort of "corruption" and restore the republican ideals of Jefferson's day invigorated the interest of many Americans in politics—especially the followers of Andrew Jackson. They sought control of government in order to tear the banks from its protective embrace, to substitute hard money for bank notes, and even to abolish the banks altogether. Opposed to the Jacksonians were those persons who favored the current banking system and, more generally, who believed that the federal government had a legitimate role to play in promoting economic growth.

The Missouri Compromise likewise awakened many Americans, especially white southerners, to the importance of politics. The spectacle of organized northern resistance to admission of Missouri as a slave state aroused fears in the white South about further federal aggressions against states' rights—especially the right to perpetuate slavery. Many white southerners became involved in politics in order to prevent that result.

Economic distress and the slavery issue together raised the political stakes in the 1820s, ushering in a whole new chapter in the history of American politics. The deference, apathy, and virtually nonexistent party organizations of the Era of Good Feelings gave way to the boisterous democracy, frenzied vitality, and strong political parties of the Jacksonian era. Voter turnout rose dramatically, from about 25 percent of eligible voters in the presidential election of 1824 to 78 percent in the election of 1840. A new style of politicking emerged, as candidates made increasing use of banners, badges, parades, barbecues, free drinks, and baby kissing in an effort to "get out the vote." The old suspicion of political parties as illegitimate disrupters of society's natural harmony was replaced by an acceptance of the sometimes wild contentiousness of political life. Vigorous political conflict even came to be celebrated as necessary for the health of democracy.

Everywhere the people flexed their political muscles. To an increasing degree, members of the Electoral College were being chosen directly by the people, rather than by state legislatures. Presidential nominations by a secret congressional caucus were now condemned as furtive, elitist, and subversive of democracy. Crying "Down with King Caucus," the voters in 1824 turned against the candidate (Crawford) who had been selected by the congressional clique. A search developed for a more democratic method of nominating presidential candidates. For a brief period nominations were made by some of the state legislatures. But these did not seem democratic either, and in 1831 the first of the circus-like national nominating conventions was held (by the short-lived but significant Anti-Masonic party). Here the people appeared to exercise greater control, though their will was often thwarted by paunchy bosses in smoke-filled rooms.

The Adams-Clay "Corrupt" Bargaining

The woods were full of presidential timber in 1824. Four candidates towered above the others: Andrew Jackson of Tennessee, the tall, silver-maned, and hollow-cheeked "Old Hero" of New Orleans; Henry Clay of Kentucky, the gamy and gallant "Harry of the West"; William H. Crawford of Georgia, a giant of a man, able but ailing; and John Quincy Adams of Massachusetts, highly intelligent, experienced, and aloof.

All four rivals professed to be "Republicans." Well-organized parties had not yet emerged, as illustrated by the fact that John C. Calhoun appeared as the vice-presidential candidate on both the Adams and the Jackson tickets.

The results of the noisy campaign were interesting but confusing. Jackson, the war hero, clearly had the strongest personal appeal, especially in the West. Foreshadowing the themes that would later shape his presidency, his campaign appealed for the salvation of republicanism from the forces of corruption and privilege in government. He polled nearly as many popular votes as his next two rivals combined, but he failed to win a majority of the electoral vote. In such a deadlock the House of Representatives, as directed by the Twelfth Amendment (see the Appendix), must choose among the top three candidates. Clay was thus eliminated, yet as a popular Speaker of the House, he was in a position to throw the election to the candidate of his choice.

Clay reached his fateful decision by a process of elimination. Crawford, recently felled by a paralytic stroke, was out of the picture. Clay hated the "military chieftain" Jackson, who in turn bitterly resented Clay's public denunciation of his Florida foray in 1818. The only candidate left was the puritanical Adams, with whom Clay—a free-living gambler and duelist—had never established cordial personal relations. But the two men had much in common politically: both were fervid nationalists and advocates of the American System. Shortly before the final ballot in the House, Clay met privately with Adams and assured him of his support.

Decision day came early in 1825. The House of Representatives met amid tense excitement, with sick members being carried in on stretchers. On the first ballot, thanks largely to Clay's behind-the-scenes influence, Adams was elected president. A few days later, the victor announced that Henry Clay would be the new secretary of state.

Masses of angered Jacksonians roared in protest against the "Corrupt Bargain." Jackson condemned

Election of 1824

Candidates	Electoral Vote	Popular Vote	Popular Percentage
Jackson	99	153,544	42.16%
Adams	84	108,740	31.89
Crawford	41	46,618	12.95
Clay	37	47,136	12.99

Clay as the "Judas of the West," and John Randolph of Virginia said of Clay, "He shines and stinks like . . . a rotten mackerel by moonlight." No positive evidence has yet been unearthed to prove that Adams and Clay entered into a formal bargain, corrupt or otherwise. But appearances were so damning as to render denials unconvincing.

A Yankee Misfit in the White House

John Quincy Adams was a chip off the old family glacier. Short (5 feet 7 inches; 1.7 meters), thickset, and billiard-bald, he was even more frigidly austere than his presidential father, John Adams. Shunning people, he often went for early morning swims, sometimes stark naked, in the then-pure Potomac River. Essentially a closeted thinker rather than a politician, he was irritable, sarcastic, and tactless. Yet few men have ever come to the presidency with a more brilliant record in statecraft, especially in foreign affairs. He ranks as one of the most successful secretaries of state, yet one of the least successful Presidents.

A man of puritanical honor, Adams entered upon his four-year "sentence" in the White House smarting under charges of "bargain," "corruption," and "usurpation." Fewer than one-third of the voters had voted for him. As the first "minority President," he would have found it difficult to win popular support even under the most favorable conditions. Possessing almost none of the arts of the politician, he had achieved high office by commanding respect rather than by courting popularity. In an earlier era, an aloof John Adams could win the votes of propertied men by sheer ability. But with the raw New Democracy in the driver's seat, his cold-fish son could hardly hope for success at the polls.

The old Jeffersonian Republican party was breaking into fragments, most of which tended to coalesce around a common hatred of the Adams-Clay partnership. The flinty President refused to recognize that the popular tide was turning away from the post-Ghent nationalism toward states' rights and sectionalism. Confirmed nationalist that he was, Adams urged upon Congress in his first annual message the construction of roads and canals. He renewed George Washington's proposal for a national university, and went so far as to advocate a federal astronomical observatory.

The public reaction to these proposals was prompt and unfavorable. To many workaday Americans grubbing out stumps, astronomical observatories seemed like a scandalous waste of public funds. The South, in particular, bristled up, reasoning that if the federal government could meddle in local concerns like education and roads, it might try to lay its hand on the "peculiar institution" of black slavery. If it took on such heavy financial burdens, it would have to continue the hated tariff duties.

The Tricky "Tariff of Abominations"

The touchy tariff issue became one of Adams's biggest headaches. Congress had increased the general tariff in 1824, from about 23 percent on dutiable goods to about 37 percent. But wool manufacturers, dissatisfied with their share of protection, bleated for still-higher barriers.

Rabid Jacksonites, seeking to unhorse Adams, proposed a politically designed bill that would push duties as high as 45 percent on manufactured items and impose a heavy duty on certain raw materials, notably wool. They thought that New Englanders, who needed these materials, would vote against the entire measure, thus giving Adams a political black eye and boosting Jackson. But the New Englanders were so eager to preserve the principle of protection that they voted to swallow the whole measure. Daniel Webster, who had earlier fought the mild Tariff of 1816, and John C. Calhoun, who had sponsored it, had by this time completely reversed their positions. They and others now clearly saw that the future of New England lay in the factory, rather than on the waves, while the destiny of the South lay in the cotton fields.

Southerners, as heavy consumers of manufactured goods, were shocked by what they regarded as the outrageous rates of the Tariff of 1828. Hotheads promptly branded it the "Tariff of Abominations," and several southern states adopted formal protests.

Why did the South, especially South Carolina, react so angrily against the tariff? Underlying the southern outcry were growing anxieties about possible federal interference with the institution of slavery. The congressional debate on the Missouri Compromise had kindled those anxieties, and they were further fed by an ominous slave rebellion in Charleston in 1822, led by a free black, Denmark Vesey. The South Carolinians, still closely tied to the British West Indies, also knew full well how their slaveowning West Indian cousins were feeling the mounting pressure that British abolitionists were putting on the London government. Abolitionism in America might similarly use the power of the government in Washington to suppress slavery in the South. If so, now was the time, and the tariff was the issue, for taking a strong stand on principle against all federal encroachments on states' rights.

Nearer the surface was the real economic distress of the Old South—the seaboard area first settled. It was now the least flourishing of all the sections. Overcropped acres of the Old South were petering out, and the price of cotton was falling sharply. Southerners were seeking a scapegoat for their economic distress, but there was also a sound basis for their belief that the "Yankee tariff" discriminated against them. They sold their cotton and other farm produce in a world market completely unprotected by tariffs and were forced to buy their manufactured goods in an American market heavily protected by tariffs.

The plight of the South may be illustrated by a hypothetical case. Suppose that in 1828 an English manufacturer sold shoes in South Carolina at $1.25 a pair, whereas a Massachusetts shoemaker, paying higher wages, would have to charge $1.50 for a pair of equal quality. South Carolinians would naturally buy the British footwear. But if a tariff of $0.50 a pair were levied on foreign shoes at the Charleston customshouse, the British shoes would cost $1.75 a pair. The Massachusetts shoemaker could safely raise the price to anything less than $1.75—say, $1.74—and still undercut the British competitor by selling the

cheapest shoes in South Carolina. South Carolinians would thus be forced to pay higher prices, while the profits of the Yankee manufacturer were commensurately fattened.

The South also objected to other consequences of lowered tariffs. If higher prices led Americans to buy fewer English textiles, the British would in turn buy less southern cotton with which to make the textiles. Southerners thus would suffer both as consumers and producers, as importers and exporters.

South Carolinians took the lead in protesting against the "Tariff of Abominations." Their legislature went so far as to publish in 1828, though without formal endorsement, a pamphlet known as "The South Carolina Exposition." It had been secretly written by John C. Calhoun, one of the few top-flight political theorists ever produced by America. (As Vice-President, he was forced to conceal his authorship.) "The Exposition" boldly denounced the recent tariff as unjust and unconstitutional. Going a stride beyond the Kentucky and Virginia resolutions of 1798, it bluntly proposed that the states should nullify the tariff—that is, declare it null and void within their borders.

Calhoun found himself caught in an awkward straddle. Still a Unionist and a nationalist, he was also a Southern sectionalist. He therefore desperately sought a formula that would protect the minority in the South from the "tyranny of the majority" in the North and West. Seizing upon nullification, he undertook by this explosive device to preserve the Union and prevent secession. Calhoun's intention was to salvage the Union by quieting the fears of those forces that might destroy it, even though nullification, if implemented, would have undermined the constitutional powers of the federal government.

Calhoun's "Exposition," at least immediately, was a false alarm. No other state joined South Carolina in her heated antitariff protest. But the disruptive theory of nullification was further publicized, foreshadowing the even more dangerous doctrine of secession. South Carolina was not then prepared to force the controversy to a showdown. The election of Carolina-born Andrew Jackson to the presidency had occurred two weeks earlier, and the "Old Hero"—a fellow cotton planter and slaveowner—was expected to sympathize with the plight of the South.

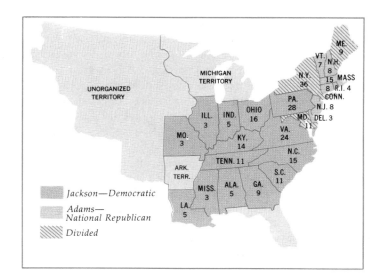

Presidential Election of 1828 (with electoral vote by state).   *Note that Jackson swept the South and West, while Adams retained the old Federalist stronghold of the Northeast. Yet Jackson's inroads in the Northeast were decisive. He won 20 of New York's electoral votes, and all 28 of Pennsylvania's. If those votes had gone the other way, Adams would have been victorious—by a margin of one vote.*

Map legend: Jackson—Democratic; Adams—National Republican; Divided

Going "Whole Hog" for Jackson in 1828

The presidential campaign for Andrew Jackson had started early. It began on February 9, 1825, the day of John Quincy Adams's election by the House, and continued noisily for nearly four years.

Even before the election of 1828, the temporarily united Republicans of the Era of Good Feelings had split into two camps. One was the National Republicans, with the ultra-nationalistic Adams as their leader. The other was the Democratic-Republicans, with the fiery Jackson heading their ticket.

"Shall the people rule?" was the chief issue of 1828, at least to Jacksonians. They argued that the will of the voters had been thwarted in 1825 by the back-stairs "bargain" of Adams and Clay. The only way to right the wrong was to seat Jackson, who would then bring about "reform" by sweeping out the "dishonest" Adams gang.

Mudslinging reached a disgraceful level, partly as a result of the taste of the new mass electorate for bare-knuckle politics. Adams would not resort to gutter tactics, but his backers were less squeamish. They described Jackson's mother as a prostitute, recounted his numerous duels and his hanging of six militiamen, and branded him an adulterer for marrying his wife Rachel before her divorce was officially granted.

Jackson men also hit below the belt. They turned Adams's White House billiard tables into "gambling furniture" in the "presidential palace," mocked Adams's long service on the federal payroll, and even accused him of serving as a pimp to a lusty Russian nobleman while on duty as minister to Russia.

When the nasty campaign was over, General Jackson was as victorious at the ballot box as he had been on the battlefield. The popular tally was 647,286 votes for him to 508,064 for Adams, with an electoral count of 178 to 83. Support for Jackson came mainly from the West and South, and to a considerable extent from the sweat-stained laborers of the eastern seaboard. Generally speaking, the common people—though by no means all of them—voted for the Hero of New Orleans. Adams won the backing of his own New England and the propertied "better elements" of the Northeast.

The election of 1828 has often been called the "Revolution of 1828." Actually, as in 1800, there was no upheaval or landslide that swept out the incumbent. But the concept of a *political* revolution in 1828 is not completely farfetched. It was a peaceful revolution, achieved by ballots instead of bullets, by counting heads instead of crushing them. In the struggle between the poorer masses and the entrenched classes, the homespun folk scored a resounding triumph. America hitherto had been ruled by an elite of brains and wealth, whether aristocratic Federalist shippers or aristocratic Jeffersonian planters. Jackson's victory accelerated the transfer of national power from the countinghouse to the farmhouse, from the East to the West, and from the snobs to the mobs. The plowholders were now ready to take over the government—their government.

The Advent of "Old Hickory" Jackson

Andrew Jackson cut a striking figure—tall (6 feet 1 inch; 1.86 meters), gaunt, and with bushy iron-gray hair brushed high above a prominent forehead, craggy eyebrows, and blue eyes. His irritability and emaciated condition (140 pounds; 64 kilograms) probably had resulted in part from longterm bouts with dysentery, malaria, tuberculosis, and lead poisoning from two bullets that he carried in his body from near-fatal duels. His autobiography was largely written in his lined face.

To a considerable degree, Jackson personified the New West. He reflected its individualism, its Jack-of-all-trades versatility, its opportunism, its energy, its directness, and its prejudices. He was a genuine folk hero—an uncommon common man. Born in the Carolinas and early orphaned, "Mischievous Andy" grew up without parental restraints. As a youth, he displayed much more interest in brawling and cockfighting than in his scanty opportunities for reading and spelling. Although he ultimately learned to express himself in writing with vigor and clarity, his grammar was always rough-hewn and his spelling was often original.

The youthful Carolinian had the foresight to emigrate "up West" to Tennessee, where a fighting man was more highly regarded than a writing man. There—through native intelligence, force of personality, and powers of leadership—he became a judge and a member of Congress. His passions were so terrible that on occasion he would choke into silence when he tried to speak. He won his greatest fame as a commander of militia troops, who dubbed him "Old Hickory" in honor of his toughness. Afflicted with a violent temper, he early became involved in numerous duels, stabbings, and other bloody frays. But, rough and forthright as democracy itself, he made things happen.

The first President from the West, and the first without a college education, except Washington, Jackson was unique. His university was adversity. He had risen from the masses, but he was not one of them, except insofar as he shared many of their prejudices. Essentially a frontier aristocrat, he owned many slaves, cultivated broad acres, and lived in one of the finest mansions in America—the Hermitage, near Nashville, Tennessee.

As befitted an authentic man of the people and hero of the "one-suspender" common man, Jackson's political ideas had a stark simplicity. He considered the federal government a bastion of privilege dangerously removed from popular scrutiny, and was therefore determined to reduce it "to that simple machine which the Constitution created." This meant, among other things, hostility to the active federal economic role envisioned in Henry Clay's American System. Conversely, he and especially his followers were generally friendly toward the frothy democracy bubbling up in the states and looked with some favor on economic activism on the part of state government.

While President, Jackson proved to be a storm center. As a former military man, he demanded prompt and loyal support from his subordinates. Cherishing strong ideas as to his constitutional prerogatives, he ignored the Supreme Court on several conspicuous occasions. He likewise defied or dominated Congress as few Presidents have done. His six predecessors had wielded the veto ten times; during his two terms he employed it twelve times, sometimes on grounds of personal distaste rather than constitutional principle. Jackson's modest use of the veto ax was perfectly legitimate, but his numerous enemies condemned him as "King Andrew the First."

Jackson's inauguration symbolized the newly won ascendancy of the masses. "Hickoryites" poured into Washington from far places, sleeping on hotel floors or in hallways. They were curious to see their hero take office, and perhaps to pick up a well-paying office for themselves. Nobodies mingled with notables as the White House, for the first time, was thrown open to the multitude. A milling crowd of clerks, shopkeepers, hobnailed artisans, and grimy laborers surged in, wrecking the china and furniture, and threatening the "people's champion" with cracked ribs. Jackson was hastily spirited through a side door, and the White House miraculously emptied itself when the word was passed that huge bowls of well-spiked punch had been placed on the lawns.

To conservatives, this orgy seemed like the end of the world. "King Mob" reigned triumphant as Jacksonian vulgarity replaced Jeffersonian simplicity. Old ladies of both sexes shuddered, drew their blinds, and recalled the opening scenes of the French Revolution.

Jackson Nationalizes the Spoils System

Under Jackson the spoils system—that is, rewarding political supporters with appointment to public office—was introduced into the federal government on a large scale. The name came from Senator Marcy's remark in 1832, "To the victors belong the spoils of the enemy," but the basic idea was as old as politics. The system had already secured a firm hold in New York and Pennsylvania, where well-greased political machines were run by professional politicians who made a full-time occupation out of politics by ladling out the "gravy" of office.

A housecleaning of some sort in Washington was clearly needed. No party overturn had occurred since the defeat of the Federalists in 1800. A few officeholders, their commissions signed by President Washington, were lingering on into their eighties, drawing their breath and salary but doing little else. Elected as a reformer, Jackson believed that the swiftest road to reform was to sweep out the Adams-Clay gang and bring in his own trusted henchmen. Furiously aroused against his foes, he agreed that the old Adams "barnacles" must "be scraped clean from the Ship of State."

The spoilsmen now had their inning. Office seekers hounded Jackson at every turn and even invaded his privacy; for every appointee there were seemingly ten disappointees. In view of such pressures, one may marvel that he removed so few incumbents rather than so many. During his eight years, only about one-fifth of the old civil servants were dismissed, leaving more than 9,000 out of the original 11,000. The "clean sweeps" were to come in later administrations.

Even so, a demoralizing practice was begun on a national scale. Fitness, merit, and the ideal of public service were subordinated, while offices were prostituted to political ends. The questions were not "What can he do for the country?" but "What has he done for the Party?" and "Is he loyal to Jackson?"

Scandal inevitably accompanied the new system. Men were appointed to high office who had openly bought their posts by campaign contributions. Illiterates, incompetents, and plain crooks were given positions of public trust; they lusted for the spoils of office rather than the toils of office. Samuel Swartwout, despite ample warnings of his untrustworthiness, was awarded the high-salaried post of collector of the customs of the port of New York. Nearly nine years later he "Swartwouted out" for England, leaving his accounts more than a million dollars short—the first man to steal a million dollars from the Washington government.

Finally, the spoils system built up a potent, personalized political machine. Its delicate gears were lubricated by gifts from expectant party members, and by percentage levies on the salaries of officeholders—a kind of political job insurance. The system at length secured such a tenacious hold that more than half a century passed before its grip could be partially loosened.

Cabinet Crises and Nationalistic Setbacks

Jackson's cabinet was mediocre; its members were used primarily as executive clerks. The only person of conspicuous ability was the smooth-tongued and keen-witted secretary of state, Dutch-descended Martin Van Buren of New York, who shone as a gifted conciliator and wire-puller. A balding, sharp-featured little man, he was affectionately addressed by Jackson as "Matty." But he was known to his enemies as the "Little Magician."

The official cabinet of six was privately supplemented by an extra-official cabinet of about thirteen ever-shifting members. It grew out of Jackson's informal meetings with his advisers, some of whom were newspapermen who kept him in touch with the fickle winds of public opinion. The enemies of the President branded these shirt-sleeved cronies "the Kitchen Cabinet."

The regular cabinet was wrecked in 1831, as a result of the "Eaton malaria." Secretary of War Eaton had married the daughter of a Washington boarding-house keeper, pretty Peggy O'Neal, whom the tongue of scandal had perhaps unfairly linked with the male boarders. She was consequently snubbed by the ladies of Jackson's official family, conspicuously by the blue-blooded wife of Vice-President Calhoun. The President, whose own spouse had been victimized by scandalmongers, was chivalrously aroused in behalf of Mrs. Eaton's chastity. With a zeal worthy of a better cause, he tried to force the social acceptance of the black-haired beauty. In spite of his efforts, the all-conquering general finally had to acknowledge defeat in the "Petticoat War" at the hands of the female phalanx.

The Eaton scandal played directly into the hands of Secretary Van Buren. As a fancy-free widower, he further curried favor with Jackson by paying marked attention to Mrs. Eaton, whose physical charms lightened this self-imposed task. Jackson turned increasingly against Calhoun, and finally broke with him completely. Followers of the South Carolinian were purged from the cabinet in 1831. Calhoun himself, resigning the vice-presidency the next year, entered the Senate as a champion of South Carolina.

It would be absurd to say that Peggy Eaton caused the Civil War. But up to this time Calhoun had publicly been a strong nationalist, despite his secret espousal of nullification in "The South Carolina Exposition" of 1828. As vice-president, he thought himself in line for the presidency after Jackson had served one term. The open break with the incumbent, though foreshadowed earlier, blighted his hopes. He gradually abandoned his weakening nationalism and became an inflexible defender of southern sectionalism. Seeking extreme medicines for protecting the states and preserving the Union, the "Great Nullifier" contributed to the almost fatal illness of the Union.

Jackson himself dealt nationalism a body blow by his hostility to localized roads and canals. It is true that he signed a number of measures which appropriated federal funds for ambitious internal improvements. But his states'-rights principles rebelled against spending money from the pinched Washington Treasury for roads built entirely within individual states and unrelated to an interstate network. He headlined his antagonism in 1830, when he vig-

orously vetoed a bill for improving the Maysville Road, which lay completely within Henry Clay's Kentucky (but which was connected with an interstate artery). This setback was incidentally a slap at the internal improvements aspect of the American System, so ardently championed by Clay, the "corrupt bargainer" whom Jackson never forgave. "Old Hickory's" veto was also a signal victory for eastern and southern states' rightism in its struggle with Jackson's own West.

The Webster-Hayne Forensic Duel

Sectional jealousies found a spectacular outlet in the Senate during 1829–1830. Hidebound New England, resenting the marvelous expansion of the West, was determined to call a halt. The lavish distribution of western acreage was draining off Eastern population, while further upsetting the political balance. Late in 1829, therefore, a New England senator introduced a resolution designed to curb the sale of public lands.

Sectional passions flared forth angrily in the Senate, as the western senators sprang furiously to the defense of their interests. The South, seeking sectional allies in its controversies with the Northeast, promptly sided with the West. Its most persuasive spokesman was Robert Y. Hayne, of South Carolina, one of the silver-tongued orators of his generation.

Hayne's oratorical effort in the Senate was impressive. He roundly condemned the obvious disloyalty of New England during the war of 1812, as well as her selfish inconsistency on the protective tariff. Airing in detail the grievances of the South, he reserved his heavy fire for the "Tariff of Abominations" (1828). He then acclaimed Calhoun's dangerous doctrine of nullification as the only way to safeguard the minority interests of his section.

The "Godlike Daniel" Webster, spokesman for New England, now took the floor and began a nine-day running debate with Hayne in January of 1830. Matchless orator and leader of the American bar, Webster awed audiences by his majestic presence, including craglike brows, flashing eyes, a sonorous voice, a noble head, and a well-chested frame.

After defending New England with vigor, if not complete candor, Webster, the ex-Federalist, passed on to the larger issue of Union. Insisting that the *people* and not the *states* had framed the Constitution (here he was on shaky historical ground*), he decried the insidious doctrine of nullification. Either the Supreme Court would judge the constitutionality of laws, or the Republic would be torn by revolution. If each of the twenty-four states was free to go its separate way in obeying or rejecting federal statutes, there would be no union but only a "rope of sand." Webster's concluding outburst, which brought tears to people's eyes, was a magnificent tribute to the Union, ending with those imperishable words: "Liberty and Union, now and forever, one and inseparable."

Websterian Cement for the Union

Webster did not overpower Hayne with his thunderous oratory; Hayne did not defeat Webster with his seductive eloquence. There were no official judges. The polished Southerner was sounder on historical and economic grounds; the impassioned New Englander was sounder on constitutional practicalities and common sense—on things as they were rather than as they had been. Each section was satisfied with its champion.

The impact of Webster's reply was spectacular. About forty thousand copies were printed in three months, and arguments for the Union were seared into the minds of countless Northerners. Among them was young Abraham Lincoln, just turning twenty-one and moving from Indiana to the Illinois frontier. Webster's inspirational peroration was printed in the school readers, and was memorized by tens of thousands of impressionable lads—the Boys in Blue who in 1861–1865 were willing to lay down their lives for the Union.

Webster, beyond a doubt, had a large hand in winning the Civil War. He probably did more than any other person to arouse the oncoming generation of northerners to fight for the ideal of Union. His admirers have claimed that the nation was saved

---

*The original preamble of the Constitution of 1787 had read: "We the people of the states of"—and then they were listed by name. But when it was objected that all the states might not ratify, the formula "We the people of the United States" was adopted. (For the text of the Preamble, see Appendix.)

"The man who has filled the measure of his Country's Glory."
JEFFERSON.

Jackson,

DEMOCRACY,   And our Country.

"*The Union must be Preserved.*"

A Jackson Campaign Poster, 1832.   *Note the emphasis on democracy and union. (Tennessee State Library and Archives)*

hardly less by the thunder of Webster's replies to Hayne than by the thunder of General Grant's replies to the cannonading of General Lee.

Hot-tempered "Old Hickory" had meanwhile been keeping strangely silent on Southern grievances. States' rights leaders, at a Jefferson Day banquet in 1830, schemed to smoke him out. Their strategy was to devise a series of toasts in honor of Jefferson, one-time foe of centralization, that would lean toward states' rights and nullification. The plotters assumed that the "Old Hero"—a fellow Southerner—would be swept along by the tenor of the toasts and speak up in favor of states' rights.

Jackson, forewarned and inwardly fuming, had carefully prepared his response. At the proper moment he rose to his full height, fixed his eyes on Calhoun, and with dramatic intensity proclaimed:

"Our Union: It must be preserved!"

The Southerners were dumbfounded, and Calhoun haltingly replied, in part:

"The union, next to our liberty, most dear!"

Some seventy other anti-climactic toasts followed, but in effect the party was over.

Jackson's military ire was aroused. As commander-in-chief, he would stand for no back talk from the states, particularly from the hated Calhoun. But, as fate decreed, the showdown with defiant South Carolina was postponed for over two years.

VARYING VIEWPOINTS

Aristocratic nineteenth-century historians damned Andrew Jackson as a backwoods barbarian. They criticized Jacksonianism as democracy run riot— an irresponsible, backcountry outburst that overturned the electoral system and raised hob with the national financial structure. Early twentieth-century "progressive" historians followed the lead of Frederick Jackson Turner in his famous 1893 essay "The Significance of the Frontier in American History." They saw the frontier as the fount of democratic virtue, and they hailed Jackson as a popular hero sprung from the forests of the West. But with the publication of Arthur M. Schlesinger, Jr.'s *The Age of Jackson* in 1945, the focus of the debate on Jacksonianism shifted. Contending that the urban working people of the Northeast formed the backbone of Jackson's support, Schlesinger argued that its identification with a social class, rather than a geographic section, was the most important characteristic of Jacksonianism. In the last twenty years, historical discussion has again shifted, from considerations of class to an emphasis on ethnic and religious conflict. This "ethnocultural school," following Lee Bensen's pioneering study of New York, sees disputes between ethnic groups, especially those concerning local issues, as the basis for political alignments in the Jacksonian era.

SELECT READINGS

Primary Source Documents

Davy Crockett's *Exploits and Adventures in Texas** (1836) is a lively description of the democratic political order of Jacksonian America. C.W. Janson, *The Stranger in America, 1793–1806** (1807), exposes the seamier aspects of American egalitarianism. On the Tariff of Abominations and its implications, see the "Webster-Hayne Debate"* (1830). Webster's reply to Hayne is one of the greatest specimens of American political oratory.

Secondary Sources

A still-living classic treatise on the Jacksonian period is Alexis de Tocqueville, *Democracy in America* (1835, 1840). General introductions are Glyndon G. Van Deusen, *The Jacksonian Era* (1959) and Edward Pessen, *Jacksonian America: Society, Personality, and Politics* (rev. ed., 1978). The latter volume sharply disputes Tocqueville's findings. Marvin Meyers, *The Jacksonian Persuasion* (1957) and John William

Ward, *Andrew Jackson: Symbol for an Age* (1955) examine the broader cultural significance of Old Hickory and his supporters. Arthur M. Schlesinger, Jr., in his seminal *The Age of Jackson* (1945) stresses the support of eastern labor for Jackson, a view that has come under attack in Lee Bensen, *The Concept of Jacksonian Democracy: New York as a Test Case* (1961). On the evolution of mass-based political parties, see Richard P. McCormick, *The Second American Party System* (1966) and two books by Ronald P. Formisano, *The Birth of Mass Political Parties: Michigan, 1827–1861* (1971) and *The Transformation of Political Culture: Massachusetts Parties, 1790s–1840s* (1983). Samuel Flagg Bemis, *John Quincy Adams and the Union* (1956) is the second volume of a distinguished biography, as is Robert V. Remini, *Andrew Jackson and the Course of American Freedom, 1822–1832* (1981). The standard on the subject is Frank W. Taussig, *The Tariff History of the United States* (1931).

15

Jacksonian Democracy at Flood Tide

**The vain threats of resistance by those who [in South Carolina] have
raised the standard of rebellion shew their madness and folly....
In forty days, I can have within the limits of So. Carolina
fifty thousand men.... The Union will be preserved.**

Andrew Jackson, 1832

"Nullies" in South Carolina

The "abominable" Tariff of 1828 continued to rankle
with hot-blooded South Carolinians. They persisted
in seeing it not only as economically punitive in the
short run, but as a possible entering wedge for later
federal interference with slavery in the southern
states. The nullifiers—"nullies," they were called—
tried strenuously to muster the necessary two-thirds
vote for nullification in the South Carolina legislature.
But they were blocked by a determined minority of
Unionists, scorned as "submission men."

Back in Washington, Congress touched off the fuse
by passing the new Tariff of 1832, which fell far short
of meeting all Southern demands. The measure did
pare away the worst of the "abominations" of 1828,
and it did lower the imposts to about the level of the
moderate Tariff of 1824—roughly 35 percent, or a
reduction of 10 percent. Yet the new law was frankly

protective and to many Southerners it had a disquieting air of permanence.

South Carolina was now nerved for drastic action.
Nullifiers and Unionists clashed head-on in the state
election of 1832. "Nullies," defiantly wearing the state
symbol of palmetto ribbons on their hats, emerged
with more than a two-thirds majority. The state legislature then called for a special convention. Several
weeks later the delegates, meeting in Columbia, solemnly declared the existing federal tariff to be null
and void within South Carolina. The hotheaded
assemblage also called upon the state legislature to
undertake any necessary military preparations.
Finally, the convention defiantly threatened to take
South Carolina out of the Union if the Washington
regime attempted to collect the customs duties by
force.

President-General Jackson, his military instincts aroused, reacted violently. Hating Calhoun and pledged to uphold the Union, he privately threatened to hang the nullifiers. But fortunately for compromise, he was much less pugnacious in public.

Henry Clay of Kentucky had no desire to see his old enemy Jackson win new laurels by crushing the Carolinians and returning with Calhoun's scalp dangling from his belt. Clay therefore threw his influence behind a compromise bill that would gradually reduce the Tariff of 1832 by about 10 percent.

The compromise Tariff of 1833 finally squeezed through Congress. But at the same time, and partly as a face-saving device, Congress passed the Force Bill, known among Carolinians as the "Bloody Bill." It authorized using the army and navy, if necessary, to collect federal tariff duties.

Militant South Carolinians welcomed this opportunity to extricate themselves without loss of face from a dangerously tight corner. To the consternation of the Calhounites, no other Southern states had sprung to their support. Moreover, an appreciable Unionist minority within South Carolina was gathering guns, organizing militia, and nailing the Stars and Stripes to flagpoles. Faced with civil war within and invasion from without, the Columbia convention met again and repealed the ordinance of nullification. As a final but futile gesture of fist-shaking, it nullified the unnecessary Force Act and adjourned.

A Victory for Both Union and Nullification

South Carolina actually emerged with colors flying. Although confronted with overwhelming odds, it had forced a reduction of the tariff to as reasonable a level as it could have expected. It had not only saved face but it had surrendered no principle. Unrepentant and defiant, it felt that it had won; and the people of Charleston—the "Cradle of Secession"—gave a gala "victory ball" for the volunteer troops. But ominously the South Carolinians gradually abandoned nullification in favor of the more extreme remedy of secession.

Later generations, gazing back through the smoke of the Civil War, have condemned the "appeasement" of South Carolina in 1833 as sheer folly. Unbloody and

unbowed, she could have been voted the state most likely to secede. (In 1860 she was the first to go.) If Jackson had only strangled the serpent of secession in the cradle, so the argument runs, there might have been no Civil War.

Yet force was the risky solution. The flare-up in South Carolina was no mere Whiskey Rebellion, and the nation was not yet ready to drink the cup of blood. Violence tends to beget violence. Armed invasion might have aroused other southern states and touched off a civil war, at a time when the Unionists were even worse prepared for fighting than in 1861. Force is a confession that statesmanship has failed. Reasonable compromise was in the American tradition, and in 1833 any other course seemed unwise.

The Bank as a Political Football

A man of violent dislikes, President Jackson came to share the prejudices of his own West against the "moneyed monster," the Bank of the United States (B.U.S.). The hated Henry Clay aroused his ire by supporting a premature move in the Senate to recharter the Bank in 1832—four years early.

Clay's scheme was to ram a recharter bill through Congress, and then send it on to the White House. If Jackson signed it, he would alienate his worshipful western followers. If he vetoed it, as seemed certain, he would presumably lose the presidency in the forthcoming election by alienating the wealthy and influential groups in the East. The President growled privately, "The Bank . . . is trying to kill me, but I will kill it."

The recharter bill slid through Congress on greased skids, as planned, but was killed by a scorching veto from Jackson. The "Old Hero" assailed the plutocratic and monopolistic Bank as unconstitutional. Of course the Supreme Court had earlier declared it constitutional in the case of *McCulloch* v. *Maryland* (1819), but Jackson acted as though he regarded the executive branch as superior to the judicial branch. He had taken an oath to uphold the Constitution as he understood it, not as his foe, John Marshall, understood it.

Jackson's veto message went on to condemn the bank as not only antiwestern but anti-American. A substantial minority of its stockholders were foreigners, chiefly Britons, for whom Americans still harbored a war-born hate. Thus, at one bold stroke, Jackson succeeded in mobilizing the prejudices of the West against the East. He was setting the log cabin against the business office, the anxious debtor against the steely-eyed creditor. More than that, he was arousing the "native" American against the foreigner, the states'-righter against the centralizer.

The gods continued to misguide Henry Clay. Delighted with the financial fallacies of Jackson's message, but blind to its political appeal, he arranged to have thousands of copies printed as a campaign document. The President's sweeping accusations may indeed have seemed demagogic to the moneyed men of the country, but they made good sense to the common men. The bank issue was now thrown into the noisy arena of the Clay-Jackson presidential canvass of 1832.

Brickbats and Bouquets for the Bank

What of Jackson's vigorous charges? The bank was undeniably antiwestern in its strong hostility to the wobbly "wildcat banks" that provided financial fuel—often volatile paper—for western expansion. It had foreclosed on many western farms, and had thus drained "tribute" into its eastern coffers. For that era, it was a mammoth super-bank—a "monster monopoly"—and hence out of touch with the sweaty New Democracy. It was undeniably plutocratic, run by an elite moneyed aristocracy, headed by the able but high-handed Nicholas Biddle (dubbed "Czar Nicholas I"). The bank was also in some degree autocratic, especially when it turned the screws on the weak "rag money" banks.

The charge that the Bank was a "hydra of corruption" contained much truth. Biddle cleverly lent funds where they would make influential friends. In 1831 alone, a total of fifty-nine members of Congress borrowed sums from "Biddle's Bank" totaling about a third of a million dollars. Even a dog does not ordinarily bite the hand that feeds him. During one period Daniel Webster was a director of the bank, its chief paid counsel, its debtor in the sum of thousands of dollars, and a member of the United States Senate, where he eloquently battled for his employer's interests. Judicious loans by Biddle to newspaper editors

likewise ensured a "good press" and led to the sneer "Emperor Nick of the Bribery Bank." Whomever he could not corrupt, it was believed, he crushed.

Yet the bank had much to commend it. An eminently sound organization, it was the only national financial institution of its kind in American history. It kept the fly-by-night Western banks under some restraint—banks that often consisted of little more than a few chairs and a suitcase full of printed notes. It reduced bank failures and, at a time when the country was flooded with depreciated paper money, issued sound banknotes ("Old Nick's Money"). It helped the west expand by making credit and sound currency reasonably abundant. It was a safe depository for the funds of the Washington government, which it also served by transferring and disbursing money. Admittedly it had a monopoly of surplus federal funds, but that monopoly had been specifically authorized by the people's representatives in Congress.

The Bank, in short, was a highly important and useful institution which had fallen into the hands of a wealthy clique. Its officers were not only arrogant but also neglectful of their responsibilities to society in the management of a public trust.

"Old Hickory" Crushes Clay in 1832

Clay, as a National Republican, and Jackson, as a Democrat, were the chief gladiators in the presidential contest of 1832. The gaunt old general, who had earlier favored one term for a president and rotation in office, was easily persuaded by his cronies not to rotate himself out of office.

Novel features made the campaign of 1832 especially memorable. For the first time, a third party entered the field—the newborn Anti-Masonic party, which opposed the fearsome secrecy of the Masonic order. The Anti-Masonic party quickly became a potent political force in New York and spread its influence throughout the middle Atlantic and New England states. The Anti-Masons appealed to long-standing American suspicion of secret societies, which they condemned as citadels of privilege and monopoly—a note that harmonized with the democratic chorus of the Jacksonians. But since Jackson himself was a Mason, and publicly gloried in his membership, the Anti-Masonic party was also an

"Race Over Uncle Sam's Course." *Clay, with his American System, is supposed to gain the White House as Jackson, with his veto club and Van Buren as running mate, falls on the bank issue in 1832. A falsely optimistic Whig cartoon. (Boston Public Library)*

anti-Jackson party. Moreover, the Anti-Masons attracted support from many evangelical Protestant groups seeking to use political power to effect moral and religious reforms, such as prohibiting mail deliveries on Sundays and otherwise keeping the Sabbath holy.

A further novelty of the presidential contest in 1832 was the calling of national nominating conventions (three of them) to name candidates. The Anti-Masons and a group of National Republicans added still another innovation when they adopted formal platforms, publicizing their positions on the issues.

Henry Clay and his overconfident National Republicans enjoyed impressive advantages. Ample funds flowed into their campaign chest, including $50,000 in "life insurance" from the B.U.S. Most of the newspaper editors, some of them "bought" with Biddle's bank loans, dipped their pens in acid when they wrote of Jackson.

Yet Jackson won easily over the sparkling Kentuckian. The popular count stood at 687,502 to 530,189; the electoral count at 219 to 49. A Jacksonian wave swept over the West and South, washed into Pennsylvania and New York, and even broke into rock-ribbed New England.

Badgering Biddle's Bank

A vindictive Jackson was not one to let the financial octopus die in peace. He was convinced that he now had a "mandate" from the voters, and he had good reason to fear that the slippery Biddle might try to manipulate the Bank (as he did) so as to force its recharter. Jackson therefore decided to "remove" the federal deposits gradually, thus cushioning the final shock when the bank expired in four years. He would accomplish his objective by depositing no more funds with Biddle, and by using existing deposits to pay the daily bills of the government.

"Removing" the deposits involved nasty complications. Jackson, his dander up, was forced to reshuffle his cabinet before he could find a secretary of the treasury who would bend to his iron will. Surplus federal funds henceforth were placed in several dozen state institutions—the so-called pet banks or Jackson's pets.

Compelled to retrench after losing federal deposits, Biddle called in loans with unnecessary severity. A number of wobbly banks were driven to the wall by "Biddle's Panic." The teetering financial structure received an additional shock in 1836 when Jackson issued a "Specie Circular" requiring all public lands to be purchased with "hard" metallic money. With "wildcat" Western currency so unreliable, this step was long overdue, but coming at that time it gave the speculative bubble another sharp prick. Hard money brought hard feelings and hard times for the West.

Transplanting the Tribes

Wondrous indeed was the continued expansion of the American population. The unflagging fertility of the people, reinforced by immigration, brought the total figure to nearly 13 million by 1830—or more than three times that of 1790.* Most of the states east of the Mississippi had been admitted, leaving islands of Indians marooned on lands coveted by their white neighbors.

President Jackson, the veteran Indian fighter known as "Big Knife," was convinced of the folly of continuing to regard the tribes as separate nations within the individual states. When Georgia attempted to exercise control over the Cherokees, and the Supreme Court thrice upheld the rights of the Indians, Jackson viewed continued defiance by the state with unaccustomed composure. A state might flout federal law if white men thereby profited at the Indians' expense. In a callous sneer at the defender of the Indians, Jackson reportedly snapped, "John Marshall has made his decision; now let him enforce it."

Yet Jackson also harbored protective feelings toward the Indians. Their present condition, he told Congress in 1829, "contrasted with what they once were, makes a most powerful appeal to our sympathies." Could not something be done, he implored, to preserve "this much injured race"? Jackson proposed a bodily removal of the remaining eastern tribes— chiefly Cherokee, Creek, Choctaw, and Chickasaw— beyond the Mississippi. Individual Indians might remain if they adopted white men's ways. Emigration should be voluntary, since it would be "cruel and unjust to compel the aborigines to abandon the graves of their fathers."

---

*For population figures since 1790, see Appendix.

Southern Tribes Before Transplanting.

Jackson's policy was high-sounding, but it led to the more or less forcible uprooting of more than 100,000 Indians in the 1830s. Many died on the "Trail of Tears" to the newly established Indian Territory (present Oklahoma), where they were to be "permanently" free of white encroachments. The Bureau of Indian Affairs was established in 1836 to administer relations with America's original inhabitants. But as the landhungry "palefaces" pushed west faster than anticipated, the government's guarantees went up in smoke. The "permanent" frontier lasted about fifteen years.

Suspicious of white intentions from the start, braves from Illinois and Wisconsin, ably led by Black Hawk, resisted eviction. They were bloodily crushed in 1832 by regular troops, including Lieutenant Jefferson Davis of Mississippi, and by volunteers, including Captain Abraham Lincoln of Illinois.

In Florida the Seminole Indians, joined by runaway black slaves, retreated to the swampy Everglades. For seven years (1835–1842) they waged a bitter guerrilla war that took the lives of some 1,500 soldiers and proved to be the costliest Indian conflict in American experience. The spirit of the Seminoles was at last broken in 1837, when the American field commander treacherously seized their half-breed leader, Osceola, under a flag of truce. Some fled deeper into the Everglades, where their descendants now live, but about four-fifths of them were moved to present Oklahoma, where about three thousand of the tribe survive.

The Lone Star of Texas Flickers

Americans, greedy for land, continued to covet the vast expanse of Texas, which the United States had abandoned to Spain when acquiring Florida in 1819. The Spanish authorities were desirous of populating this virtually unpeopled area, but before they could carry through their contemplated plans, the Mexicans won their independence. A new regime in Mexico City thereupon concluded arrangements in 1823 for granting a huge tract of land to Stephen Austin, with the understanding that he would bring in 300 American families. Immigrants were to be of the established Roman Catholic faith, and were to become properly Mexicanized.

These two restrictions were largely ignored. Hardy Texan pioneers remained Americans at heart, resenting the trammels imposed by a "foreign" government. They were especially annoyed by the presence of Mexican soldiers, many of whom were ragged ex-convicts.

Virile and prolific, Texas-Americans numbered about thirty thousand by 1835. Among the adventurers who had migrated to Texas were Davy Crockett, the fabulous rifleman, and James Bowie, the presumed inventor of the murderous knife that bears his name. A distinguished latecomer and leader was

an ex-governor of Tennessee, Sam Houston. His life had been temporarily shattered in 1829 when his bride of a few weeks left him and he took up transient residence with the Arkansas Indians, who dubbed him "Big Drink." He subsequently took the pledge of temperance.

The pioneer individualists who came to Texas were not easy to push around. Friction rapidly increased between Mexicans and Texans over such issues as slavery, immigration, and local rights. Slavery was a particularly touchy issue. Mexico emancipated its slaves in 1830 and prohibited their further importation into Texas, as well as further settlement by troublesome Americans. The Texans refused to honor this decree. They kept their slaves in bondage, and new American settlers kept bringing more slaves into Texas. The explosion finally came in 1835, when Mexican dictator Santa Anna wiped out all local rights and started to raise an army to suppress the upstart Texans.

Early in 1836 the Texans declared their independence and unfurled their Lone Star flag—with Sam Houston as commander in chief. Santa Anna, at the head of about six thousand men, swept ferociously into Texas. Trapping a band of nearly two hundred pugnacious Texans at the Alamo in San Antonio, he wiped them out to a man after a thirteen-day siege. A short time later a band of about four hundred surrounded and defeated American volunteers, having thrown down their arms at Goliad, were butchered as "pirates."

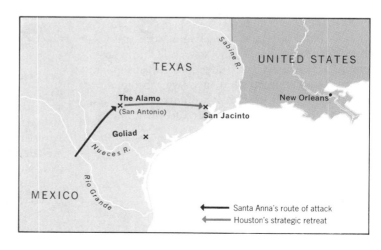

The Texas Revolution, 1835–1836. *General Houston's strategy was to retreat and use defense in depth. His line of supply from the United States was shortened as Santa Anna's lengthened. The Mexicans were forced to bring up supplies by land because the Texas navy controlled the sea. This force consisted of only four small ships, but it was big enough to do the job.*

The Alamo. *An abandoned mission at San Antonio, the Alamo occupies a glorious spot in Texas history. Known as "The Cradle of Texas Liberty," the Alamo was constructed as a Franciscan chapel in the days of Spanish colonization in the eighteenth century. It had been abandoned for some time prior to its famous use as a fort in 1836. Destroyed in the Mexican attack, the Alamo was purchased by the state of Texas in 1883 and subsequently restored. (Courtesy, Texas State Library)*

Texan war cries—"Remember the Alamo!" "Remember Goliad!" and "Death to Santa Anna!"— swept up into the United States. Scores of vengeful Americans seized their rifles and rushed to the aid of relatives, friends, and compatriots. But despite their efforts, the Lone Star was in grave danger of being dimmed forever as General Sam Houston's small army continued its thirty-seven-day eastward retreat.

But Houston proved equal to the occasion. A commanding figure of a man and a natural leader of the Texans, he lured the pursuers onward to San Jacinto, near the site of the city that now bears his name. The invaders numbered about thirteen hundred men; the Texans about nine hundred. Suddenly, on April 21, 1836, Houston turned. Taking full advantage of the Mexican siesta hour, he wiped out the invading force and captured Santa Anna, who was found cowering in the tall grass near the battlefield. Confronted with thirsty Bowie knives, the quaking dictator was speedily induced to sign two treaties. By their terms he agreed to withdraw Mexican troops and to recognize the Rio Grande as the extreme southwestern boundary of Texas. When released, he repudiated the whole agreement as illegal and as extorted under duress.

Texas: An International Derelict

Mexico no doubt had a genuine grievance against the United States. The Texans, though courageous, could hardly have won their independence without unneutral help in men and supplies from their American cousins. The Washington government, as the Mexicans bitterly complained, had a solemn obligation under international law to enforce its leaky neutrality statutes. But American public opinion, overwhelmingly favorable to the Texans, openly nullified the existing legislation. The federal authorities were powerless to act.

Jackson's heart was torn by the Texas issue. He disliked the Mexican overlords and admired the heroism of Sam Houston, his old comrade-in-arms against the Indians. But he was in no haste to recognize Texas formally as an independent republic. To do so would touch off the whole explosive issue of slavery, at a time when he was trying to engineer the election of his handpicked successor, Martin Van Buren. But after Van Buren had come safely under the wire, Jackson extended the right hand of recognition, the day before he left office in 1837.

Texas had every reason to expect a union with the United States, for what nation in its right mind would refuse so princely a dowry? The radiant Texan bride, officially petitioning for annexation in 1837, presented herself for marriage. But the expectant groom, Uncle Sam, was jerked back by the black hand of the slavery issue. Antislavery zealots in the North were opposing annexation with increasing vehemence; they contended that the whole scheme was merely a conspiracy cooked up by the Southern "slavocracy" to bring new slave pens into the Union.

The jilted Texas bride was left in a dangerous predicament. Fearing the return of the "villain," Santa Anna, she understandably went so far as to flirt openly with Britain and France for support. An ugly situation, involving balance-of-power politics, began to develop in this underbelly of the United States. It could not be allowed to go on indefinitely.

The Birth of the Whigs and the Election of 1836

New political parties were gelling as the 1830s lengthened. As early as 1828, the Democratic-Republicans of Andrew Jackson had unashamedly adopted the once-tainted name of "Democrats." Jackson's opponents condemned him as "King Andrew I" and began to coalesce as *Whigs*—a name deliberately chosen to recollect eighteenth-century and Revolutionary American opposition to the monarchy.

The Whig party contained so many diverse elements that it was mocked at first as "an organized incompatibility." Hatred of Jackson and his "executive usurpation" was its only apparent cement in its formative days. Coalescing first in the Senate in opposition to Jackson's bank policies, the Whigs rapidly evolved into a potent national political force by attracting other groups alienated by Jackson: supporters of Clay's American System; southern states' righters offended by Jackson's stand on nullification; the larger northern industrialists and merchants; and eventually many of the evangelical Protestants associated with the Anti-Masonic party.

As the presidential election of 1836 neared, the still-ramshackle organization of the Whigs showed in their inability to nominate a single presidential candidate. Their long-shot strategy was instead to run several prominent "favorite sons" who would so scatter the vote that no candidate would win a majority.

Martin Van Buren of New York, a smooth-as-silk politician, was Jackson's choice for "appointment" as his successor. Leaving nothing to chance, the general carefully rigged the nominating convention and rammed his favorite down the throats of the delegates. Van Buren was supported by the Jacksonites without wild enthusiasm, even though he had promised "to tread generally" in the military-booted footsteps of his predecessor.

In retrospect, the Jackson years were yeasty ones. The rough-hewn general—through forthrightness, energy, and strength of character—left a lasting imprint on the presidency. He demonstrated anew the value of strong executive leadership; he led the common people into national politics; he united them into the powerful and long-lived Democratic party; and he proved that they could be trusted with the vote. Reasserting the power of the presidency, he amazed weak-kneed politicians by showing that the courageous course often wins the most votes.

The other side of the ledger is less satisfying. Jackson cannot escape blame for his encouragement of the spoils system and of unsound finance, with its heartbreaking legacy of a century of thousands of bank failures. No one can deny that the B.U.S. was a powerful and ultimately a corrupting monopoly, which needed to have its wings clipped. But chopping off its head instead of its wings was of dubious benefit to the entire nation.

Big Woes for the "Little Magician"

Martin Van Buren, the eighth president, was the first to be born under the American flag. Bland of face, bald of head, slender of figure, the adroit little New Yorker has been described as "a first-class second-rate man." An accomplished wire-puller and spoilsman—"the wizard of Albany"—he was also a statesman of wide experience in both legislative and administrative life. In intelligence, education, and training, he was above the average of the presidents since Jackson. The myth of his complete mediocrity sprouted from a series of misfortunes over which he had no control.

From the outset, the new politician-president labored under severe handicaps. As a machine-made candidate, he incurred the resentment of many Democrats—the men who objected to having a "bastard politician" smuggled into office beneath the tails of the old general's military coat. Jackson, the master showman, had been the dynamic type of executive whose administration had resounded with furious quarrels and cracked heads. Easygoing Martin Van Buren seemed to rattle about in the military boots of his testy predecessor. The people felt let down. Inheriting Jackson's mantle without his popularity, the polished New Yorker also inherited the ex-president's many vengeful enemies.

Worst of all, Van Buren inherited the makings of a searing depression from Jackson. Much of his energy had to be devoted to the purely negative task of battling the panic, and there were not enough rabbits in the "Little Magician's" tall silk hat. Hard times ordinarily blight the reputation of a President—and Van Buren was no exception.

Depression Doldrums and the Independent Treasury

The panic of 1837 was a symptom of the financial sickness of the times. Its basic cause was evidently overspeculation, prompted by a mania of get-rich-quickism. Gamblers in Western lands were doing a "land-office business" on borrowed capital, much of it in the shaky currency of "wildcat banks." The speculative craze spread to canals, roads, railroads, and slaves.

But speculation alone did not cause the crash. Jacksonian finance, including the Bank War and the Specie Circular, gave an additional jolt to an already teetering structure. Failures of wheat crops, ravaged by the Hessian fly, deepened the distress. Grain prices were forced so high that mobs in New York City, three weeks before Van Buren took the oath, stormed warehouses and broke open flour barrels.

Financial stringency abroad likewise left its imprint on America. Late in 1836, while Jackson was still President, the failure of two prominent British banks created tremors and these in turn caused English investors to call in foreign loans. The resulting pinch in the United States, combined with other setbacks, heralded the beginning of the panic.

Hardship was acute and widespread. American banks collapsed by the hundreds, including some "pet banks," which carried down with them several millions in government funds. Commodity prices drooped, sales of public lands fell off, and customs revenues dried to a rivulet. Factories closed their doors; unemployed workers darkened the streets.

Increasingly, the Whigs were coming forward with proposals for active government remedies for the economy's ills. They called for the expansion of bank credit, higher tariffs, and subsidies for internal improvements. But Van Buren, shackled by the Jacksonian philosophy of keeping the government's paws off the economy, scorned all such ideas.

The beleaguered Van Buren tried to apply vintage Jacksonian medicine to the ailing economy through his controversial "Divorce Bill." Convinced that some of the financial fever was fed by the injection of federal funds into private banks, he championed the principle of "divorcing" the government from banking altogether. By establishing a so-called independent treasury, the government could lock its surplus money in vaults. Government funds would thus be safe, but they would also be denied to the banking system as reserves, thereby shriveling available credit resources. Van Buren's desire for political purity triumphed over enlightened economics.

Van Buren's "divorce" scheme was never highly popular. It was supported only lukewarmly by his fellow Democrats, many of whom longed for the risky but lush days of the "pet banks." The new policy was condemned by the Whigs, primarily because it would dampen their hopes for a revived Bank of the United States. After a prolonged struggle, the Independent Treasury Bill passed Congress in 1840. Repealed the next year by the victorious Whigs, the scheme was reenacted by the triumphant Democrats in 1846, and then continued until merged with the Federal Reserve System in the next century.

"Tippecanoe" Versus "Little Van"

Van Buren, though panic-tainted, was renominated by the Democrats in 1840, albeit without great enthusiasm. They had no acceptable alternative to what the Whigs called "Martin Van Ruin."

The Whigs, hungering for the spoils of office, scented victory in the breeze. Pangs of the panic were still being felt; and voters blindly blamed their woes on the party in power. The Whigs turned again not to their ablest statesman—Clay or Webster—but to their presumably ablest vote-getter: General Harrison, a coarse-featured military chieftain, with a long, thin face and medium build (5 feet 8 inches; 1.72 meters).

The aging hero, nearly sixty-eight when the campaign ended, was a small-bore candidate. Despite an inflated reputation, he had been only moderately successful in civilian and military life, notably at the Battles of Tippecanoe (1811) and the Thames (1813). "Old Tippecanoe" was then living quietly in a sixteen-room mansion, located on a three thousand-acre farm near North Bend, Ohio. His views on current issues were only vaguely known. He was nominated primarily because he was issueless and enemyless—and a most unfortunate precedent was thus set. John Tyler of Virginia, an afterthought, was selected as his vice-presidential running mate.

The Whigs played this political game with the cards close to their vests. They published no platform, fearing to make bothersome commitments and unwilling to reveal the deep divisions within their own patchwork party. They hoped to sweep their hero in by a frothy huzza-for-Harrison campaign.

A dull-witted Democratic editor played directly into Whig hands. Stupidly insulting the West, he sneered at Harrison as an impoverished old farmer who would be content with a pension, a log cabin, and a barrel of hard cider—the poor westerner's champagne. The Whigs thereupon gleefully took up the challenge and, stressing the hard cider and log cabin theme, turned the campaign into a huge political revival meeting.

A nonexistent candidate rapidly began to take shape in the hands of Whig mythmakers. The real Harrison was not lowborn, but from one of the FFV's (First Families of Virginia). He was not poverty-stricken; he did not live in a one-room log cabin; he did not swill down gallons of hard cider (he evidently preferred whiskey); and he did not plow his fields with his own "huge paws."

Whig propagandists made merry with little "Matty" Van Buren, the "Flying Dutchman." Although reared in poverty, he was denounced as a supercilious aristocrat, who wore corsets and ate French food with golden teaspoons from golden plates. Jackson's rough-timbered Democratic party, deeply rooted in the West, was thus saddled with a simpering dandy from the aristocratic East.

The Log Cabins and Hard Cider of 1840

Eager Democrats, who had hurrahed Jackson into the White House, now discovered to their chagrin that this was a game two could play. Acres of Whig audiences and miles of Whig marchers shouted such slogans as: "Harrison, Two Dollars a Day and Roast Beef" and "With Tip and Tyler We'll Bust Van's Biler." Log cabins were dished up in every conceivable form. Bawling Whigs, stimulated by fortified cider, rolled huge inflated balls from village to village and state to state—balls that represented the snowballing majority for "Tip and Ty." As they pushed, they sang:

> Tippecanoe, and Tyler too.
> And with them we'll beat little Van, Van, Van,
> Oh! Van is a used-up man.

Claptrap was king, as the electoral debauch reached an all-time intellectual low. There was little sober discussion of solid issues. Democrats inquired earnestly about the bank, internal improvements, and the tariff. The replies were "log cabin," "hard cider," "Harrison is a poor man." Van Burenites, protesting futilely, were drowned in a virtual tidal wave of apple juice as America experienced its first mass-turnout election.

Harrison won by the surprisingly close margin of 1,275,016 popular votes to 1,129,102, but by the overwhelming electoral count of 234 to 60. The hard-ciderites had seemingly received a mandate to go to Washington, tear down the White House, and erect a log cabin.

Basically, the vote was a protest against hard times—a thunderous shout of "Out with the old and in with the new." But the blatant bunkum and silly slogans set an unfortunate example for future campaigns. Democracy calls for hard thinking, not hard cider; for dignity, not delirium. Yet an able, well-organized, and well-entrenched political party, committed to solid principles, was hooted out of office by an inane hoopla campaign.

The Democrats were baffled. They complained with much bitterness and no little truth that they had been shouted down, sung down, lied down, and drunk down. Yet, though out-sloganed, they had kept their ranks intact. Even in defeat they were a stronger party than the Whigs. Though temporarily overdosed with hard cider, they would be heard from again.

Politics for the Common Man.   *Artist George Caleb Bingham here gently satirizes the drinking and wheeler-dealing that sometimes marred the electoral process in the boisterous age of Jacksonian politics. (Boatman's National Bank of St. Louis)*

The Two-Party System Emerges

The Jeffersonians of an earlier day had been so successful in absorbing the programs of their Federalist opponents that a full-blown two-party system had never truly emerged in the subsequent Era of Good Feelings. The idea had prevailed that parties of any sort smacked of conspiracy and "faction" and were injurious to the health of the body politic in a virtuous republic.

But the American political world changed dramatically in the era of the New Democracy. One of Andrew Jackson's most lasting legacies was the impetus he gave to the formation of a vigorous and durable two-party system, which had fully come of age by 1840.

Both parties, the Democrats as well as the Whigs, grew out of the rich soil of Jeffersonian repub-

licanism, and each laid claim to different aspects of the republican inheritance. Jacksonians glorified the liberty of the individual and were fiercely on guard against the inroads of "privilege" into government. Whigs trumpeted the natural harmony of society and the value of community over individualism and self-interest, and were willing to use government to realize their objectives.

Democrats clung to states' rights and federal restraint in social and economic affairs as their basic doctrines. Whigs, on the other hand, tended to favor a renewed national bank; protective tariffs; internal improvements; public schools; and increasingly, moral reforms, such as the prohibition of liquor and eventually the abolition of slavery.

The two parties were thus separated by real differences of philosophy and policy. But they also had much in common. Both were mass-based "catchall" parties that tried deliberately to mobilize as many voters as possible for their cause. Though it is true that Democrats tended to be more humble folk and Whigs more prosperous, both parties nevertheless commanded the loyalties of all kinds of Americans, from all social classes and in all sections. The social diversity of the two parties fostered horse-trading compromises *within* each party that prevented either from assuming extreme positions. By the same token, the geographical diversity of the two parties retarded the emergence of sectional political parties—temporarily suppressing, through compromise, the ultimately uncompromisable issue of slavery. When the two-party system began to creak in the 1850s, the Union was mortally imperiled.

VARYING VIEWPOINTS

As the debate over Jacksonianism shifted from a concern with geography to a consideration of social class, and later to an analysis of religion and ethnicity, historical evaluations of the rival parties have also changed. Patrician historians of the nineteenth century made the Whigs the champions of enlightened civilization against the excesses of the Jacksonian rabble. The progressive historians of the early years of this century reversed those assessments. They praised the Jacksonians as the representatives of freedom and equality and damned the Whigs as self-serving, aristocratic snobs. That view held sway until recent times, when historians began exploring the operation of the party system on a local level and the variations in party positions from state to state. Studies such as those by Ronald Formisano and Michael Holt stress the two parties' connections with various religious and immigrant groups and have encouraged a more balanced assessment of the merits of both parties.

SELECT READINGS

Primary Source Documents

An incisive commentary on Jacksonian politics is novelist James Fenimore Cooper's *The American Democrat** (1838). On the Bank War, see Andrew Jackson's "Veto Message" (July 10, 1832), in James D. Richardson, ed., *Messages and Papers of the Presidents* (1896), vol. II, pp. 576 ff,* and Daniel Webster's "Speech on Jackson's Veto of the U.S. Bank Bill" (1832), in Richard Hofstadter, ed., *Great Issues in American History*.

Secondary Sources

Glyndon G. Van Deusen, *The Jacksonian Era, 1828–1848* (1959) is an excellent introduction. More thorough is the concluding volume of Robert V. Remini's biography, *Andrew Jackson and the Course of American Democracy, 1833–1845* (1984). Incisive analysis can be found in Richard Hofstadter's essay on Jackson in *The American Political Tradition* (1948). A superior monograph is William W. Free-

hling, *Prelude to Civil War: The Nullification Controversy in South Carolina* (1966). Jacksonian banking policy is broadly treated in John McFaul, *The Politics of Jacksonian Finance* (1972). Robert V. Remini focuses on the political conflict over economic issues in *Andrew Jackson and the Bank War* (1967). Jackson's Indian policies are scrutinized in Ronald N. Satz, *American Indian Policy in the Jacksonian Era* (1975) and Michael P. Rogin's heavily psychoanalytic *Fathers and Children: Andrew Jackson and the Subjugation of the American Indians* (1975). Important political transformations are handled in the Ronald P. Formisano and Richard P. McCormick volumes cited in Chapter 14. See also the opening chapters of Michael F. Holt's *The Political Crisis of the 1850s* (1978). Daniel W. Lowe provides a stimulating analysis of Jackson's opponents in *The Political Culture of the American Whigs* (1980). The color of the frothy presidential campaign of 1840 comes through in Robert G. Gunderson, *The Log-Cabin Campaign* (1957).

16

Manifest Destiny in the Forties

Our manifest destiny [is] to overspread the continent allotted by Providence for the free development of our yearly multiplying millions.

John L. O'Sullivan, 1845*

The Accession of "Tyler Too"

A horde of hard-ciderites descended upon Washington in 1841, clamoring for the spoils of office. The real leaders of the Whig party regarded "Old Tippecanoe" as little more than an impressive figurehead. Daniel Webster, as secretary of state, and Henry Clay, the uncrowned king of the Whigs and their ablest spokesman in the Senate, would grasp the helm.

Unluckily for Clay and Webster, their schemes soon hit a fatal snag. Before the new term had fairly started, Harrison came down with pneumonia, and died after only four weeks in the White House—the shortest administration by far in American history.

The "Tyler too" part of the Whig ticket, hitherto only a rhyme, now claimed the spotlight. Six feet (1.83

meters) tall, slender, blue-eyed, and fair-haired, with classical features and a high forehead, Tyler was a Virginia gentleman of the old school—gracious and kindly, yet stubbornly attached to principle. He had earlier resigned from the United States Senate, quite unnecessarily, rather than accept distasteful instructions from the Virginia legislature. Still a lone wolf, he had forsaken the Jacksonian Democratic fold for that of the Whigs, largely because he could not stomach the dictatorial tactics of Jackson.

Tyler's enemies accused him of being a Democrat in Whig clothing, but this charge was only partially true. The Whig party, like the Democratic party, was something of a catchall, and the accidental president belonged to the minority wing, which embraced a number of Jeffersonian states' righters. Tyler had in fact been put on the ticket partly to attract the vote of this influential group.

---

*Earliest known use of the term *Manifest Destiny,* sometimes called "manifest desire."

It was true, however, that on virtually every major issue the obstinate Virginian was at odds with the majority of his Whig party, which was probank, pro–protective tariff, and pro–internal improvements. "Tyler too" rhymed with "Tippecanoe," but there the harmony ended. As events turned out, President Harrison, the Whig, served for only four weeks, while Tyler, the ex-Democrat who was still largely a Democrat at heart, served for 204 weeks.

John Tyler: A President Without a Party

After their hard-won, hard-cider victory, the Whigs brought their secret platform out of Clay's waistcoat pocket. To the surprise of no one, it outlined a strongly nationalistic program.

Financial reform came first. The Whig Congress hastened to pass a law ending the Independent Treasury system, and President Tyler, disarmingly agreeable, signed it. Clay next drove through Congress a bill for a "Fiscal Bank," which would establish a new Bank of the United States.

Tyler's hostility to a centralized bank was notorious, and Clay—the "Great Compromiser"—would have done well to conciliate him. But the Kentuckian, robbed repeatedly of the presidency by lesser men, was in an imperious mood and riding for a fall. When the bank bill reached the presidential desk, Tyler flatly vetoed it on both practical and constitutional grounds. A drunken mob gathered late at night near the White House and shouted insultingly, "Huzza for Clay!" "A Bank! A Bank!" "Down with the Veto!"

Whig extremists, boiling with indignation, condemned Tyler as "His Accidency." To the delight of Democrats, the stiff-necked Virginian was formally expelled from his party by a caucus of Whig congressmen, and a serious attempt to impeach him was made in the House of Representatives. His entire cabinet resigned in a body, except Secretary of State Webster.

The proposed Whig tariff also felt the prick of the President's well-inked pen. Tyler vetoed a tariff bill that included a scheme for distributing revenues from sale of public land to the states. But he reluctantly signed the revised Clayite tariff of 1842, pushing rates back down to the moderately protective level of 1832, about 32 percent.

Manipulating the Maine Maps

Hatred of England during the nineteenth century came to a head periodically and had to be lanced by treaty settlement or by war. The poison had festered ominously in the late 1830s, especially because of private American involvement in an unsuccessful Canadian rebellion.

Then, Anglo-American controversy exploded in the early 1840s over the disputed Maine boundary. The St. Lawrence River is icebound several months of the year, as the British, remembering the War of 1812, well knew. They were determined, as a defensive precaution against the Yankees, to build a road westward from the seaport of Halifax to Quebec. But the proposed route ran through disputed territory—claimed also by Maine under the misleading peace treaty of 1783. Tough-knuckled lumberjacks from both Maine and Canada entered the disputed no-man's-land of the tall-timbered Aroostook River Valley. Ugly fights flared up; both sides summoned the local militia. The small-scale lumberjack clash, dubbed the "Aroostook War," threatened to widen into a shooting war.

As the crisis deepened in 1842, the London Foreign Office took an unusual step. It sent to Washington a non-professional diplomat, the conciliatory financier Lord Ashburton, who had married a wealthy American woman. He speedily established cordial relations with Secretary Webster, who had recently been lionized during a visit to England.

The two statesmen, their nerves frayed by protracted negotiations in the heat of a Washington summer, finally agreed to compromise on the Maine boundary. On the basis of a rough, split-the-difference arrangement, the Americans were to retain some 7,000 square miles (18,130 square kilometers) of the 12,000 square miles (31,080 square kilometers) of wilderness in dispute. The British got less land, but won the desired Halifax-Quebec route.

An overlooked bonus was won in the same treaty when the British, in adjusting the boundary to the west, surrendered 6,500 square miles (16,835 square kilometers). The area was later found to contain the priceless Mesabi iron ore of Minnesota.

The Lone Star of Texas Shines Alone

The jilted Texan bride, during the uncertain eight years since 1836, had led a precarious existence. Mexico, refusing to recognize her independence, regarded the Lone Star Republic as a province in revolt, to be reconquered in the future. Mexican officials loudly threatened war if the American eagle should gather the fledgling republic under its protective wings.

The Texans were forced to maintain a costly military establishment. Vastly outnumbered by their Mexican foe, they could not tell when he would strike again. Mexico actually did make two half-hearted raids which, though ineffectual, foreshadowed more fearsome efforts. Confronted with such perils, Texas was driven to open negotiations with England and France, in the hope of securing the defensive shield of a protectorate. In 1839 and 1840, the Texans concluded treaties with France, Holland, and Belgium.

Britain was intensely interested in an independent Texas. Such a republic would check the southward surge of the American colossus, whose bulging biceps posed a constant threat to nearby British possessions in the New World.

British abolitionists were also busily intriguing for a foothold in Texas. If successful in freeing the few blacks there, they presumably would inflame the nearby slaves of the South. In addition, British merchants regarded Texas as a potentially important free-trade area—an offset to the tariff-walled United States. British manufacturers likewise perceived that those vast Texan plains constituted one of the great cotton-producing areas of the future. An independent Texas would relieve British looms of their fatal dependence on American fiber—a supply which might be cut off in time of crisis by embargo or war.

The Belated Texas Nuptials

Partly because of the fears aroused by British schemers, Texas became a leading issue in the presidential campaign of 1844. The pro-expansion Democrats under James K. Polk finally triumphed over the Whigs under Henry Clay, the hardy perennial candidate. Lame-duck President Tyler thereupon interpreted the narrow Democratic victory, with dubious accuracy, as a "mandate" to acquire Texas.

Eager to crown his troubled administration with this splendid prize, Tyler deserves much of the credit for shepherding Texas into the fold. Many "conscience Whigs" feared that Texas in the Union would be red meat to nourish the lusty "slave power." Tyler

despaired of securing the needed two-thirds vote for a treaty in the Senate, and he made haste to arrange for annexation by a joint resolution. This solution required only a simple majority in both houses of Congress. After a spirited debate, the resolution passed early in 1845, and Texas was formally invited to become the twenty-eighth star on the American flag. After some coyness, the waiting bride, grown weary of her many years in limbo, unpacked her mildewing wedding dress and was formally embraced as a full-fledged state.

Mexico angrily charged that the Americans had despoiled her of Texas. This was to some extent true in 1836, but hardly true in 1845, for the area was no longer Mexico's to be despoiled of. As the years stretched out, realistic observers could see that the Mexicans would not be able to reconquer their lost province. Yet Mexico left the Texans dangling by denying their right to dispose of themselves as they chose.

By 1845, the Lone Star Republic had become a danger spot, inviting foreign intrigue that menaced the American people. Its continued existence as an independent nation threatened to involve the United States in a series of ruinous wars, both in America and in Europe.

What other power would have spurned the imperial domain of Texas? The bride was so near, so rich, so fair, so willing. Whatever the peculiar circumstances of the Texas revolution, the United States can hardly be accused of unseemly haste in achieving annexation. Nine long years were surely a decent wait between the beginning of the courtship and the consummation of the marriage.

"Oregon Fever" Populates Oregon

The so-called Oregon Country was an enormous wilderness. It sprawled magnificently west of the Rockies to the Pacific Ocean, and north of California to the line of 54° 40′—the present southern tip of the Alaska panhandle. All or substantial parts of this immense area were claimed at one time or another by four nations: Spain, Russia, Britain, and the United States.

Two claimants dropped out of the scramble. Spain, though the first to raise her banner in Oregon, bartered away her claims to the United States in the so-

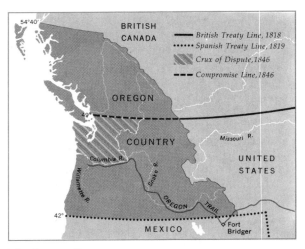

The Oregon Controversy.

called Florida Treaty of 1819. The Russian bear retreated to the line of 54° 40' by the treaties of 1824 and 1825 with America and Britain. These two remaining rivals now had the field to themselves.

British claims to Oregon were strong—at least to that portion north of the Columbia River. They were based squarely on prior discovery and exploration, on treaty rights, and on actual occupation. The most important colonizing agency was the far-flung Hudson's Bay Company, which was trading profitably with the Indians of the Pacific Northwest for their furs.

Americans, for their part, could also point pridefully to exploration and occupation. Captain Robert Gray in 1792 had stumbled upon the majestic Columbia River, which he named after his ship; and the famed Lewis and Clark expedition of 1804–1806 had ranged overland through the Oregon Country to the Pacific. This shaky American toehold was ultimately strengthened by the presence of missionaries and other settlers, a sprinkling of whom reached the grassy Willamette River Valley, south of the Columbia, in the 1830s. These men of God, in saving the soul of the Indian, were instrumental in saving the soil of Oregon for the United States. They stimulated interest in a faraway domain which countless Americans had earlier assumed would not be settled for centuries.

Scattered American and British pioneers in Oregon continued to live peacefully side by side. At the time of negotiating the Treaty of 1818, the United States had sought to divide the vast domain by the 49th parallel. But the British, who regarded the Columbia River as the St. Lawrence of the West, were unwilling to yield this vital artery. A scheme for peaceful "joint occupation" was thereupon adopted, pending a future settlement.

The handful of Americans in the Willamette Valley was suddenly multiplied in the early 1840s, when "Oregon fever" seized hundreds of restless pioneers. In ever-increasing numbers their creaking covered wagons jolted over the 2,000-mile long (3,200-kilometer) Oregon Trail as the human rivulet widened into a stream. By 1846 there were about five thousand American settlers south of the Columbia River.

The British, in the face of this rising torrent of humanity, could muster only seven hundred or so subjects north of the Columbia. Losing out lopsidedly in the population race, they were beginning to see the wisdom of arriving at a peaceful settlement before being engulfed by their neighbors.

A curious fact is that only a relatively small segment of the Oregon Country was in actual controversy by 1845. The area in dispute consisted of the rough triangle between the Columbia River on the south and the 49th parallel on the north. Britain had repeatedly offered the line of the Columbia; America had repeatedly offered the 49th parallel. The whole fateful issue was now tossed into the presidential election of 1844.

A Mandate (?) for Manifest Destiny

The two major parties nominated their presidential standard-bearers in May 1844. Ambitious but often-frustrated Henry Clay, easily the most popular man in the country, was enthusiastically chosen by the Whigs at Baltimore. The Democrats, meeting later in the same city, nominated James K. Polk of Tennessee. Speaker of the House of Representatives for four years and governor of Tennessee for two terms, Polk was a determined, industrious, ruthless, and intelligent public servant. Whigs attempted to jeer him into oblivion with the taunt, "Who is James K. Polk?" They soon found out.

The campaign of 1844 was in part an expression of the mighty emotional upsurge known as Manifest

Destiny. Countless citizens in the 1840s and 1850s, feeling a sense of mission, believed that Almighty God had "manifestly" destined the American people for a hemispheric career. They would irresistibly spread their uplifting and ennobling democratic institutions over at least the entire continent, and possibly over South America as well. Land greed and ideals were thus conveniently conjoined.

Expansionist Democrats were strongly swayed by the intoxicating spell of Manifest Destiny. They came out flat-footedly in their platform for the "Reannexation of Texas"* and the "Reoccupation of Oregon," all the way to 54° 40'. The Whigs countered with such slogans as "Hooray for Clay" and "Polk, Slavery, and Texas, or Clay, Union, and Liberty."

On the crucial issue of Texas, the acrobatic Clay tried to ride two horses at once. The "Great Compromiser" compromised away the presidency when he stated that he favored annexing Texas—an appeal to the South—but that he also favored postponement— an appeal to the North. By straddling the issue this way, Clay alienated ardent anti-slaveryites.

In the stretch drive, Polk nipped Henry Clay at the wire, 170 to 105 in the Electoral College and 1,337,243 to 1,299,062 in the popular column. Clay would have won if he had not lost New York by a scant 5,000 votes. There the tiny antislavery Liberty party absorbed nearly 16,000 votes, many of which would otherwise have gone to the unlucky Kentuckian. Ironically, the anti-Texas Liberty party, by helping to elect the pro-Texas Polk, hastened the annexation of Texas. The victorious Democrats proclaimed that they had received a mandate from the voters to take Texas, and three days before leaving office President Tyler signed the joint resolution of annexation.

Polk the Purposeful

"Young Hickory" Polk, unlike "Old Hickory" Jackson, was not an impressive figure. Of middle height (5 feet 8 inches; 1.72 meters), lean, white-haired (worn

President Polk's Flimsy House of Cards. *He appears to be hatching troublesome eggs relating to vexatious issues. (Yankee Doodle)*

long), gray-eyed, and stern-faced, he took life seriously and drove himself mercilessly into a premature grave. His burdens were increased by an unwillingness to delegate authority. Methodical and hardworking but not brilliant, he was shrewd, narrow, conscientious, and persistent. "What he went for he fetched," wrote a contemporary. Purposeful in the highest degree, he developed a positive four-point program, and with remarkable success achieved it completely in less than four years.

Polk first wanted to lower the tariff. Wispy Robert Walker, his Secretary of the Treasury, lobbied through Congress a tariff-for-revenue bill that lowered the average rates of the Tariff of 1842 from about 32 percent to 25 percent. The Walker Tariff of 1846 proved to be an excellent revenue producer.

---

*The United States had given up its claims to Texas in the so-called Florida Purchase Treaty with Spain in 1819 (see p. 140). The slogan "Fifty-four forty or fight" was evidently not coined until two years later, in 1846.

A second objective of Polk was the restoration of the independent treasury, which was unceremoniously dropped by the Whigs in 1841. Pro-Bank Whigs in Congress raised a storm of opposition, but victory at last rewarded the President's efforts in 1846.

The third and fourth points on Polk's "must list" were the acquisition of California and the settlement of the Oregon dispute.

"Reoccupation" of the "whole" of Oregon had been promised Northern Democrats in the campaign of 1844. But Southern Democrats, once they had "reannexed" Texas, rapidly cooled off. Polk, himself a Southerner, had no intention of insisting on the 54° 40' pledge of his own platform. But feeling bound by the offers of his predecessors, he again proposed the compromise line of 49°.

British antiexpansionists ("Little Englanders") were now persuaded that the Columbia River after all was not the St. Lawrence of the West, and that the turbulent American hordes might one day seize the Oregon Country. Why fight a hazardous war over this wilderness on behalf of an unpopular monopoly, the Hudson's Bay Company, which had already "furred out" much of the area anyhow? Early in 1846 the British, hat in hand, came around and themselves proposed the line of 49°. The senators speedily accepted the offer and approved the subsequent treaty, despite a few diehard shouts of "Fifty-four forty forever!"

Satisfaction with the Oregon settlement among Americans was not unanimous. The northwestern states, hotbed of Manifest Destiny and "fifty-four fortyism," joined the antislavery men in condemning what they regarded as a base betrayal by the South. Why *all* of Texas and not *all* of Oregon? Because, sneered the expansionist Senator Benton of Missouri, "Great Britain is powerful and Mexico is weak."

So Polk, despite all the campaign bluster, got neither "fifty-four forty" nor a fight. But he did get something that in the long run was better; a reasonable compromise without shedding a drop of blood.

Misunderstandings with Mexico

Faraway California was another worry of Polk's. He and other disciples of Manifest Destiny had long coveted its verdant valleys, and especially the spacious bay of San Francisco. This splendid harbor was widely regarded as America's future gateway to the Pacific Ocean.

The population of California in 1845 was curiously mixed. It consisted of some seven thousand sun-blessed Spanish-Mexicans, plus more than ten times as many dispirited Indians. There were fewer than a thousand foreigners, mostly Americans, some of whom had "left their consciences" behind them as they rounded Cape Horn. Given time, these transplanted Yankees might yet bring California into the Union by "playing the Texas game."

Polk was eager to buy California from Mexico. But relations with Mexico City were dangerously embittered, partly over unpaid claims but mostly over Texas. After threatening war if the United States should acquire the Lone Star Republic, the Mexican government had completely broken diplomatic relations following annexation.

Deadlock with Mexico over Texas was further tightened by a question of boundaries. During the long era of Spanish-Mexican occupation, the southwestern boundary of Texas had been the Nueces River. But the expansive Texans, on rather farfetched grounds, were claiming the more southerly Rio Grande instead. Polk, for his part, felt a strong moral obligation to defend Texas in her claim, once she was annexed.

The Mexicans were far less concerned about this boundary quibble than the United States. In their eyes all of Texas was still theirs, although temporarily in revolt, and a dispute over the two rivers seemed pointless. Yet Polk was careful to keep American troops out of virtually all of the explosive no-man's-land between the Nueces and the Rio Grande, as long as any real prospect of peaceful adjustment still remained.

The golden prize of California continued to cause Polk much anxiety. Disquieting rumors (now known to have been ill-founded) were circulating that the British lion was about to buy or seize California—a grab that Americans could not tolerate under the Monroe Doctrine. In a last desperate throw of the dice, Polk dispatched John Slidell to Mexico City as minister late in 1845. The new envoy, among other alternatives, was instructed to offer a maximum of $25 million for California and territory to the east. But the proud Mexicans would not even permit Slidell to present his "insulting" proposition.

American Blood on American (?) Soil

A frustrated Polk was now prepared to force a show-down. On January 13, 1846, he ordered four thousand men, under General Zachary Taylor, to march from the Nueces River to the Rio Grande, provocatively near Mexican forces. Polk's presidential diary reveals that he expected at any moment to hear of a clash. When none occurred after an anxious wait, he informed his cabinet on May 9, 1846, that he proposed to ask Congress to declare war on the basis of (1) unpaid claims and (2) Slidell's rejection. These, at best, were rather flimsy pretexts. Two cabinet members spoke up and said that they would feel better satisfied if Mexican troops should fire first.

That very evening, as fate would have it, news of bloodshed arrived. On April 25, 1846, Mexican troops had crossed the Rio Grande and attacked General Taylor's command, with a loss of sixteen Americans killed or wounded.

Polk, further aroused, sent a vigorous war message to Congress. He declared that despite "all our efforts" to avoid a clash, hostilities had been forced upon the country by the shedding of "American blood on the American soil." A patriotic Congress overwhelmingly voted for war, and enthusiastic volunteers cried, "Ho for the Halls of the Montezumas!" and "Mexico or Death!" Inflamed by the war fever, even antislavery Whig centers joined with the rest of the nation, though they later condemned "Jimmy Polk's war." As James Russell Lowell of Massachusetts lamented,

> Massachusetts, God forgive her,
> She's akneelin' with the rest.

In his message to Congress Polk was making history—not writing it. If he had been a historian, he would have explained that American blood had been shed on soil which the Mexicans had good reason to regard as their own. A gangling, rough-featured Whig congressman from Illinois, one Abraham Lincoln, introduced certain resolutions that requested information as to the precise "spot" on American soil where American blood had been shed. He pushed his

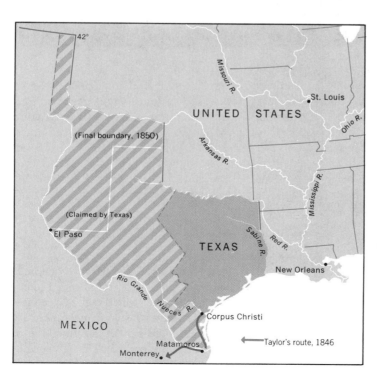

Texas, 1845–1846. *Texas President Mirabeau Buonaparte Lamar, flushed with imperial dreams, tried to secure the Texas claim to the large striped area on this map by leading a military expedition in 1841 against the Mexicans at Santa Fe. But the weak and outgunned "army" of the Lone Star Republic, made up mostly of American drifters and adventurers, was speedily smashed. The Texans drew in their horns thereafter, and with renewed vigor sought annexation to the United States, rather than further expansion to the West of their precariously independent nation.*

War News from Mexico. *The new-fangled telegraph kept the nation closely informed of events in far-off Mexico. (National Academy of Design)*

"spot" resolutions with such persistence that he came to be known as the "spotty Lincoln," who could die of "spotted fever."

Did Polk provoke war? California was an imperative point in his program, and Mexico would not sell it at any price. The only way to get it was to use force, or wait for an internal American revolt. Yet delay seemed dangerous, for the claws of the British lion might snatch the ripening California fruit from the talons of the American eagle. In 1846, patience had ceased to be a virtue as far as Polk was concerned. So he pushed the quarrel to a bloody showdown.

Both sides, in fact, were spoiling for a fight. Hotheaded Americans, especially Southwestern expansionists, were eager to teach the Mexicans a lesson. The Mexicans, in turn, were burning to humiliate the "Bullies of the North." Possessing a considerable standing army, heavily overstaffed with gener-

als, they boasted of invading the United States, freeing the black slaves, and lassoing whole regiments of Americans. They were hoping that the quarrel with Britain over Oregon would blossom into a full-dress war, as it came near doing, and further pin down the hated *Yanquis.* A conquest of Mexico's vast and arid expanses seemed fantastic, especially in view of the bungling American invasion of Canada in 1812.

The Mastering of Mexico

Polk wanted California—not war. But when war came he hoped to fight it on a limited scale, and then pull out when he had won the prize. The dethroned Mexican dictator Santa Anna, then exiled with his teenage bride in Cuba, let it be known that if the American blockading squadron would permit him to slip into Mexico, he would sell out his country. This discredita-

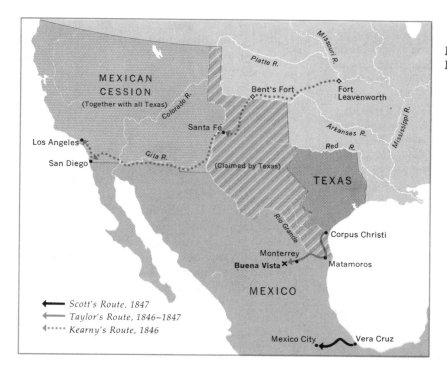

Major Campaigns of the Mexican War.

ble intrigue was finally carried through. But the double-crossing Santa Anna, self-styled "Napoleon of the West," rallied the Mexicans to a desperate defense of their soil.

American operations in the Southwest and in California were completely successful. In 1846 General Stephen W. Kearny led a detachment of seventeen hundred troops over the famous Santa Fe trail, from Fort Leavenworth to Santa Fe. This sunbaked outpost, with its drowsy plazas, was easily captured. But before Kearny could reach California, the fertile province was won. When war broke out, Captain John C. Frémont, the dashing explorer, just "happened" to be there with several dozen well-armed men. In helping to overthrow Mexican rule in 1846, he collaborated with American naval officers and with the local Americans, who had hoisted the banner of the short-lived California Bear Flag Republic.

General Zachary Taylor meanwhile had been spearheading the main thrust. Known as "Old Rough and Ready" because of his iron constitution and incredibly unsoldierly appearance—he sometimes wore a Mexican straw hat—he fought his way across the Rio Grande into Mexico. After several gratifying victories, he reached Buena Vista. There, on February 22–23, 1847, his weakened force of five thousand men was attacked by some twenty thousand march-weary troops under Santa Anna. The Mexicans were finally repulsed with extreme difficulty, and overnight Zachary Taylor became the "Hero of Buena Vista."

Sound American strategy now called for a crushing blow at the enemy's vitals—Mexico City. General Taylor, though a good leader of modest-sized forces, could not win decisively in the semi-deserts of northern Mexico. The command of the main expedition, which pushed inland from the coastal city of Vera Cruz early in 1847, was entrusted to General Winfield Scott. A handsome giant of a man, Scott had emerged as a hero from the War of 1812 and had later earned the nickname of "Old Fuss and Feathers" because of his resplendent uniforms and strict discipline. Scott succeeded in battling his way up to Mexico City by September 1847 in one of the most brilliant campaigns in American military annals.

Fighting Mexico for Peace

Polk was anxious to end the shooting as soon as he could secure his territorial goals. Accordingly, he sent along with Scott's invading army the chief clerk of the State Department, Nicholas P. Trist. Negotiating a treaty with a sword in one hand and a pen in the other was ticklish business. But Trist, grasping a fleeting opportunity to negotiate, signed the Treaty of Guadalupe Hidalgo on February 2, 1848, and forwarded it to Washington.

The terms of the treaty were breathtaking. They confirmed the American title to Texas, and yielded the enormous area stretching westward to Oregon and the ocean and embracing coveted California. This total expanse, including Texas, was about one-half of Mexico. The United States agreed to pay $15 million for the land, and to assume the claims of its citizens against Mexico in the amount of $3,250,000.

Polk submitted the treaty to the Senate. Speed was imperative. The antislavery Whigs in Congress—dubbed "Mexican Whigs"—were condemning this "damnable war" with increasing heat. Having secured control of the House in 1847, they were even threatening to vote down supplies for the armies in the field. If they had done so, Scott probably would have been forced to retreat, and the fruits of victory might have been tossed away.

Another peril impended. A swelling group of expansionists, intoxicated by Manifest Destiny, was clamoring for all of Mexico. If America had seized it, the nation would have been saddled with an expensive and vexatious policing problem. Farseeing Southerners like Calhoun, alarmed by the mounting anger of antislavery agitators, realized that the South would do well not to be too greedy. The treaty was finally approved by the Senate, 38 to 14. Oddly enough, it was condemned both by opponents who wanted all of Mexico and by opponents who wanted none of it.

Profit and Loss in Mexico

As wars go, the Mexican War was a small one. It cost some 13,000 American lives, most of them taken by disease. But the fruits of the fighting were enormous.

America's total expanse, already vast, was increased by about one-third (counting Texas)—an addition even greater than that of the Louisiana Purchase. A sharp stimulus was given to the spirit of Manifest Destiny for, as the proverb has it, the appetite comes with eating.

As fate ordained, the Mexican War was the blood-spattered schoolroom of the Civil War. The campaigns provided priceless field experience for most of the officers destined to become leading generals in the forthcoming conflict, including Captain Robert E. Lee and Lieutenant U. S. Grant. The Military Academy at West Point, founded in 1802, fully justified its existence through the well-trained officers. Useful also was the navy, which did valuable work in throwing a crippling blockade around Mexican ports. The Marine Corps, in existence since 1798, won new laurels, and to this day sings, in its stirring hymn, about the Halls of Montezuma.

The army waged war without defeat and without a major blunder, despite formidable obstacles and a half-dozen or so achingly long marches. Chagrined British critics, as well as other foreign skeptics, reluctantly revised upward their estimate of Yankee military prowess. Opposing armies, moreover, emerged with increased respect for each other. The Mexicans, though poorly led, fought heroically. At Chapultepec, near Mexico City, the teenage lads of the military academy there (*los niños*) perished to a boy.

Long-memoried Mexicans have never forgotten that their northern enemy tore away about half of their country. The argument that they were lucky not to lose all of it, and that they had been paid something for their land, did not lessen their bitterness. The war also marked an ugly turning point in the relations between the United States and Latin America as a whole. Hitherto, Uncle Sam had been regarded with some complacency, even friendliness. Henceforth, he was increasingly feared as the "Colossus of the North." Suspicious neighbors to the south condemned him as a greedy and untrustworthy bully, who might next despoil them of their soil.

Most ominous of all, the war rearoused the snarling dog of the slavery issue, and the beast did not stop yelping until drowned in the blood of the Civil War. Abolitionists assailed the Mexican conflict as one

PLUCKED:

THE MEXICAN EAGLE BEFORE THE WAR! OR. THE MEXICAN EAGLE AFTER THE WAR!

A Cartoon from *Yankee Doodle*, 1847. *This satiric drawing was symbolic of the "lick all creation" spirit of the times.*

provoked by the Southern "slavocracy" for its own evil purposes.

Quarreling over slavery extension also erupted on the floors of Congress. In 1846, shortly after the shooting started, Polk requested an appropriation of $2 million with which to buy a peace. Representative David Wilmot of Pennsylvania, fearful of the Southern "slavocracy," introduced a fateful amendment. It barred slavery in any territory wrested from Mexico.

The disruptive Wilmot amendment twice passed the House, but not the Senate. Southern members, unwilling to be robbed of prospective slave states, fought the restriction tooth and nail. Antislavery men,

in Congress and out, battled no less bitterly for the exclusion of slaves. The "Wilmot Proviso" soon came to symbolize the burning issue of slavery in the territories.

In a broad sense, the opening shots of the Mexican War were the opening shots of the Civil War. President Polk left the nation the splendid physical heritage of California and the Southwest but also the ugly moral heritage of an embittered slavery dispute. Mexicans could later take some satisfaction in knowing that the territory wrenched from them had proved to be a frightful apple of discord that could well be called Santa Anna's revenge.

VARYING VIEWPOINTS

Historians have long probed for the real meaning behind the pulse-stirring phrase *Manifest Destiny*. Some have emphasized the idealistic impulses behind continental expansion. Others have stressed the supposed "superiority" of Anglo-Saxon culture over Indian and Spanish civiliza-

tions. Still other writers have seen American expansion as simply another chapter in the familiar story of territorial conquest. In recent years, many historians, no doubt influenced by the general reappraisal of America's relations with the rest of the world, have stressed the "imperialistic" forces behind America's territorial growth. These writers identify economic considerations—the quest for markets, the desire for cheap land, the demands for the expansion of slavery—as the motivations for conquest. Scholars have also begun to show more interest in, and sympathy for, the people displaced or absorbed in America's sweep to the western sea. They condemn the racial doctrines that had for several generations been used to justify expansionism.

SELECT READINGS

Primary Source Documents

The colorful reminiscences of the pioneers are collected in Dale Morgan, ed., *Overland in 1846: Diaries and Letters of the California-Oregon Trail* (1963). The outbreak and conduct of the Mexican War come alive in the fascinating *Diary of James K. Polk,* edited by Milo Milton Quaife (1910).

Secondary Sources

A brief introduction is Ray A. Billington, *The Far Western Frontier, 1830–1860* (1956); more comprehensive is his *Westward Expansion* (rev. ed., 1974). Still useful is Albert K. Weinberg, *Manifest Destiny* (1935), though it should be supplemented by two works of Frederick Merk, *Manifest Destiny and Mission in American History* (1963) and *Monroe Doctrine and Expansionism, 1843–1859* (1966). For the Pacific region, see Francis Parkman's classic *The California and Oregon Trail* (1849) and Norman A. Graebner's general account, *Empire on the Pacific* (1955). On the conflict with Mexico, see K. Jack Bauer, *The Mexican-American War, 1846–1848* (1974). The other side's perspective is given in Gene M. Brack, *Mexico Views Manifest Destiny, 1821–1846* (1976). John H. Schroeder analyzes an important aspect of the conflict in *Mr. Polk's War: American Opposition and Dissent, 1846–1848* (1973). David M. Pletcher gives an overall view in *The Diplomacy of the Annexation of Texas, Oregon, and the Mexican War* (1973). William R. Brock summarizes the politics of the 1840s in *Parties and Political Conscience: American Dilemmas, 1840–1850* (1979). Unusually colorful social history of the westward movement is provided in John Mack Faragher, *Women and Men on the Overland Trail* (1979) and John D. Unruh, Jr., *The Plains Across: The Overland Emigrants and the Trans-Mississippi West, 1840–1860* (1979). Julie Roy Jeffrey focuses on *Frontier Women* (1979).

17

Shaping the National Economy

**The progress of invention is really a threat [to monarchy].
Whenever I see a railroad I look for a republic.**

Ralph Waldo Emerson, 1866

The March of Mechanization

A gifted group of British inventors, beginning about 1750, perfected a series of machines for the mass production of textiles. This enslavement of steam multiplied the power of man's muscles some ten thousandfold, and ushered in the modern factory system.

The factory system gradually spread from England—"the world's workshop"—to other lands. It took a generation or so to reach western Europe, and then the United States. Why was the youthful American Republic, destined to be an industrial giant, so slow to embrace the machine?

For one thing, virgin soil in America was cheap. Land-starved descendants of land-starved peasants were not going to coop themselves up in smelly factories when they might till their own acres in God's fresh air and sunlight. Labor was therefore generally scarce, and enough nimble hands to oper-

ate the machines were hard to find. Money for capital investment, moreover, was not plentiful in pioneering America. Raw materials lay undeveloped, undiscovered, or unsuspected.

Just as labor was scarce, so were consumers. The young country at first lacked a domestic market large enough to make factory-scale manufacturing profitable.

Long-established British factories, which provided cutthroat competition, posed another problem. Their superiority was attested by the fact that a few unscrupulous Yankee manufacturers, out to make a dishonest dollar, learned to stamp their own products with faked English trademarks.

The British also enjoyed a monopoly in the textile machinery, whose secrets they were anxious to hide from foreign competitors. Parliament enacted laws, in harmony with the mercantilistic system, forbidding the export of the machines, or the emigration of mechanics able to reproduce them.

Although a number of small manufacturing enterprises existed in the early Republic, the future industrial colossus was still snoring. Not until well past the middle of the nineteenth century did the value of the output of the factories exceed that of the farms.

Whitney Ends the Fiber Famine

Samuel Slater has been acclaimed the "Father of the Factory System" in America, and seldom can the paternity of a movement more properly be ascribed to one person. A skilled British mechanic of twenty-one, he was attracted by bounties being offered to English workmen familiar with the textile machines. After memorizing the plans for the machinery, he escaped in disguise to America, where he won the backing of Moses Brown, a Quaker capitalist in Rhode Island. Laboriously reconstructing the essential apparatus with the aid of a blacksmith and a carpenter, he put into operation in 1791 the first efficient American machinery for the spinning of cotton thread.

The ravenous mechanism was now ready, but where was the cotton fiber? Handpicking 1 pound (0.45 kilogram) of lint from 3 pounds (1.36 kilograms) of seed was a full day's work for one slave, and this process was so expensive that cotton cloth was relatively rare.

Another mechanical genius, Massachusetts-born Eli Whitney, now made his mark. After graduating from Yale College, he journeyed to Georgia to serve as a private tutor while preparing for the law. There he was told that the poverty of the South would be relieved if someone could only invent a workable device for separating the seed from the short-staple cotton fiber. Within ten days in 1793, he constructed a crude machine called the cotton gin (short for en*gine*) that was fifty times more efficient than the handpicking process.

Few machines have ever wrought so wondrous a change. The gin affected not only the history of America but that of the world. Almost overnight

the raising of cotton became highly profitable, and the South was tied hand and foot to the throne of King Cotton. Human bondage had been dying out, but the insatiable demand for cotton reriveted the chains on the limbs of the luckless Southern blacks.

South and North both prospered. Slave-driving planters cleared more acres for cotton, pushing the Cotton Kingdom westward off the depleted tidewater plains, over the Piedmont, and onto the black loam bottomlands of Alabama and Mississippi. Humming gins poured out avalanches of snowy fiber for the spindles of the Yankee machines. The American phase of the Industrial Revolution, which first blossomed in cotton textiles, was well on its way.

Factories at first flourished most actively in New England, though branching out into the more populous areas of New York, New Jersey, and Pennsylvania. The South, increasingly wedded to the production of cotton, could boast of comparatively little manufacturing. Its capital was bound up in slaves; its local consumers for the most part were desperately poor.

New England was singularly favored as an industrial center for several reasons. Her narrow belt of stony soil discouraged farming and hence made manufacturing more attractive than elsewhere. A relatively dense population provided labor; shipping brought in capital; and snug seaports made easy the import of raw materials and the export of the finished products. Finally, the rapid rivers—most notably the Merrimack in Massachusetts—provided abundant water power to turn the cogs of the machines. By 1860, more than 400 million pounds (182,000 metric tons) of Southern cotton were pouring annually into the gaping maws of over 1,000 mills, mostly in New England.

Marvels in Manufacturing

America's factories spread slowly until about 1807, when there began the fateful sequence of the embargo, non-intercourse, and the War of 1812. The stoppage of European shipping drove both capital and labor from the waves onto the factory floor. "Buy American" and "Wear American" became popular slogans, as patriotism prompted the wearing of baggy homespun garments. President Madison donned some at his inauguration, where he was said to have been a walking argument for the better processing of native wool.

The manufacturing boomlet broke abruptly with the Peace of Ghent in 1815, as British competitors unloaded their dammed-up surpluses at ruinously low prices. Responding to pained outcries, Congress provided some relief when it passed the mildly protective Tariff of 1816.

As the factory system flourished, it embraced numerous other industries in addition to textiles. Prominent among them was the manufacturing of firearms, and here the wizardly Eli Whitney again appeared with an epochal contribution. Frustrated in his earlier efforts to monopolize the cotton gin, he turned to the mass production of muskets for the United States army. Up to this time each part of a firearm had been hand-tooled, and if the trigger of one broke, the trigger of another might or might not fit. About 1798 Whitney seized upon the idea of having machines make each part, so that all the triggers, for example, would be as much alike as the successive imprints of a copperplate engraving. Journeying to Washington, he reportedly dismantled ten of his new muskets in the presence of skeptical officials, scrambled the parts together, and then quickly reassembled ten different muskets.

The principle of interchangeable parts was widely adopted by 1850, and it ultimately became the basis of modern mass-production, assembly-line methods. It gave to the North the vast industrial plant which ensured its eventual military preponderance over the South. The Yankee Eli Whitney, by perfecting the cotton gin, gave slavery a renewed lease on life, and perhaps made inevitable the Civil War. The same Whitney, by popularizing the principle of interchangeable parts, caused factories to flourish in the North, and contributed heavily to the winning of that war by the Union.

The sewing machine, invented by Elias Howe in 1846 and perfected by Isaac Singer, gave another strong boost to northern industrialization. The sewing machine became the foundation of the ready-made clothing industry, which took root about the time of the Civil War. It drove many a seamstress from the shelter of the private home to the factory where, like a human robot, she tended the clattering mechanisms.

Each momentous new invention seemed to stimulate still more imaginative inventions. For the decade ending in 1800 only 306 patents were registered in Washington, but the decade ending in 1860 saw the amazing total of 28,000. Yet in 1838 the clerk of the Patent Office had resigned in despair, complaining that all worthwhile inventions had been discovered.

Technical advances spurred equally important changes in the form and legal status of business organizations. The principle of limited liability aided the concentration of capital by permitting the individual investor, in cases of legal claims or bankruptcy, to risk no more than his own share of the corporation's stock. Laws of "free incorporation," first passed in New York in 1848, meant that businessmen could create corporations without applying for individual charters from the legislature.

Samuel F. B. Morse's telegraph was among the inventions that tightened the sinews of an increasingly complex business world. A distinguished but poverty-stricken portrait painter, Morse finally secured from Congress, to the accompaniment of the usual jeers, an appropriation of $30,000 to support his experiment with "talking wires." In 1844 Morse strung a wire 40 miles (64 kilometers) from Washington to Baltimore, and tapped out the historic message, "What hath God wrought?" The invention brought fame and fortune to Morse, as he put distantly separated people in almost instant communication with one another.

Northern "Wage Slaves"

One ugly offspring of the factory system was an increasingly acute labor problem. Hitherto, manufacturing had been done in the home, or in the small shop, where the master craftsman and his apprentice, rubbing elbows at the same bench, could maintain an intimate and friendly rela-

Textile Workers of Lawrence (Massachusetts). *Engraving by Winslow Homer, a famous painter. Born in Boston in 1836, Homer first became famous as a magazine illustrator. His drawings of battlefield scenes for* Harper's Weekly *during the Civil War made the conflict come to life for thousands of home-bound readers. He abandoned illustration in 1876 and gained even greater renown as a painter in oils and watercolors, especially with his depictions of marine scenes and life among blacks.* (Harper's Weekly, 1868)

tionship. The Industrial Revolution submerged this personal association in the impersonal ownership of stuffy factories in "spindle cities." Around these, like tumors, the slum-like hovels of the "wage slaves" tended to cluster.

Clearly the early factory system did not shower its benefits evenly on all. While many owners waxed fat, workingpeople often wasted away at their workbenches. Hours were long, wages were low, and meals were skimpy and hastily gulped. Workers were forced to toil in unsanitary buildings that were poorly ventilated, lighted, and heated. They were forbidden by law to form labor unions, for such cooperative activity was regarded as a criminal conspiracy. Not surprisingly, only twenty-four recorded strikes occurred before 1835.

Women and children were also sucked into the clanging mechanism of factory production. They typically toiled six days a week, earning a pittance for dreary stints of twelve or thirteen hours— "from dark to dark." The Boston Associates pridefully pointed to their textile mill at Lowell, Massachusetts, as a showplace factory. The workers were virtually all New England farm girls, carefully supervised on and off the job by watchful matrons. Escorted regularly to church from their company boardinghouses, forbidden to form unions, they were as disciplined and docile a labor force as any employer could wish.

Even more vulnerable to exploitation than women were child workers. In 1820, half the nation's industrial toilers were children under ten years of age. Victims of factory labor, many children were mentally blighted, emotionally starved, physically stunted, and even brutally whipped in special "whipping rooms." In Samuel Slater's mill of 1791, the first machine tenders were seven boys and two girls, all under twelve.

By contrast, the lot of most adult male wage workers improved markedly in the 1820s and 1830s. Newly armed with the ballot, they pushed for such goals as the ten-hour day, better wages and working conditions, public education, and an end to the inhuman practice of imprisonment for debt.

Employers, abhorring the rise of the "rabble" in politics, fought the ten-hour day to the last ditch. But labor registered a red-letter gain in 1840 when President Van Buren established the ten-hour day for federal employees on public works, and in ensuing years a number of states gradually fell into line by reducing hours for working people.

Day laborers at last learned that their strongest weapon was to lay down their tools, even at the risk of prosecution under the law. Dozens of strikes erupted in the 1830s and 1840s, most for higher wages or the ten-hour day. The workers lost more strikes than they won, for the employer could resort to such tactics as importing strikebreakers—often derisively called "scabs" or "rats," and often fresh off the boat from the Old World. Labor long raised its voice against the unrestricted inpouring of wage-depressing and union-busting immigrant workers.

By 1830 some 300,000 workers belonged to trade unions, but union membership shriveled because of unemployment during the severe depression of 1837. A more hope-giving sign of the future came in 1842 from the Massachusetts Supreme Court ruling in the case of *Commonwealth* v. *Hunt* that labor unions were not illegal conspiracies, provided that their methods were "honorable and peaceful." This enlightened decision pointed the way to the future, even though strikes remained illegal in most of the country and unions still had nearly a century to go before they could meet management on relatively even terms.

Western Farmers Reap a Revolution in the Fields

As smoke-belching factories altered the eastern skyline, flourishing farms were changing the face of the West. The trans-Allegheny region—especially

McCormick Reaper Works, 1850s. *This scene illustrates the new factory methods of "mass production," which were replacing the older handicraft methods of the small shops. (McCormick Collection, State Historical Society of Wisconsin)*

the Ohio-Indiana-Illinois tier—was fast becoming the nation's breadbasket. Before long, it would become a granary to the world.

Pioneer farmers first hacked a clearing out of the forest, and then planted their painfully furrowed fields to corn. The yellow grain was amazingly versatile. It could be fed to hogs ("corn on the hoof") or distilled into liquor ("corn in the bottle"). Both these products could be more easily transported than the bulky grain itself, and they became the early Western farmer's staple market items. So many hogs were butchered, traded, or shipped at Cincinnati that the city was known as the "Porkopolis" of the West.

Western farmers, who at first floated most of their produce down the Ohio-Mississippi system to feed the booming Cotton Kingdom, continuously sought ways to bring more and more acres into cultivation. Frustrated by thickly matted soil that snagged and snapped fragile wooden plows, farmers rejoiced in 1837 when John Deere finally produced a sharp steel plow light enough to be pulled by horses, rather than oxen.

Virginia-born Cyrus McCormick contributed the most wondrous contraption of all: a mechanical mower-reaper. The clattering cogs of McCormick's horse-drawn machine were to the Western farmers what the cotton gin was to the Southern planters. Seated on his red-chariot reaper, a single husbandman could do the work of five men with sickles and scythes.

No other American invention cut so wide a swath. It made ambitious capitalists out of humble plowmen, who now scrambled for more acres on which to plant more fields of billowing wheat. Large-scale ("extensive"), specialized, cash-crop agriculture came to dominate the trans-Allegheny West. With it followed mounting indebtedness, as farmers bought more land and more machinery to work it. Soon hustling farmer-businessmen were annually harvesting a larger crop than the South could devour. They began to dream of markets elsewhere—in the mushrooming factory towns of the East, or across the faraway Atlantic. But they were still largely landlocked. Commerce moved north and south on the river systems. Before it

could begin to move east-west in bulk, a transportation revolution would have to occur.

Highways and Steamboats

In 1789, when the Constitution was launched, primitive methods of travel were still in use. Waterborne commerce, whether along the coast or on the rivers, was slow, uncertain, and often dangerous. Stagecoaches and wagons lurched over boneshaking roads. Passengers would be routed out to lay nearby fence rails across muddy stretches, and occasionally horses would drown in muddy pits while wagons sank slowly out of sight.

Cheap and efficient carriers were imperative if raw materials were to be transported to the factories, and if the finished product was to be delivered to the consumer.

A promising change came in the 1790s, when a private company completed the Lancaster turnpike, a broad, hard-surfaced highway that thrust 62 miles (100 kilometers) westward from Philadelphia to Lancaster, Pennsylvania. The highly successful Lancaster Pike returned dividends as high as 15 percent annually to its stockholders, attracted a rich trade to Philadelphia, stimulated the westward migration of the canvas-covered Conestoga wagons, and touched off a turnpike-building boom that lasted about twenty years.

Always expensive, Western roads also encountered opposition from states'-righters, who opposed federal aid to local projects, and from eastern states, which protested against being bled of their populations. Westerners scored a notable triumph in 1811 when the federal government began to construct the elongated National or Cumberland Road. When finally completed in 1852, after interruptions caused by the War of 1812 and states'-rights shackles on internal improvements, the highway stretched 591 miles (952 kilometers) from Cumberland, Maryland, to Vandalia, Illinois.

The steamboat craze, which overlapped the turnpike-building era, was touched off by an ambitious painter-engineer named Robert Fulton. In 1807 Fulton installed a powerful steam engine in the vessel *Clermont*, dubbed "Fulton's Folly" by a dubious public. Belching sparks from its single smokestack, the quaint little ship steadily churned up the Hudson River from New York City to Albany, making the 150-mile (242-kilometer) trip in 32 hours.

The success of the steamboat was sensational. Man could now in large degree defy wind, wave, tide, and downstream current. Within a few years Fulton had changed all of America's navigable streams into two-way arteries, thereby doubling their carrying capacity. Hitherto, keelboats had been pushed up the Mississippi, with quivering poles and raucous profanity, at less than one mile an hour—a process that was prohibitively costly. Now the steamboats could churn rapidly against the current, ultimately attaining speeds in excess of 10 miles (16 kilometers) an hour. The mighty Mississippi had finally met her master.

By 1820 some sixty steamboats were plying the Mississippi and its tributaries; by 1860, about one thousand were cruising the inland waters, some of them luxurious river palaces. Chugging steamboats played a vital role in the opening of the West and South, both of which were richly endowed with navigable rivers. Like bunches of grapes on a vine, population clustered along the banks of the broad-flowing streams. Cotton growers and other farmers made haste to take up the now-profitable virgin soil. Not only could they float their produce out to market but, hardly less important, they could ship in, at low cost, their shoes, hardware, and other manufactured necessities.

Canals and Iron Horses

A canal-cutting craze paralleled the boom in turnpikes and steamboats. Led by dynamic Governor DeWitt Clinton, New York state started the trend when it dug the Erie Canal linking the Hudson River to the Great Lakes.

Begun in 1817, the canal eventually ribboned 363 miles (585 kilometers). On its completion in 1825, a garland-bedecked canal boat glided from Buffalo, on Lake Erie, to the Hudson River and on to New York harbor. There, with colorful ceremony, Governor Clinton emptied a cask of water

from the lake to symbolize "the marriage of the waters."

The water from Clinton's cask baptized an Empire State. Mule-drawn passengers and bulky freight could now be handled with cheapness and dispatch, at the dizzy speed of 5 miles (8 kilometers) an hour. The cost of shipping a ton of grain from Buffalo to New York City fell from $100 to $5, and the time of transit from about twenty days to six.

Ever-widening economic ripples followed the completion of the Erie Canal. The value of land along the route skyrocketed, and new cities—like Rochester and Syracuse—blossomed. Industry in the state boomed. The new profitableness of farming in the Old Northwest—notably in Ohio, Michigan, Indiana, and Illinois—attracted thousands of European immigrants to the unaxed and untaxed lands now available. Flotillas of steamships soon plied the Great Lakes, connecting with waiting canal barges at Buffalo. Interior waterside villages like Cleveland, Detroit, and Chicago exploded into mighty cities.

Other profound economic and political changes followed the completion of the canal. The price of potatoes in New York City was cut in half, and many dispirited New England farmers, no longer able to face this ruinous competition, abandoned their rocky holdings and went elsewhere. Some became mill hands, thus speeding the industrialization of America. Others, finding it easy to go west over the Erie Canal, took up new farmlands south of the Great Lakes, where they were joined by countless thousands of New Yorkers and other northerners. Still others shifted to fruit, vegetable, and dairy farming. These transformations in the Northeast showed how long-established local market structures could be swamped by the emerging behemoth of a continental economy.

The most significant contribution to the development of such an economy proved to be the railroad. It was fast, reliable, cheaper than canals to construct, and not frozen over in winter. Able to go almost anywhere, even through the Allegheny barrier, it defied terrain and weather. The first railroad appeared in the United States in 1828. By 1860, only

The Stourbridge Lion.   *On August 8, 1829, at Honesdale, Pennsylvania, this smoke-belching beast made the first successful trip in America by a steam locomotive. (The Bettmann Archive)*

thirty-two years later, the United States boasted 30,000 miles (48,000 kilometers) of railroad track, three-fourths of it in the rapidly industrializing North.

At first the railroad faced strong opposition from vested interests, especially canal backers. Anxious to protect its investment in the Erie Canal, the New York legislature in 1833 prohibited the railroads from carrying freight—at least temporarily. Early railroads were also considered a dangerous public menace, for sparks set fire to haystacks and houses, and appalling accidents turned the wooden "miniature hells" into flaming funeral pyres for their riders.

Railroad pioneers had to overcome other obstacles as well. Arrivals and departures were conjectural, and numerous differences in gauge (the distance between the rails) meant frequent changes of trains for passengers. In 1840 there were seven transfers between Philadelphia and Charleston. But gauges gradually became standardized, safety devices were adopted, and the Pullman "sleeping palace" was introduced in 1859. America at long last was being bound together with ribs of iron, later to be made of steel.

The Transport Web Binds the Union

More than anything else, the desire of the East to tap the West stimulated the "transportation revolution." Until about 1830, the produce of the western region drained southward to the cotton belt or to the heaped-up wharves of New Orleans. The steamboat vastly aided the reverse flow of finished goods up the watery western arteries, and helped bind West and South together. But the truly revolutionary changes in commerce and communication came in the three decades before the Civil War, as canals and railroad tracks radiated out from the East, across the Alleghenies, and into the blossom-

Railroads in Operation in 1850.

Railroads in Operation in 1860.

ing heartland. The ditchdiggers and tie-layers were attempting nothing less than a conquest of nature itself. They would offset the "natural" flow of trade on the interior rivers by laying down an impressive grid of "internal improvements."

The builders succeeded beyond their wildest dreams. The Mississippi was increasingly robbed of its traffic, as goods moved eastward on chugging trains, puffing lake boats, and mule-tugged canal barges. Governor Clinton had in effect picked up the mighty Father of Waters and flung it over the Alleghenies, forcing it to empty into the sea at New York City. By the 1840s Buffalo was handling more Western produce than New Orleans. Between 1836 and 1860, grain shipments through Buffalo increased a staggering sixtyfold. New York City became the seaboard queen of the nation, a gigantic port through which a vast hinterland poured its wealth, and to which it daily paid economic tribute.

By the eve of the Civil War, a truly continental economy had emerged. The principle of division of labor, which spelled productivity and profits in the factory, applied on a national scale as well. Each region now specialized in a particular type of economic activity. The South raised cotton for export to New England and old England; the West grew grain and livestock to feed eastern factory workers; the East made machines and textiles for the other two regions.

The economic pattern thus woven had fateful political and military implications. Many Southerners regarded the Mississippi as a silver chain that naturally linked together the upper valley states and the Cotton Kingdom. They were convinced, as secession approached, that some or all of these states would have to secede with them or be strangled. But they overlooked the man-made links that now bound the upper Mississippi Valley to the East in intimate commercial union. Southern rebels would have to fight not only Northern armies, but the tight bonds of an interdependent continental economy. Economically, the two northerly sections were Siamese twins.

The emergence of a specialized, continental-scale economy also had far-reaching social effects. As more and more Americans—mill hands as well as farmers, women as well as men—linked their economic fate to the burgeoning market economy, the self-sufficient households of colonial days were transformed. Most families had once raised all their own food, spun their own wool, and bartered with their neighbors for the few necessities they could not make themselves. In growing numbers, they now scattered to work for wages in the mills, or they planted just a few crops for sale and market and used the money to buy goods made by strangers in far-off factories. As store-bought fabrics, candles, and soap replaced home-made products, a quiet revolution occurred in the household division of labor and status. Traditional women's work was rendered superfluous and devalued. The home itself, once a center of economic production in which all family members cooperated, grew into a place of refuge from the world of work, a refuge that became increasingly the special and separate sphere of women.

Wealth and Poverty

Revolutionary advances in manufacturing and transportation brought increased prosperity to all Americans, but they also widened the gulf between the rich and the poor. Millionaires had been rare in the early days of the Republic, but by the eve of the Civil War several specimens of colossal financial success were strutting across the national stage. Spectacular was the case of fur trader and real-estate speculator John Jacob Astor, who left an estate of $30 million on his death in 1848.

Cities bred the greatest extremes of economic inequality. Unskilled workers, then as always, fared worst. Many of them came to make up a floating mass of "drifters," buffeted from town to town by the shifting prospects for menial jobs. These wandering workers accounted, at various times, for up to half the population of the brawling industrial centers. Although their numbers were large, they left little behind them but the homely fruits of their transient labor. Largely unstoried and unsung, they are among the forgotten men and women of American history.

Many myths about "social mobility" grew up over the buried memories of these luckless day laborers. Mobility did exist in industrializing America—but not in the proportions that legend often portrays. Rags-to-riches success stories were relatively few.

Yet America, with its dynamic society and its wide open spaces, undoubtedly provided much more "opportunity" than did the contemporary countries of the Old World—which is why millions of immigrants packed their bags and headed for New World shores. Moreover, a rising tide lifts all boats, and the improvement in overall standards of living was real. Wages for unskilled workers in labor-hungry America rose about 1 percent a year from 1820 to 1860. This general prosperity helped to defuse the potential class conflict that otherwise might have exploded—and that did explode in several European countries.

Cables, Clippers, and Pony Riders

A new pattern of American foreign trade also emerged in the antebellum years, though businessmen concentrated on developing the wondrously rewarding domestic market. (Foreign commerce seldom added up to more than 7 percent of the national product.) Abroad as at home, cotton was king and regularly accounted for more than half the value of all American exports. After the repeal of the British exclusionary Corn Laws in 1846, the wheat gathered by McCormick's reapers began to play an increasingly important role in trade with Great Britain. Americans generally exported agricultural products and imported manufactured goods—and they generally imported more than they exported.

A crucial step came in 1858 when Cyrus Field, called "the greatest wire puller in history," finally stretched a cable under the deep North Atlantic waters from Newfoundland to Ireland. Although this initial cable went dead after three weeks of public rejoicing, a heavier cable laid in 1866 permanently linked the American and European continents.

The United States merchant marine encountered rough sailing during much of the early nineteenth century. American vessels had been repeatedly laid up by the embargo, the War of 1812, and the panics of 1819 and 1837. American naval designers made few contributions to maritime progress. A pioneer American steamer, the *Savannah,* had crept across the Atlantic in 1819, but she used sail most of the time and was pursued for a day by a British captain who thought her afire.

In the 1840s and 1850s a golden age dawned for American shipping. Yankee naval yards, notably Donald McKay's at Boston, began to send down the ways sleek new craft called clipper ships. Long, narrow, and majestic, they glided across the sea under towering masts and clouds of canvas. In a fair breeze they could outrun any steamer.

The stately clippers sacrificed cargo space for speed, and their captains made killings by hauling high-value cargoes in record times. They wrested much of the tea-carrying trade between the Far East and England from their slower-moving British competitors, and they sped thousands of impatient adventurers to the gold fields of California and Australia.

But the hour of glory for the clipper was relatively brief. On the eve of the Civil War the British had clearly won the world race for maritime ascendancy with their iron tramp steamers ("tea-kettles"). Though slower and less romantic than the clipper, these vessels were steadier, more capacious, more reliable, and hence more profitable.

No story of rapid American communication would be complete without including the Far West.

By 1858 horse-drawn overland stages, immortalized by Mark Twain's *Roughing It*, were a familiar sight. Their dusty tracks stretched from the bank of the muddy Missouri River clear to California.

Even more dramatic was the Pony Express, established in 1860 to carry mail speedily the 2,000 lonely miles (3,220 kilometers) from St. Joseph, Missouri, to Sacramento, California. Daring, lightweight riders, leaping onto wiry ponies saddled at stations approximately 10 miles (16 kilometers) apart, could make the trip in an amazing ten days. These unarmed horsemen galloped on, summer or winter, day or night, through dust or snow, past red Indians and white bandits. The speeding postmen missed only one trip, though the whole enterprise lost money heavily and folded after only eighteen legend-leaving months.

Just as the clippers had succumbed to steam, so were the express riders unhorsed by Morse's clacking keys, which began tapping messages to California in 1861. The swift ships and the fleet ponies ushered out a dying technology of wind and muscle. In the future, machines, rather than manpower, would be in the saddle.

VARYING VIEWPOINTS

Economic history was once simply a tale of industrious inventors and inventive industrialists. But economics has become a sophisticated science, and so has the story of the material past. Historians now seek to know just why economic growth occurred. Many scholars emphasize the plentiful resources of the United States. These resources, especially abundant land, limited the industrial labor supply, thus driving up wages and inducing manufacturers to adopt labor-saving machinery. Thus, the natural bounty of the continent set off a chain reaction that unleashed explosive economic growth.

Other historians stress the contribution of human resources to America's economic progress. They focus on the large population of natives and immigrants to till the soil and fill the factories, the exploitation of slaves, legal and political innovations such as the tariff and the general incorporation laws, and the technical genius of the American people.

Historians are also increasingly interested in the question: Which people benefited most from economic growth? This is known as the "welfare" question, as distinct from the fact of growth alone. Recently, labor historians, such as Sean Wilentz, have described the emergence of an increasingly self-conscious working class in industrial America. These studies reveal the efforts of urban workers to protect themselves from the dislocations of industrialization and to secure a fair share of the benefits of the economic development that was rapidly occurring in the new nation.

SELECT READINGS

Primary Source Documents

Seth Luther, *An Address to the Working-Men of New-England** (1833), is the eloquent appeal of an uneducated working-class labor reformer. On the transportation revolution, see John H. B. Latrobe's *Western Waters** (1871) and Mark Twain's classic *Life on the Mississippi* (1883). Lemuel Shaw's decision of 1842 in *Commonwealth v. Hunt,* 4 Metc. III (in Henry Steele Commager, *Documents of American History*) is regarded as the "Magna Charta of American labor organization."

Secondary Sources

Solid introductions are George R. Taylor, *The Transportation Revolution, 1815–1860* (1951); Clarence H. Danhoff, *Change in Agriculture: The Northern United States, 1820–1870* (1969); and Douglas C. North, *Economic Growth in the United States, 1790–1860* (1961). The events of the period are placed in a larger context of economic history in Stuart Bruchey, *The Roots of American Eco-* *nomic Growth, 1607–1861* (1965) and in Walt W. Rostow, *The Stages of Economic Growth* (rev. ed., 1971). The laboring classes are chronicled in Joseph Rayback, *History of American Labor* (1966). Consult also Herbert Gutman's path-breaking *Work, Culture, and Society in Industrializing America* (1976) and Sean Wilentz's insightful *Chants Democratic: New York City and the Rise of the American Working Class, 1788–1850* (1984). On the introduction of technology, see the provocative anthology edited by S. B. Saul, *Technological Change: The U.S. and Britain in the Nineteenth Century* (1970). Ideological aspects of this process are described in John F. Kassen, *Civilizing the Machine: Technology and Republican Values in America, 1776–1900* (1976). On railroads, consult Robert Fogel, *Railroads and American Economic Growth* (1964), which presents the startling thesis that the iron horse in fact did little to promote growth. For a different view, see Albert Fishlow, *American Railroads and the Transformation of the Ante-Bellum Economy* (1965).

18

Creating an American Character, 1790–1860

America was bred in a cabin.

Morris Birkbeck, 1817

American Children of Environment

"In the United States," wrote Gertrude Stein, "there is more space where nobody is than where anybody is. This is what makes America what it is." Even today, although a highly industrialized and technologically sophisticated people, Americans have not fully shaken off the effects of their centuries-long battle with the wilderness.

The West, with its raw frontier, was the most typically American part of America. As Ralph Waldo Emerson wrote in 1844, "Europe stretches to the Alleghenies; America lies beyond."

The "go-aheaditive" Americans sprang from a restless breed of people. Born hustlers—always "a-doin"—they were footloose and frequently on the move. One "tall tale" of the frontier described chickens that voluntarily crossed their legs every spring, waiting to be tied for the annual move west. Even in repose, Americans were often whittling, sewing, chewing, jiggling, or rocking. The rocking chair—"the chair that travels but stays at home"—was a typically American device. At the dinner table, the rule seemed to be "gobble, gulp, and go." Americans had no time for four o'clock tea, as the English did. There was too much cream to be skimmed off the continent—furs, timber, wildlife—with a consequent wasting of soil and natural resources in some areas. All this restlessness came partly from youth; as late as 1850 the majority of Americans were under thirty.

The West attracted these nervous particles of human energy like a magnet. Already by 1840 the "demographic center" of the American population map had crossed the Alleghenies. On the eve of the Civil War, it had marched beyond the Ohio River. Legend portrays an army of muscular axmen triumphantly carving civilization out of the Western

Westward Movement of the Center of Population, 1790–1984. *Note the remarkable equilibrium of the north-south pull from 1790 onward, and the strong spurt west and south after 1940. The 1980 census revealed that the nation's center of population had at last moved west of the Mississippi River.*

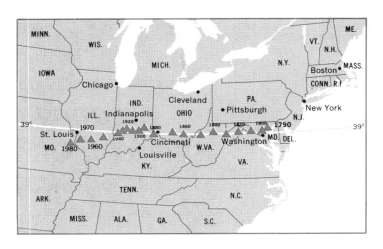

woods. But in reality life was downright grim for most pioneer families. Poorly fed, ill-clad, housed in hastily erected shanties, they were perpetual victims of disease, depression, and premature death. Above all, there was the awful loneliness, especially for women, who sometimes cracked under the strain. They were often cut off from human contact, especially neighbors, for whole days or even weeks, while confined to the cramped orbit of a dark cabin erected in a crude and secluded clearing. Breakdowns and even madness were all too frequently the "opportunities" that the frontier offered to pioneer women.

Rugged Pioneers

A mad scramble for riches led not only to waste but to superficiality. Wooden bridges were flung across streams, until time permitted the hurry-up American to build stone spans. The breathless pursuit of treasure inevitably led to accusations of money-chasing and crass materialism. John Stuart Mill, the noted English writer, remarked in the 1840s that in America the life of one sex was "devoted to dollar hunting, and of the other to the breeding of dollar hunters." Wealth was everywhere recognized as the badge of success and the symbol of power.

The rough-and-tough American—especially the Westerner—was often crude, ruthless, brutal. Tobacco chewing and indelicate spitting—"the salivary propensity"—became a national scandal in the decades before the Civil War. One visiting Briton suggested that the spittoon, not the eagle, should be America's national emblem; and a group of Japanese visitors in 1860 noted that the white man had brown saliva. Frontier wrestling, often of the no-holds-barred type, sanctioned such niceties as the biting off of noses or the gouging out of eyes. "Look out, or I'll measure the length of your eye-strings [eye muscles]" was an expressive frontier warning. Nor was brutality directed solely at fellow white men. The Indians stood in the way of expansion, and when they fought back they were brushed aside or killed off, like the wild animals.

Average Americans were strenuous, courageous, aggressive—overendowed with the "lick all creation" spirit. They had unshakeable faith in their military prowess, untrained though they might be. They were tough and tenacious. Learning to laugh at adversity, they fought the elements, the wild animals ("varmints"), their Canadian and Mexican neighbors, and, above all, the Indians.

Gamblers All

Marooned by geography, Americans were self-centered, provincial, and isolationist, whether in their hometowns or in the world community. First and foremost they were individualists. The men depended on their own trusty axes and especially their rifles, which, in the Western phrase, made them all "equally tall." Their political and social beliefs might not bear a radical stamp, for many observers noted the remarkable conformity of American opinion. But they were convinced that their way in the world was for them alone to make. Emerson's popular lecture-essay, "Self-Reliance," struck a deeply responsive chord. Popular literature of the period abounded in portraits of heroically unique, even isolated, figures like Cooper's Natty Bumppo and Melville's Captain Ahab—just as Jacksonian politics aimed to emancipate the lonewolf, enterprising businessperson. Vast space and fabulous economic abundance fostered this fond self-image, and gave it a certain reality. Yet even in this heyday of "rugged individualism" there were exceptions. Pioneers, in tasks clearly beyond their own individual resources, would call upon their neighbors for logrolling and barnraising, and upon their federal government for help in building internal improvements.

Americans in general were confident, buoyant, optimistic—born boosters, tellers of "tall tales," admirers of the giant lumberjack, the fabled Paul Bunyan. Pessimism was a kind of treason; "knockers" were not wanted. Immigrants had to be courageously optimistic to undertake the stormy Atlantic crossing.

Those who reached the New World were all gamblers. They gambled their lives against disease and Indians, and their crops and fortunes against the elements. The American people are distilled not only from a select group of brave men and women but also from a long line of risk-takers.

Americans were boastful—a trait growing out of their easy optimism. The game of poker ("brag"), with its premium on successful bluffing, attained great popularity in the West, especially with Henry Clay. Americans were painfully aware of their nation's many physical and cultural shortcomings and while smarting under the sneers of monocled foreigners, they would brag loudly and defensively about the splendid cities that would one day spring from their malarial swamps. Significantly, they boasted of the future, while Europeans boasted of their past. They also learned to worship bigness, partly because America excelled in size. Above all, they had unbounded faith in the future, in progress, in the "American dream."

The Torch of Democracy

The American people were essentially democratic except, conspicuously, for the blight of slavery. In their social democracy, especially beyond the mountains, they set little store by caste, tradition, or family trees. The first question was not "Who are you?" but "What can you do?" The very first sentence of Alexis de Tocqueville's great treatise entitled *Democracy in America* (1835) proclaimed: "Nothing struck me more forcibly than the general equality of conditions among the people."

Political democracy was one of the nation's proudest boasts. White manhood suffrage came to be the rule. The people realized that the world was skeptically watching their vast experiment in political democracy, and this awareness contributed further to self-conscious boastfulness. Emerson once observed that the American eagle was something of a peacock.

Americans, moreover, were lovers of freedom. Responding to the flattery of imitation, they applauded democratic revolutions whenever they occurred, and often assisted them with money and volunteers. They cheered as thrones crashed, and they openly pitied people who did not have the "gumption" to rise up and break their autocratic chains. Mark Twain caught the spirit of anti-monarchical America when he had Huck Finn remark, "Sometimes I wish we could hear of a country that's out of kings."

The March of the Millions

An amazing multiplication of people continued decade after decade, without serious slackening. By midcentury the population was still doubling approximately every twenty-three years, as in fertile colonial days.

By 1860 the original thirteen states had more than doubled in number: thirty-three stars graced the American flag. The United States was the fourth most populous nation in the Western world, exceeded by only three European countries—Russia, France, and Austria.

Urban growth continued explosively. In 1790 only two cities could boast 20,000 or more souls:

Philadelphia and New York. By 1860 there were forty-three; and about three hundred other places claimed over 5,000 inhabitants apiece. New York was the metropolis; New Orleans, the "Queen of the South;" and Chicago, the swaggering lord of the Midwest, destined to be "hog butcher for the world."

Such overrapid urbanization unfortunately brought undesirable by-products. It intensified the problems of smelly slums, feeble street lighting, inadequate policing, impure water, foul sewage, ravenous rats, and improper garbage disposal. Hogs poked their scavenging snouts about many city streets as late as the 1840s. Boston in 1823 pioneered with a sewage system; and New York in 1842 abandoned wells for a piped-in water supply. The city thus unknowingly eliminated the breeding places of many disease-carrying mosquitoes.

A continuing high birthrate accounted for most of the increase in population, but by the 1840s the tides of immigration were adding hundreds of thousands more. Before this decade, immigrants had been flowing in at the rate of about 60,000 a year, but suddenly the influx was tripled in the 1840s, and then quadrupled in the 1850s. During these two feverish decades, over a million and a half Irish, and nearly as many Germans, swarmed down the gangplanks. Why did they come?

The immigrants came partly because Europe seemed to be running out of room. The population of the Old World more than doubled in the nineteenth century, and Europe began to generate a great seething pool of apparently "surplus" people. They were displaced and footloose in their homelands before they felt the tug of the American magnet. Indeed, at least as many people moved about *within* Europe as crossed the Atlantic.

Although many of these people went elsewhere, it was America that beckoned most strongly to the struggling masses of Europe. About 35 million of the nearly 60 million people who abandoned Europe in the century after 1840 headed for "the land of freedom and opportunity," where no aristocratic caste or state church suppressed the individual. Much-read letters sent home by immigrants—"America letters"— described in glowing terms the richer life: low

taxes, no compulsory military service, and "three meat meals a day." The introduction of transoceanic steamships also meant that the immigrants could come speedily, in a matter of ten or twelve days instead of ten or twelve weeks. They were still jammed into unsanitary quarters, thus suffering an appalling death rate, but the nightmare was more endurable because it was shorter.

The Emerald Isle Moves West

Ireland, already groaning under the heavy hand of British overlords, was prostrated in the mid-1840s. A terrible rot attacked the potato crop, on which the people had become dangerously dependent, and about one-fourth of them were swept away by disease and hunger. Starved bodies were found dead by the roadsides with grass in their mouths. All told, about 2 million perished.

Tens of thousands of destitute souls, fleeing the Land of Famine for the Land of Plenty, flocked to America in the "Black Forties." Ireland's great export has been population; and the Irish take their place beside the Jews as a dispersed people.

These uprooted newcomers swarmed into the larger seaboard cities, such as Boston and New York, which rapidly became the largest Irish city in the world.

The luckless Irish received no red-carpet treatment. They were scorned by the older American stock, especially "proper" Protestant Bostonians, who regarded the scruffy Catholic newcomers as a social menace. Barely literate "Biddies" (Bridgets) took jobs as kitchen maids. Broad-shouldered "Paddies" (Patricks) were pushed into pick-and-shovel drudgery on canals and railroads, where thousands left their bones as victims of disease and accidental explosions. It was said that an Irishman lay buried under every railroad tie. Even so, the Irish were hated by native workers. "No Irish Need Apply" was a sign commonly posted at factory gates, and was often abbreviated to NINA. The Irish, in turn, fiercely resented the blacks, with whom they shared society's basement. Race riots between black and Irish dockworkers flared up in several port cities, and the Irish were always cool to the abolitionist cause.

Irish and German Immigration by Decade

Years	Irish	German	All Others	Grand Total
1820–1830	Unknown	Unknown	Unknown	151,824
1831–1840	207,381	152,454	239,290	599,125
1841–1850	780,719	434,626	497,906	1,713,251
1851–1860	914,119	951,667	732,428	2,598,214
1861–1870	435,778	787,468	1,091,578	2,314,824
1871–1880	436,871	718,182	1,657,138	2,812,191
1881–1890	655,482	1,452,970	3,138,161	5,246,613
1891–1900	388,416	505,152	2,793,996	3,687,564

The friendless Irish were forced to fend for themselves. The Ancient Order of Hibernians, a semi-secret society founded in Ireland to fight rapacious landlords, served in America as a benevolent society, aiding the downtrodden. It also helped to spawn the "Molly Maguires," a shadowy Irish miners' union that rocked the Pennsylvania coal districts in the 1860s and 1870s.

The Irish tended to remain in low-skill occupations, but gradually improved their lot, usually by acquiring modest amounts of property. The education of children was cut short as families struggled to save money to purchase a home. But for humble Irish peasants, cruelly cast out of their homeland, owning property was a grand "success."

Politics quickly attracted these gregarious Gaelic newcomers. They soon began to gain control of powerful city machines, notably New York's Tammany Hall, and reaped the patronage rewards. Before long, beguilingly brogued Irishmen dominated police departments in many big cities, where they now drove the "Paddy wagons" that had once carted their brawling forebears to jail.

The German Forty-Eighters

The influx of refugees from Germany between 1830 and 1860 was hardly less spectacular than that from Ireland. During these troubled years, over a million and a half thrifty Germans stepped onto American soil. The bulk of them were uprooted farmers, displaced by crop failures and by other hardships. But a strong sprinkling were liberal political refugees. Saddened by the collapse of the democratic revolutions of 1848, they had decided to leave the autocratic fatherland and flee to America—the brightest hope of democracy.

Germany's loss was America's gain. Zealous German liberals like the lanky and public-spirited Carl Schurz, a relentless foe of slavery and public corruption, contributed richly to the elevation of American political life.

Many of the German newcomers, unlike the Irish, possessed a modest amount of this world's goods. Most of them pushed out to the lush lands of the Middle West, notably Wisconsin, where they settled and established model farms.

The hand of Germans in shaping American life was widely felt in still other ways. They had fled from the militarism and wars of Europe, and consequently came to be a bulwark of isolationist sentiment in the upper Mississippi Valley. Better educated on the whole than the stump-grubbing Americans, they strongly supported public schools, including their *Kindergarten* (children's garden). They likewise did much to stimulate art and music. As outspoken champions of freedom, they became relentless enemies of slavery during the fevered years before the Civil War.

Yet the Germans—often dubbed "damned Dutchmen"—were occasionally regarded with suspicion by their old-stock American neighbors. Seeking to preserve their language and culture, they sometimes settled in compact "colonies" and kept aloof from the surrounding community. Accustomed to the "Continental Sunday" and uncurbed by Puritan tradition, they made merry on the Sabbath and drank huge quantities of an amber beverage called *Bier* (beer), which dates its real popularity in America to their coming.

Flare-ups of Antiforeignism

The invasion by this so-called immigrant "rabble" in the 1840s and 1850s inflamed the hates of American "nativists." Not only did the newcomers take jobs from "native" Americans, but the bulk of displaced Irishmen were Roman Catholics, as were a substantial minority of the Germans. The Church of Rome was still widely regarded by many old-line Americans as a "foreign" church.

Roman Catholics were now on the move. Seeking to protect their children from Protestant indoctrination in the public schools, they began in the 1840s to construct an entirely separate Catholic school system—an enormously expensive undertaking for a poor immigrant community, but one that revealed the strength of its religious commitment. A negligible minority in colonial days, Catholics became a powerful religious group with the enormous influx of the Irish and Germans in

the 1840s and 1850s. In 1840 they ranked fifth, behind the Baptists, Methodists, Presbyterians, and Congregationalists. By 1850, with some 1.8 million communicants, they had bounded into first place—a position they have never lost.

"Native" Americans were alarmed by these mounting figures. They professed to believe that in due time the "alien riffraff" would "establish" the Catholic church at the expense of Protestantism and would introduce "Popish idols." The noisier American "nativists" rallied for political action. In 1849 they formed the Order of the Star-Spangled Banner, which soon developed into the formidable American, or "Know-Nothing" party—a name derived from its secretiveness. "Nativists" agitated for rigid restrictions on immigration and naturalization and for laws authorizing the deportation of alien paupers.

Anti-Catholic sentiment occasionally burst out in ugly mass violence. As early as 1834 a Catholic convent near Boston was burned by a howling mob, and in ensuing years there were a few scattered attacks on Catholic schools and churches. The most frightful flare-up occurred during 1844 in Philadelphia, where the Irish Catholics fought

Crooked Voting. *A bitter "nativist" cartoon charging Irish and German immigrants with "stealing" elections. (New York Public Library)*

back against the threats of the "nativists." The City of Brotherly Love did not quiet down until two Catholic churches had been burned and some thirteen citizens had been killed and fifty wounded in several days of fighting.

Reviving Religion

Church attendance was still a regular ritual for about three-fourths of the 23 million Americans in 1850. Alexi de Tocqueville declared that there was "no country in the world where the Christian religion retains a greater influence over the souls of men than in America." Yet the old Calvinist rigor had long been seeping out of the American churches.

The rationalist ideas of the French Revolutionary era had done much to soften the older orthodoxy. Many of the Founding Fathers, including Paine, Jefferson, and Franklin, embraced the liberal doctrines of Deism, which relied on reason rather than revelation, on science rather than the Bible. Deists rejected the concept of original sin and denied Christ's divinity, but believed in a Supreme Being who had endowed human beings with a capacity for moral behavior.

Deism helped to inspire an important spin-off from Puritanism—the Unitarian faith, which began to gather momentum in New England at the end of the eighteenth century. Unitarians held that God existed in only *one* person (hence *uni*tarian) and not in the orthodox Trinity. Although denying the divinity of Jesus, Unitarians stressed the essential goodness of human nature, the possibility of salvation through good works, and God as a loving Father rather than a stern Creator. Embraced by many leading thinkers (including Ralph Waldo Emerson), the Unitarian movement appealed

A Camp Meeting at Sing Sing, New York.   *Note the preacher with uplifted hands under the canopy at the left. A British visitor wrote in 1839 of a revival meeting: "In front of the pulpit there was a space railed off and strewn with straw, which I was told was the anxious seat, and on which sat those who were touched by their consciences." (Library of Congress)*

mostly to intellectuals whose rationalism and optimism contrasted sharply with the Calvinist doctrines of predestination and human depravity.

A boiling reaction against the growing liberalism in religion set in about 1800. A fresh wave of roaring revivals, beginning on the southern frontier but soon rolling even into the cities of the Northeast, sent a Second Great Awakening surging across the land. The Second Awakening was one of the most momentous episodes in the history of American religion, a tidal wave of spiritual fervor that left in its wake countless converted souls, shattered and reorganized churches, and new sects. The Awakening was spread to the masses on the frontier by huge "camp meetings" where as many as twenty-five thousand spiritually starved souls would gather for an encampment of several days. In the East, many converts were moved to engage in missionary work in the Indian backwoods, in Hawaii, and in faraway Asia. Everywhere the Second Awakening encouraged an effervescent evangelicism that bubbled up into innumerable areas of American life—including prison reform, the temperance cause, the women's movement, and the crusade to abolish slavery.

Methodists and Baptists reaped the biggest harvest of souls from the fields fertilized by revivalism. Both sects stressed personal conversion (contrary to predestination), relatively democratic control of church affairs, and rousing emotionalism. As a frontier jingle ran:

> The Devil hates the Methodist
> Because they sing and shout the best.

Many prominent evangelists spread the spirit of revival across the American continent. Powerful Peter Cartwright (1785–1872), a Methodist "circuit rider" or traveling frontier preacher, ranged for a half-century from Tennessee to Illinois, calling upon sinners to repent. This ill-educated but sinewy servant of the Lord not only lashed the devil with his bellowing voice, but with his fists he knocked out rowdies who tried to break up his meetings. Bell-voiced Charles Grandison Finney, the greatest of the revival preachers, abandoned his career as a lawyer to·become an evangelist after a deeply moving conversion experience. Finney held

huge crowds spellbound with the power of his oratory. He led massive revivals in Rochester and New York City in 1830 and 1831. Holding out the promise of a perfect Christian kingdom on earth, Finney denounced both alcohol and slavery. He eventually served as president of Oberlin College in Ohio, which he helped to make a hotbed of revivalist activity and abolitionism.

Denominational Diversity

Revivals also furthered the fragmentation of religious faiths. Western New York, where many descendants of New England Puritans had settled, was so blistered by sermonizers preaching "hell-fire and damnation" that it came to be known as the "Burned-Over District."

Like the First Great Awakening, the Second Great Awakening tended to widen the lines between classes and regions. The more prosperous and conservative denominations in the East were little touched by revivalism; Episcopalians, Presbyterians, Congregationalists, and Unitarians continued to rise mostly from the wealthier, better-educated levels of society. Methodists, Baptists, and the members of the other new sects spawned by the swelling evangelistic fervor tended to come from less prosperous, less "learned" communities in the rural South and West.

Religious diversity further reflected social cleavages when the churches faced up to the slavery issue. By 1844–1845 both the Southern Baptists and the Southern Methodists had split with their Northern brethren over human bondage. In 1857 the Presbyterians, North and South, parted company. The secession of the southern churches foreshadowed the secession of the southern states. First the churches split, then the political parties split, and then the Union split.

A Desert Zion in Utah

The smoldering spiritual embers of the Burned-Over District kindled one especially ardent flame in 1830. In that year Joseph Smith—a tall, powerfully built visionary—reported that he had received some golden plates from an angel. When

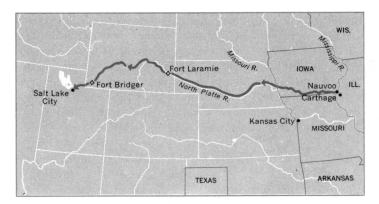

The Mormon Trek, 1846–1847.
Accompanied by livestock, the first pioneer band, led by Brigham Young, set out for Utah in 1846. The party consisted of 146 young men and women driving 73 wagons.

deciphered, they constituted the Book of Mormon, and the Church of Jesus Christ of Latter-Day Saints (Mormons) was launched. It was a native American product, one of the few American-born denominations to spread its influence worldwide.

After establishing a religious oligarchy, Smith ran into serious opposition from his non-Mormon neighbors, first in Ohio and then in Missouri and Illinois. His cooperative sect rasped rank-and-file Americans, who were individualistic and dedicated to free enterprise. The Mormons aroused further antagonism by voting as a unit and by openly but understandably drilling their militia for defensive purposes. Accusations of polygamy likewise arose and increased in intensity, for Joseph Smith was reputed to have several wives.

Continuing hostility finally drove the Mormons to desperate measures. In 1844 Joseph Smith and his brother were murdered and mangled by a mob in Carthage, Illinois, and the movement seemed near collapse. But the falling torch was seized by a remarkable Mormon Moses named Brigham Young, an aggressive leader, an eloquent preacher, and a gifted administrator. Determined to escape further persecution, Young in 1847–1848 led his oppressed and despoiled Latter-Day Saints over vast rolling plains to Utah as they sang "Come, Come, Ye Saints."

Overcoming pioneer hardships, the Mormons soon made the desert bloom like a new Eden by means of ingenious and cooperative methods of irrigation. The crops of 1848, threatened by hordes of crickets, were saved when flocks of gulls

appeared, as if by a miracle, to gulp down the invaders. (A monument to the sea gulls stands in Salt Lake City today.)

Semiarid Utah grew remarkably. By the end of 1848 some five thousand settlers had arrived, and other large bands were to follow. Many dedicated Mormons in the 1850s actually made the 1,300-mile (2,090-kilometer) trek across the plains pulling two-wheeled carts.

Under the rigidly disciplined management of Brigham Young, the community became a prosperous frontier theocracy and a cooperative commonwealth. Young married as many as twenty-seven women—some of them wives in name only—and begot fifty-six children.

A crisis developed when the Washington government was unable to control the hierarchy of Brigham Young, who had been made territorial governor in 1850. A federal army marched in 1857 against the Mormons, who harassed its lines of supply and rallied to die in their last dusty ditch. Fortunately, the quarrel was finally adjusted without serious bloodshed. The Mormons later ran afoul of the anti-polygamy laws passed by Congress in 1862 and 1882, and their unique marital customs delayed statehood for Utah until 1896.

Daily Diversions

As the log-clearing phase passed, the masses were left with more leisure to enjoy the good things of life. The stage took on greater respectability as the nineteenth century unfolded, even in Boston, where the Puritans had frowned upon the theater as "the Devil's chapel." Classical English dramas continued their popularity, while in the 1850s *Uncle Tom's Cabin* and *Ten Nights in a Barroom,* a Prohibitionist melodrama, played to packed houses.

Sports continued to relieve the monotony of everyday drudgery. Horse racing continued to attract an enthusiastic and open-pursed following. Embryonic baseball had attained so much popularity by 1845 that a uniform set of rules was adopted. Flashy and flammable showboats were churning the main rivers, bringing their variety shows to a gaping public. The traveling circus was drawing appreciative crowds, although the huge three-ring spectacles were not introduced until after the Civil War.

The most famous showman of the era was Phineas T. Barnum (1810–1891), a shrewd and cynical Connecticut Yankee, "the Prince of Humbug." He got his start during the 1830s and 1840s in New York City, where he displayed bearded ladies and other freaks. Realizing that the American public loved to be "humbugged," he declared that a "sucker" was born every minute.

For the upper crust, fashionable "watering places" were established at Saratoga Springs (New York) and Newport (Rhode Island). These resorts were frequented by the gaudily dressed elite, including many cotton-rich southerners. Growing numbers of wealthier Americans were also making the "Grand Tour" of Europe.

Culturally, by 1860 America had traveled a long and uphill road since crude pioneering days. But a high degree of polish and sophistication, at least by European standards, lay in the lap of the future.

Free Schools for a Free People

Tax-supported primary schools were scarce in the early years of the Republic. They had the odor of pauperism about them, since they existed chiefly to educate the children of the poor—the so-called ragged schools. Advocates of "free" public education met stiff opposition.

Well-to-do, conservative Americans gradually saw the light. If they did not pay to educate "other folkses brats," the brats might grow up into a dangerous, ignorant rabble—armed with the vote. Taxation for education was an insurance premium that the wealthy paid for stability and democracy.

Tax-supported public education, though lagging in the slavery-cursed South, triumphed between 1825 and 1850. Grimy-handed laborers wielded increased influence and demanded instruction for their children. Most important was the gaining of manhood suffrage for whites in Jackson's day. A free vote cried aloud for free education. A civilized nation that was both ignorant and free, declared Thomas Jefferson, "never was and never will be."

The famed little red schoolhouse—with one room, one stove, one teacher, and often eight grades—became the shrine of American democracy. Regrettably, it was an imperfect shrine. Early free schools stayed open only a few months of the year. Schoolmasters were too often ill trained, ill tempered, and ill paid. These knights of the blackboard often "boarded around" in the community, and some knew scarcely more than their older pupils. They usually taught only the "Three Rs"—"readin', 'ritin', and 'rithmetic."

Reform was urgently needed. Into the breach stepped Horace Mann (1796–1859), a brilliant and idealistic graduate of Brown University. As secretary of the Massachusetts Board of Education, he campaigned effectively for more and better schoolhouses, longer school terms, higher pay for teachers, and an expanded curriculum. His influence radiated out to other states, and impressive improvements were chalked up. Yet education remained an expensive luxury for many communities. As late as 1860 the nation counted only a few hundred public secondary schools—and nearly a million white adult illiterates.

Educational advances were aided by improved textbooks, notably those of Noah Webster (1758–1843), a Yale-educated Connecticut Yankee who was known as the "Schoolmaster of the Republic." He devoted twenty years to his famous dictionary, published in 1828, which helped to standardize the American language.

Equally influential was Ohioan William H. McGuffey (1800–1873), a teacher-preacher of rare power. His grade-school readers, first published in the 1830s, sold 122 million copies in the following decades. *McGuffey's Readers* hammered home lasting lessons in morality, patriotism, and idealism.

Higher Goals for Higher Learning

Higher education was likewise stirring. The religious zeal of the Second Great Awakening, beginning about 1800, led to the planting of many small, denominational, liberal arts colleges, chiefly in the South and West.

The first state-supported universities sprang up in the South, beginning with North Carolina in 1795. Federal land grants nourished the growth of state institutions of higher learning.

Women's higher education was frowned upon in the early decades of the nineteenth century. A woman's place was in the home, and training in needlecraft seemed more important than training in algebra. In an era when the clinging-vine bride was the ideal, co-education was regarded as frivolous. Prejudices also prevailed that too much learning injured the feminine brain, undermined health, and rendered a young lady unfit for marriage. The teachers of Susan B. Anthony, the future feminist, refused to instruct her in long division.

Women's schools at the secondary level began to attain some respectability in the 1820s, thanks in part to the dedicated work of Emma Willard (1787–1870). In 1821 she established the Troy (New York) Female Seminary. Oberlin College, in Ohio, shocked traditionalists in 1837 when it opened its doors to women as well as men. In the same year, Mary Lyon established an outstanding women's school, Mount Holyoke Seminary (later College), in South Hadley, Massachusetts.

Traveling lecturers helped to carry learning to the masses through the lyceum lecture associations, which numbered about three thousand by 1835. The lyceums provided platforms for speakers on science, literature, and moral philosophy. Talented talkers like Ralph Waldo Emerson journeyed thousands of miles on the lyceum circuits, casting their pearls of culture before appreciative audiences hungry for education.

Magazines flourished in the pre–Civil War years, but most of them withered after a short life. The *North American Review,* founded in 1815, was the long-lived leader of the intellectuals. *Godey's Lady's Book,* founded in 1830, survived until 1898, and attained the enormous circulation (for those days) of 150,000. It was devoured devotedly by countless millions of women.

The Changing American Family

The rustling pages of publications like *Godey's Lady's Book,* perused in parlors all over America, quietly heralded a subtle, slow-moving, but even-

Godey's Lady's Book.   *The most popular women's magazine of the era. (Schlesinger Library, Radcliffe College; photo by Barry Donahue)*

tually sweeping revolution in American society. In a world where male and female sexual roles were becoming more sharply divided, women were growing more conscious of themselves as individuals, and as one another's "sisters." This dawning of self-consciousness was beginning to change women's lives—and to transform society's most fundamental institution, the family.

It was still a man's world, in America and Europe, when the nineteenth century opened. A wife was supposed to immerse herself in her home and subordinate herself to her lord and master. Like black slaves, she could not vote; like black slaves, she could be legally beaten by her overlord "with a reasonable instrument." When she married, she could not retain title to her property; it passed to her husband. But as the decades unfolded, women increasingly emerged to breathe the air of freedom and self-determination. In contrast to colonial times, many women avoided marriage altogether—about 10 percent of adult women remained "spinsters" at the time of the Civil War.

Opportunities for women to be economically self-supporting were still scarce, and consisted mainly of low-paying factory jobs, nursing, teaching, and domestic service. Perhaps one white family in ten employed servants at midcentury, most of whom were poor white, immigrant, or black women. About 10 percent of white women were working for pay outside their own homes in 1850, and estimates are that about 20 percent of all women had worked at some time prior to marriage.

The vast majority of working women were single. Upon marriage, they left their paying jobs and took up their new work (without wages) as wives and mothers. In the home they were enshrined in a "cult of domesticity," a widespread cultural creed that glorified the traditional functions of the homemaker. From their pedestal, married women commanded immense moral power, and they increasingly made decisions that altered the character of the family itself.

Families are like air—they surround most people so completely and so constantly that they have tended to be invisible, historically speaking. But though they long went unrecorded, important changes were overtaking the life of the nineteenth-century home—the traditional "women's sphere." Love, not parental "arrangement," more and more frequently determined the choice of a spouse—yet parents often retained the power of veto. Families thus became more closely knit and affectionate, providing the emotional refuge that made the threatening impersonality of big-city industrialism tolerable to many people.

Most striking, families grew smaller. The average household had nearly six members at the end of the eighteenth century, but fewer than five members a century later. The "fertility rate," or number of births among women aged 14 to 45, dropped sharply among white women after the Revolution, and in the course of the nineteenth century as a whole, fell by half. Birth control was still a taboo topic for polite conversation, and contraceptive technology was primitive, but clearly some form of family limitation was being practiced quietly and effectively in countless families, rural and urban alike. Women undoubtedly played a large part—perhaps the leading part—in decisions to have fewer children.

Smaller families, in turn, meant child-centered families, because where children are fewer parents can lavish more care on them individually. European visitors to the United States in the nineteenth century often complained about the unruly behavior of American "brats." But what Europeans saw as permissiveness was in reality the consequence of an emerging new idea of child rearing, in which the child's will was not to be simply broken, but shaped. In the little republic of the family, as in the Republic at large, good citizens were raised not to be meekly obedient to authority, but to be independent individuals who could make their own decisions on the basis of internalized moral standards. Thus the outlines of the "modern" family were clear by midcentury: it was small, affectionate, child-centered, and provided a special arena for the talents of women. Feminists of a later day might decry the stifling atmosphere of the Victorian home, but to many women of the time it seemed a big step upward from the conditions in which their mothers had lived.

VARYING VIEWPOINTS

Ever since its publication in 1835, Alexis de Tocqueville's *Democracy in America* has defined the terms for discussion of the American character. Most accounts of the era between the Revolution and the Civil War have ratified Tocqueville's claims that individualism and equality formed the distinguishing values of antebellum American life.

Nearly twenty-five years ago, the historian David M. Potter raised a challenge to Tocqueville. How would our conception of the American character change, Potter asked, if we remembered that half of all Americans were women? How did the ideal of equality apply to women? Does a focus on women cause us to revise the belief that individualism and suspicion of the "community" were hallmarks of the national character? In the last ten years, historians such as Nancy Cott have offered answers to Potter's question. Women's concern for their families and for a larger network of human associations, these scholars argue, nurtured strong traditions of community ties and reform activity in antebellum America.

SELECT READINGS

Primary Source Documents

Joseph Smith, *The Pearl of Great Price** (1829), contains an account of the Mormon leader's religious visions, which capture the religious ferment of the age. William H. McGuffey, *Fifth Eclectic Reader** (1879), was the most popular school text of the age. Catherine Beecher and Harriet Beecher Stowe, *The American Woman's Home** (1869), discusses the role of women. Stowe's classic *Uncle Tom's Cabin* (1852) offers an emotional appeal against slavery and a fascinating portrait of slavery, religion, and family life in antebellum America.

Secondary Sources

Satisfying detail may be found in Russell B. Nye, *The Cultural Life of the New Nation, 1776–1830* (1960) and the same author's *Society and Culture in America, 1830–1860* (1974). Alexis de Tocqueville's classic account of life in the young Republic is brilliantly analyzed by James R. Schieffler in *The Making of Tocqueville's "Democracy in America"* (1980). Richard A. Easterlin analyzes *Population, Labor Force, and Long Swings in Economic Growth: The American Experience* (1968). Maldwyn Jones, *American Immigration* (1960) is a standard work. Sydney E. Ahlstrom, *Religious History of the American People* (1972) is sweeping. On revivalism, see William G. McLoughlin, *Modern Revivalism: Charles Grandison Finney to Billy Graham* (1959) and Whitney Cross's absorbing *The Burned-Over District* (1950). McLoughlin's *Revivals, Awakenings, and Reform: An Essay on Religion and Social Change in America, 1607–1977* (1978) is highly original. On education, see Lawrence A. Cremin, *American Education: The National Experience, 1789–1860* (1980). An alternative interpretation of the rise of public education can be found in Michael Katz, *The Irony of Early School Reform* (1968) and Samuel Bowles and Herbert Gintis, *Schooling in Capitalist America* (1976). Recent works of note on women and the family include Carl N. Degler, *At Odds: Women and the Family in America from the Revolution to the Present* (1980); Mary P. Ryan, *Cradle of the Middle Class: The Family in Oneida County, New York* (1981); and Nancy Cott's particularly sensitive *The Bonds of Womanhood: "Woman's Sphere" in New England, 1780–1835* (1977).

19

The Ferment of Reform and Culture, 1790–1860

We [Americans] will walk on our own feet;
we will work with our own hands;
we will speak our own minds.

Ralph Waldo Emerson, "The American Scholar," 1837

An Age of Reform

As the young Republic grew, reform campaigns of all types flourished in sometimes bewildering abundance. There was not "a reading man" who was without some scheme for a new utopia in his "waistcoat pocket," claimed Ralph Waldo Emerson. Reformers promoted rights for women as well as miracle medicines, communal living, polygamy, celibacy, rule by prophets, and guidance by spirits. Societies were formed against alcohol, tobacco, profanity, and the transit of mail on the Sabbath. Eventually overshadowing all other reforms was the crusade against slavery.

Many reformers were simply crackbrained cranks. But most were intelligent, inspired idealists, usually touched by the fire of evangelical religion then licking through the pews and pulpits of American churches. The optimistic promises of the Second Great Awakening inspired countless souls to do battle against earthly evils. These modern idealists dreamed anew the old Puritan vision of a perfected society: free from cruelty, war, intoxicating drink, discrimination, and—ultimately—slavery. Women were particularly prominent in these reform crusades, especially in their own struggle for suffrage. For many middle-class women, the reform campaigns provided a unique opportunity to escape the confines of home and enter the arena of public affairs.

In part, the practical, activist Christianity of these reformers resulted from their desire to reaffirm traditional values as they plunged ever further into a world disrupted and transformed by the turbulent forces of a market economy. Often blissfully unaware that they were witnessing the dawn of the industrial era, they either ignored the problems of factory workers or blamed them on bad habits. Reformers sometimes applied conventional virtue to refurbishing an older order—while events hurtled them headlong into the new.

Imprisonment for debt continued to be a nightmare. As late as 1830 hundreds of penniless persons were languishing in filthy holes, sometimes for owing less than one dollar. The poorer working classes were especially hard hit by this merciless practice. But as the embattled laborer won the ballot and asserted himself, state legislatures gradually abolished debtors' prison.

Criminal codes in the states were likewise being softened. The number of capital offenses was being reduced, and brutal punishments, such as whipping and branding, were slowly being eliminated. A refreshing idea was taking hold that prisons should reform as well as punish—hence "reformatories," "houses of correction," and "penitentiaries" (for penance).

Sufferers from so-called insanity were still being treated with incredible cruelty. The mentally deranged were considered willfully perverse and depraved, and often chained like beasts in jails or poorhouses. A quiet New England teacher-author, Dorothea Dix (1802–1887) spent eight years observing these conditions at first hand, and presented her damning findings to the Massachusetts legislature in 1843. Her description of cells so foul that visitors were driven back by the stench turned legislative stomachs and hearts. Her persistent prodding resulted in improved conditions and in a gain for the concept that the demented were not willfully perverse but mentally ill.

Agitation for peace also gained some momentum in the pre–Civil War years. In 1828 the American Peace Society was formed, with a ringing declaration of war on war. The American peace crusade, linked with the European crusade, was making promising progress by midcentury, when it was set back by the bloodshed of the Crimean War in Europe and the Civil War in America.

Demon Rum—The "Old Deluder"

The ever-present drink problem also attracted dedicated reformers. Widespread heavy drinking caused labor inefficiency and increased the danger of accidents on the job. Weddings and funerals all too often became disgraceful brawls, and occasionally a drunken man would fall into the open grave with the corpse. Drunkenness also fouled the sanctity of the family, threatening the spiritual welfare and physical safety of women and children.

After earlier and feebler efforts, the American Temperance Society was founded in Boston in 1826. Within a few years about a thousand local groups sprang into existence. They implored drinkers to sign the temperance pledge and organized children's clubs, known as the "Cold Water Army." Temperance crusaders also made effective use of pictures, pamphlets, and lurid lecturers, some of whom were reformed drunkards.

The most popular antialcohol tract of the era was T. S. Arthur's melodramatic novel, *Ten Nights in a Barroom and What I Saw There* (1854). It described in shocking detail how a once-happy village was ruined by Sam Slade's tavern. The book was second only to Stowe's *Uncle Tom's Cabin* as a best seller in the 1850s, and it enjoyed a highly successful run on the stage.

Early foes of Demon Drink adopted two major lines of attack. One was to stiffen the individual's will to resist the wiles of the little brown jug. Moderate reformers thus stressed "temperance" rather than "teetotalism," or the total elimination of intoxicants. But less patient zealots gradually came to believe that temptation should be removed by legislation. Prominent among this group was Neal S. Dow of Maine, a blue-nosed reformer who, as a mayor of Portland and an employer of labor, had often witnessed the debauching effect of alcohol.

Dow—the "Father of Prohibition"—sponsored the so-called Maine Law of 1851. This drastic new statute, hailed as "the law of Heaven Americanized," prohibited the sale and manufacture of intoxicating liquor. Other states in the North followed Maine's example, and by 1857 about a dozen had passed various prohibitory laws.

Women in Revolt

Sexual differences were strongly emphasized in nineteenth-century America—largely because the burgeoning market economy was increasingly separating women and men into sharply distinct economic roles. Women were thought to be physically and emotionally weak, but also artistic and refined. Endowed with finely tuned moral sensibilities, they were the keepers of society's conscience, with special responsibility for the young. Men were considered strong but crude, always in danger of slipping into some savage or beastly way of life if not guided by the gentle hands of their loving ladies.

But if sexual roles were sharply separated, men and women could still be regarded as equals. As a sign of the prestigious position of American women, French visitor Alexis de Tocqueville noted that in his native France rape was punished only slightly, while in America it was one of the few crimes punishable by death.

The home was woman's special sphere. But some women increasingly felt that the glorified sanctuary of the home was in fact a gilded cage. They yearned to tear down the bars that separated the private world of women from the public world of men.

The clamorous female reformers gathered strength as the century neared its halfway point. Most of them were broad-gauge battlers; while demanding rights for women, they participated in the general reform movement of the age, fighting for temperance and the abolition of slavery. Like men, they had been touched by the evangelical spirit that offered the alluring promise of earthly reward for human endeavor. Neither foul eggs nor foul words, when hurled by disapproving men, could halt women heartened by these doctrines.

The woman's rights movement was mothered by some arresting characters. Prominent among them was Lucretia Mott, a sprightly Quaker whose ire had been aroused when she and her fellow female delegates to the London antislavery convention of 1840 were not recognized. Elizabeth Cady Stanton, a mother of seven who had insisted on leaving the word *obey* out of her marriage vows, shocked fellow feminists by going so far as to advocate suffrage for women. Quaker-reared Susan B. Anthony, a militant lecturer for women's rights, exposed herself to rotten garbage and vulgar epithets. She became such a conspicuous advocate of

Stellar Suffragists. *Elizabeth Cady Stanton* (left) *and Susan B. Anthony* (right) *were two of the most persistent battlers for women's rights. (Brown Brothers)*

female rights that progressive women everywhere were called "Suzy Bs."

Other feminists challenged the man's world. Dr. Elizabeth Blackwell, a pioneer in a previously forbidden profession for women, was the first female graduate of a medical college. Precocious Margaret Fuller edited a transcendentalist journal, *The Dial.* The talented Grimké sisters, Sarah and Angelina, spoke at antislavery gatherings and aroused the ire of conservatives. Lucy Stone retained her maiden name after marriage—hence the latter-day "Lucy Stoners," who follow her example. Amelia Bloomer revolted against the current "street sweeping" female attire by donning a semi-masculine short skirt with Turkish trousers—"bloomers," they were called—amid much bawdy ridicule about "Bloomerism" and "loose habits." A jeering male rhyme of the times jabbed:

> Gibbey, gibbey gab
> The women had a confab
> And demanded the rights
> To wear the tights
> Gibbey, gibbey gab.

Fighting feminists met at Seneca Falls, New York, in a memorable Woman's Rights Convention (1848). The defiant Mrs. Stanton read a "Declaration of Sentiments," which in the spirit of the Declaration of Independence declared that "all men *and women* are created equal." One resolution formally demanded the ballot for females. The Seneca Falls meeting, which launched the modern women's rights movement, not surprisingly became the object of scorn and denunciation from press and pulpit.

The crusade for women's rights was eclipsed by that against slavery in the decade before the Civil War. Male idiots could still vote; women could not. Yet women were being gradually admitted to colleges, and some states, beginning with Mississippi in 1839, were even permitting wives to own property after marriage.

Wilderness Utopias

Leaders of the women's rights movement often marched arm in arm with other reformers. Professional "do-gooders" popped up at every hand, giving the 1840s the distinction of being the "hot air period" of American history.

Various reformers, ranging from the high-minded to the "lunatic fringe," set up more than forty communities of a more or less cooperative, communistic, or "communitarian" nature. Seeking human betterment, a wealthy and idealistic Scottish textile manufacturer, Robert Owen, established in 1825 a communal society of about a thousand persons at New Harmony, Indiana. Little harmony prevailed in the colony, which, in addition to hardworking visionaries, attracted a sprinkling of radicals, lazy theorists, and outright scoundrels. The enterprise sank in a morass of contradiction and confusion.

Brook Farm in Massachusetts, comprising 200 acres of grudging soil, was started in 1841 with the brotherly cooperation of about twenty intellectuals. They prospered reasonably well until 1846, when they lost by fire a large new communal building shortly before its completion. The whole experiment in "plain living and high thinking"

then collapsed in debt. Although a financial failure, Brook Farm was in some ways a social and educational success.

A more radical experiment was the Oneida Colony, founded in New York in 1848. It practiced free love ("complex marriage"), birth control, and the eugenic selection of parents to produce superior offspring. The leader finally fled to Canada to escape prosecution for adultery. This curious enterprise flourished for more than thirty years, largely because its craftsmen made superior steel traps and Oneida Community (silver) Plate. In 1879–1880 the group embraced monogamy and abandoned communism.

Perhaps the longest-lived communitarian sect was the Shakers who, beginning in 1776, set up the first of a score or so religious communities. They attained a membership of about 6,000 in 1840, but because they opposed both marriage and free love, they were virtually extinct by 1940.

Artistic Endeavors and Achievements

Architecturally, America contributed little of note in the first half of the century. The rustic republic continued to imitate European models. Public buildings and other important structures followed Greek and Roman lines, which seemed curiously out of place in a wilderness setting. A remarkable Greek revival came between 1820 and 1850. About midcentury, strong interest developed in a revival of Gothic forms, with their emphasis on pointed arches and large windows.

Talented Thomas Jefferson, architect of revolution, was probably the ablest American architect of his generation. He brought a classical design to his Virginia hilltop home, Monticello—perhaps the most stately mansion in the nation (see p. 98). The quadrangle of the University of Virginia at Charlottesville, another creation of Jefferson, remains one of the finest examples of classical architecture in America.

Painting, like the theater, suffered from the Puritan prejudice that art was a sinful waste of time—and often obscene. When Edward Everett, the eminent Boston scholar and orator, placed a statue of Apollo in his home, he had its naked limbs draped.

Competent painters nevertheless emerged. Gilbert Stuart (1775–1828) wielded his brush in England, in competition with the best artists. He produced several portraits of Washington, all of them somewhat idealized and dehumanized. Charles Wilson Peale (1741–1827) painted some sixty portraits of Washington, who patiently sat for about fourteen of them. John Trumbull (1756–1843), who had fought in the Revolutionary War, recaptured its scenes and spirit on scores of striking canvases.

During the nationalistic upsurge after the War of 1812, American portrait painters turned increasingly from human landscapes to romantic mirrorings of local landscapes. The Hudson River School excelled in this type of art. At the same time, portrait painters gradually encountered some unwelcome competition from the invention of a crude photograph known as the daguerreotype, perfected about 1839 by a Frenchman, Louis Daguerre.

The Blossoming of a National Literature

"Who reads an American book?" sneered a British critic in 1820. The painful truth was that the nation's rough-hewn, pioneering civilization gave little encouragement to "polite" literature. America produced political essays, sermons, and autobiographies, but imported or plagiarized most of its imaginative reading matter from England.

The first creative outburst of a genuinely American literature came after the wave of nationalism that followed the War of Independence and especially the War of 1812. By 1820 the older seaboard areas were sufficiently removed from tree-chopping so that literature could be supported as a profession. The Knickerbocker Group in New York blazed brilliantly across the literary heavens, thus enabling America for the first time to boast of a literature to match her magnificent landscapes.

Washington Irving (1783–1859), born in New York City, was the first American to win international recognition as a literary figure. Steeped in the traditions of New Netherland, he published in 1809 his *Knickerbocker's History of New York,* with its amusing caricatures of the Dutch. When the family business failed, Irving was forced to turn to the goose-feather pen. In 1819–1820 he published *The Sketch Book,* which brought him immediate fame at home and abroad. Combining a pleasing style with delicate charm and quiet humor, he used English as well as American themes, and included such immortal Dutch-American tales as "Rip Van Winkle" and "The Legend of Sleepy Hollow." Europe was amazed to find at last an American with a feather in his hand, not in his hair.

The novelist James Fenimore Cooper (1789–1851) also made New World themes internationally respectable. He first achieved fame in 1821 with his novel *The Spy*—an absorbing tale of the American Revolution. But his most enduring achievement was the series of *Leatherstocking Tales,* such as *The Last of the Mohicans,* in which the noble rifleman Natty Bumppo meets stirring adventures with the Indians. Although many Europeans who read Cooper's novels came to think of all Americans as born with a tomahawk in hand, the author actually sought to portray the good society somewhere between the anarchy of the wilderness and the artificiality of modern civilization.

A third member of the Knickerbocker group in New York was the belated Puritan William Cullen Bryant (1794–1878), transplanted from Massachusetts. At age sixteen he wrote the meditative and melancholy "Thanatopsis" (published in 1817), which was one of the first high-quality poems produced in the United States. Critics could hardly believe that it had been written on "this side of the water."

Trumpeters of Transcendentalism

A golden age in American literature dawned in the second quarter of the nineteenth century, when an amazing outburst shook New England. One of the mainsprings of this literary flowering was transcendentalism, especially in the Boston area, which preened itself as "the Athens of America."

The transcendentalist movement of the 1830s

resulted in part from a liberalizing of the strait-jacket Puritan theology. It also owed much to foreign thinkers, including the German romantic philosophers. The transcendentalists rejected the prevailing theory, derived from John Locke, that all knowledge comes to the mind through the senses. Truth, rather, "transcends" the senses: it cannot be found by observation alone. Every person possesses an inner light that can illuminate the highest truth and put the individual in direct touch with God, or the "Oversoul."

These mystical doctrines of transcendentalism defied precise definition, but they underlay concrete beliefs. Foremost was a stiff-backed individualism in matters religious as well as social. Closely associated was a commitment to self-reliance, self-culture, and self-discipline. These traits naturally bred hostility to authority and to formal institutions of any kind, as well as to all conventional wisdom. Finally came exaltation of the dignity of the individual, whether black or white—the mainspring of a whole array of humanitarian reforms.

Best known of the transcendentalists was Boston-born Ralph Waldo Emerson (1803–1882). Tall, slender, and intensely blue-eyed, he mirrored serenity in his noble features. Trained as a Unitarian minister, he early forsook his pulpit and ultimately reached a wider audience by pen and platform. He was a never-failing favorite as a lyceum lecturer, and for twenty years took a Western tour every winter. Perhaps his most thrilling public effort was a Phi Beta Kappa address, "The American Scholar," delivered at Harvard College in 1837. This brilliant appeal was an intellectual Declaration of Independence, for it urged American writers to throw off European traditions and delve into the riches of their own backyards.

Hailed as both a poet and a philosopher, Emerson was not of the highest rank as either. He was more influential as a practical philosopher, and through his fresh and vibrant essays enriched countless thousands of humdrum lives. Catching the individualistic mood of the Republic, he stressed self-reliance, self-improvement, optimism, and freedom. The secret of Emerson's popularity lay largely in the fact that his ideals reflected those of an expanding America. Among his most-quoted observations are: "Whoso would be a man, must be a non-conformist" and "A foolish consistency is the hobgoblin of little minds."

Henry David Thoreau (1817–1862) was one of Emerson's close associates—a poet, a mystic, a transcendentalist, and a nonconformist. Condemning a government that supported slavery, he refused to pay his Massachusetts poll tax, and was jailed for a night.* A gifted prose writer, he is well known for *Walden: Or Life in the Woods* (1854). The book is a record of Thoreau's two years of simple existence in a hut which he built on the edge of Walden Pond, near Concord, Massachusetts. A rugged individualist, he believed that he should reduce his bodily wants so as to gain time for a pursuit of truth through study and meditation. Thoreau's *Walden* and his essay *Civil Disobedience* exercised a strong influence in furthering idealistic thought, both in America and abroad. His writings later encouraged Mohandas Gandhi to resist British rule in India.

Bold, brassy, and swaggering was the open-collared figure of Brooklyn's Walt Whitman (1819–1892). In his famous collection of poems, *Leaves of Grass* (1855), he gave free rein to his gushing genius with what he called a "barbaric yawp." Highly romantic, emotional, and unconventional, he dispensed with titles, stanzas, rhymes, and at times even regular meter. He handled sex with shocking frankness.

Whitman's *Leaves of Grass* was at first a financial failure. The only three enthusiastic reviews that it received were written by the author himself—anonymously. But in time the once-withered *Leaves of Grass,* revived and honored, won for Whitman an enormous following in both America and Europe.

Leaves of Grass gained for Whitman the informal title "Poet Laureate of Democracy." Singing with transcendental abandon of his love for the

---

*The story (probably apocryphal) is that Emerson visited Thoreau at the jail and asked, "Why are you here?" The reply came, "Why are you not here?"

Walt Whitman. *This portrait of the young poet appeared in the first edition of* Leaves of Grass *(1855). (Rare Book Division, New York Public Library, Astor, Lenox and Tilden Foundations)*

masses, he caught the exuberant enthusiasm of an expanding America that had turned her back on the Old World:

> All the Past we leave behind;
> We debouch upon a newer, mightier world, varied
>   world;
> Fresh and strong the world we seize—world of
>   labor and the march—
> Pioneers! O Pioneers!

Here at last was the native art for which critics had been crying.

Glowing Literary Lights

Certain other literary giants were not actively associated with the transcendentalist movement, though not completely immune to its influences. Professor Henry Wadsworth Longfellow (1807–1882), a man who for many years taught modern languages at Harvard College, was one of the most popular poets ever produced in America. His wide knowledge of European literature sup-

plied him with many themes, but some of his most admired poems were based on American traditions—*Evangeline, Hiawatha,* and *The Courtship of Miles Standish.* Immensely popular in Europe, Longfellow was the only American ever to be honored with a bust in the Poets' Corner of Westminster Abbey.

A fighting Quaker, John Greenleaf Whittier (1807–1892), was the uncrowned poet laureate of the antislavery crusade. His poems cried aloud against inhumanity, injustice, and intolerance, against

> The outworn rite, the old abuse,
> The Pious fraud transparent grown.

Undeterred by insults and the stonings of mobs, Whittier helped arouse a calloused America on the slavery issue. A great conscience rather than a great poet or intellect, Whittier was preeminently the poet of human freedom.

Many-sided James Russell Lowell (1819–1891), who succeeded Professor Longfellow at Harvard, is remembered as a political satirist in his *Biglow Papers,* especially those of 1846 dealing with the Mexican War. Written partly as poetry in the Yankee dialect, the *Papers* condemned in blistering terms the alleged slavery-expansion designs of the Polk administration.

Slender Dr. Oliver Wendell Holmes (1809–1894), who lectured in anatomy with a sparkle at Harvard Medical School, was a prominent poet, essayist, novelist, lecturer, and wit. A nonconformist and a fascinating conversationalist, he shone among a group of literary lights who regarded Boston as "the hub of the universe." His poem "The Last Leaf," in honor of the last "white Indian" of the Boston Tea Party, came to apply to himself. Dying at age eighty-five, he was the "last leaf" among his distinguished contemporaries.*

A noteworthy literary figure produced by the South before the Civil War was novelist William Gilmore Simms (1806–1870). Eighty-two books flowed from his ever-moist pen, winning for him

---

*Oliver Wendell Holmes had a son with the same name who became a distinguished justice of the Supreme Court (1902–1932) and who lived to be ninety-four, less two days.

the title "the Cooper of the South." His themes dealt with the southern frontier in colonial days and with the South during the Revolutionary War.

Literary Individualists and Dissenters

Not all writers in these years believed so keenly in human goodness and social progress. Edgar Allan Poe (1809–1849), who spent much of his youth in Virginia, was an eccentric genius. Orphaned at an early age, cursed with ill health, and married to a child-wife of fourteen who fell fatally ill of tuberculosis, he suffered hunger, cold, poverty, and debt. Failing at suicide, he took refuge in the bottle and dissipated his talent early. Poe was a gifted lyric poet, as "The Raven" attests. A master stylist, he also excelled in the short story, especially of the horror type, in which he shared his alcoholic nightmares with fascinated readers. If he did not invent the modern detective novel, he at least set new high standards in tales like "The Gold Bug."

Poe was fascinated by the ghostly and ghastly, as in "The Fall of the House of Usher" and other stories. He reflected a morbid sensibility distinctly at odds with the usually optimistic tone of American culture. Partly for this reason, Poe has perhaps been even more prized by Europeans than by his own countrymen. His brilliant career was cut short when he was found drunk in a Baltimore gutter and shortly thereafter died.

Two other writers reflected the continuing Calvinist obsession with original sin and with the never-ending struggle between good and evil. In somber Salem, Massachusetts, Nathaniel Hawthorne grew up in an atmosphere heavy with the memories of his Puritan forebears and the tragedy of his father's premature death on an ocean voyage. His masterpiece was *The Scarlet Letter* (1850), which described the Puritan practice of forcing an adulteress to wear a scarlet A on her clothing. The tragic tale chronicles the psychological effects of sin on the guilty heroine and her secret lover (the father of her baby), a minister of the gospel in Puritan Boston.

Herman Melville (1819–1891), an orphaned and ill-educated New Yorker, went to sea as a youth and served eighteen adventuresome months on a whaler. "A whale ship was my Yale College and my Harvard," he wrote. Jumping ship in the South Seas, he lived among cannibals, from whom he providentially escaped uneaten. His masterpiece, *Moby Dick* (1851), was a complex allegory of good and evil, told in terms of the conflict between a whaling captain, Ahab, and a giant white whale, Moby Dick. Captain Ahab, who lost a leg to the marine monster, swore revenge. His pursuit finally ended when Moby Dick rammed and sank Ahab's ship, leaving only one survivor. The whale's exact identity and Ahab's motives remained obscure. In the end the sea, like the terrifyingly impersonal and unknowable universe of Melville's imagination, simply rolled on.

Moby Dick was widely ignored at the time of its publication; people were accustomed to more straightforward and upbeat prose. A disheartened Melville continued to write unprofitably for some years, part of the time eking out a living as a customs inspector, and then died in relative obscurity and poverty. Ironically, his brooding masterpiece about the mysterious white whale had to wait until the more jaded twentieth century for readers and proper recognition.

Portrayers of the Past

A distinguished group of American historians was emerging at the same time that other writers were winning distinction. Energetic George Bancroft (1800–1891), who as secretary of the navy helped found the Naval Academy at Annapolis in 1845, has deservedly received the title "Father of American History." He published a spirited, super-patriotic history of the United States to 1789 in six (originally ten) volumes (1834–1876), a work that grew out of his vast researches in dusty archives in Europe and America.

Two other historians are read with greater pleasure and profit today. William H. Prescott (1796–1859) published classic accounts of the conquest of Mexico (1843) and Peru (1847). Francis Parkman penned a brilliant series of volumes, beginning in 1851. In epic style he chronicled the struggle between France and England in colonial times for the mastery of North America.

Early American historians of prominence were almost without exception New Englanders, largely because the Boston area provided well-stocked libraries and a stimulating literary tradition. These writers numbered abolitionists among their relatives and friends, and hence were disposed to view unsympathetically the slave-cursed South. The writing of American history for generations to come was to suffer from an antisouthern bias perpetuated by this early "made in New England" interpretation. Not until the twentieth century was the South to produce historians who achieved eminence at the national level.

VARYING VIEWPOINTS

Early chronicles of the antebellum period universally lauded the reformers, portraying them as disinterested, idealistic persons intent on improving American society. After World War II, however, historians began searching for selfish motivations underlying the apparent benevolence of the reformers. This view described the advocates of reform as conservative, upper-class women and men who felt threatened by the ferment of life in antebellum America. The pursuit of reforms like prohibition, asylums, and mandatory education represented a means of asserting "social control." In this vein, David H. Donald identified one reform movement as "the anguished protest of an aggrieved class against a world they never made." The wave of reform activity in the 1960s coincided with a resurgence in the reputation of antebellum reformers. Recent interpretations stress the religious commitments of reformers and especially the participation of women, who sought various social improvements as an extension of their role as protectors of the home and family.

SELECT READINGS

Primary Source Documents

On the women's movement, see the "Seneca Falls Manifesto"* (1848), which set the stage for later feminist agitation. Henry D. Thoreau's *Walden** is a classic of the period, as is Ralph Waldo Emerson's "The American Scholar," in *Collected Works of Ralph Waldo Emerson* (1971), edited by Robert E. Spiller.

Secondary Sources

General intellectual histories are Merle Curti, *The Growth of American Thought* (3d ed., 1964) and Ralph H. Gabriel, *The Course of American Democratic Thought* (2d ed., 1956). Ronald Walters summarizes *American Reformers, 1815–1860* (1978). An older but still useful discussion of reform is Alice F. Tyler, *Freedom's Ferment* (1944).

Women's history for this period has recently blossomed in a number of fine studies, including Ellen Carol Dubois, *Feminism and Suffrage* (1978); Barbara J. Berg, *The Remembered Gate: Origins of American Feminism—The Woman and the City, 1800–1860* (1977); Ruth Bordin, *Women and Temperance* (1981); Estelle B. Freedman, *Their Sisters' Keepers: Women's Prison Reform in America, 1830–1930* (1981); Keith E. Melder, *The Beginnings of Sisterhood* (1977); and, emphasizing intellectual and literary history, Ann Douglas, *The Feminization of American Culture* (1977). F. O. Mathiessen's masterful *American Renaissance* (1941) is indispensable on the writers of the 1840s and 1850s, as is Alfred Kazin's *An American Procession* (1984). D. H. Lawrence, *Studies in Classic American Literature* (1923) is a classic in its own right.

20

The South and the Slavery Controversy

If you put a chain around the neck of a slave, the other end fastens itself around your own.

Ralph Waldo Emerson, 1841

"Cotton is King!"

When George Washington first took the presidential oath, the economic wheels of the South were creaking badly. They were burdened with depressed prices, unmarketable products, overcropped lands, and the dead weight of an unprofitable slave system. Some Southern statesmen, including Thomas Jefferson, were talking openly of freeing their slaves, and confidently predicting that slavery would gradually die of economic anemia.

But the introduction of Whitney's cotton gin in 1793 changed the scene. The newly popularized short-staple cotton, which brought a premium price, gradually became the dominant Southern crop, eclipsing tobacco, rice, and sugar. Slavery was reinvigorated, the slave chained to the gin, and the planter to the slave.

As time passed, the Cotton Kingdom developed into a huge agricultural factory, pouring out avalanches of the fluffy fiber. Quick profits drew planters to the virgin bottom lands of the gulf states. As long as the soil was still vigorous, the yield was bountiful and the rewards were high. Caught up in an economic spiral, the planters bought more slaves and land to grow more cotton, so as to buy still more slaves and land.

Northern shippers reaped a large part of the profits from the cotton trade. They would load bulging bales of cotton at southern ports, transport them to England, sell them for pounds sterling, and buy needed manufactured goods for sale in the United States. To a large degree the prosperity of both North and South rested on the bent backs of southern slaves.

Cotton accounted for half the value of all American exports after 1840. It even held foreign nations in partial bondage. Britain's most important single manufacture in the 1850s was cotton cloth, from which about one-fifth of her population, directly or indirectly, drew its livelihood. About 80 percent of this precious supply of fiber came from the South.

Southern statesmen were fully aware that England was tied to them by cotton threads, and this dependence gave them a heady sense of power. In their eyes "Cotton was King," the gin was his throne, and the black bondsmen were his henchmen. If war should ever break out between North and South, northern warships would presumably cut off the outflow of cotton. Fiber-famished British factories would then close their gates, starving mobs would force the London government to break the blockade, and the South would triumph. Cotton was a powerful monarch indeed.

Slaves of the Slave System

Before the Civil War the South was in some respects not so much a democracy as an oligarchy—or a government by the few, in this case heavily influenced by a planter aristocracy. In 1850 only 1,733 families owned more than 100 slaves

each, and this select group provided the cream of the political and social leadership of the section and nation. Here was the mint-julep South of the tall-columned and white-painted plantation mansion—the "big house," where dwelt the "cottonocracy."

The planter aristocrats, with their blooded horses and Chippendale chairs, enjoyed a lion's share of Southern wealth. They could educate their children in the finest schools, often in the North or abroad. Their money provided the leisure for study, reflection, and statecraft, as was notably true of men like John C. Calhoun (a Yale graduate) and Jefferson Davis (a West Point graduate).

Unhappily, the moonlight-and-magnolia tradition concealed much that was worrisome, distasteful, and sordid. Plantation agriculture was wasteful, largely because King Cotton and his money-hungry subjects despoiled the good earth. Quick profits led to excessive cultivation or "land butchery," which in turn caused a heavy leakage of population to the West and Northwest.

The economic structure of the South became increasingly monopolistic. As the land wore thin,

Southern Cotton Production, 1860

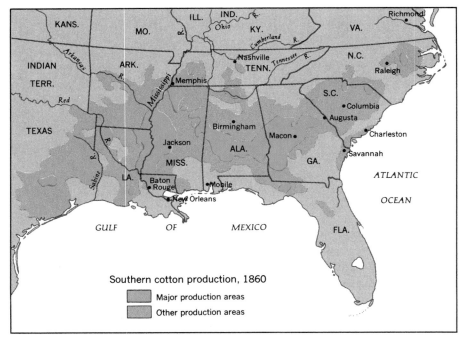

Southern cotton production, 1860
- Major production areas
- Other production areas

many small farmers sold their holdings to more prosperous neighbors. The big got bigger and the small smaller. When the Civil War finally broke, a large number of southern families had lost the farms originally cleared by their ancestors.

Another cancer in the bosom of the South was the financial instability of the plantation system. The temptation to overspeculate in land and slaves caused many a planter, including Andrew Jackson in his later years, to plunge in beyond his depth. The slaves represented a heavy investment of capital, perhaps $1,200 each in the case of prime field hands; and they might deliberately injure themselves or run away.

Dominance by King Cotton likewise led to a dangerous dependence on a one-crop economy, whose price level was at the mercy of world conditions. The whole system discouraged a healthy diversification of the economy, particularly the development of manufacturing, for which the South was almost ideally fitted.

Southern planters resented watching the North grow fat at their expense. They were pained by the heavy outward flow of commissions and interest to northern middlemen, bankers, agents, and shippers. True sons of the South, especially by the 1850s, deplored the fact that when born they were wrapped in Yankee-made swaddling clothes, and that they spent the rest of their lives in servitude to Yankee manufacturing. When they died, they were laid in coffins made with Yankee nails, and were buried in graves dug with Yankee shovels. The South furnished the corpse and the hole in the ground.

The Cotton Kingdom also repelled large-scale European immigration, which added so richly to the manpower and wealth of the North. In 1860 only 4.4 percent of the Southern population was foreign born, as compared with 18.7 percent for the North.

The White Majority

Only a handful of southern whites lived in Grecian-pillared mansions. Below those 1,733 families in 1850 who owned a hundred or more slaves were the less wealthy slaveowners. They totaled in 1850 some 345,000 families. Over two-thirds of these families—255,268 in all—owned fewer than ten slaves each. All told, only about one-fourth of white southerners owned slaves or belonged to a slaveowning family.

The smaller slaveowners did not own a majority of the slaves, but they made up a majority of masters. With the striking exception that their household contained a slave or two, the style of their lives probably resembled that of small farmers in the North more than it did that of the southern planter aristocracy. They lived in modest farmhouses and sweated beside their bondsmen in the cotton fields.

Beneath the slaveowners was the great body of whites who owned no slaves at all. By 1860 their numbers had swelled to 6,120,825 persons—three-quarters of the southern white population. Shouldered off the richest bottomlands by the mighty planters, they scratched a simple living from the thinner soils of the backcountry and mountain val-

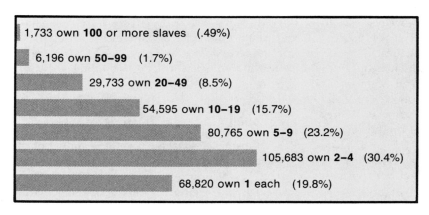

1,733 own **100** or more slaves   (.49%)

6,196 own **50–99**   (1.7%)

29,733 own **20–49**   (8.5%)

54,595 own **10–19**   (15.7%)

80,765 own **5–9**   (23.2%)

105,683 own **2–4**   (30.4%)

68,820 own **1** each   (19.8%)

Slaveowning Families, 1850. *The philosopher Ralph Waldo Emerson, a New Englander, declared in 1856: "I do not see how a barbarous community and a civilized community can constitute a state. I think we must get rid of slavery or we must get rid of freedom."*

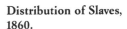

Distribution of Slaves, 1860.

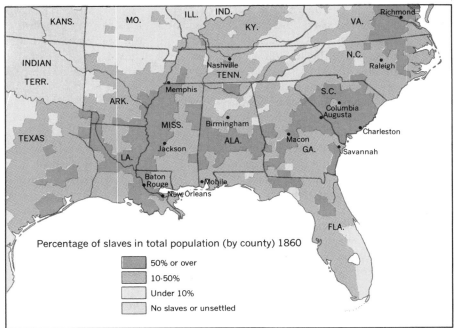

Percentage of slaves in total population (by county) 1860

- 50% or over
- 10-50%
- Under 10%
- No slaves or unsettled

leys. These red-necked yeomen participated in the market economy scarcely at all. As subsistence farmers, they raised corn and hogs, not cotton, and lived often isolated lives. Some of the least prosperous nonslaveholding whites were scorned even by slaves as "poor white trash" or "hillbillies."

All these whites without slaves had no direct stake in the preservation of slavery, yet they were among the stoutest defenders of the slave system. Why? The answer is not far to seek.

The carrot on the stick ever dangling before their eyes was the hope of buying a slave or two and of parlaying their holdings into riches—all in accord with the "American dream" of upward social mobility. They also took fierce pride in their presumed racial superiority, which would be watered down if the slaves were freed. Many of the poorer whites were hardly better off economically than the slaves, but even the most wretched whites could take perverse comfort from the knowledge that they outranked in status the still more wretched Afro-American bondsman. Thus did the logic of economics join with the illogic of racism in buttressing the slave system.

In a special category among white southerners were the mountain whites, more or less marooned in the valleys of the Appalachian range that stretched from western Virginia to northern Georgia and Alabama. As independent small farmers, hundreds of miles distant from the heart of the cotton kingdom and rarely if ever in sight of a slave, these mountain whites had little in common with the whites of the flatlands. Many of them, including future President Andrew Johnson of Tennessee, hated both the haughty planters and their gangs of blacks. When the Civil War came, the tough-fibered mountain whites constituted a vitally important peninsula of Unionism jutting down into the secessionist Southern sea. They ultimately played a significant role in crippling the Confederacy.

Free Blacks: Slaves Without Masters

Precarious in the extreme was the standing of the South's free blacks, who numbered about 250,000 by 1860. In the upper South, the free black population traced its origins to a wavelet of emancipation inspired by the idealism of Revolutionary days. In the deeper South, many free blacks were mulattoes, usually the emancipated children of a white planter and his black mistress. Throughout the South were some free blacks who had purchased their freedom with earnings from labor after hours.

The free blacks in the South were a kind of "third race." They were prohibited from certain occupations, and always vulnerable to being high-jacked back into slavery by unscrupulous slave traders. As free men and women they were walking examples of what might be achieved by emancipation, and hence were resented and detested by defenders of the slave system.

Free blacks were also unpopular in the North, where about another 250,000 of them lived. Several states forbade their entrance, most denied them the right to vote, and some barred blacks from public schools. Much of the agitation in the North against the spread of slavery into the new territories in the 1840s and 1850s grew out of race prejudice, not humanitarianism.

Antiblack feeling was in fact frequently stronger in the North than in the South. It was sometimes observed that white southerners, who were often suckled and reared by black nurses, liked the black as an individual but despised the race. The white northerner, on the other hand, often professed to like the race but disliked individual blacks.

Plantation Slavery

In society's basement in the South of 1860 were nearly 4 million black human chattels.. Their numbers had quadrupled since the dawn of the century, as the booming cotton economy created a seemingly unquenchable demand for slave labor. Despite the ending of the legal slave trade by Congress in 1808, the price of "black ivory" was so high that uncounted thousands of slaves continued to be smuggled into the South. Yet the huge bulk of the increase in the slave population came not from imports but instead from natural reproduction—a fact that distinguished slavery in America from other New World societies and implied much

Slave Deck of the Slaver *Wildfire*.   *Captured by the U.S. Navy, this slave ship was brought into Key West, Florida, in April 1860. The blacks were freed. (From a daguerreotype [photograph] published in* Harper's Weekly, *June 2, 1860)*

about the tenor of the slave regime and the conditions of family life under slavery.

Above all, the planters regarded the slaves as investments, into which they had sunk nearly $2 billion by 1860. Slaves were the primary form of wealth in the South, and as such they were cared for as any asset is cared for by a prudent capitalist. Masters sometimes hired cheap Irish wage laborers to perform dangerous work rather than risk the life of a prime field hand, worth $1,800 by 1860 (a price that had quintupled since 1800).

Slavery was profitable for the great planters, though it hobbled the economic development of the region as a whole. The profits from the cotton boom sucked ever more slaves from the upper to the lower South, so that by 1860 the Deep South states of South Carolina, Florida, Mississippi, Alabama, and Louisiana each had a majority or near-majority of blacks.

Breeding slaves in the way that cattle are bred was not openly encouraged. But women who bore thirteen or fourteen babies were prized as "rattlin' good breeders." White masters, all too frequently,

The Cruelty of Slavery.   (left) *Held captive in a net, a slave sits on the Congo shore, waiting to be sold and shipped. (Collection Photothèque Musée de 'Homme)* (above) *The device was riveted around a slave's neck. Its attached bells, like a cow bell, made it impossible for the wearer to hide from his or her owner.*

would force their attention on female slaves, fathering a sizable mulatto population, most of which remained enchained.

Slave auctions were brutal sights. The open selling of human flesh under the hammer was among the most revolting aspects of slavery. On the auction block families were separated with distressing frequency, usually for economic reasons such as bankruptcy or the division of "property" among heirs. The sundering of families in this fashion was perhaps slavery's greatest psychological horror. Abolitionists decried the practice, and Harriet Beecher Stowe seized on the emotional power of this theme by putting it at the heart of the plot of *Uncle Tom's Cabin.*

Life Under the Lash

White southerners often romanticized about the happy life of their singing, dancing, banjo-strumming, joyful "darkies," but how did the slaves actually live? There is no simple answer to this question. Conditions varied greatly from region to region, from large plantation to small farm, and from mas-

ter to master. Everywhere, of course, slavery meant hard work, ignorance, and oppression. The slaves—both men and women—usually toiled from dawn to dusk in the fields, under the watchful eyes and ready whip-hand of a white overseer or black "driver." They had no civil or political rights, and even the minimal protection from murder or unusually cruel punishment was difficult to enforce, since slaves were forbidden to testify in court.

Floggings were common, for the whip was the substitute for the wage-incentive system and the most visible symbol of the planter's mastery. Strong-willed slaves were sometimes sent to "breakers," whose technique consisted mostly in lavish laying on of the lash. As an abolitionist song of the 1850s lamented:

> To-night the bond man, Lord
> Is bleeding in his chains;
> And loud the falling lash is heard
> On Carolina's plains!

But savage beatings made sullen laborers, and lash marks hurt resale values. There are, to be sure, sadistic monsters in any population, and the planter class contained its share. But for financial as well as humane reasons, the typical planter did not customarily go out and beat to death a valuable field hand before breakfast.

By 1860 most slaves were concentrated in the "black belt" of the Deep South that stretched from South Carolina and Georgia into the new south-west states of Alabama, Mississippi, and Louisiana. A majority of blacks lived on larger plantations that harbored communities of twenty or more slaves. In some counties of the Deep South, especially along the lower Mississippi River, blacks accounted for more than 75 percent of the population. There the family life of slaves tended to be relatively stable, and a distinctive Afro-American slave culture developed. Forced separation of spouses, parents, and children were evidently more common on smaller plantations and in the upper South. Slave marriage vows sometimes proclaimed, "Until death or *distance* do you part."

With impressive resilience, blacks managed to sustain family life in slavery, and most slaves were raised in stable two-person households. Continuity of family identity across generations was evidenced in the widespread practice of naming children for grandparents or adopting the surname not of a current master, but of a forebear's master. Afro-Americans also displayed their African cultural roots when they avoided marriage between first cousins, which white society then permitted.

African roots were also visible in slave religious practices. Though heavily Christianized by itiner-ant evangelists of the Second Great Awakening, blacks in slavery molded their own distinctive religious forms from a mixture of Christian and African elements. They emphasized those aspects of the Christian heritage that seemed most perti-nent to their own situation—especially the cap-tivity of the Israelites in Egypt. One of the most haunting spirituals implored:

> Tell old Pharaoh
> "Let my people go."

And another lamented:

> Nobody knows de trouble I've had
> Nobody knows but Jesus

African practices also persisted in the "responsor-ial" style of preaching, in which the congregation frequently punctuates the minister's remarks with assents and *amens*—an adaptation of the give-and-take between caller and dancers in the African ringshout dance.

The Burdens of Bondage

Slavery was intolerably degrading to the victims. They were deprived of the dignity and sense of responsibility that come from independence and the right to make choices. They were denied an education, because reading brought ideas, and ideas brought discontent. Many states passed laws forbidding their instruction. For all slaves—indeed for all blacks, slave or free—the "American dream" of bettering one's lot through study and hard work was a cruel and empty mockery.

Not surprisingly, victims of the "peculiar institution" devised countless ways to throw sand in its gears. Slaves often slowed the pace of their labor to the barest minimum that would spare them the lash, thus fostering the myth of black "laziness" in the minds of whites. They filched food from the "big house" and other goods that had been pro-duced by their labor. They sometimes sabotaged expensive equipment and occasionally even put poison in their master's food.

The slaves also universally pined for freedom. Many took to their heels as runaways, frequently in search of a separated family member. Others rebelled, though never successfully. In 1800 a slave named Gabriel led an armed insurrection in Rich-mond, Virginia, and in 1822 Denmark Vesey, a free black, organized another rebellion in Charleston. In both cases the rebels were betrayed by informers and hanged. In 1831 the semiliterate Nat Turner, a visionary black preacher, led an uprising that slaughtered about sixty Virginians, mostly women and children. Reprisals were swift and bloody.

The dark taint of slavery also left its mark on the whites. It fostered the brutality of the whip, the bloodhound, and the branding iron. White south-erners increasingly lived in a state of imagined siege, surrounded by potentially rebellious blacks inflamed by abolitionist propaganda from the North. Their fears bolstered an intoxicating theory of biological racial superiority and turned the

South into a reactionary backwater in an era of progress. The defenders of slavery were forced to degrade themselves, along with their victims. As Booker T. Washington, a distinguished black leader and ex-slave, later observed, a white man cannot hold a black man in a ditch without getting down there with him.

Early Abolitionism

The inhumanity of the "peculiar institution" gradually caused antislavery societies to sprout forth. The first stirrings of abolitionist sentiment occurred at the time of the Revolution, especially among leading Quakers. Because of the widespread loathing of blacks, some of the earliest abolitionist efforts focused on transporting the blacks bodily back to Africa. The American Colonization Society was founded for this purpose in 1817, and in 1822 the Republic of Liberia was established for former slaves on the West African coast.

In the 1830s the abolitionist movement took on new energy and momentum, mounting to the proportions of a crusade. American abolitionists took heart in 1833 when their British counterparts unchained the slaves in the West Indies. Most important, the religious spirit of the Second Great Awakening now inflamed the hearts of many abolitionists against the sin of slavery.

Prominent among them was lanky, plain-speaking Theodore Dwight Weld, who had been evangelized by Charles Grandison Finney in the 1820s. In 1832 Weld enrolled at Lane Theological Seminary in Cincinnati, which was presided over by Lyman Beecher, the formidable father of novelist Harriet Beecher Stowe, feminist Catharine Beecher, and preacher-abolitionist Henry Ward Beecher. Expelled along with several other students in 1834 for organizing an eighteen-day debate on slavery, Weld and his fellow "Lane Rebels"—full of the energy and idealism of youth—fanned out across the Old Northwest preaching the antislavery gospel. Weld also assembled a potent propaganda tract, *American Slavery As It Is* (1839), which influenced Harriet Beecher Stowe's *Uncle Tom's Cabin*.

Radical Abolitionism

On New Year's Day, 1831, a shattering abolitionist blast came from the bugle of William Lloyd Garrison, a mild-looking, emotionally high-strung reformer of twenty-six. A spiritual child of the Second Great Awakening, Garrison published in Boston the first issue of his militantly antislavery newspaper *The Liberator.* With this mighty paper broadside Garrison triggered a thirty-year war of words and in a sense fired one of the opening guns of the Civil War.

Stern and uncompromising, Garrison proclaimed in strident tones that under no circumstances would he tolerate the poisonous weed of slavery:

> I will be as harsh as truth and as uncompromising as justice. . . . I am in earnest—I will not equivocate—I will not excuse—I will not retreat a single inch—and I WILL BE HEARD!

Other dedicated abolitionists rallied to Garrison's standard, and in 1833 they founded the American Anti-Slavery Society.

Black abolitionists distinguished themselves as living monuments to the cause of Afro-American freedom. Their ranks included the incendiary David Walker, who advocated violent revolt against white supremacy. Also noteworthy were Sojourner Truth, a freed black woman who fought tirelessly for black emancipation and women's rights, and Martin Delany, one of the few black leaders who advocated black recolonization in Africa.

The greatest of the black abolitionists was Frederick Douglass. Escaping from bondage in 1838 at the age of twenty-one, Douglass was "discovered" by the abolitionists three years later when he gave a stunning impromptu speech at an antislavery meeting in Massachusetts. Thereafter he lectured widely for the cause, despite frequent beatings and threats against his life. In 1845 he published his classic autobiography, *Narrative of the Life of Frederick Douglass.*

Douglass was just as flexibly practical as Garrison was stubbornly principled. Garrison often

Frederick Douglass (c. 1817–1895). *Born a slave in Maryland, Douglass escaped to the North and became the most prominent black abolitionist. Gifted as an orator, writer, and editor, he continued to battle for the civil rights of his people after emancipation. Near the end of a distinguished career, he served as U.S. minister to Haiti. (Library of Congress)*

appeared to be more interested in his own righteousness than in the substance of the slavery evil itself, and repeatedly demanded that the "virtuous" North secede from the "wicked" South. Renouncing politics, on the Fourth of July, 1854, he publicly burned a copy of the Constitution as "a covenant with death and an agreement with hell." Douglass, on the other hand, along with other abolitionists, increasingly looked to politics to end the blight of slavery. These political abolitionists backed the Liberty party in 1840, the Free Soil party in 1848, and eventually the Republican party in the 1850s.

High-minded and courageous, the abolitionists were men and women of goodwill and various colors who faced the cruel choice that people in many ages have had thrust upon them: When is evil so enormous that it must be denounced, even at the risk of precipitating bloodshed and butchery?

The South Lashes Back

Antislavery sentiment was not unknown in the South, but after about 1830 the voice of white southern abolitionism was silenced. Nat Turner's rebellion sent a wave of hysteria sweeping over the white cotton fields, and planters in increasing numbers slept with pistols by their pillows.

The nullification crisis in 1832 further implanted haunting fears in southern minds, which conjured up nightmares of black incendiaries and abolitionist devils. Jailings, whippings, and lynchings now greeted rational efforts to discuss the slavery problem in the South.

Proslavery whites responded by launching a massive defense of slavery as a positive good. In doing so, they forgot their own section's previous doubts about the morality of the "peculiar institution." Slavery, they claimed, was supported by the authority of the Bible and the wisdom of Aristotle. It was good for the Africans, who were lifted from the barbarism of the jungle and clothed with the blessings of Christian civilization.

White apologists also pointed out that master-slave relationships really resembled those of a family. On many plantations, especially those in the Old South of Virginia and Maryland, this argument had a certain plausibility.

Southern whites were quick to contrast the "happy" lot of their "servants" with that of the overworked northern wage slaves, including sweated women and stunted children. The blacks mostly toiled in the fresh air and sunlight, not in dark and stuffy factories. They did not have to worry about slack times or unemployment, as did the "hired hands" of the North. Provided with a jail-like form of Social Security, they were cared for in sickness and old age, unlike the northern workers, who were turned adrift.

These curious proslavery arguments only widened the chasm between a backward-looking South and a forward-looking North—and indeed much of the rest of the Western world. The Southerners reacted to the pressure of their own fears and the merciless nagging of the northern abolitionists. Increasingly the white South turned in upon itself and grew hotly intolerant of any embarrassing questions about the status of slavery.

Regrettably, also, the controversy over free men endangered free speech in the entire country. Piles of petitions poured in upon Congress from the antislavery reformers; and in 1836 sensitive Southerners drove through the House the so-called gag resolution. It required all such antislavery appeals to be tabled without debate.

Southern whites likewise resented the flooding of their mails with incendiary abolitionist literature. In 1835 a mob in Charleston, South Carolina, looted the local post office and burned a pile of abolitionist propaganda. Capitulating to southern pressures, the Washington government in the 1830s ordered southern postmasters to destroy abolitionist material and called on southern state officials to arrest federal postmasters who did not comply. Such was "freedom of the press" as guaranteed by the Constitution.

The Abolitionist Impact in the North

Abolitionists—especially the extreme Garrisonians—were for a long time unpopular in many parts of the North. Northerners had been brought up to revere the Constitution and to regard the clauses on slavery as a lasting bargain. The ideal of Union, hammered home by the thundering eloquence of Daniel Webster and others, had taken deep root; and Garrison's wild talk of secession grated harshly on northern ears.

The North also had a heavy economic stake in Dixieland. By the late 1850s the southern planters owed northern bankers and other creditors about $300 million, and much of this immense sum would be lost—as, in fact, it later was—should the Union dissolve. New England textile mills were fed with cotton raised by the slaves, and a disrupted labor system might cut off this vital supply and bring unemployment. The Union during these critical years was partly bound together with cotton threads, tied by lords of the loom in collaboration with the so-called lords of the lash. It was not surprising that strong hostility developed in the North against the boat-rocking tactics of the radical antislaveryites.

Repeated tongue-lashings by the extreme abolitionists provoked many mob outbursts in the North, some led by respectable gentlemen. A gang of young toughs broke into Lewis Tappan's New York house in 1834 and demolished its interior, while a crowd in the street cheered. In 1835 Garrison, with a rope tied around him, was dragged through the streets of Boston by the so-called Broadcloth Mob but escaped almost miraculously. Reverend Elijah P. Lovejoy, of Alton, Illinois, not content to assail slavery, impugned the chastity of Catholic women. His printing press was destroyed four times, and in 1837 he was killed by a mob, thus becoming "the martyr abolitionist." So unpopular were the antislavery zealots that ambitious politicians, like Lincoln, usually avoided the taint of Garrisonian abolition like the plague.

Yet by the 1850s the abolitionist outcry had made a deep dent in the northern mind. Many citizens had come to see the South as the land of the unfree and the home of a hateful institution. Few northerners were prepared to abolish slavery outright, but a growing number, including Abraham Lincoln, opposed extending it to the territories in the West. People of this stamp, commonly called "free-soilers," swelled their ranks as the Civil War approached.

VARYING VIEWPOINTS

In his pioneering study *American Negro Slavery* (1918), Ulrich Bonnell Phillips argued that planters, contrary to abolitionist charges of ruthless exploitation, treated their chattels with kindly paternalism, and that slaves were passive and dim by nature and did not abhor the institution. Scholars no longer accept Phillips's views of racial inferiority, but they still debate the nature of the master-slave relationship and its effect on the slave personality.

Beginning in the late 1950s, historians such as Stanley Elkins emphasized the harshness of the slave system, which they even compared to the Nazi concentration camps, and its "infantil- izing" effect on the slaves' personalities. Recently, scholars such as Eugene Genovese have criticized these views. Without diminishing the deprivations and pains of slavery, these stu- dents of the "peculiar institution" concede that slavery embraced a strong form of paternalism, a system that reflected not the benevolence of southern slaveholders but their need to protect

and coax work out of their often recalcitrant "investment."

Other historians agree with Elkins that slav- ery was a brutal institution, but differ with his portrait of the slaves as simply passive, infan- tilized victims. Kenneth Stampp stressed the frequency and variety of violent and peaceful slave resistance. Scholars such as Herbert Gut- man and Lawrence Levine emphasize the tenac- ity with which slaves maintained their own culture, despite the hardships of bondage. Point- ing to the slaves' capacity for clever initiative, they see the "Sambo" stereotype as an act, an image that the slaves employed in order to con- found their masters without incurring punish- ment.

SELECT READINGS

Primary Source Documents

Two influential abolitionist documents are Theodore Dwight Weld, *American Slavery As It Is* * (1839), and the inaugural editorial of William Lloyd Garrison's *The Liber- ator* * (1831). Roy P. Basler, ed., *The Collected Works of Abraham Lincoln* (1933), contains the Great Eman- cipator's assessment of abolitionism in 1854. For southern perspectives, see James Henry Hammond's famous "Cotton Is King" speech, *Congressional Globe,* 36 Cong., 1 sess. p. 961 (March 3, 1858).*

Secondary Sources

A good introduction to southern history is Clement Eaton, *A History of the Old South: The Emergence of a Reluctant Nation* (1975). Wilbur J. Cash, *The Mind of the South* (1941) is an engagingly written classic. Always incisive is C. Vann Woodward, *The Burden of Southern History* (1960) and *American Counterpoint* (1971). The literature on slavery and Afro-Americans is enormous; the best place to start is John Hope Franklin, *From Slavery to Freedom* (5th ed., 1980), and consult also Nathan Irving Huggins' sometimes lyrical *Black Odyssey* (1977). The

modern debate on slavery began with Ulrich B. Phillips' classic *American Negro Slavery* (1918); a darker view of the same subject is found in Kenneth M. Stampp, *The Peculiar Institution* (1956). Consult also Stanley Elkins' stimulat- ing essay, *Slavery* (2d ed., 1968), which also has interesting observations on the abolitionists. A major study of the slaves and their relations to their masters is Eugene Gen- ovese, *Roll, Jordan, Roll* (1974). Carl N. Degler compares slavery and race relations in Brazil and the United States in *Neither Black Nor White* (1971). David B. Davis provides indispensable background to the history of abolitionism in *The Problem of Slavery in Western Culture* (1966) and *The Problem of Slavery in the Age of Revolution* (1975). The best brief history of the abolitionists is James B. Stewart, *Holy Warriors* (1976). Aileen Kraditor is favora- bly disposed toward Garrison in *Means and Ends in Amer- ican Abolitionism: Garrison and His Critics* (1977). White attitudes toward race and slavery can be studied in Winthrop Jordan's masterful *White Over Black* (1968) and George Frederickson's insightful *The Black Image in the White Mind* (1971).

21

Renewing the Sectional Struggle, 1848–1854

> **Secession! Peaceable secession!**
> **Sir, your eyes and mine are never destined to see that miracle.**
>
> Daniel Webster, Seventh of March speech, 1850

The Popular Sovereignty Panacea

The year 1848, highlighted by a rash of revolutions in Europe, was filled with unrest in America. The Treaty of Guadalupe Hidalgo had officially ended the war with Mexico, but it had initiated a new and perilous round of political warfare in the United States. The vanquished Mexicans had been forced to relinquish an enormous tract of real estate from Texas to California. The acquisition of this huge domain raised anew the burning issue of extending slavery into the territories. Northern anti-slaveryites had rallied behind the Wilmot Proviso, which flatly prohibited slavery in any territory acquired in the Mexican War. Southern senators had blocked the passage of the proviso, but the issue would not die (see p. 177).

Ominously, debate over slavery in the area of the Mexican Cession threatened to disrupt the ranks of both Whigs and Democrats and split national politics along North-South sectional lines. Each of the two great political parties was a vital bond of national unity, for each enjoyed powerful support in both North and South. If they should be replaced by two purely sectional groupings, the Union would be in peril. To politicians, the wisest strategy seemed to be to sit on the lid of the slavery issue and ignore the boiling beneath. Even so, the cover bobbed up and down ominously in response to the agitation of zealous northern abolitionists and hot-headed southern "fire-eaters."

With illness-plagued President Polk pledged to a single term, anxious Democrats sought a new standard-bearer in 1848. They turned to aging General Lewis Cass, an experienced but pompous senator whose enemies dubbed him "General

Gass." The Democratic platform was silent on the burning issue of slavery in the territories. But Cass himself was a well-known advocate of "popular sovereignty," the doctrine that the people of a territory, under the principles of the Constitution, should themselves determine the status of slavery.

Popular sovereignty had a persuasive appeal. The public liked it because it accorded with the democratic tradition of self-determination. Politicians liked it because it seemed a comfortable compromise between a ban on slavery in the territories and southern demands that Congress protect slavery in the territories. Popular sovereignty tossed the slavery problem into the laps of the people in the various territories. Advocates of the doctrine thus hoped to dissolve the most stubborn national issue of the day into a series of local issues. Yet popular sovereignty had one fatal defect: it might serve to spread the blight of slavery.

Meeting in Philadelphia, the Whigs turned away from controversy-ridden Henry Clay and nominated Zachary Taylor, the "Hero of Buena Vista," who had never held civil office or even voted for president.

As usual, the Whigs pussyfooted in their platform. Eager to win at any cost, they dodged all the troublesome issues and merely extolled the homespun virtues of their candidate. Taylor had not committed himself on the issue of slavery extension, but as a wealthy Louisiana sugar planter he owned scores of slaves.

Aroused by the conspiracy of silence in the Democratic and Whig platforms, ardent antislavery men organized the Free-Soil Party. It stood four-square for the Wilmot Proviso and against slavery in the territories. The new party trotted out wizened ex-President Van Buren, shouting, "Free soil, free speech, free labor, and free men."

With the slavery issue officially shoved under the rug by the two major parties, politicians on both sides carefully kept the focus on personalities. The Whigs closely watched the amateurish Taylor lest his indiscreet pen puncture his puffed-up military reputation. Taylor won with 1,360,099 popular and 163 electoral votes compared with Cass's 1,220,544 popular and 127 electoral votes. Free-soiler Van Buren polled 291,263 votes and won no

states, but apparently diverted enough Democratic strength from Cass in the crucial state of New York to throw the election to Taylor.

Sectional Balance and the Underground Railroad

The South of 1850 was relatively well off. It had seated in the White House the war hero Zachary Taylor, a Virginia-born, slave-owning planter from Louisiana. It had a majority in the Cabinet and on the supreme bench. If outnumbered in the House, the South had equality in the Senate, where it could hope to exercise a veto voice. Its cotton fields were expanding, and the price of the snowy fiber was profitably high. Few sane people, North or South, believed that slavery was seriously threatened where it already existed below the Mason-Dixon line.* The fifteen slave states could easily veto any proposed constitutional amendment.

Yet the South was deeply worried, as it had been for several decades, by the ever-tipping political balance. There were then fifteen slave states and fifteen free states. The admission of California would destroy the delicate equilibrium in the Senate, perhaps forever. The fate of California might well establish a precedent for the rest of the Mexican Cession territory.

Texas nursed an additional grievance of its own. It claimed a huge area east of the Rio Grande and north to the forty-second parallel, part of present New Mexico. The federal government was proposing to detach this prize, while hot-blooded Texans were threatening to descend upon Santa Fe and seize what they regarded as rightfully theirs. The explosive quarrel foreshadowed shooting.

Many southerners were also angered by the nagging agitation in the North for the abolition of slavery in the District of Columbia. They looked with alarm on the prospect of a ten-mile-square oasis of free soil, thrust between slaveholding Maryland and slaveholding Virginia.

Even more disagreeable to the South was the loss of runaway slaves, many of whom were assisted

---

*Originally the southern boundary of colonial Pennsylvania.

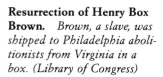

Resurrection of Henry Box Brown. *Brown, a slave, was shipped to Philadelphia abolitionists from Virginia in a box. (Library of Congress)*

north by the Underground Railroad. It consisted of an informal chain of "stations" (antislavery homes), through which scores of "passengers" (runaway slaves) were spirited by "conductors" (usually white and black abolitionists) from the slave states to the free-soil sanctuary of Canada.

The most amazing of these "conductors" was a runaway slave from Maryland, fearless Harriet Tubman. During nineteen forays into the South, she rescued more than 300 slaves, including her aged parents, and deservedly earned the title "Moses."

By 1850 Southerners were demanding a new and more stringent fugitive-slave law. The old one, passed by Congress in 1793, had proved inadequate to cope with runaways, especially since unfriendly state authorities failed to cooperate.

Estimates indicate that the South in 1850 was losing perhaps 1,000 runaways a year, out of its total of some 4 million slaves. In fact, the owners probably freed more blacks voluntarily than ever escaped.

Twilight of the Senatorial Giants

Southern fears were such that Congress was confronted with catastrophe in 1850. Free-soil California was banging on the door for admission, and

"fire-eaters" in the South were voicing ominous threats of secession. The crisis brought into the congressional forum the most distinguished assemblage of statesmen since the Constitutional Convention of 1787—the Old Guard of the dying generation and the young gladiators of the new. That "immortal trio"—Clay, Calhoun, and Webster—appeared together for the last time.

Henry Clay, now seventy-three years of age, played a crucial role by proposing a series of compromises. Ably seconded by Senator Stephen A. Douglas of Illinois, the "Little Giant," Clay urged that the North and South both make concessions.

Senator John C. Calhoun, then sixty-eight and dying of tuberculosis, championed the South in his last formal speech. Too weak to deliver it himself, he sat bundled up in the Senate chamber, his eyes glowing in his stern face, while a younger colleague read his fateful words. Passionately rejecting Clay's proposed concessions, Calhoun's plea was to leave slavery alone, return runaway slaves, give the South its rights as a minority, and restore the political balance. Calhoun died in 1850, before the debate was over, uttering the sad words, "The South! The South! God knows what will become of her."

Daniel Webster, now sixty-eight years old and ailing, next took the Senate spotlight to uphold Clay's compromise measures in his last great

Compromise of 1850

Concessions to the North	Concessions to the South
California admitted as a free state	The remainder of the Mexican Cession area to be formed into the territories of New Mexico and Utah, without restriction on slavery, hence open to popular sovereignty
Territory disputed by Texas and New Mexico to be surrendered to New Mexico	Texas to receive $10 million from the federal government as compensation
Abolition of the slave trade (but not slavery) in the District of Columbia	A more stringent Fugitive Slave Law, going beyond that of 1793

speech. Webster urged all reasonable concessions to the South, including a new fugitive-slave law. Because climate would prevent the spread of cotton production to the Mexican Cession territory, Webster argued, it was unnecessary to legislate on slavery there.* The old orator's eloquent plea visibly strengthened Union sentiment, and especially pleased Northern banking and commercial interests, which stood to lose millions of dollars by secession. But abolitionists, who had mistakenly regarded Webster as sympathetic to their cause, upbraided him as a traitor.

The stormy Congressional debate of 1850 was not finished, for the Young Guard from the North were yet to have their say. Led by wiry William Seward of New York, this new generation of antislavery politicians were more interested in purifying the Union than in patching it. Seward flatly opposed further concessions to the South, appealing to a moral "higher law" than the Constitution to exclude slavery from the territories.

As the great debate in Congress ran its heated course, deadlock seemed certain. In response to the threats of Texas to seize Santa Fe, blunt old President Taylor seemed ready to lead an army into Texas and hang all the "damned traitors." If the troops had marched, the South probably would have seceded, and the Civil War might have erupted in 1850.

---

*Webster was wrong on this point; within 100 years California had become one of the great cotton-producing states of the Union.

Breaking the Congressional Logjam

At the height of the crisis, President Taylor unknowingly made compromise possible by suddenly dying. The colorless vice-president, Millard Fillmore, took the reins. As presiding officer of the Senate, he had been impressed with the arguments for conciliation, and now he gladly signed the delicate series of compromises that passed Congress.

The struggle to get these measures accepted by the country was hardly less heated than in Congress. In the North, "Union savers" like Clay, Webster, and Douglas orated on behalf of compromise. Clay alone delivered more than seventy speeches. Their cause was aided by a feeling of relief that the crisis was over and by an upsurge of prosperity.

But Southern "fire-eaters" were still violently opposed to concessions. They organized in Nashville, Tennessee, to condemn the compromise. A southern boycott of northern goods made some headway. But in the end southern Unionists, aided by the warm glow of prosperity, persuaded reluctant southern opinion to reject the extremists.

Like the calm after a storm, a second Era of Good Feelings dawned. Both North and South were determined that the compromises should finally bury the explosive issue of slavery. But this reign of reason proved all too brief.

Balancing the Compromise Scales

Who got the better of the Compromise of 1850?

The answer is clearly the North. California, as a free state, tipped the Senate balance permanently

Slavery After the Compromise of 1850.

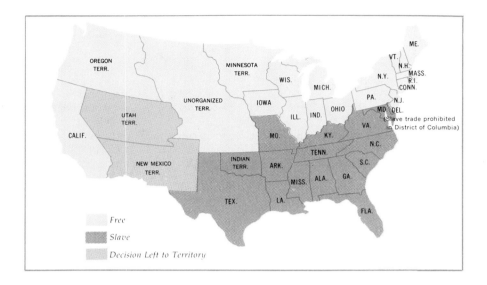

Free

Slave

Decision Left to Territory

against the South. The territories of New Mexico and Utah were open to slavery on the basis of popular sovereignty. But the iron law of nature—the "highest law" of all—had loaded the dice in favor of free soil. The Southerners urgently needed more slave territory to restore the "sacred balance." If they could not carve new states out of the recent conquests from Mexico, where could they get them?

Even the apparent gains of the South rang hollow. Disgruntled Texas was to be paid $10 million toward discharging her indebtedness, but in the long run this was a modest sum. The immense area in dispute had been torn from the side of slaveholding Texas, and was almost certain to be free. The South had halted the drive toward abolition in the District of Columbia, at least temporarily, by permitting the outlawing of the slave traffic. But even this move was an entering wedge toward complete emancipation in the nation's capital.

Most alarming of all, the drastic new Fugitive Slave Law—"the Bloodhound Bill"—stirred up a storm of opposition in the North. The fleeing slave could not testify in his own behalf, and he was denied a jury trial. These harsh practices threatened to create dangerous precedents for the whites. The federal commissioner who handled the case would receive five dollars if the runaway was freed,

and ten dollars if not—an arrangement that strongly resembled a bribe. Freedom-loving northerners who aided the slave to escape were liable to heavy fines and jail sentences. They might even be ordered to join the slavecatchers, and this possibility rubbed salt into old sores.

So savage was this "Man-Stealing Law" that it touched off an explosive chain reaction in the North. Many shocked moderates, hitherto passive, were driven into the swelling ranks of the abolitionists.

The Underground Railroad stepped up its timetable, while infuriated northern mobs rescued slaves from their pursuers. Massachusetts, in a move toward nullification suggestive of South Carolina in 1832, made it a penal offense for any state official to enforce the new federal statute. Other states passed "personal liberty laws," which denied local jails to federal officials and otherwise hampered enforcement. The abolitionists rent the heavens with their protests against the man-stealing statute. A meeting presided over by Garrison in 1851 declared, "We execrate it, we spit upon it, we trample it under our feet."

Beyond question, the Fugitive Slave Law was an appalling blunder on the part of the South. No single irritant of the 1850s was more persistently galling to both sides, and none did more to awaken

A Ride for Liberty. *This famous painting by New England artist Eastman Johnson brilliantly evokes the anxiety of fleeing slaves. (The Brooklyn Museum. Gift of Miss Gwendolyn O.L. Conkling)*

in the North a spirit of antagonism against the South. The southerners in turn were embittered because the northerners would not in good faith execute the law—the one real and immediate "gain" from the Great Compromise. Slavecatchers, with some success, redoubled their efforts.

Should the shooting showdown have come in 1850? From the standpoint of the secessionists, yes; from the standpoint of the Unionists, no. Time was fighting for the North. With every passing decade this huge section was forging farther ahead in population and wealth—in crops, factories, foundries, ships, and railroads.

Delay also added immensely to the moral strength of the North—to its will to fight for the Union. In 1850 countless thousands of northern moderates were unwilling to pin the South to the rest of the nation with bayonets. But the inflam-

matory events of the 1850s did much to bolster the Yankee will to resist secession, whatever the cost. This one feverish decade gave the North time to accumulate the physical and moral strength that provided the margin of victory. Thus the Compromise of 1850, from one point of view, won the Civil War for the Union.

Defeat and Doom For the Whigs

Meeting in Baltimore in 1852, the Democratic convention chose as its nominee an obscure New Hampshire lawyer-politician, Franklin Pierce. Weak and indecisive, Pierce was called the "Fainting General" by his opponents because he had fallen off a horse. Chosen for his acceptability to the slavery wing of the Democratic party, Pierce came out for the finality of the Compromise of 1850, Fugitive Slave Law and all.

The Whigs, also convening in Baltimore, foolishly bypassed figures associated with the Compromise of 1850, such as President Fillmore and Senator Webster. Having won in the past only with military heroes, they turned to another, "Old Fuss and Feathers," General Winfield Scott. The huge and haughty Scott's personality repelled the masses, and Democrats cried exultantly, "We Polk-ed 'em in '44; we'll Pierce 'em in '52."

Scott was an inept candidate, but an even greater boon for the Democrats was the hopeless split in the Whig party. Antislavery Whigs swallowed Scott but deplored his platform, which endorsed the hated Fugitive Slave Law. Southern Whigs, who doubted Scott's loyalty to the Compromise of 1850 and especially to the Fugitive Slave Law, swallowed the platform but spat on the candidate. Stabbed in the back by his fellow Whigs in the South, Scott received 1,386,580 popular votes, but only 42 electoral votes. The pliant Pierce won handily with 1,601,274 popular votes and 254 electoral votes.

The election of 1852 was fraught with frightening significance, though it may have seemed tame at the time. It marked the effective end of the disorganized Whig party, and within a few years its complete death. The Whigs were governed at times by the crassest opportunism, and they won only two presidential elections (1840, 1848) in their colorful career, both with war heroes. They finally choked to death trying to gag down the Fugitive Slave Law. But their great contribution—and a noteworthy one indeed—was to help implant and uphold the ideal of Union through leaders like Clay and Webster. Both of these statesmen, by unhappy coincidence, died during the campaign. But the good that they had done lived after them, and contributed powerfully to the preservation of a united United States.

The Expansionist Legacy of the Mexican War

From the outset the Pierce administration displayed vigor in pursuing expansion. The new president's cabinet contained aggressive southerners,

including Secretary of War Jefferson Davis, future president of the Confederacy. The men of Dixie were determined to acquire more slave territory, and the compliant Pierce was their willing tool.

The intoxicating victories of the Mexican War stimulated the lust for new slave territory among "slaveocrats." Many Americans were also looking for potential canal routes across Central America in Nicaragua and Panama, and favored expansion into the islands flanking them, notably Spain's Cuba.

Nicaragua was of vital concern to Great Britain. Fearing that the grasping Yankees would monopolize trade there, the British seized a solid foothold at Greytown, the eastern end of the proposed Nicaraguan canal route, and an ugly armed clash threatened. But the crisis was surmounted in 1850 by the Clayton-Bulwer Treaty, which stipulated that neither America nor Britain would secure exclusive control over any future Isthmian waterway.

America had become a Pacific power with the acquisition of California and Oregon. American shippers already traded with China, and they now urged Washington to push for commercial intercourse with Japan, which had been closed to the European world for two hundred years.

The government responded in 1853 by dispatching a fleet of awesome, smoke-belching warships, commanded by Commodore Matthew C. Perry. Through a judicious combination of force and tact, Perry persuaded the Japanese to sign a memorable treaty in 1854 that proved to be the first step of an epochal relationship.

Sugar-rich Cuba, lying off the nation's southern doorstep, was the prime objective of Manifest Destiny in the 1850s. Supporting a large population of enslaved blacks, it was coveted by the South as the most desirable slave territory available. Carved into several states, it would once more restore the political balance in the Senate.

Polk, the expansionist, had already offered the Spanish $100 million for Cuba, but they had replied that they would see it sunk into the ocean before they would sell it to Americans at any price. With purchase out of the question, seizure was apparently the only way to pluck the fruit.

Private adventurers from the South now

undertook to shake the tree of Manifest Destiny. During 1850–1851, two filibustering expeditions, each numbering several hundred armed men, descended upon Cuba. These efforts were repelled, and fifty of the invaders were shot or hanged.

When Spanish officials in Cuba seized an American steamer in 1854, southern-dominated President Pierce decided to provoke a war with Spain and seize Cuba. An incredible cloak-and-dagger episode followed. On the instructions of the secretary of state, the American ministers to Spain, England, and France met in Ostend, Belgium, and drew up a top-secret plan to acquire Cuba. Their document, known as the Ostend Manifesto, said that the United States should offer $120 million for Cuba; if Spain refused to sell, the United States would "be justified in wresting" the island from her grasp.

When the secret Ostend Manifesto leaked out, Northern free-soilers burst out in wrath against the "manifesto of brigands." The red-faced Pierce administration was forced to drop its brazen schemes to grab Cuba. The shackled black hands of Harriet Beecher Stowe's Uncle Tom, who had already roused the North, held the South back from Cuba.

Promoting a Pacific Railroad

Acute transportation problems were another legacy of the Mexican War. The newly acquired prizes of California and Oregon might just as well have been islands some eight thousand miles (thirteen thousand kilometers) west of the nation's capital. The sea routes to and from the Isthmus, to say nothing of those around South America, were too long. Covered-wagon travel past bleaching animal bones was possible, but it was slow and dangerous. A popular song recalled:

> They swam the wide rivers and crossed the tall peaks,
> And camped on the prairie for weeks upon weeks.
> Starvation and cholera and hard work and slaughter,
> They reached California spite of hell and high water.

Feasible land transportation was imperative—or the newly won possessions on the Pacific Coast might break away. Camels were even proposed as the answer, but a transcontinental railroad was clearly the only real solution to the problem. The South was especially eager to extend a railway to the Pacific, lest it lose the economic race with the North. The best route across the Southwest ran south of the Mexican border. Secretary of War Jefferson Davis had South Carolina railroad man James Gadsden appointed minister to Mexico, and in 1853 he negotiated a treaty to purchase the desired territory for $10 million. The Gadsden Purchase aroused northern criticism, but the Senate approved the pact.

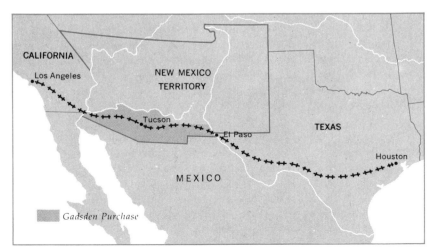

Gadsden Purchase, 1853. *Also shown is the future route of the Southern Pacific Railroad, completed in 1882.*

Southerners now argued that because their proposed line ran through the organized New Mexico territory, the southern route should be built first. Northern railroad boosters quickly replied that if organized territory was the test, then Nebraska should be organized. But the southerners in Congress greeted all schemes for organizing the Nebraska territory with apathy or hostility. Why should the South help create new free-soil states, and thus cut its own throat by facilitating a northern railroad?

Douglas's Kansas-Nebraska Scheme

At this point in 1854 Senator Stephen A. Douglas of Illinois delivered a counterstroke to offset the Gadsden thrust for southern expansion westward. A squat, bull-necked, and heavy-chested figure, the "Little Giant" radiated the energy and breezy optimism of the self-made man. An ardent booster for the West, he longed to break the North-South deadlock over westward expansion and stretch a line of settlements across the continent. He had also invested heavily in Chicago real estate and railway stock, and was eager to have the Windy City become the eastern terminus of the proposed Pacific railroad. He would thus endear himself to Illinois voters, benefit his section, and enrich his purse.

A veritable "steam engine in breeches," Douglas threw himself behind a legislative scheme that would enlist the support of a reluctant South. The proposed Territory of Nebraska would be carved into two territories, Kansas and Nebraska. Their status regarding slavery would be settled by popular sovereignty—a democratic concept to which Douglas and his Western constituents were deeply attached. Kansas, which lay due west of slaveholding Missouri, would presumably choose to become a slave state. But Nebraska, lying west of free-soil Iowa, would presumably become a free state.

Douglas's Kansas-Nebraska scheme ran headlong into a formidable political obstacle. The Missouri Compromise of 1820 had forbidden slavery in the Nebraska Territory, which lay north of the sacred 36°30′ line. The only way to open the region to popular sovereignty was to repeal the ancient compact outright. This bold step Douglas was prepared to take, even at the risk of shattering the truce patched up by the Great Compromise of 1850.

Many southerners, who had not conceived of Kansas as slave soil, rose to the bait. Here was a chance to gain one more slave state. The pliable President Pierce, under the thumb of Southern advisers, threw his full weight behind the Kansas-Nebraska Bill.

But the Missouri Compromise, now thirty-four years old, could not be brushed aside lightly. Whatever Congress passes it can repeal, but by this time the North had come to regard the sectional pact as almost as sacred as the Constitution itself. Free-soil members of Congress struck back furiously. They met their match in the violently gesticulating Douglas, who was the ablest rough-and-tumble debater of his generation. Employing twisted logic and oratorical fireworks, he rammed the bill through Congress, with strong support from many southerners. So heated were political passions that bloodshed was barely averted. Some members carried a concealed revolver or a bowie knife—or both.

Douglas's motives in prodding anew the snarling dog of slavery have long puzzled historians. His personal interests have already been mentioned. In addition, his foes accused him of angling for the presidency in 1856. Yet his admirers have argued in his defense that if he had not championed the ill-omened bill, someone else would have.

The truth seems to be that Douglas acted somewhat impulsively and recklessly. His heart did not bleed over the issue of slavery, and he declared repeatedly that he did not care whether it was voted up or down in the territories. What he failed to perceive was that hundreds of thousands of his fellow countrymen in the North *did* feel deeply on this moral issue. They regarded the repeal of the Missouri Compromise as an intolerable breach of faith, and they would henceforth resist to the last trench all future demands of the South for slave territory.

A genuine leader, like a skillful chess player, must foresee the possible effects of their moves. Douglas predicted a "hell of a storm," but he grossly underestimated its proportions. His critics in the North, branding him a "Judas" and a "traitor," greeted his name with frenzied boos, hisses, and "three groans for Doug." But he still enjoyed a high degree of popularity among his own loyal following in the Democratic party, especially in Illinois, a stronghold of popular sovereignty.

Congress Legislates a Civil War

The Kansas-Nebraska Act—a curtain raiser to a terrible drama—was one of the most momentous measures ever to pass Congress. By one way of reckoning, it led directly down the slippery slope to Civil War.

Antislavery Northerners were angered by what they condemned as an act of bad faith by the "Nebrascals" and their "Nebrascality." All future compromise with the South would be immeasurably more difficult, and without compromise there was bound to be conflict.

Henceforth the Fugitive Slave Law of 1850, previously enforced in the North only halfheartedly, was a dead letter. The Kansas-Nebraska Act wrecked two compromises: that of 1820, which it repealed specifically, and that of 1850, which northern opinion repealed indirectly. Emerson wrote, "The Fugitive [Slave] Law did much to unglue the eyes of men, and now the Nebraska Bill leaves us staring."

Northern abolitionists and Southern "fire-eaters" alike were stirred to new outbursts. The growing legion of anti-slaveryites gained numerous recruits, who resented the grasping move by the "slavocracy" for Kansas. The southerners, in turn, became inflamed when the free-soilers attempted to control Kansas, contrary to the presumed "deal."

The proud Democrats—a party now over half a century old—were shattered by the Kansas-Nebraska Act. They managed to elect a President two years later, but he was the last one they were to send to the White House for twenty-eight years.

Undoubtedly the most durable offspring of the Kansas-Nebraska blunder was the new Republican party. It sprang up spontaneously in the Middle West, notably in Wisconsin and Michigan, as a mighty moral protest against the gains of slavery. Gathering together dissatisfied elements, it soon included disgruntled Whigs (including Abraham Lincoln), Democrats, Free-Soilers, Know-Nothings, and other foes of the Kansas-Nebraska Act. The hodgepodge party spread eastward with the rapidity of a prairie fire and with the zeal of a religious crusade. Unheard of and unheralded at the beginning of 1854, it elected a Republican speaker of the House of Representatives within two years. Never really a third-party movement, it erupted with such force as to become almost overnight the second major political party—and a purely sectional one.

At long last the dreaded sectional rift had appeared. The new Republican party would not be allowed south of the Mason-Dixon line. Countless southerners subscribed wholeheartedly to the sentiment that it was "a nigger stealing, stinking, putrid, abolition party." The Union was in dire peril.

VARYING VIEWPOINTS

Historical analysts of the 1850s have long been preoccupied with the mounting controversy over slavery. Why, they have asked, did the long-simmering slavery issue finally boil to a head in the decade of the 1850s, eventually exploding in the brutal Civil War of 1861–1865? Many scholars, most notably David M. Potter, have argued that the irreconcilable differences between free and slavery societies—moral, political, economic, and social—increasingly eroded the ties between the sections and inexorably set the United States on the road to Civil War. In this process, no event was more important than the breakdown of the Jacksonian party system.

In recent years, historians of the "ethnocultural" school, especially Michael Holt, have challenged this traditional view. In their view, it was a temporary *consensus* between the two parties on almost all *other* national issues that shoved slavery to the fore, encouraging the emergence of Republicans in the North and secessionists in the South. In the absence of normal two-party conflict, these purely regional parties identified their opponents not simply as competitors for power but as threats to their way of life, even to the life of the Republic itself. This approach suggests an answer to the question of why the Civil War came when it did: sectional strife had existed at least since the Missouri Compromise, but, paradoxically, it was only with the collapse of traditional partisan conflict in the 1850s that it led to war.

SELECT READINGS

Primary Source Documents

The *Congressional Globe* for 1850 contains the dramatic orations of a dying generation of American statesmen on the Compromise of 1850. See the speeches by Webster,* Calhoun,* and Clay (in Richard Hofstadter, ed., *Great Issues in American History*). The debate on the Kansas-Nebraska Bill can be found in the 1854 volume of the same source, which includes addresses by Stephen A. Douglas* and his Republican opponent, Salmon P. Chase.*

Secondary Sources

The best account of the events of the 1850s is David M. Potter's masterful *The Impending Crisis, 1848–1861* (1976). Sketchy but penetrating is Roy F. Nichols, *The Stakes of Power, 1845–1877* (1961); see also his more detailed *The Disruption of American Democracy* (1948). Comprehensive treatments may be found in James G. Randall and David Donald, *The Civil War and Reconstruction* (rev. ed., 1969), and Allan Nevins, *Ordeal of the Union* (2 vols., 1947). David Potter offers illuminating insights in *The South and the Sectional Conflict* (1968). The standard work is Holman Hamilton, *Prologue to Conflict: The Crisis and Compromise of 1850* (1964). The emergence of the Republican party can be studied in Eric Foner's brilliant discussion of ideology, *Free Soil, Free Labor, Free Men* (1970); William Gienapp, *The Origins of the Republican Party* (1985); and Michael Holt's perceptive *Forging a Majority: The Formation of the Republican Party in Pittsburgh* (1969). Foner's ideas can be pursued further in his *Politics and Ideology in the Age of Civil War* (1980), while Holt has developed his views in *The Political Crisis of the 1850s* (1978), an unusually provocative book. Richard H. Sewell, *Ballots for Freedom: Antislavery Politics in the United States, 1837–1860* (1976) is a standard work.

22

Drifting Toward Disunion, 1854–1861

A house divided against itself cannot stand.
I believe this government cannot endure permanently half slave and half free.

Abraham Lincoln, 1858

Stowe and Helper: Literary Incendiaries

Sectional tensions were further strained in 1852, and later, by an inky phenomenon. Harriet Beecher Stowe, a wisp of a woman and the mother of a half-dozen children, published her heartrending novel *Uncle Tom's Cabin.* Dismayed by the passage of the Fugitive Slave Law, she was determined to awaken the North to the wickedness of slavery by laying bare its terrible inhumanity, especially the cruel splitting of families. Her book was distinguished by powerful imagery and touching pathos. "God wrote it," she explained in later years—a reminder that the sources of her antislavery sentiments lay in the religious crusades of the Second Great Awakening.

The success of the novel at home and abroad was sensational. Several hundred thousand copies were published in the first year, and the totals soon ran into the millions as the tale was translated into more than a score of languages. It was also put on the stage in "Tom shows" for lengthy runs. No other novel in American history—perhaps in all of world history—can be compared with it as a political force. To millions of people it made slavery appear almost as evil as it really was.

When Mrs. Stowe was introduced to President Lincoln in 1862, he reportedly remarked with twinkling eyes, "So you're the little woman who wrote the book that made this great war." The truth is that *Uncle Tom's Cabin* helped start the Civil War—and win it.

Uncle Tom, endearing and enduring, left a profound impression on the North. Uncounted thousands of readers swore that henceforth they would have nothing to do with the enforcement of the Fugitive Slave Law. The tale was devoured by millions of impressionable youths in the 1850s—the

Harriet Beecher Stowe (1811–1896). *She was a remarkable woman whose pen helped to change the course of history. (The Metropolitan Museum of Art, gift of I. N. Phelps Stokes, Edward S. Hawes, Alice Mary Hawes, and Marion Augusta Hawes, 1937)*

later Boys in Blue who volunteered to fight the Civil War through to its grim finale. The memory of a beaten and dying Uncle Tom helped sustain their determination to wipe out the plague of slavery.

Another trouble-brewing book appeared in 1857, five years after the debut of Uncle Tom. Entitled *The Impending Crisis of the South,* it was written by Hinton R. Helper, a nonaristocratic white from North Carolina. Hating both slavery and blacks, he attempted to prove by an array of statistics that indirectly the nonslaveholding whites were the ones who suffered most from the millstone of slavery. Helper's book, with its "dirty allusions," was banned in the South, where book-burning parties were held. But in the North countless thousands of copies, many in condensed form, were

distributed as campaign literature by the Republicans.

The North-South Contest for Kansas

The rolling plains of Kansas had meanwhile been providing a horrible example of the workings of popular sovereignty. Newcomers who ventured into Kansas were a motley lot. Most of the northerners were just ordinary westward-moving pioneers. But a small part of the inflow was financed by groups of northern abolitionists or free-soilers, especially the New England Emigrant Aid Company, which sent about 2,000 persons to the troubled area to forestall the South—and also to make a profit. Shouting "Ho for Kansas," many of them carried the deadly new breech-loading Sharps rifles, nicknamed "Beecher's Bibles" after the prominent clergyman who had helped raise money for their purchase. Many of the Kansas-bound pioneers sang Whittier's marching song (1854):

> We cross the prairie as of old
> The pilgrims crossed the sea,
> To make the West, as they the East,
> The homestead of the free!

Southern spokesmen, now more than ordinarily touchy, raised furious cries of betrayal. They had supported the Kansas-Nebraska scheme of Douglas with the informal understanding that Kansas would become slave and Nebraska free. The Northern "Nebrascals" were now apparently out to "abolitionize" *both* Kansas and Nebraska.

Quick to respond in kind, a few Southern hotheads attempted to "assist" small groups of wellarmed slaveowners to Kansas. But despite such efforts slavery never really came to Kansas. The census of 1860 found only 2 slaves among 107,000 souls in the territory, and only fifteen in Nebraska. Critics persuasively charged that the whole quarrel revolved around "an imaginary Negro in an impossible place."

Crisis conditions in Kansas rapidly worsened. When the day came in 1855 to elect members of the first territorial legislature, pro-slavery "border ruffians" poured in from Missouri to vote early and often. The slavery men triumphed, and then set up their own puppet government at Shawnee Mission. The free-soilers, unable to stomach this fraudulent conspiracy, established an extralegal regime of their own in Topeka. Confused Kansans thus had their choice between two governments—one based on fraud, the other on illegality. Tension mounted in 1856 when a gang of proslavery raiders shot up and burned a part of the free-soil town of Lawrence. This outrage was but the prelude to a bloodier tragedy.

Kansas in Convulsion

The fanatical figure of John Brown now stalked upon the Kansas battlefield. Spare, gray-bearded, iron-willed, and narrowly ignorant, he was dedicated to the abolitionist cause. The power of his glittering gray eyes was such, so he claimed, that his stare could force a dog or cat to slink out of a room. Brooding over the recent attack on Lawrence, "Old Brown" of Osawatomie led a band of his followers to Pottawatomie Creek, in May 1856. There they literally hacked to pieces five surprised men, allegedly proslaveryites. This fiendish butchery brought vicious retaliation from proslavery men. Civil war in Kansas thus flared forth in 1856, and continued intermittently until it merged with the large-scale Civil War of 1861–65.

The proslavery forces intensified the conflict in 1857 when they attempted to bring Kansas into the Union under a tricky document known as the Lecompton Constitution. Although the majority of Kansans were free-soilers, the vote on the proposed constitution was arranged so that it was impossible to prohibit all black bondage and still obtain statehood. With infuriated free-soilers boycotting the election, proslavery forces won outright, and Kansas applied for admission as a slave state in 1857.

The new President, James Buchanan, just as much under Southern influence as Pierce, threw his weight behind the notorious Lecompton Constitution. But Senator Douglas, who championed true popular sovereignty, would have none of this semi-popular fraudulency. Deliberately tossing away his strong support in the South for the presidency,

Douglas successfully fought for a fair popular vote on the *entire* Lecompton Constitution. Free-soilers thereupon snowed it under at the polls, ending Kansas's hopes for statehood until 1861.

President Buchanan, by antagonizing the numerous Douglas Democrats in the North, hopelessly divided the once-powerful Democratic party. Until then, it had been the only remaining *national* party, for the Whigs were dead and the Republicans were sectional. With the disruption of the Democrats came the snapping of one of the last important strands in the rope that was barely binding the Union together.

"Bully" Brooks and His Bludgeon

"Bleeding Kansas" also splattered blood on the floor of the United States Senate. Cold, brooding Senator Charles Sumner of Massachusetts delivered a blistering speech in 1856 entitled, "The Crime Against Kansas," in which he condemned proslavery men as "hirelings picked from the drunken spew and vomit of an uneasy civilization." The speech also insulted white-haired Senator Butler of South Carolina.

Hot-tempered South Carolina Congressman Preston Brooks, Butler's nephew, took vengeance into his own hands. On May 22, 1856, he approached Sumner, then sitting at his Senate desk, and pounded the orator with a heavy cane until it broke. The victim fell bleeding and unconscious to the floor, suffering serious injuries to his head and nervous system.

Bleeding Sumner thus joined Bleeding Kansas as a political issue. South Carolina triumphantly reelected Brooks, while Massachusetts did the same for Sumner, even though the battered abolitionist was unable to take his seat. Aroused Northerners bought tens of thousands of copies of Sumner's abusive speech, while Southern admirers deluged Brooks with canes to replace the one he had broken.

The Sumner-Brooks clash and the ensuing reactions revealed how dangerously inflamed passions were becoming, North and South. It was ominous that the cultured Sumner should have

Sumner Beaten by Brooks. *Note that the cartoonist has two of the senators smiling or laughing and one of them preventing interference with his cane. Note also that Sumner is defending himself with a quill pen while Brooks is wielding a club. (Courtesy the New York Public Library, Astor, Lenox, and Tilden Foundations)*

SOUTHERN CHIVALRY — ARGUMENT versus CLUB'S.

used the language of a barroom bully, and that the gentlemanly Brooks should have employed the tactics and tools of a thug. Emotion was displacing thought. The blows rained on Sumner's head were, broadly speaking, among the first blows of the Civil War.

"Old Buck" Versus "The Pathfinder"

With bullets whining in Kansas, Democrats met in Cincinnati to nominate the presidential standard-bearer of 1856. Both weak-kneed President Pierce and dynamic Senator Douglas were too blackened by the Kansas-Nebraska Act to win the election, so the party turned to a well-to-do Pennsylvania lawyer, James Buchanan, who had fortunately been abroad as minister to London during the Kansas-Nebraska uproar. Although his "Kansasless" neutrality made him acceptable to the party, "Old Buck" was mediocre, irresolute, confused—a pygmy in a time that called for giants.

The fast-growing Republican party, meeting in Philadelphia, passed over "Higher Law" Seward, their most conspicuous leader, and chose a dashing but erratic explorer-soldier-surveyor, John C. Frémont. Republicans hoped that the "Pathfinder of the West," like Buchanan untarred with the Kansas

brush, would find them the path to the White House. Vigorously condemning the extension of slavery into the territories, Republicans sang:

> Arise, arise ye brave!
> And let our war-cry be
> Free speech, free press, free soil, free men,
> Fre-mont and victory!

Although the slavery question loomed largest in the campaign, it was almost overshadowed by an ugly dose of antiforeignism. The recent horde of immigrants from Ireland and Germany had alarmed many "nativist" old-stock Protestants. They organized the American party, called the Know-Nothing party because of its secretiveness, and in 1856 they nominated lackluster former President Fillmore. Antiforeign and anti-Catholic, the super-patriotic Know-Nothings competed for ex-Whig support and cut into Republican strength.

A bland Buchanan, although polling less than a majority of the popular vote, won handily. His tally in the Electoral College was 174 to 114 for Frémont, with Fillmore garnering 8. The popular vote was 1,832,955 for Buchanan to 1,339,932 for Frémont, with 871,731 for Fillmore.

Although the Democrats got the hapless "Old Buck" into office, it was the infant Republicans who could rightfully claim a "victorious defeat" in 1856. Against the third-party Know-Nothing competition and loud threats of southern secession if they won, the spanking new party had pulled nearly even with the old Democratic machine. Whittier pointedly asked:

> Then sound again the bugles,
> Call the muster-roll anew;
> If months have well-nigh won the field,
> What may not four years do?

The question cast a long shadow forward, as politicians peered anxiously toward 1860.

The Dred Scott Bombshell

The Dred Scott decision, handed down by the Supreme Court on March 6, 1857, abruptly ended the two-day presidential honeymoon of the unlucky bachelor, James Buchanan.

Basically, the case was simple. Dred Scott, a black slave, had lived with his master for five years in Illinois and Wisconsin Territory. Backed by interested abolitionists, he sued for freedom on the basis of his long residence on free soil.

The Supreme Court proceeded to turn a simple legal case into a complex political issue. It ruled, not surprisingly, that Dred Scott was a black slave and not a citizen, and hence could not sue in federal courts.* The tribunal could then have thrown out the case on these technical grounds alone. But a majority decided to go further, under the leadership of emaciated Chief Justice Taney from the slave state of Maryland.

Taney's thunderclap rocked the free-soilers back on their heels. A majority of the Court had decreed that because a slave was private property, he or she could be taken into *any* territory and held there. The reasoning was that the Fifth Amendment clearly forbade Congress to deprive persons of their property without due process of law. The Court, to be consistent, went further. The Missouri Compromise, banning slavery north of 36°30′, had

been repealed three years earlier by the Kansas-Nebraska Act. But its spirit was still venerated in the North. Now the Court had ruled that the Compromise of 1820 had been unconstitutional all along: Congress had no power to ban slavery from the territories, regardless of what the territorial legislatures might want.

While Southerners exulted over this unexpected victory, champions of popular sovereignty, including Senator Douglas and most northern Democrats, were aghast. The decision thus drove another lethal wedge between the northern and southern wings of the once-united Democratic party.

Foes of slavery extension, especially the Republicans, furiously denounced the Dred Scott decision. Because a majority of the court were southerners, Republicans considered the opinion purely political, and declared it no more binding than the views of a "Southern debating society." Southerners, in turn, wondered how long they could remain married to a section that refused to honor the Supreme Court and, in their opinion, the constitutional compact that had established it.

The Financial Crash of 1857

Bitterness caused by the Dred Scott decision was deepened by hard times, which dampened a period of feverish prosperity. Late in 1857, a panic burst about Buchanan's harassed head. Over 5,000 businesses failed within a year, and unemployment, especially in urban areas, became widespread.

The North, including the grain growers, was hardest hit. The South, enjoying favorable cotton prices abroad, rode out the storm with flying colors. Panic conditions seemed further proof that cotton *was* king, and that his economic kingdom was stronger than that of the North. This fatal delusion helped drive the overconfident southerners closer to a shooting showdown.

One side effect of the economic distress was an intensified northern demand for a policy of free homesteads in the West. Eastern industrialists, worried about losing their labor force, together with southern slaveholders, fearful of spreading free-soilism, had long blocked the scheme. In 1860

---

*This part of the ruling, denying blacks their citizenship, seriously menaced the precarious position of the South's quarter-million "free" blacks.

Congress finally passed a homestead act that made 160 acres available to any pioneer at the nominal sum of twenty-five cents an acre. But the pro-southern Buchanan stabbed the bill to death with his veto pen.

The Panic of 1857 also created a clamor for higher tariffs. The Tariff of 1857 had lowered duties to about 20 percent, but no sooner were the revised rates in place than the financial distress descended like a black pall. Northern manufacturers blamed their misfortunes on the low tariff and appealed for relief. Thus the Panic of 1857 gave the Republicans two sure-fire issues for 1860: protection for the unprotected and farms for the farmless.

An Illinois Rail Splitter Emerges

The Illinois senatorial election of 1858 now claimed the national spotlight. Senator Douglas's term was about to expire, and the Republicans decided to run against him a rustic Springfield lawyer, one Abraham Lincoln. The candidate—6 feet 4 inches (1.93 meters) in height and 180 pounds (81.7 kilograms) in weight—presented an awkward but arresting figure. His legs, arms, and neck were grotesquely long; his head was crowned by coarse, black, and unruly hair; and his face was sad, sunken, and weather-beaten.

Lincoln was no silver-spoon child of destiny. Born in a Kentucky log cabin to impoverished parents, he attended a frontier school for not more than a year; being an avid reader, he was mainly self-educated. All his life he said "git," "thar," "heered." Though narrow-chested and somewhat stoop-shouldered, he shone in his frontier community as a wrestler and weight-lifter, and spent some time, among other pioneering pursuits, as a splitter of logs for fence rails. Although a superb teller of earthy and amusing stories, he would also periodically plunge into protracted periods of melancholy.

Lincoln's private and professional life was not especially noteworthy. He married "above himself" socially, into the influential Todd family of Kentucky; and the temperamental outbursts of his highstrung wife, known by her enemies as the "she wolf," helped to school him in patience and forebearance. After reading a little law, he gradually emerged as one of the dozen or so better-known trial lawyers in Illinois, although still accustomed to carrying important papers in his stovepipe hat. He was widely referred to as "Honest Abe," partly because he would refuse cases that he could not conscientiously defend.

The rise of Lincoln as a political figure was less than rocket-like. After making his mark in the Illinois legislature as a Whig politician of the log-rolling variety, he served one undistinguished term in Congress, 1847–1849. Until 1854, when he was forty-five years of age, he had done nothing to establish a claim to statesmanship. But the passage of the Kansas-Nebraska Act in that year lighted within him unexpected fires. After mounting the Republican bandwagon, he emerged as one of the foremost politicians and orators of the Northwest. At the Philadelphia convention of 1856, where Frémont was nominated, Lincoln actually received 110 votes for the vice-presidential nomination.

The Great Debate: Lincoln Versus Douglas

Lincoln, as Republican nominee for the Senate seat, boldly challenged Douglas to a series of joint debates. This was a rash act, because the stumpy senator was probably the nation's most devastating debater. Douglas promptly accepted the challenge, and seven meetings were arranged from August to October 1858.

The most famous of the forensic clashes came at Freeport, Illinois, where Lincoln neatly impaled his opponent on the horns of a dilemma. Suppose, he queried, the people of a territory should vote slavery down? The Supreme Court in the Dred Scott decision had decreed that they could not. Who would prevail, the Court or the people?

Douglas, the "Little Giant," replied that no matter how the Supreme Court ruled, slavery would stay down if the people voted it down. Laws to protect slavery would have to be passed by the territorial legislatures. These would not be forthcoming in the absence of popular approval, and

Lincoln and Douglas Debate, 1858. *Thousands of persons attended each of the seven Lincoln-Douglas debates. Douglas is shown here sitting to Lincoln's right in the debate at Charleston, Illinois, in September. On one occasion, Lincoln quipped that Douglas's logic would prove that a horse chestnut was a chestnut horse. (Illinois State Historical Library)*

black bondage would soon disappear. Douglas, in truth, had American history on his side. Where public opinion does not support the federal government, as in the case of Jefferson's embargo, the law is almost impossible to enforce.

The upshot was that Douglas defeated Lincoln for the Senate seat. The "Little Giant's" loyalty to popular sovereignty, which still had a powerful appeal in Illinois, probably was decisive. But in winning Illinois, Douglas further split his splintering party. Coming on top of his opposition to the Lecompton Constitution for Kansas, Douglas's defiance of the Supreme Court at Freeport guaranteed that Southern Democrats would break the party and the Union rather than accept him. The Lincoln-Douglas debate platform thus proved to be one of the preliminary battlefields of the Civil War.

John Brown: Murderer or Martyr?

The gaunt, grim figure of John Brown of Kansas fame now appeared again in a more terrible way. His crackbrained scheme was to invade the South secretly with a handful of followers, call upon the slaves to rise, furnish them with arms, and establish a kind of black free state as a sanctuary. Brown secured several thousand dollars for firearms from northern abolitionists, and finally arrived in hilly western Virginia with some twenty men. He seized the federal arsenal at scenic Harpers Ferry in October 1859, incidentally killing seven innocent people, including a free black, and injuring ten or so more. But the slaves refused to rise, and the wounded Brown and the remnants of his tiny band were quickly captured. "Old Brown" was convicted of murder and treason, after a hasty but nevertheless legal trial.

Brown—"God's angry man"—was given every opportunity to pose and to enjoy martyrdom. Though probably of unsound mind, he was clever enough to see that he was worth much more to the abolitionist cause dangling from a rope than in any other way.

So the hangman's trap was sprung, and Brown plunged not into oblivion but into world fame. A memorable marching song of the impending Civil War ran:

> John Brown's body lies a-mould'ring in
> the grave,
> His soul is marching on.

The effects of Harpers Ferry were calamitous. In the eyes of the South, already embittered, "Osawatomie Brown" was a wholesale murderer and an apostle of treason. Many southerners asked how they could possibly remain in the Union while a "murderous gang of abolitionists" were financing armed bands to "Brown" them. Moderate northerners, including Republican leaders, openly deplored this mad exploit. But the South naturally concluded that the violent abolitionist view was shared by the entire North, dominated by "Brown-loving" Republicans.

Abolitionists and other ardent free-soilers were infuriated by Brown's execution. On the day of his death, free-soilers in the North tolled bells, fired guns, half-masted flags, and held mass meetings in protest.

Democrats Divide and Republicans Rally

The issue of civil war hung over the election of 1860, the most fateful in American history. Deeply divided, the Democrats met in Charleston. Northern Democrats looked to Douglas as their leader, but southern "fire-eaters" regarded him as a traitor. Cotton-state delegates walked out of the convention after a bitter platform fight. The southerners' departure from the Democratic convention was the first tragic secession. Resolution of conflict by secession unfortunately became habit-forming.

The Democrats tried again in Baltimore. With northern Douglas Democrats firmly in the saddle,

the cotton-state delegates again took a walk, and the rest of the convention enthusiastically nominated their hero. Angered southern Democrats promptly organized a rival convention in Baltimore and selected as their nominee the stern-jawed vice-president, John C. Breckinridge, from the border state of Kentucky. Their platform favored the extension of slavery into the territories and the annexation of slave-populated Cuba.

A middle-of-the-road group, fearing for the Union, hastily organized the Constitutional Union party. Consisting mainly of old Whigs and Know-Nothings, this "gathering of graybeards" met in Baltimore and nominated John Bell of Tennessee for the presidency on a platform of "the Union, the Constitution, and the Enforcement of the Law."

With their opponents hopelessly split into three factions, elated Republicans scented victory in the breeze. The favorite as they gathered for their convention in Chicago was William H. Seward. But Seward's Rochester speech in 1858 referring to an "irrepressible conflict" between slavery and freedom had tarred him as a radical, even though he had not meant by the phrase a necessarily bloody conflict. Because rail-splitting Abraham Lincoln of Illinois had fewer enemies than Seward, and was many delegates' second choice, he was nominated over the New Yorker on the third ballot.

The Republican platform appealed to almost every important nonsouthern group. To the free-soilers, it promised the nonextension of slavery; to the northern manufacturers, a protective tariff; to the immigrants, no abridgement of rights; and to Westerners and farmers, internal improvements, free homesteads, and a Pacific railroad.

Southern secessionists promptly served notice that the election of the "abolitionist baboon" Lincoln would split the Union. Although Lincoln was in fact no abolitionist, he campaigned quietly and made no new statements in response to these threats. The most active opposition to southern extremism came from "Little Doug" Douglas, who waged a vigorous speaking campaign, even in the South, and threatened to put the hemp with his own hands around the neck of the first secessionist.

The returns, breathlessly awaited, proclaimed a sweeping victory for Lincoln (see map).

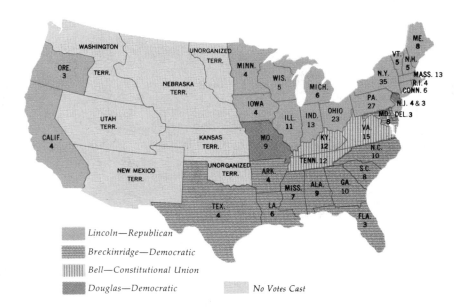

Presidential Election of 1860 (with electoral vote by state). *A surprising fact is that Lincoln, often rated among the greatest presidents, ranks near the bottom in percentage of popular votes. In all the eleven states that seceded, he received only a scattering of one state's votes—about 1.5 percent in Virginia.*

Lincoln—Republican
Breckinridge—Democratic
Bell—Constitutional Union
Douglas—Democratic   No Votes Cast

The Electoral Upheaval of 1860

Awkward "Abe" Lincoln had run a curious race. To a greater degree than any other president (except J. Q. Adams), he was a minority president. Sixty percent of the voters preferred some other candidate. He was also a sectional president, for in ten Southern states, where he was not allowed on the ballot, he polled no popular votes. The election of 1860 was virtually two elections: one in the North, the other in the South. South Carolinians rejoiced over Lincoln's victory; they now had their excuse to secede. In winning the North the "Rail Splitter" had split off the South.

Douglas, though scraping together only 12 electoral votes, made an impressive showing. He drew important strength from all sections, and ranked a fairly close second in the popular-vote column. In fact, the Douglas Democrats and the Breckinridge Democrats together amassed 366,484 more votes than Lincoln. But even if all the Democrats and Constitutional Unionists had united behind the "Little Giant," Lincoln would have carried the populous northern states, and therefore would have won in the electoral college by only a slightly smaller margin than his actual majority of 180 to 123 for his three opponents.

Significantly, the election displayed no strong southern sentiment in favor of secession. The "fire-eaters'" candidate, John Breckinridge, polled fewer votes in the slave states than Douglas and Bell combined. Although southern hotheads saw Lincoln's victory as the end of slavery, more rational southerners could see that their section still controlled the Supreme Court, both Houses of Congress, and sufficient states to block any attempt to end slavery by constitutional amendment.

The Secessionist Exodus

Nevertheless, a tragic chain reaction of secession now began to explode. South Carolina had threatened to go out if the "Illinois baboon" were elected, and in December 1860 a special convention called by the legislature carried out the threat by voting unanimously to secede. During the next six weeks, six other states of the lower South followed South Carolina over the precipice.

As the Union disintegrated, the crisis was deepened by the "lame duck" interlude.* Although elected President in November 1860, Lincoln could not take office until four months later, March

---

*The "lame duck" period was shortened to ten weeks in 1933 by the 20th Amendment (See Appendix).

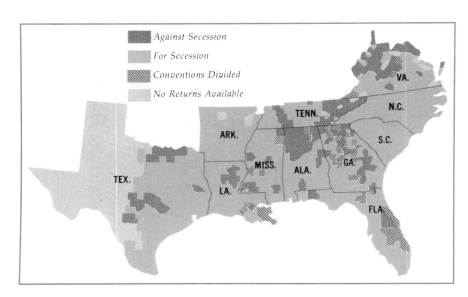

Southern Opposition to Secession, 1860–1861 (showing vote by county). *This county vote shows the opposition of the antiplanter, antislavery mountain whites in the Appalachian region. There was also considerable resistance to secession in Texas, where Governor Sam Houston, who led the Unionists, was deposed by secessionist hotheads.*

4, 1861. As a private citizen, Lincoln could only watch as the seven states pulled out of the Union during this period of protracted uncertainty.

Meanwhile, the aging President Buchanan chose to wring his hands rather than secessionist necks. Buchanan was wedded to the Constitution and convinced that the southern states could not legally secede. But the never-vigorous old bachelor lawyer was surrounded by southern advisers, and he could find no authority in the Constitution for stopping secession with guns.

Even though Buchanan has been blamed for his inaction, there were good reasons for not resorting immediately to force. The tiny standing army of 15,000 was widely scattered, fighting Indians in the West. Public opinion in the North, at that time, was far from willing to unsheathe the sword. Fighting would merely shatter all prospects of adjustment, and until the guns began to boom there was still a flickering hope of reconciliation rather than a contested divorce. The weakness lay not so much in Buchanan as in the Constitution and in the Union itself. Ironically, Lincoln as president essentially continued Buchanan's wait-and-see policy.

The Collapse of Compromise

Impending bloodshed spurred final, frantic attempts at compromise, most notably by Senator Crittenden of Kentucky. Crittenden proposed several constitutional amendments designed to appease the South. Slavery in the territories was to be prohibited north of 36°30′, but south of that line it was to be given federal protection in all territories existing or "hereafter to be acquired" (such as Cuba). Future states, north or south of 36°30′, could come into the Union with or without slavery, as they should choose. In short, the slavery men were to be guaranteed full rights in the southern territories, as long as they were territories, regardless of the wishes of the majority under popular sovereignty. Federal protection in a territory south of 36°30′ might conceivably, though improbably, turn the entire area permanently to slavery.

Lincoln flatly rejected the Crittenden scheme, which offered some slight prospect of success, and all hope of compromise fled. For this refusal he must bear a heavy responsibility. Yet he had been elected on a platform that opposed the extension of slavery, and he felt that as a matter of principle he could not afford to yield, even though gains for slavery in the territories might be only temporary. Larger gains might come later in Cuba and Mexico.

As for the supposedly spineless "Old Fogy" Buchanan, how could he have prevented the Civil War by starting a civil war? No one has yet come up with a satisfactory answer. If he had used force on

South Carolina in December 1860, the fighting almost certainly would have erupted three months sooner than it did, and under less favorable circumstances for the Union. The North would have appeared as the heavy-handed aggressor. And the crucial Border States, so vital to the Union, might have been driven into the arms of their "wayward sisters."

With the failure of the Crittenden compromise the last hopes of preserving the Union disappeared. The seven seceding states formally met at Montgomery, Alabama, in February 1861 to create a government known as the Confederate States of America. As their president they chose Jefferson Davis, a dignified and austere recent member of the United States Senate from Mississippi. He was a West Pointer and a former Cabinet member with wide military and administrative experience.

Farewell to Union

Secessionists who parted company with their sister states left for a number of avowed reasons, mostly relating in some way to slavery. They were alarmed by the inexorable tipping of the political balance against them—"the despotic majority of numbers." The "crime" of the North, observed James Russell Lowell, was the census returns. Southerners were also dismayed by the triumph of the new sectional Republican party, which seemed to threaten their rights as a slaveholding minority. They were weary of free-soil criticism, abolitionist nagging, and northern interference, ranging from the Underground Railroad to John Brown's raid. "All we ask is to be let alone," declared president Jefferson Davis in an early message to his congress.

Many southerners supported secession because they felt sure that their departure would be unopposed, despite "Yankee yawp" to the contrary. They were confident that the clodhopping and codfishing Yankee would not or could not fight. They believed that northern manufacturers and bankers, so heavily dependent on Southern cotton and markets, would not dare to cut their own economic throats with their own swords. But should war come, the immense debt owed to northern creditors by the South—happy thought—could be promptly repudiated, as it later was.

Southern leaders regarded secession as a golden opportunity to cast aside their generations of "vassalage" to the North. An independent Dixieland could develop its own banking and shipping, trade directly with Europe, and forever rid itself of the threat of high tariffs. For decades these issues had caused friction between the manufacturing North and the agrarian South.

The principles of self-determination—of the Declaration of Independence—seemed to many southerners to apply perfectly to them. Few, if any, of the seceders felt that they were doing anything wrong or immoral. The thirteen original states had voluntarily entered the Union and now seven—ultimately eleven—southern states were voluntarily withdrawing from it.

Historical parallels ran even deeper. In 1776, thirteen American colonies, led by the rebel George Washington, had seceded from the British Empire by throwing off the yoke of King George. In 1860–1861, eleven American states, led by the rebel Jefferson Davis, were seceding from the Union by throwing off the yoke of "King" Abraham Lincoln. With that burden gone, the South was confident that it could work out its own peculiar destiny more quietly, happily, and prosperously.

VARYING VIEWPOINTS

Few issues have generated as much heat among American historians as the causes of the War for Southern Independence. The very names chosen to describe the conflict—notably "Civil War" or "War Between the States"—reveal much about various authors' points of view. Opinions have naturally differed according to section, but in general the appraisals of the war have gone through four phases.

The so-called nationalist school in the late

nineteenth century found slavery and Union to be the fundamental causes of the bloodletting, and approved the war because it ended slavery and preserved the Union. In the early twentieth century, some writers, notably Charles Beard, argued that the war was not about slavery per se, but about the basic economic conflict between an industrial North and an agricultural South.

After the disappointing results of World War I, some historians argued that the Civil War itself had been a great mistake, traceable not to any fundamentally "irreconcilable conflict," whether racial or economic, but to the breakdown of political institutions and the ineptitude of a blundering generation of leaders. But since World War II, a "neo-nationalist" view has generally prevailed. It pictures the Civil War as an all-but-inevitable clash between two cultures and two sets of social values, ending in victory for the forces of virtue and progress.

SELECT READINGS

Primary Source Documents

Harriet Beecher Stowe's *Uncle Tom's Cabin* (1852) and Hinton R. Helper's *Impending Crisis of the South,** (1852) are vivid and important. The Lincoln-Douglas debates* (1858) frame the issues of the 1850s and remain classics of American oratory.

Secondary Sources

Refer to the previous chapter for the titles by Roy F. Nichols, James G. Randall, and David Donald. Richly detailed is Allan Nevins, *The Emergence of Lincoln* (2 vols., 1950). Lincoln's rise is also developed in Don F. Fehrenbacher, *Prelude to Greatness* (1962). On the Lincoln-Douglas debates see Harry V. Jaffa, *Crisis of the House Divided* (1959). Don E. Fehrenbacher brilliantly and thoroughly dissects *The Dred Scott Case* (1978). The final moments before the fighting began are scrutinized in David M. Potter, *Lincoln and His Party in the Secession Crisis* (1942) and in Kenneth M. Stampp, *And the War Came* (1950). Stephen B. Oates paints a vivid portrait of John Brown in *To Purge This Land with Blood* (1970). Thomas J. Pressley reviews the copious literature about the war in *Americans Interpret Their Civil War* (1954). George Forgie offers a psychoanalytic explanation of the coming of the war in *Patricide in the House Divided: A Psychological Interpretation of Lincoln and His Age* (1979).

23

The War for Southern Independence

**My paramount object in this struggle is to save the Union,
and is not either to save or to destroy slavery.**

Abraham Lincoln, 1862

President of the Disunited States of America

Abraham Lincoln solemnly took the oath of office on March 4, 1861, after having slipped into Washington at night, partially disguised to thwart assassins. He thus became President, not of the *United* States of America, but of the *disunited* states of America. Seven had departed; eight more were teetering on the edge. The girders of the unfinished Capitol dome loomed nakedly in the background, as if to symbolize the imperfect state of the Union.

Lincoln's inaugural address was firm yet conciliatory: there would be no conflict unless the South provoked it. Secession, the President declared, was wholly impracticable, because "Physically speaking, we cannot separate."

Here Lincoln put his finger on a profound geographical truth. The North and South were Siamese twins, bound inseparably together. If they had been divided by the Pyrenees Mountains or the Danube River, a sectional divorce would have been more feasible. But the Appalachian Mountains and the mighty Mississippi River both ran crosswise to the ideological division.

Uncontested secession would only create new controversies. What share of the national debt should the South be forced to take with it? What portion of the jointly held federal territories, if any, should the Confederate states be allotted—areas so largely purchased with Southern blood? How would the fugitive-slave issue be dealt with? The Underground Railroad would certainly redouble its activity, and it would have to transport its passengers only across the Ohio River, not all the way to Canada. Was it conceivable that all such problems could have been solved without ugly armed clashes?

A united United States had hitherto been the top-dog republic in the Western Hemisphere. If this powerful democracy should break into two hostile parts, the European nations would be delighted. They could gleefully transplant to America their hoary concept of the balance of power. Playing the no less hoary game of divide and conquer, they could incite one snarling fragment of the dis-United States against the other. The colonies of the European powers in the New World, notably those of Britain, would thus be made safer against the rapacious Yankees. And European imperialists, with no unified republic to stand across their path, could the more easily defy the Monroe Doctrine and seize territory in the Americas.

The South Assails Fort Sumter

The issue of the divided Union came to a head over the matter of federal forts in the South. As the seceding states left, they had seized the United States arsenals, mints, and other public property within their borders. When Lincoln took office, only two significant forts in the South still flew the Stars and Stripes. The more important of the pair was square-walled Fort Sumter, in Charleston Harbor, with fewer than 100 men.

Ominously the choices presented to Lincoln by Fort Sumter were all bad. This stronghold had provisions that would last only a few weeks—until the middle of April 1861. If no supplies were forthcoming, its commander would have to surrender without firing a shot. Lincoln, quite understandably, did not feel that such a weak-kneed course squared with his obligation to protect federal property. But if he sent reinforcements, the South Carolinians would undoubtedly fight back; they could not tolerate a federal fort blocking the mouth of their most important Atlantic seaport.

After agonizing indecision, Lincoln adopted a middle-of-the-road solution. He notified the South Carolinians that an expedition would be sent to *provision* the garrison, though not to *reinforce* it. But in Southern eyes any such "provisioning" spelled "reinforcement."

A Union naval force was next started on its way to Fort Sumter—a move that the South regarded as an act of aggression. On April 12, 1861, the cannon of the Carolinians opened fire on the fort, while crowds in Charleston applauded and waved handkerchiefs. After a thirty-four-hour bombardment, which took no life, the dazed garrison surrendered.

The firing on the fort electrified the North, which at once responded with cries of "Remember Fort Sumter" and "Save the Union." Hitherto countless Northerners had been saying that if the

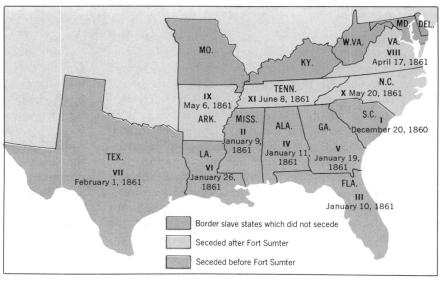

Seceding States (with dates and order of secession). *Note the long period of time between the secession of South Carolina, the first state to go, and that of Tennessee, the last state to leave the Union. These six months were a time of terrible trial for moderate Southerners. When a Georgia statesman pleaded for restraint and negotiations with Washington, he was rebuffed with the cry: "Throw the bloody spear into this den of incendiaries!"*

MD. DEL.

W.VA. VA.
VIII
April 17, 1861

MO.

KY.

N.C.
X May 20, 1861

TENN.
XI June 8, 1861

IX
May 6, 1861

ARK.

S.C.
I
December 20, 1860

MISS.
II
January 9, 1861

ALA.
IV
January 11, 1861

GA.
V
January 19, 1861

TEX.
VII
February 1, 1861

LA.
VI
January 26, 1861

FLA.
III
January 10, 1861

Border slave states which did not secede

Seceded after Fort Sumter

Seceded before Fort Sumter

Southern states wanted to go, they should not be pinned to the rest of the nation with bayonets. "Wayward sister, depart in peace" was a common sentiment.

But the assault on Fort Sumter provoked the North to a fighting pitch: the fort was lost, but the Union was saved. Lincoln had contrived to win a great strategic victory. Southerners had wantonly fired upon the glorious Stars and Stripes, and honor demanded an armed response. Lincoln promptly (April 15) issued a call to the states for seventy-five thousand militiamen; and volunteers sprang to the colors in such enthusiastic numbers that many were turned away—a mistake not often repeated. On April 19 and 27 the President proclaimed a leaky blockade of Southern seaports.

The call for troops, in turn, aroused the South much as the attack on Fort Sumter had aroused the North. Lincoln was now waging war—from the Southern view an aggressive war—on the Confederacy. Virginia, Arkansas, and Tennessee, all of which had earlier voted down secession, reluctantly joined their embattled sister states, as did North Carolina. Thus the seven became eleven as the "submissionists" and "Union shriekers" were overcome. Richmond, Virginia, replaced Montgomery, Alabama, as the Confederate capital.

Brothers' Blood and Border Blood

The only slave states left were the crucial Border States. This group consisted of Missouri, Kentucky, Maryland, Delaware, and later West Virginia—the "mountain white" area that somewhat illegally tore itself from the side of Virginia in mid-1861. If the North had fired the first shot, some or all of these doubtful states probably would have seceded, and the South might well have succeeded. The Border group actually boasted a white population more than half that of the entire Confederacy. Lincoln reportedly said that he hoped to have God on his side, but he *had* to have Kentucky.

In dealing with the Border States, the President used methods of dubious legality. In Maryland he declared martial law where needed and sent in troops. He also deployed Union soldiers in western Virginia and notably in Missouri, where they fought

beside Unionists in a local civil war within the larger Civil War.

Any official statement of the North's war aims was profoundly influenced by the teetering Border States. An antislavery declaration would no doubt have driven the Border States into the welcoming arms of the South. Lincoln had to insist repeatedly—even though weakening his moral cause—that his primary purpose was to preserve the Union at all costs. Thus the war began not as one between slave soil and free soil, but one for the Union with slaveholders on both sides.

Unhappily, the conflict between "Billy Yank" and "Johnny Reb" was a brothers' war. There were many Northern volunteers from the Southern states, and many Southern volunteers from the Northern states. The "mountain whites" of the South sent north some 50,000 men, and the loyal slave states contributed some 300,000 soldiers to the Union. In many a family of the Border States, one brother rode north to fight with the Blue, another south to fight with the Gray. Senator Crittenden of Kentucky, who fathered the abortive Crittenden Compromise, fathered two sons: one became a general in the Union army, the other a general in the Confederate army.

Europe's Aristocracy Sticks Together

Confederates were inspirited by the open sympathy of Europe's ruling classes. European aristocrats had from the beginning abhorred the American democratic experiment. They had long felt more akin to the semifeudal, aristocratic society of the South. Reflecting these pro-Southern sentiments, the British and French Foreign Offices welcomed the breakup of the United States.

Leaders of British industrial and commercial life likewise hailed the newly born Confederacy. For one thing, it would provide the long-coveted independent cotton supply. For another, it would increase the opportunities of British shippers and manufacturers to make profits from the South, without the hurdle of a Yankee protective tariff.

On the other hand, millions of workers in England, and to some extent in France, were pulling or praying for the North. Many of them had read *Uncle Tom's Cabin,* and they sensed that a victory for the Union would result in freeing the slaves. The ending of human bondage anywhere would further dignify free labor everywhere.

The common folk in Britain could not yet cast the ballot, but they could cast the brick. Their certain hostility to any official intervention on behalf of the South evidently had a sobering effect on the British Cabinet. Thus the dead hands of Uncle Tom helped Uncle Sam by restraining the British and French ironclads from breaking the Union blockade.

The Balance of Forces

When war broke out, the South seemed to have great advantages. The Confederacy could fight defensively behind interior lines. The North had to invade the vast territory of the Confederacy, conquer it, and drag it bodily back into the Union. In fact, the South did not have to win the war in order to win its independence. If it merely fought the invader to a draw and thereby discouraged him, Confederate independence would be won. Fighting on their own soil for self-determination and preservation of their way of life, Southerners at first enjoyed an advantage in morale as well.

Militarily, the South had the most talented officers right from the beginning of the war. Most conspicuous among a dozen or so first-rate commanders was gray-haired General Robert E. Lee, whose knightly bearing and sense of honor embodied the Southern ideal. President Lincoln had unofficially offered him the command of the Northern armies, but when Virginia seceded Lee felt honor-bound to go with his native state. Lee's chief lieutenant for much of the war was black-bearded Thomas J. ("Stonewall") Jackson, a tactical theorist whose use of "foot cavalry" made him a master of speed and deception.

Besides their brilliant leaders, ordinary Southerners were also bred to fight. Accustomed to managing horses and bearing arms from boyhood, they made excellent cavalrymen and foot soldiers.

As one immense farm, the South seemed to be handicapped by the scarcity of its factories. Yet by seizing federal weapons, running Union blockades, and developing their own ironworks, Southerners managed to obtain sufficient weaponry. "Yankee ingenuity" was not confined to Yankees.

Nevertheless, as the war dragged on and the North cut railroad supply lines, grave shortages of shoes, uniforms, and blankets did appear in the South. Even with immense stores of food on Southern farms, civilians and soldiers often went hungry because of supply problems. "Forward, men! They have cheese in their haversacks," cried one Southern officer as he attacked the Yankees.

The economy was the greatest Southern weakness; it was the North's greatest strength. The North was not only a huge farm but a sprawling factory as well. Yankees boasted about three-fourths of the nation's wealth, including three-fourths of the thirty thousand miles (forty-eight thousand kilometers) of railroads.

The North also controlled the sea. With its vastly superior navy, it established a blockade that choked off Southern supplies and eventually shattered Southern morale. Its sea power also enabled the North to exchange huge quantities of grain for munitions and supplies from Europe, thus adding the factories of Europe to its own.

The Union also enjoyed a much larger reserve of manpower. The loyal states had a population of some 22 million; the seceding states had 9 million people, including about 3.5 million slaves. The Northern advantage in military enlistments ran 1,556,000 to 1,082,000, giving Northern generals a considerable manpower advantage.

Adding to the North's population strength was the large immigrant population from Europe, which continued to pour into the North even during the war. Over 800,000 newcomers arrived between 1861 and 1865, most of them British, Irish, and German. Large numbers of them were induced to enlist in the Union armies. Altogether about one-fifth of the Union forces were foreign born, and in some units military commands were given in four different languages.

Whether immigrant or native, ordinary Northern boys were much less prepared than their Southern counterparts for military life. Yet the Northern "clodhoppers" and "shopkeepers" eventually adjusted themselves to soldiering, and became known for their discipline and determination.

The North was much less fortunate in its higher commanders. It was forced to use a costly trial-and-error method to sort out effective leaders from the many incompetent political officers, until it finally uncovered a general, Ulysses Simpson Grant, who would crunch his way to victory.

In the long run, as the Northern strengths were brought to bear, they outweighed those of the South. But when the war began, the chances for Southern independence were unusually favorable—certainly better than the prospects for success of the thirteen colonies in 1776. The turn of a few events could easily have produced a different outcome.

The might-have-beens are fascinating. *If* the Border States had seceded, *if* the uncertain states of the upper Mississippi Valley had turned against the Union, *if* a wave of Northern defeatism had demanded an armistice, and *if* England and/or France had broken the blockade, the South probably would have won. All of these possibilities almost became realities, but none of them actually occurred. Successful revolutions, including the American Revolution of 1776, have generally succeeded because of foreign intervention. The South counted on it, did not get it, and lost.

Black Men Battle Bondage

Altogether about 180,000 blacks served in the Union armies, most of them from the slave states but many from the free-soil North. Blacks accounted for about 10 percent of the total enlistments in Union forces, on land or sea.

Black volunteers were at first rejected. Race prejudice, fear of arming blacks, and a feeling that white men should fight their own war raised a forbidding hand. But as manpower ran low and emancipation was proclaimed, black enlistees were welcomed, although at first they were not paid as well as the whites. Strangely enough, the blacks had to fight for the privilege of fighting for freedom.

Black fighting men unquestionably had their hearts in a war against slavery. They participated in about five hundred engagements, major and minor, and received twenty-two Congressional Medals of Honor—the highest military award. Their casualties were extremely heavy; over thirty-eight thousand died, whether from battle, sickness, or reprisals by vengeful masters. A small number were

Black Union Soldiers. *Former slaves, recruited into the Union army in Tennessee, helped to man an artillery battery during the battle of Nashville. (Chicago Historical Society)*

put to death as slaves in revolt, because it was not until 1864 that the South began to recognize them as prisoners of war.

For reasons of pride, prejudice, and principle, the Confederacy could not bring itself to enlist slaves until a month before the war ended and then it was too late. Meanwhile tens of thousands were impressed into labor battalions, the building of fortifications, the supplying of armies, and other war-connected activities. Slaves moreover were "the stomach of the Confederacy," for they kept the farms going while the white men fought.

Ironically, the great mass of Southern slaves did little to help their Northern liberators, white or black. A thousand scattered torches in the hands of a thousand slaves would have brought the Southern soldiers home, and the war would have ended. Through the "grapevine," the blacks learned of Lincoln's Emancipation Proclamation. Yet the bulk of them, whether because of lethargy, loyalty, lack of leadership, or strict policing, did not cast off their chains. But tens of thousands revolted "with their feet," when they abandoned their plantations upon the arrival or imminent arrival of Union armies, with or without emancipation proclamations. About 25,000 joined Sherman's march through Georgia in 1864, and their presence in such numbers created problems of supply and discipline.

Dethroning King Cotton

Textile mills in Britain were fatally dependent on Southern cotton, and the Confederates were supremely confident that the British fleet would break the blockade. Why did King Cotton fail them?

English manufacturers had on hand, when the shooting started in 1861, a heavy oversupply of fiber. The real pinch did not come until about a year and a half later, when thousands of hungry operatives were thrown out of work. But by this time Lincoln had announced his slave-emancipation policy, and the "wage slaves" of England would not demand a war for the slaveowners of the South.

The direst effects of the "cotton famine" in England were relieved in several ways. Hunger among unemployed workers was partially eased when certain kindhearted Americans sent over several shiploads of foodstuffs. As Union armies penetrated the South, they captured or bought considerable supplies of cotton and shipped them to England; and the Confederates also ran a limited quantity through the blockade. In addition, the cotton growers of Egypt and India, responding to high prices, increased their output. Finally, booming war industries in England, which supplied both North and South, relieved unemployment.

The North's King Wheat and King Corn proved to be more potent potentates than King Cotton. Blessed with ideal weather and the efficient harvesting of McCormick's mechanical reaper, the North produced bumper crops during the war years. The grain was purchased by Britain, which suffered a series of bad harvests at the same time. The British became so dependent on the Northern granary that they were unwilling to cut off this precious supply by breaking the blockade.

President Davis Versus President Lincoln

The Confederate government, like King Cotton, betrayed fatal weaknesses. Its constitution, borrowing liberally from that of the Union, had one deadly defect. Created by secession, it could not logically deny future secession to its states. Jefferson Davis, while making his bow to states' rights, had in view a well-knit central government. But determined states' rights supporters fought him bitterly to the end. The Richmond regime even encountered difficulty in persuading the troops of some states to serve outside their own borders.

Unlike Lincoln, Davis was somewhat imperious and inclined to defy rather than lead public opinion. No one could doubt his courage, sincerity, integrity, and devotion to the South, but the task proved beyond his powers. It was probably beyond the powers of any mere mortal.

Lincoln also had his troubles, but on the whole they were less prostrating. The North enjoyed the prestige of a long-established government, financially stable and fully recognized, both at home and abroad. Lincoln, the inexperienced prairie politician, proved superior to the more

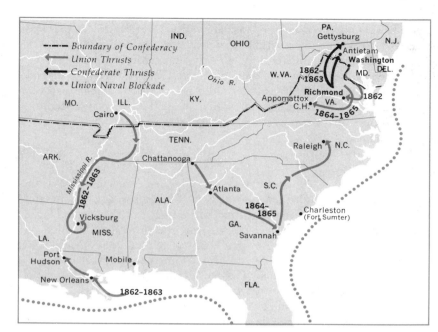

Main Thrusts, 1861–1865.
Northern strategists at first believed that the rebellion could be snuffed out quickly by a swift, crushing blow. But the stiffness of Southern resistance to the Union's early probes revealed that the conflict would be a war of attrition, long and bloody.

experienced but less flexible Jefferson Davis. Able to relax with droll stories at critical times, "Old Abe" grew as the war dragged on. Tactful, quiet, patient, yet firm, he developed a genius for interpreting and leading a fickle public opinion. Holding aloft the banner of Union with inspiring utterances, he revealed charitableness toward the South.

Strangulation of the South by Sea

As finally developed, the general plan of Northern attack had four phases. First, slowly suffocate the South by blockading its coasts. Second, cut it in half by seizing control of the Mississippi River backbone. Third, chop it to pieces (a later idea) by sending troops through Georgia, and then North into the Carolinas. Fourth, strangle it by capturing its capital (Richmond) and by pounding its remaining armies into submission. The overall strategy called for slowly beating down the enemy rather than delivering a knockout punch.

The blockade started leakily: it was not clamped down all at once but extended by degrees. Blockading was simplified by concentrating on the principal ports and inlets. Only at such places were

dock facilities available for loading bulky bales of cotton. The blockade was also strengthened when Britain recognized it as binding and warned her shippers that they ignored it at their peril.

Blockade-running soon became riskily profitable, as the growing scarcity of Southern goods drove prices skyward. The most successful runners were swift, gray-painted steamers, scores of which were specially built in Scotland. A leading rendezvous was the West Indian port of Nassau, in the British Bahamas, where at one time thirty-five of the speedy ships were counted. The low-lying craft would take on cargoes of arms brought in by tramp steamers from England, leave with fraudulent papers for "Halifax" (Canada), and return a few days later with a cargo of cotton. The risks were great, but the profits would mount to 700 percent and more for lucky gamblers. The lush days of blockade-running finally passed as Union squadrons gradually pinched off the leading Southern ports, from New Orleans to Charleston.

The most alarming Confederate threat to the blockade came in 1862. Resourceful Southerners raised and reconditioned a former wooden United States warship, the *Merrimack,* and plated its sides with old iron railroad rails. Renamed the *Virginia,* this clumsy but powerful monster easily destroyed two wooden ships of the Union navy in the Virginia waters of Chesapeake Bay; it also threatened the entire Yankee blockading fleet. (Actually the home-made ironclad was not a seaworthy craft.)

A tiny Union ironclad, the *Monitor,* built in about 100 days, arrived on the scene in the nick of time. For four hours, on March 9, 1862, the little "Yankee cheesebox on a raft" fought the wheezy *Merrimack* to a standstill. Britain and France had already built several powerful ironclads, but the first battle-testing of these new craft heralded the doom of wooden warships. A few months after the historic battle, the Confederates destroyed the *Merrimack* to keep her from the grasp of advancing Union troops.

The Runners of Bull Run

By the summer of 1861, a Union army of some 30,000 men was being drilled near Washington. It was ill-prepared for battle, but Northern news-paper editors, eager to end the war in a hurry, raised the cry, "On to Richmond!"

The preliminaries of the clash at Bull Run, on July 21, 1861, seemed like those of a sporting event. The raw Yankee recruits marched or straggled from the capital, accompanied by congressmen, ladies, and others riding out with lunch baskets to see the fun. The ill-trained Union force encountered a smaller Confederate army at Bull Run (Manassas Junction), some thirty miles (forty-eight kilo-meters) southwest of Washington. At first the battle went well for the Yankees. But "Stonewall" Jack-son's gray-clad warriors stood like a stone wall (here he won his nickname), and Confederate reinforce-ments arrived unexpectedly. Panic suddenly seized the weary Union soldiers, many of whom fled in disgraceful confusion. The Confederates, too ex-hausted or too disorganized to pursue effectively, feasted on captured lunches.

The "military picnic" at Bull Run, though not decisive militarily, was significant psychologically. Defeat was better than victory for the Union, because it dispelled all illusion of a one-punch war and caused the Northerners to buckle down to the staggering task at hand. Conversely, the victory was worse than a defeat for the South, because it inflated an already dangerous overconfidence. Many soldiers deserted, some boastfully to display their trophies, others sure that the war was over. Southern enlistments fell off sharply, and prepara-tions for a protracted war slackened.

"Tardy George" McClellan

Northern hopes brightened later in 1861, when General George B. McClellan was given command of the Army of the Potomac, as the major Union force near Washington was now called. Red-haired and red-mustached, strong and stocky, McClellan was a brilliant, thirty-four-year-old West Pointer.

Cocky George McClellan embodied a curious mixture of virtues and defects. He was a superb organizer and drillmaster, and he injected splendid morale into the Army of the Potomac. Hating to sacrifice his troops, he was idolized by his men, who affectionately called him "Little Mac." But he was a perfectionist who seems not to have realized that an army is never ready to the last button, and that wars cannot be won without running some risks. He consistently but erroneously believed that the enemy outnumbered him, partly because his intel-ligence reports from the head of Pinkerton's Detec-tive Agency were unreliable. He was over-cautious—Lincoln once accused him of having "the slows"—and he addressed the president in an arrogant tone which a less forgiving person would never have tolerated. Privately the general referred to his Chief as a "baboon." After threatening to "borrow" the army if it was not going to be used, Lincoln finally issued firm orders to move.

A reluctant McClellan decided upon a water-borne flanking approach to Richmond. Choosing the route up the peninsula formed by the James and York Rivers, he warily advanced toward the city in the spring of 1862 with about 100,000 men. After taking a month to capture historic Yorktown, which bristled with imitation wooden cannon, he finally came within sight of the spires of Richmond. Then General Lee suddenly struck with about 70,000 troops. Brilliantly assisted by "Stonewall" Jackson, he slowly drove McClellan back to his base on Chesapeake Bay. Although the Union army was still in fighting shape, the whole Peninsular Campaign was abandoned as a costly failure.

McClellan was now given a less active command, amid a storm of controversy. His enemies accused "Mac the Unready" of having moved too timorously. His defenders claimed that he would have captured Richmond if Lincoln had not withdrawn troops for the defense of Washington, which had been jeopardized by the lightning feints of General Jackson in the Shenandoah Valley. It is worth noting that McClellan was never decisively defeated, and that after the war Lee rated him the ablest of his many opponents.

The Antietam Pivotal Point

Lee now undertook a daring thrust into Maryland. He hoped to win a victory that would not only encourage foreign intervention, but also seduce the wavering Border States from the Union.

Events finally shaped up for a critical battle at Antietam Creek, Maryland. Lincoln, responding to popular pressures, hastily restored "Little Mac" to active command of the main Northern army. The soldiers tossed their caps into the air and hugged his horse as they hailed his return. At Antietam, on September 17, 1862, McClellan succeeded in halting Lee in one of the bloodiest days of the war. Antietam was more or less a draw militarily. Lee, finding his thrust parried, retired across the Potomac.

The landmark Battle of Antietam was the most decisive of the Civil War—probably one of the most decisive of world history. Jefferson Davis was perhaps never again so near victory as on that fateful summer day. The British and French governments were on the verge of diplomatic mediation in the American conflict, a move that would have boosted the cause of Confederate independence and caused angry resentment in the North. But both Paris and London cooled off when the Union displayed unexpected power at Antietam, and their chill deepened with the passing months.

Bloody Antietam also provided the long-awaited "victory" which Lincoln needed for launching his Emancipation Proclamation. The abolitionists had long been clamoring for action.

Confederate Corpses at Antietam. *Unknown to Lee, who had dangerously divided his army, McClellan had somehow obtained a copy of the Confederate battle plan. The Union forces thus had a great tactical advantage, and the result was appalling slaughter. The twelve-hour fight at Antietam Creek ranks as the bloodiest day of the war, with more than ten thousand Confederate casualties and even more on the Union side. "At last the sun went down and the battle ended," one historian wrote, "smoke heavy in the air, the twilight quivering with the anguished cries of thousands of wounded men." (Library of Congress)*

By midsummer of 1862, with the Border States safely in the fold, Lincoln was ready to move. But he believed that to issue such an edict on the heels of a series of military disasters would be folly.

The halting of Lee's offensive was just enough of a victory to justify Lincoln's issuing, on September 23, 1862, the preliminary Emancipation Proclamation. This hope-giving document announced that on January 1, 1863, the President would issue a final proclamation. On the scheduled date he fully redeemed his promise, and the Civil War became more of a moral crusade.

A Proclamation Without Emancipation

Lincoln's Emancipation Proclamation of 1863 declared "forever free" the slaves in those Confederate states still in rebellion. The blacks in the loyal Border States were not affected, nor were those in specific conquered areas in the South—all told, about 800,000. The tone of the document was dull and legalistic: there was no clarion call for a holy war to achieve freedom. Lincoln in fact is on record, as late as February of 1865, as favoring cash compensation to the owners of all slaves.

The presidential pen did not formally strike the shackles from a single slave. Where Lincoln could presumably free the slaves—that is, in the loyal Border States—he refused to do so, lest he spur disunion. Where he could not—that is, in the Confederate states—he tried to. In short, where he *could* he would not, and where he *would* he could not. Thus the Emancipation Proclamation was stronger on proclamation than emancipation.

Yet much unofficial do-it-yourself liberation did take place. Thousands of jubilant slaves, learning of the proclamation, flocked to the invading Union armies, stripping already run-down plantations of their work force. In this sense the Emancipation Proclamation was heralded by the patter of running feet. But many fugitives would have come anyhow, as they had from the war's outset. Actually, Lincoln did not go so far as legislation already passed by Congress for freeing enemy-owned slaves. His immediate goal was not so much to liberate the slaves as to strengthen the moral cause of the Union at home and abroad. This he

succeeded in doing. At the same time his proclamation, though of dubious constitutionality, clearly foreshadowed the ultimate doom of slavery. This was legally achieved by action of the individual states and by their ratification of the Thirteenth Amendment in 1865, eight months after the war had ended. (For text, see Appendix.)

Public reactions to the long-awaited proclamation of 1863 were varied. "God bless Abraham Lincoln," exulted the antislavery editor Horace Greeley in his New York *Tribune.* But many ardent abolitionists complained that Lincoln had not gone far enough. On the other hand, formidable numbers of Northerners, especially in the Old Northwest and the Border States, felt that he had gone too far.

Opposition mounted in the North against supporting an "abolition war." Many Boys in Blue, especially from the Border States, had volunteered to fight for the Union, not against slavery. Desertions increased sharply. The crucial congressional elections in the autumn of 1862 went heavily against the administration, particularly in New York, Pennsylvania, and Ohio. Democrats even carried Lincoln's Illinois, although they failed to secure control of Congress.

The Emancipation Proclamation caused an outcry to rise from the South that "Lincoln the fiend" was trying to stir up the "hellish passions" of a slave insurrection. Aristocrats of Europe, noting that the proclamation applied only to rebel slaveholders, were inclined to sympathize with Southern protests. But the Old World working classes, especially in England, reacted otherwise. They sensed that the proclamation spelled the ultimate doom of slavery, and many laborers were more determined than ever to oppose intervention. Gradually the diplomatic position of the Union improved.

Bisecting the Confederacy

Luckily the spectacular rise of Ulysses S. Grant provided Lincoln at last with an able general. As a mediocre student at West Point, Grant had distinguished himself only in horsemanship, although he did fairly well in mathematics. After participat-

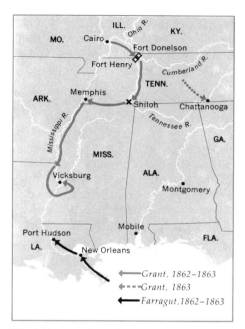

The Mississippi River and Tennessee, 1862–1863.

ing with credit in the Mexican War, he was stationed at lonely frontier posts, where boredom and loneliness drove him to drink. Resigning from the army to avoid a court martial for drunkenness, he failed at various business ventures, and when war came he was working in his father's leather store in Illinois at $50 a month.

Grant did not cut much of a figure. The shy and silent shopkeeper was short, stooped, awkward, stubble-bearded, and sloppy in dress. He managed with some difficulty to secure a colonelcy in the volunteers. From then on his military experience—combined with boldness, resourcefulness, and doggedness—brought a meteoric rise.

Grant's first signal success came in the northern Tennessee theater. After heavy fighting, he succeeded in capturing Fort Henry and Fort Donelson on the Tennessee and Cumberland Rivers in February 1862. When the Confederate commander at Fort Donelson asked for terms, Grant demanded "an unconditional and immediate surrender."

This triumph in Tennessee was of major significance. Kentucky was riveted more securely to the Union, and the gateway was opened to the rest of

Tennessee as well as to Georgia and the heart of the South. Grant's exploit also captured the imagination of the victory-starved North, and infused badly needed life into the Union cause.

"Unconditional Surrender" Grant was caught napping several weeks later at Shiloh, in southern Tennessee, April 6–7, 1862. But he finally managed to beat off the enemy on one of the goriest fields of the war. Lincoln resisted all demands for his removal by saying, "I can't spare this man, he fights." When talebearers later told Lincoln that Grant drank too much, the President allegedly replied, "Find me the brand, and I'll send a barrel to each of my other generals."

Other Union thrusts were in the making. In the spring of 1862, a flotilla commanded by David G. Farragut joined with a Northern army to strike the South a staggering blow by seizing New Orleans. With Union gunboats both ascending and descending the Mississippi, the eastern part of the Confederacy was left with a precarious back door. Through this narrowing entrance, between Vicksburg and Port Hudson, flowed herds of vitally needed cattle and quantities of other provisions from Louisiana and Texas. The fortress of Vicksburg, located on a hairpin turn of the Mississippi, was the South's sentinel protecting the lifeline to the western sources of supply.

General Grant was now given command of the Union forces attacking Vicksburg, and in the teeth of grave difficulties displayed rare skill and daring. This was his best-fought campaign of the war. Vicksburg at length surrendered, on July 4, 1863, with the garrison reduced to eating mules and rats. Five days later came the fall of Port Hudson, the last southern bastion on the Mississippi. The spinal cord of the Confederacy was now severed and, in Lincoln's quaint phrase, the Father of Waters at last flowed "unvexed to the sea."

Sherman Scorches Georgia

General Grant, the victor of Vicksburg, was now transferred to the east Tennessee theater. There, in November 1863, he won a series of desperate engagements in the vicinity of Chattanooga, including Missionary Ridge and Lookout Mountain ("the

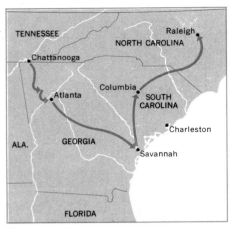

Sherman's March, 1864–1865.

Battle above the Clouds"). The state was thus cleared of Confederates, and the way was opened for an invasion of Georgia. Grant was rewarded by being made general-in-chief.

The conquest of Georgia was entrusted to General William Tecumseh Sherman. Red-haired and red-bearded, grim-faced and ruthless, he captured and burned Atlanta in September 1864. He then daringly undertook to cut loose from his base of supply, live off the country for some 250 miles (402 kilometers), and reach the sea at Savannah.

Sherman's hated "Blue Bellies," sixty thousand strong, cut a sixty-mile (ninety-seven-kilometer) swath of destruction through Georgia. They burned buildings, leaving only the blackened chimneys ("Sherman's Sentinels"). They tore up railroad rails, heated them red-hot, and twisted them into "iron doughnuts" and "Sherman's hairpins." They bayoneted family portraits and ran off with valuable "souvenirs." "War . . . is all hell," admitted Sherman later, and he proved it by his efforts to "make Georgia howl." One of his major purposes was to destroy supplies destined for the Confederate army, and to weaken the morale of the men at the front by waging war on their homes.

Sherman was a pioneer practitioner of "total war." His success in "Shermanizing" the South was attested by increasing numbers of Confederate desertions. Although his methods were brutal, he probably shortened the struggle and hence saved lives. But there can be no doubt that the discipline of his army at times broke down, as roving riffraff (Sherman's "bummers") engaged in an orgy of pillaging. "Sherman the Brute" was universally damned in the South.

After seizing Savannah as a Christmas present for Lincoln, Sherman's army veered north into South Carolina, where the destruction was even more vicious. Many Union soldiers believed that this state, the "hell-hole of secession," had wantonly provoked the war. The capital city, Columbia, burst into flames, in all probability the handiwork of the Yankee invader. Crunching steadily northward, Sherman's conquering army had rolled deep into North Carolina by the time the war ended.

Lee's Last Lunge

After Antietam, Lincoln replaced McClellan as commander of the Army of the Potomac with General A. E. Burnside, whose ornate side-whiskers came to be known as "burnsides" or "sideburns." Protesting his unfitness for this responsibility, Burnside proved it when he launched a rash frontal attack on Lee's strong position at Fredericksburg, Virginia, on December 13, 1862. A chicken could not have lived in the line of fire, remarked one Confederate officer. More than ten thousand Northern soldiers were killed or wounded in "Burnside's Slaughter Pen."

A new slaughter pen was prepared when General Burnside yielded his command to "Fighting Joe" Hooker, an aggressive officer but a headstrong subordinate. At Chancellorsville, Virginia, May 2–4, 1863, Lee daringly divided his numerically inferior force, and sent "Stonewall" Jackson to attack the Union flank. The strategy worked. Hooker, temporarily dazed by a near hit from a cannon ball, was badly beaten but not crushed. This victory was probably Lee's most brilliant, but it was dearly bought. Jackson was mistakenly shot by his own men in the gathering dusk, and died a few days later. "I have lost my right arm," lamented Lee. Southern folklore relates how Jackson outflanked the angels while getting into Heaven.

Lee now prepared to follow up his brilliant victory by invading the North again, this time through Pennsylvania. A decisive blow would add strength to the peace movement in the North, while encouraging foreign intervention. Quite by accident, the Northern army, now under General George G. Meade, took its stand on the green rolling hills near quiet little Gettysburg, Pennsylvania, and there the battle was joined. The high tide of the Confederacy was at hand.

At Gettysburg ninety-two thousand men in blue locked horns in furious combat with Lee's seventy-six thousand gray-clad warriors. The battle seesawed throughout three days, July 1–3, 1863, and the outcome was in doubt until almost the very end. The failure of General Pickett's magnificent but bloodily futile charge finally broke the back of the Confederates.

From this point on the Southern cause was doomed, for Vicksburg had surrendered on the day after the reverse at Gettysburg. Yet the men of Dixie fought on, through sweat, blood, and weariness of spirit. The Confederacy was like a cut flower—outwardly blooming but slowly dying.

Later in that dreary autumn of 1863, with the graves still fresh, Lincoln journeyed to Gettysburg to dedicate the cemetery. He read a two-minute address, following a two-hour speech by the orator of the day. Lincoln's noble remarks were branded by the London *Times* as "ludicrous" and by Democratic editors as "dishwatery" and "silly." The address attracted relatively little attention at the time, but the President was speaking for the ages.

Grant Outlasts Lee

Grant was now brought in from the West over Meade, who was blamed for failing to pursue the defeated but always dangerous Lee. Lincoln needed a general who, employing the superior resources of the North, would have the intestinal stamina to drive straight ahead, regardless of casualties. A soldier of bulldog tenacity, Grant was the man for this meat-grinder type of warfare. His overall basic strategy was to assail the enemy's armies simultaneously, so that they could not assist one another, and hence could be destroyed piecemeal. His motto was "When in doubt, fight." Lincoln urged him "to chew and choke, as much as possible."

A grimly determined Grant, with more than 100,000 men, struck for Richmond. He engaged Lee in a series of furious battles in the Wilderness of Virginia, during May and June of 1864, notably in the leaden hurricane of the "Bloody Angle" and "Hell's Half Acre." In this Wilderness Campaign Grant suffered about 50,000 casualties, or nearly as many men as Lee had at the start. But Lee lost about as heavily in proportion.

In a ghastly gamble, on June 3, 1864, Grant ordered a frontal assault on the impregnable position of Cold Harbor. The Union soldiers advanced to almost certain death with papers pinned on their backs bearing their names and addresses. In a few minutes, about 7,000 men were killed or wounded.

Public opinion in the North was appalled by this "blood and guts" type of fighting. Critics cried that "Grant the Butcher" had gone insane. But his basic strategy seemed brutally necessary; he could trade two men for one and still beat the enemy to its knees. "I propose to fight it out on this line," he wrote, "if it takes all summer." It did—and all autumn, all winter, and a part of the spring.

Early in 1865 the Confederates, tasting the bitter dregs of defeat, tried desperately to negotiate for peace between the "two countries." But Lincoln could accept nothing short of Union, and the Southerners could accept nothing short of independence. So the war had to grind on—amid smoke and agony—to its terrible climax.

The end came with dramatic suddenness. Rapidly advancing Northern troops captured Richmond and cornered Lee at Appomattox Court House in Virginia, in April 1865. Grant—stubble-bearded and informally dressed—met with Lee on Palm Sunday and granted generous terms of surrender. Among other concessions, the hungry Confederates were allowed to keep their horses to use for spring plowing.

Tattered Southern battle veterans—"Lee's Ragamuffins"—wept as they took leave of their beloved commander. The elated Union soldiers cheered, but they were silenced by Grant's stern admonition, "The war is over; the rebels are our countrymen again." Unfortunately, as the tragic sequel proved, this soldierly forgiveness was not shared by all Northern hearts.

General Ulysses S. Grant and General Robert E. Lee. *Trained at West Point, Grant (left) proved to be a better general than a president. Oddly, he hated the sight of blood and recoiled from rare beef. Lee (right), a gentlemanly general in an ungentlemanly business, remarked when the Union troops were bloodily repulsed at Fredericksburg, "It is well that war is so terrible, or we should get too fond of it." (Left and right, National Archives)*

VARYING VIEWPOINTS

Why did the North win the Civil War? The usual answer is that superior industry and transportation tipped the scales in the Union's favor. This line of reasoning leads to the conclusion that the Civil War was the first "modern" war, in which victory depended as much on home-front economic mobilization as on battlefield prowess.

Another approach focuses on military strategy. Historians of this persuasion argue that Union successes in the western theater more than compensated for the early debacles in Virginia. Victories in the West allowed the emergence of tacticians like Grant and Sherman, who were better equipped to wage a modern total war than the valiant but old-fashioned Confederate generals.

A third answer emphasizes political leadership. In this view, the Lincoln administration was able to maintain control at home and prevent unfavorable foreign intervention in the conflict. The government of Jefferson Davis had no such domestic or diplomatic success. One historian has even suggested that if the North and South had traded presidents, the Confederacy would have won its independence. Even today, heated debate continues over the relative importance of battlefront and behind-the-lines factors in accounting for the North's crushing victory.

SELECT READINGS

Primary Source Documents

Abraham Lincoln's reply in 1862 to Horace Greeley's "Prayer of Twenty Millions"* (*Collected Works of Abraham Lincoln,* edited by Roy P. Basler, 1953) is an early statement of the president's war aims. See also, in the same collection, the Emancipation Proclamation (1863). Reminiscences of the military struggle include Eliza Andrews, *The War-Time Journal of a Georgia Girl** (1908); *Memoirs of General William T. Sherman** (1887); and C. Vann Woodward, ed., *Mary Chestnut's Civil War* (rev. ed., 1981). See also Stephen Crane's classic war novel *The Red Badge of Courage* (1895).

Secondary Sources

An able survey is James G. Randall and David Donald, *The Civil War and Reconstruction* (rev. ed., 1969); greater detail appears in James G. Randall, *Lincoln the President* (4 vols., 1945–1955). Capable one-volume studies are Peter J. Parish, *The American Civil War* (1975) and James M. McPherson, *Ordeal by Fire: The Civil War and Reconstruction* (1982). Bruce Catton has a series of a dozen or so books on aspects of the Civil War, all readable and knowledgeable, including *A Stillness at Appomattox* (1953) and *This Hallowed Ground* (1956). Russell T. Weigley, *The American Way of War* (1973) puts military history in the broader context. Herman Hattaway and Archer Jones discuss *How the North Won* (1983), while Richard E. Beringer, et al., analyze *Why the South Lost the Civil War* (1986). Ben I. Wiley's descriptions of common soldiers, *The Life of Johnny Reb* (1943) and *The Life of Billy Yank* (1952), are classics. Emancipation is treated in Louis Gerteis, *From Contraband to Freedmen: Federal Policy toward Southern Blacks, 1861–1865* (1973); Herman Belz, *Emancipation and Equal Rights: Politics and Constitutionalism during the Civil War Reconstruction* (1978); and LaWanda Cox, *Lincoln and Black Freedom* (1981). On the abolitionists' role in securing emancipation, see James M. McPherson, *The Struggle for Equality* (1964). The two leading Civil War generals are masterfully treated in Douglas S. Freeman, *R. E. Lee* (4 vols., 1934–1935), and William S. McFeely, *Grant* (1981).

24

Behind the Lines: North and South

Long experience has shown that armies can not be maintained
unless desertion shall be punished by the severe penalty of death. . . .
[But] must I shoot a simple-minded soldier boy who deserts,
while I must not touch a hair of a wily agitator who induces him to desert?

Abraham Lincoln, 1863

Diplomatic Warriors Abroad

America's diplomatic front has seldom been so critical as during the Civil War. The attitude of the major European countries, particularly France and Britain, was crucial. If either power had decided to intervene, the South almost certainly would have won its independence. An infuriated North might then have turned its bayonets against British Canada, there to seek vengeance and compensation.

Britain proclaimed an official neutrality and observed it rather well, although aristocratic officials were personally more friendly to the South than to the "shopkeeping" North. To Northerners who had expected sympathy from the antislavery British, neutrality seemed more like veiled hostility.

The first real crisis with Britain came over the *Trent* affair, late in 1861. A Union warship cruising on the high seas north of Cuba stopped a British mail steamer, the *Trent*, and forcibly removed from it two Confederate diplomats who were on their way to England.

Britons were outraged: upstart Yankees could not do this sort of thing to the Mistress of the Seas. War preparations buzzed, as red-coated troops embarked for Canada with bands blaring, "I Wish I Was in Dixie." The London Foreign Office prepared an ultimatum demanding surrender of the prisoners and an apology. But luckily, slow communications gave passions on both sides a chance to cool. Lincoln came to see the *Trent* prisoners as "white elephants," and reluctantly released them.

Another major crisis in Anglo-American relations arose over the unneutral building in England of Confederate commerce-raiders, notably the *Alabama*. These vessels were not warships within the meaning of loopholed British law, because they left their shipyards unarmed and picked up their guns elsewhere. The *Alabama* escaped in 1862 to the Portuguese Azores, and there took on weapons and a crew from two English ships that followed her. Although flying the Confederate flag and officered by Confederates, she was manned by Britons and never entered a Confederate port. England was thus the chief naval base of the Confederacy.

The *Alabama* lighted the skies from Europe to the Far East with the burning hulks of Yankee merchantmen. All told, this "British pirate" captured over sixty vessels. Competing British shippers were delighted, while an angered North had to divert naval strength from its blockade for wild goose chases. The barnacled *Alabama* finally accepted a challenge from a stronger Union cruiser off the coast of France in 1864, and was quickly destroyed.

The *Alabama* was beneath the waves, but the issue of British-built Confederate raiders stayed afloat. Under prodding by the American minister, Charles Francis Adams, the British gradually perceived that allowing such ships to be built was a dangerous precedent that might be used against them. In 1863 London openly violated its own leaky laws and seized another raider being built for the South. But despite greater official efforts by Britain to remain truly neutral, Confederate commerce-destroyers, chiefly British-built, captured more than 250 Yankee ships, severely crippling the American merchant marine. Angered Americans talked openly of securing revenge by seizing Canada when the war was over.

Foreign Flare-Ups

A final Anglo-American crisis was touched off in 1863 by the Laird rams—two Confederate warships being constructed in Great Britain. Designed to destroy the wooden ships of the Union navy with their iron rams and large-caliber guns, they were far more dangerous than the swift and lightly armed *Alabama*. If delivered to the South, they probably would have sunk the blockading squadrons, and then brought Northern cities under their fire. In angry retaliation, the North doubtless would have invaded Canada, and a full-dress war with Britain would have erupted. But Minister Adams took a hard line, warning that "this is war" if the rams were released. At the last minute the London government relented, and bought the two ships for the Royal Navy. Everyone seemed satisfied—except the disappointed Confederates. Britain also eventually repented her sorry role in the *Alabama* business. She agreed in 1871 to submit the *Alabama* dispute to arbitration, and in 1872 paid American claimants $15.5 million for damages caused by wartime commerce raiders.

American anger was also directed at Canada, where despite the vigilance of British authorities, Southern agents plotted to burn Northern cities. One Confederate raid into Vermont left three banks plundered and one American citizen dead. Hatred of England burned especially fiercely among Irish-Americans, and they unleashed their fury on Canada. They raised several tiny "armies" of a few hundred green-shirted men, and launched invasions of Canada, notably in 1866 and 1870. The Canadians condemned the Washington government for permitting such violations of neutrality, but the administration was hampered by the presence of so many Irish-American voters.

As fate would have it, two great nations emerged from the fiery furnace of the American Civil War. One was a reunited United States, the other was a united Canada. The British Parliament established the Dominion of Canada in 1867. It was partly designed to bolster the Canadians, both politically and spiritually, against the possible vengeance of the United States.

Emperor Napoleon III of France, taking advantage of America's preoccupation with her own internal problems, dispatched a French army to occupy Mexico City in 1863. The following year he installed on the ruins of the crushed republic his puppet, Austrian Archduke Maximilian, as emperor of Mexico. Both sending the army and enthroning Maximilian were done in flagrant violation of the Monroe Doctrine. Napoleon was gambling that the Union would collapse and thus America would be too weak to enforce her "hands off" policy in the western hemisphere.

The North, as long as it was convulsed by war, pursued a walk-on-eggs policy toward France. But when the shooting stopped, Secretary of State

Seward, speaking with the authority of nearly a million bayonets, prepared to march south. Napoleon realized that his costly gamble was doomed. He reluctantly took "French leave" of his ill-starred puppet in 1867, and Maximilian soon crumpled ingloriously before a Mexican firing squad.

Volunteers and Draftees: North and South

Ravenous, the gods of war demanded men—lots of men. Northern armies were at first manned solely by volunteers, with each state assigned a quota based on population. But in 1863, after volunteering had slackened off, Congress passed a federal conscription law for the first time on a nationwide scale in the United States. The provisions were grossly unfair to the poor. Rich boys, including young John D. Rockefeller, could hire substitutes to go in their places, or purchase exemption outright by paying $300.

The draft was especially damned in the Democratic strongholds of the North, notably in New York City. A frightful riot broke out in 1863, touched off largely by underprivileged and anti-black Irish-Americans who shouted, "Down with Lincoln!" and "Down with the Draft!" For several days the city was at the mercy of a burning, drunken, pillaging mob, and scores of lives were lost, including many lynched blacks. Elsewhere in the North conscription met with resentment and an occasional minor riot.

Yet over 90 percent of the Union troops were volunteers, since social and patriotic pressures to enlist were strong. As able-bodied men became scarcer, generous bounties for enlistment were offered by federal, state, and local authorities.

With money flowing so freely, an unsavory crew of "bounty brokers" and "substitute brokers" sprang up, at home and abroad. They combed the poorhouses of the British Isles and Western Europe; and many an Irishman or German was befuddled with whiskey and induced to enlist. A number of the slippery "bounty boys" deserted, volunteered elsewhere, and netted another handsome haul. The rolls of the Union army recorded about 200,000 deserters of all classes, and the Confederate authorities were plagued with a problem of similar dimensions.

Like the North, the South relied mainly on volunteers. But since the Confederacy was much less populous, it scraped the bottom of its manpower barrel much more quickly. The Richmond regime, robbing both "cradle and grave" (ages 17 to 50) was forced to resort to conscription as early as April 1862, nearly a year earlier than the Union.

Confederate draft regulations also worked serious injustices. As in the North, a rich man could hire a substitute or purchase exemption. Slave-

The New York Draft Riot, 1863. *Irish workers resented competition for jobs by "nagurs." The free blacks in turn called the Irish "white niggers." (Museum of the City of New York)*

owners or overseers with twenty slaves might also claim exemption.

No large-scale draft riots broke out in the South, as in New York City. But the Confederate conscription agents often found it prudent to avoid those areas inhabited by sharp-shooting mountain whites, who were branded "Tories," "traitors," and "Yankee-lovers."

The Dollar Goes to War

Blessed with a lion's share of the wealth, the North rode through the financial breakers much more smoothly than the South. Excise taxes on tobacco and alcohol were substantially increased by Congress. An income tax was levied for the first time in the nation's history.

Customs receipts likewise proved to be important revenue-raisers. Early in 1861, after enough anti-protection Southern members had seceded, Congress passed the Morrill Tariff Act. It increased the existing duties some 5 to 10 percent, but these modest rates were soon pushed sharply upward by the war. The increases were designed partly to raise additional revenue, and partly to provide more protection for the prosperous manufacturers who were being plucked by the new internal taxes. A protective tariff thus became identified with the Republican party, as American industrialists, predominantly Republicans, waxed fat.

The Washington Treasury also issued greenbacked paper money, totaling nearly $450 million at face value. This printing-press currency was inadequately supported by gold, and hence its value was determined by the nation's credit. Greenbacks thus fluctuated with the fortunes of Union arms, and at one low point were worth only 39 cents on the gold dollar.

Yet borrowing far outstripped both greenbacks and taxes as a money-raiser. The Federal Treasury netted $2,621,916,786 through the sale of bonds, which bore interest and which were payable at a later date.

A financial landmark of the war was the National Banking System, authorized by Congress in 1863. Launched partly as a stimulant to the sale of government bonds, it was also designed to estab-lish a standard banknote currency. (The country was then flooded with depreciated "rag money" issued by unreliable bankers.) Banks that joined the National Banking System could buy government bonds and issue sound paper money backed by them. Spawned by the war, this new system continued to function for fifty years.

An impoverished South was beset by different financial problems. Customs duties were choked off as the coils of the Union blockade tightened. Large issues of Confederate bonds were sold at home and abroad, amounting to nearly $400 million. In general, the states' rights Southerners were vigorously opposed to heavy direct taxation by the central authority: only about 1 percent of the total income was raised this way.

As revenue began to dry up, the Confederate government was forced to print blue-backed paper money with complete abandon. "Runaway inflation" occurred as Southern presses continued to grind out the poorly backed treasury notes, totaling in all more than $1 billion. The Confederate paper dollar finally sank to the point where it was worth only 1.6 cents when Lee surrendered.

"Shoddy" Millionaires in the North

Wartime prosperity in the North was nothing short of miraculous. New factories, sheltered by the friendly umbrella of the new protective tariffs, mushroomed forth. Soaring prices, resulting from inflation, unfortunately pinched the day laborer and the white-collar worker to some extent. But the manufacturers and businessmen raked in "the fortunes of war." The Civil War spawned a millionaire class for the first time in American history.

Yankee "sharpness" appeared at its worst. Dishonest agents, putting profits above patriotism, palmed off aged and blind horses on government purchasers. Unscrupulous Northern manufacturers supplied shoes with cardboard soles, and fast-disintegrating uniforms of reprocessed or "shoddy" wool, rather than virgin wool. Hence the reproachful term "shoddy millionaires."

Newly invented labor-saving machinery enabled the North to expand economically, even though the cream of its manpower was being drained off to the fighting front. The sewing machine wrought wonders in fabricating uniforms and military footwear. Clattering mechanical reapers, which numbered about 250,000 by 1865, proved hardly less potent than thundering guns. They not only released tens of thousands of farm boys for the army but fed them while there. They produced vast surpluses of grain which, when sent abroad, helped dethrone King Cotton. They provided profits with which the North bought munitions and supplies from abroad.

Other industries were humming. The discovery of petroleum gushers in 1859 had led to a rush of "Fifty-Niners" to Pennsylvania. The result was the birth of a new industry, with its "petroleum plutocracy" and "coal oil Johnnies." Pioneers continued to push westward during the war, altogether an estimated 300,000 souls. Major magnets were free gold nuggets and free lands under the Homestead Act of 1862. Strong propellants were the federal draft agents. The only major Northern industry to suffer was the ocean-carrying trade, which fell prey to the *Alabama* and its sister raiders.

A Crushed Cotton Kingdom

Dismally different was the plight of the South, which had fought to exhaustion. The suffocation caused by the blockade, together with the destruction by invaders, took a terrible toll. Transportation collapsed. The South was even driven to the economic cannibalism of pulling up rails from the less-used lines to repair the main ones. Window weights were melted down into bullets; gourds replaced dishes; pins became so scarce that they were loaned with reluctance.

To the brutal end, the South revealed magnificent resourcefulness and spirit. Women buoyed up their menfolk, many of whom had seen enough of war at first hand to be heartily sick of it. A proposal was made by a number of women that they cut off their long hair and sell it abroad. But the project was not adopted, partly because of the blockade. The self-sacrificing women took pride in denying themselves the silks and satins of their Northern sisters.

The Northern Captains of Industry had conquered the Southern Lords of the Manor. A crippled South left the capitalistic North free to work its own way, with high tariffs and other benefits. The industrial giants of the North, ushering in the full-fledged industrial revolution, were destined for increased dominance over American economic and political life. Hitherto the agrarian "slavocracy" of the South, by using sectional alliances, had partially checked the rising plutocracy of the North. Now cotton capitalism had lost out to industrial capitalism. The South of 1865 was rich in little but amputees, war heroes, ruins, and memories.

Limitations on Wartime Liberties

"Honest Abe" Lincoln, when inaugurated, laid his hand on the Bible and swore a solemn oath to uphold the Constitution. Then, driven by sheer necessity, he proceeded to tear a few holes in that hallowed document. He sagely concluded that if he did not do so, and patch the parchment later, there might not be a Constitution of a *united* United States to mend. Unquestionably, the "rail splitter" was no hairsplitter.

Congress was not in session when war erupted, so Lincoln gathered the reins into his own hands. Brushing aside legal objections, he boldly proclaimed a blockade. (His action was later upheld by the Supreme Court.) He arbitrarily increased the size of the federal army—something that only Congress can do under the Constitution (see Art. I, Sec. VIII, para. 12). (Congress later approved.) He suspended the privilege of the writ of habeas corpus, so that anti-Unionists might be summarily arrested.

Lincoln's regime was also guilty of many other high-handed acts. For example, it arranged for "supervised" voting in the Border States. There the intimidated citizen, holding a colored ballot indicating his party preference, had to march between two lines of armed troops. The federal officials also ordered the suspension of some newspapers and the arrest of editors on grounds of obstructing the war.

Jefferson Davis was less able than Lincoln to exercise arbitrary power, mainly because of con-

firmed states'-righters who revealed an intense spirit of localism. To the very end of the conflict the owners of horse-drawn vans in Petersburg, Virginia, prevented the joining of the incoming and outgoing tracks of a militarily vital railroad. The South seemed willing to lose the war before it would surrender local rights—and it did.

The Curse of Copperheadism

Hundreds of Northern citizens were arrested by the military authorities, chiefly on charges of hindering the Union cause by preaching defeatism or peace-at-any-price-ism. Many were seized without a warrant and were held for prolonged periods without trial, as in czarist Russia. A large percentage of the persons thus abused were so-called Copperhead Democrats. The Copperheads were partisans who obstructed the war effort by disloyal talk—or worse—and they were named after the poisonous snake, which strikes without a warning rattle.

Notorious among the victims of autocratic arrest was a prominent Copperhead, Clement L. Vallandigham. A Southern partisan, he publicly demanded an end to the "wicked and cruel" war.

He was convicted and sentenced to prison by a military tribunal for treasonable utterances. Lincoln decided that if Vallandigham liked the Confederates so much, he ought to be banished to their lines. This was done, but Vallandigham was not so easily silenced. Working his way to Canada, he ran for the governorship of Ohio on foreign soil, and polled a substantial but insufficient vote.

Considering the hatreds aroused, civil liberties and constitutional rights fared rather well. Some of the power usurped by the chief executive was retained, but most of it was gradually restored to the courts and Congress after the shooting stopped. Wartime penalties on the whole were mild and pardons speedy. Thousands of unterrified and unmolested Copperhead Democrats openly denounced Lincoln as "the Illinois Ape," demanded an end to the "Nigger War," discouraged enlistments, and encouraged desertions.

Politics as Usual in 1864

Political infighting in the North added greatly to Lincoln's cup of woe. Factions within his own party, distrusting his ability, sought to tie his hands. Conspicuous among these critics was the group led by the overambitious Secretary of the Treasury, Salmon P. Chase. The master stroke of the anti-Lincoln Republicans was the creation of the meddlesome Congressional Committee on the Conduct of the War, which may have stirred up about as much trouble as it smoothed over. The extreme abolitionists, in addition, clamored for an immediate freeing of the slaves, regardless of the political and military consequences.

Most dangerous of all were the Northern Democrats. Deprived of the brains that had departed with the Southern wing, they were left with the taint of association with the seceders. A tragedy befell the Democrats—and the Union—when their gifted leader, Stephen A. Douglas, died of typhoid fever seven weeks after war began. Inflexibly devoted to the Union as he was, had he lived he probably could have kept much of his following on the path of loyalty.

Lacking a leader, the Democrats became badly divided. A large group of so-called War Democrats patriotically supported the Lincoln administration, but tens of thousands of Peace Democrats and regular Democrats did not. Many of the dissenters were outright Copperheads, who were especially strong in Ohio, Indiana, and Illinois, all of which contained many Southerners. Only with difficulty did the war governors of these states manage to keep them cooperating with Washington.

Lincoln Defeats McClellan at the Polls

Presidential elections come by the calendar and not by the crisis. As fate would have it, the election of 1864 fell most inopportunely in the midst of war.

The Republican party, fearing defeat, executed a clever maneuver. Joining with the War Democrats, it proclaimed itself to be the Union party. Thus the Republican party temporarily ceased to exist. Lincoln was nominated by the Union party without serious dissent.

Lincoln's running mate was ex-tailor Andrew Johnson, a loyal War Democrat from Tennessee who had been a small slaveowner when the conflict began. He was placed on the Union party ticket to "sew up" the election by attracting War Democrats

and the voters in the Border States, and not with proper regard for the possibility that Lincoln might die in office.

Embattled Democrats—both the regulars and the Copperheads—nominated the deposed and overcautious war hero, General McClellan. The Copperheads managed to force into the Democratic platform a plank denouncing the prosecution of the war as a failure. But McClellan, who could not otherwise have faced his old comrades-in-arms, repudiated this defeatist declaration.

Lincoln's reelection was at first gravely in doubt. The war was going badly, as "Butcher" Grant continued to be bogged down in the Wilderness of Virginia. Lincoln himself feared that political defeat was imminent.

But the atmosphere of gloom was changed electrically, as balloting day neared, by a succession of Northern victories. Admiral Farragut captured Mobile, Alabama, after defiantly shouting, "Damn the torpedoes! Go ahead." General Sherman seized Atlanta. General ("Little Phil") Sheridan laid waste the verdant Shenandoah Valley of Virginia so thoroughly that, in his words, "a crow could not fly over it without carrying his rations with him."

The president pulled through, but nothing more than necessary was left to chance. At election time many Northern soldiers were furloughed home to support Lincoln. One Pennsylvania veteran voted forty-nine times—once for himself and once for each absent member of his company. Other soldiers were permitted to cast their ballots at the front.

Lincoln, who could have won anyhow without the "bayonet vote," vanquished McClellan by 212 electoral votes to 21, with the loss of only Kentucky, Delaware, and New Jersey. But "Little Mac" ran a much closer race than the electoral count indicates. He netted a surprising 45 percent of the popular vote, 1,805,237 to Lincoln's 2,206,938, piling up much support in the Southerner-infiltrated states of the Old Northwest, in New York, and in his native state of Pennsylvania.

One of the most crushing defeats suffered by the South was the defeat of the Northern Demo-

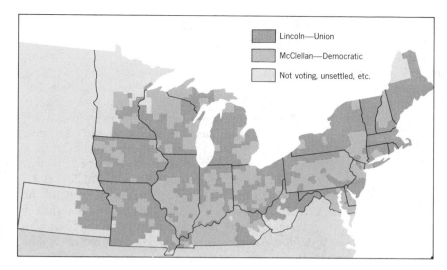

Presidential Election of 1864 (showing popular vote by county). *Lincoln also carried California, Oregon, and Nevada, but there was a considerable McClellan vote in each.*

crats in 1864. The removal of Lincoln was the last real hope for a Confederate victory. When Lincoln triumphed, desertions from the sinking Southern ship increased sharply.

The Martyrdom of Lincoln

On the night of April 14, 1865 (Good Friday), only five days after Lee's surrender, Ford's Theater in Washington witnessed its most sensational drama. A half-crazed, fanatically pro-Southern actor, John Wilkes Booth, slipped behind Lincoln as he sat in his box and shot him in the head. After lying unconscious all night, the Great Emancipator died the following morning.

Lincoln expired in the arms of victory, at the very pinnacle of his fame. From the standpoint of his reputation, his death could not have been better timed if he had hired the assassin. A large number of his countrymen had not suspected his greatness, and many others had even doubted his ability. But his dramatic death helped to erase the memory of his shortcomings, and caused his nobler qualities to stand out in clearer relief.

The full impact of Lincoln's death was not at once apparent to the South. Hundreds of bedraggled ex-Confederate soldiers cheered, as did some Southern civilians and Northern Copperheads,

when they learned of the assassination. But as time wore on, increasing numbers of Southerners perceived that Lincoln's death was a calamity for them. Belatedly they recognized that his kindliness and moderation would have been the most effective shields between them and vindictive treatment by the victors. The assassination unfortunately embittered the North, partly because of the fantastic rumor that Jefferson Davis had plotted it.

A few historians have argued that if the "Rail Splitter" had lived he would have run into serious trouble, perhaps impeachment, at the hands of embittered members of his own party who demanded harsh treatment of the South. Lincoln no doubt would have clashed with Congress; in fact, he had already found himself in some hot water. But the surefooted and experienced Lincoln could hardly have blundered into the same quicksands that engulfed Andrew Johnson, now President-by-bullet. Lincoln was a victorious President; and there is no arguing with victory. Enjoying battle-tested powers of leadership, he possessed in full measure tact, sweet reasonableness, and an uncommon amount of common sense. Andrew Johnson, hot-tempered and impetuous, lacked all of these qualities. Ford's Theater, with its tragic murder of Lincoln, set the stage for the terrible ordeal of Reconstruction.

The Aftermath of the Nightmare

The Civil War took a grisly toll in gore, about as much as all of America's subsequent wars combined. Over 600,000 men died in action or of disease, and in all, over a million were killed or seriously wounded. To its lasting hurt, the white South lost the cream of its young manhood and potential leadership.

Direct monetary costs of the conflict totaled about $15 billion. But this colossal figure does not include continuing expenses, such as pensions and interest on the national debt. The intangible costs—dislocations, disunities, wasted energies, lowered ethics, blasted lives, bitter memories, and burning hates—cannot be calculated.

The greatest constitutional decision of the century, in a sense, was written in blood and handed down at Appomattox Court House, near which Lee surrendered. The extreme states' righters were crushed. The national government, rewelded in the fiery furnace of civil war, emerged unbroken. Nullification and secession, those twin nightmares of previous decades, were laid to rest.

Beyond doubt the Civil War—the nightmare of the Republic—was the supreme test of American democracy. It finally answered the question, in the words of Lincoln at Gettysburg, whether a nation dedicated to such principles "can long endure."

Victory for Union arms also provided inspiration to the champions of democracy and liberalism the world over. The great English Reform Bill of 1867, under which Britain became a true political democracy, was passed two years after the Civil War ended. American democracy had proved itself, and its success was an additional argument used by the disfranchised British masses in securing similar blessings for themselves.

The "Lost Cause" of the South was lost, but

Prisoners from the Front. *This celebrated painting of 1866 by Winslow Homer reflected the painter's first-hand observations of the war. He brilliantly captured the enduring depths of sectional animosity. The Union officer somewhat disdainfully asserts his command of the situation; the beaten and disarmed Confederates exhibit an out-at-the-elbows pride and defiance. (The Metropolitan Museum of Art. Gift of Mrs. Frank B. Porter, 1922)*

few Americans today would argue that the end result was not for the best. With the shameful cancer of slavery sliced away, free labor was further dignified by the removal of servile competition. Grave dangers were averted, including constant friction and conflict between North and South, each bristling with guns. A strong and united nation was thus left free to fulfill its destiny as the overshadowingly powerful republic of the hemisphere—and ultimately of the world.

VARYING VIEWPOINTS

When the Civil War ended, slavery was officially defunct, secession was a dead issue, and industrial growth was surging forward. Charles Beard later hailed the war as the "Second American Revolution" because it had transformed the legal and institutional structure of government, and placed the levers of power firmly in the hands of a new business class. But did the bloody conflict neatly bisect the nation's history? In recent years many scholars have questioned the concept that the war constituted a dramatic turning point. Slavery may have formally disappeared, but blacks remained a scandalously subordinated social group. Regional differences persisted, even down to the present day. Thomas Cochran has even argued that the Civil War may have *retarded* overall industrialization. As for the rising commercial class of the postwar "Gilded Age," many historians now point to its antecedents in both the Whig and Jacksonian movements. History, it seems, is a mighty stream, which in time partially submerges even momentous events like the Civil War beneath the surface of its relentless flow.

SELECT READINGS

Primary Source Documents

The Constitution of the Confederacy* (1861) makes an interesting contrast to the United States Constitution. Two diaries that describe life behind the Confederate lines are those of John B. Jones, published as Earl S. Miers, ed., *A Rebel War Clerk's Diary** (1958), and Paul B. Barringer, *The Natural Bent** (1949). Lincoln's Gettysburg Address (1863) (in Henry Steele Commager, *Documents of American History*) poetically proclaims the president's highest war aims, as does his Second Inaugural Address (1865), in Roy P. Basler, ed., *The Collected Works of Abraham Lincoln* (1953), Vol. VIII, pp. 332-333.

Secondary Sources

See the references for the previous chapter, especially the work of James M. McPherson. The best one-volume biography is Stephen B. Oates, *With Malice toward None: The Life of Abraham Lincoln* (1977). Home-front politics are treated in James A. Rawley, *The Politics of Union* (1974) and in Joel Silbey, *A Respectable Minority: The Democratic Party in the Civil War Era* (1977). Lincoln's problems are analyzed in LaWanda Cox, *Lincoln and Black Freedom* (1981); William B. Hesseltine, *Lincoln and the War Governors* (1948); and T. Harry Williams, *Lincoln and the Radicals* (1941). For a different view of the same subject, see Hans L. Trefousse, *The Radical Republicans: Lincoln's Vanguard for Racial Justice* (1969). Mary E. Massey presents the interesting story of women in the Civil War in *Bonnet Brigades* (1966); that topic also figures in Anne Firor Scott's *The Southern Lady* (1970). On the Confederacy, see Charles P. Roland, *The Confederacy* (1960) and Emory M. Thomas, *The Confederate Nation, 1861–1865* (1979). Economic matters are handled in Ralph L. Andreano, ed., *The Economic Impact of the American Civil War* (1962) and David T. Gilchrist and W. David Lewis, eds., *Economic Change in the Civil War* (1965). The war's literary legacy is keenly analyzed in Edmund Wilson's classic *Patriotic Gore* (1962) and Daniel Aaron's *The Unwritten War: American Writers and the Civil War* (1973). For a fascinating discussion of Northern intellectuals and the conflict, consult George M. Frederickson, *The Inner Civil War* (1965).

25

The Ordeal of Reconstruction

With malice toward none, with charity for all,
with firmness in the right as God gives us to see the right, let us
strive on to finish the work we are in, to bind up the nation's wounds,
to care for him who shall have borne the battle and for
his widow and orphan, to do all which may achieve and cherish
a just and lasting peace among ourselves and with all nations.

Abraham Lincoln, Second Inaugural, March 4, 1865

The Problems of Peace

The battle was done, the buglers silent. Bone-weary and bloodied, the American people, North and South, now faced the staggering challenges of peace. Four questions loomed large. How would the South, physically devastated by war and socially revolutionized by emancipation, be rebuilt? How would the liberated blacks fare as free men and women? How would the Southern states be reintegrated into the Union? And who would direct the process of Reconstruction—the Southern states themselves, the president, or the Congress?

Other questions clamored for answers. What should be done with the captured Confederate ringleaders? During the war a popular song had been "Hang Jeff Davis to a Sour Apple Tree," and some Northerners did think Davis and others should be tried for treason. But no trials were ever held. Davis served only two years in prison, and President Johnson pardoned all "rebel" leaders as a Christmas present in 1868. Congress removed their civil disabilities thirty years later.

The Prostrate South

Dismal indeed was the picture presented by the war-racked South when the rattle of musketry faded. Not only had an age perished, but a civilization had collapsed, in both its economic and its social structure. The moonlight-and-magnolia Old South, largely imaginary in any case, had gone forever with the wind.

Handsome cities of yesteryear, such as Charleston and Richmond, were gutted. An Atlantan returned to his once-fair home town and

Richmond Devastated. *Charleston, Atlanta, and other Southern cities looked much the same, resembling bombed-out Berlin and Munich in 1945. (Library of Congress)*

remarked, "Hell has laid her egg, and right here it hatched."

Economic life had creaked to a halt. Banks and business houses had locked their doors, ruined by runaway inflation. Factories were smokeless, silent, dismantled. The transportation system had broken down completely. Efforts to untwist the rails corkscrewed by Sherman's soldiers were bumpily unsatisfactory.

Agriculture—the economic lifeblood of the South—was almost hopelessly crippled. Oncewhite cotton fields now yielded a lush harvest of nothing but green weeds. Seed was scarce, and livestock had been driven off by plundering Yankees. Pathetic instances were reported of men hitching themselves to plows, while women and children gripped the handles.

The princely planter aristocrats were humbled by the war—at least temporarily. Reduced to proud poverty, they faced charred and gutted mansions, lost investments, and almost worthless land. Their investment of more than $2 billion in slaves, their primary form of wealth, had evaporated with emancipation.

Beaten but unbent, many high-spirited white Southerners remained dangerously defiant. They cursed the "damnyankees" and spoke of "your government" in Washington instead of "our government." Conscious of no crime, these former Confederates continued to believe that their view of secession was correct and that the "lost cause" was still a just war. One popular anti-Union song ran:

> I'm glad I fought agin her, I only wish we'd won,
> And I ain't axed any pardon for anything I've done.

Such attitudes boded ill for the prospects of painlessly binding up the Republic's wounds.

Unfettered Freedmen

Confusion abounded in the still-smoldering South about the precise meaning of "freedom" for blacks. Emancipation took effect haltingly and unevenly in different parts of the conquered Confederacy, and in some regions planters stubbornly protested that slavery was legal until state legislatures or the Supreme Court might act. For many bondsmen, the shackles of slavery were not struck off in a single mighty blow; long-suffering blacks often had to struggle out of their chains link by link.

The variety of responses to emancipation, by whites as well as blacks, illustrated the sometimes startling complexity of the master-slave relationship. Unbending loyalty to "ole Massa" prompted many slaves to help their owners resist the liberating Union armies. Blacks blocked the door of the "big house" with their bodies, or stashed the plantation silverware under mattresses in their own humble huts, where it would be safe from the plundering "bluebellies." On other plantations, pent-up bitterness burst violently forth on the day of liberation. A group of Virginia slaves laid twenty lashes on the back of their former master—a painful dose of his own favorite medicine. Newly emancipated slaves sometimes eagerly accepted the invitation of Union troops to join in the pillaging of their master's possessions. One freedman said that he felt that he was entitled to steal a chicken or two, since the whites had robbed him of his labor and his children.

Emancipation followed by reenslavement, or worse, was the bewildering lot of many blacks, as Union armies marched in and out of various localities. A North Carolina slave estimated that he had celebrated emancipation about twelve times. As blacks in one Texas county flocked to the free soil of the liberated county next door, their owners bushwacked them with rifle fire as they swam for

Free at Last. *A black family in South Carolina photographed just after emancipation. Three generations are apparently present here, suggesting the cohesiveness and endurance of the Afro-American family, despite the harshness of slavery. (Library of Congress)*

freedom across the river that marked the county line. The next day, trees along the riverbank were bent with swinging corpses—a grisly warning to others dreaming of liberty.

Prodded by the bayonets of Yankee armies of occupation, all masters were eventually forced to recognize their slaves' permanent freedom. The once-commanding planter would assemble his former human chattels in front of the porch of the "big house," and announce their liberty. This "Day of Jubilo" was the occasion of wild rejoicing. Tens of thousands of blacks naturally took to the roads. They sought long-separated loved ones, as formalizing a "slave marriage" was the first goal of many newly free men and women. Others traveled in search of economic opportunity in the towns or in the still-wild West. Many moved simply to test their new freedom.

Desperately trying to bootstrap themselves up from slavery, blacks assembled in "Conventions of Freedmen" to fight for their newly gained rights. Led by ministers of God and freeborn blacks from the North, these conventions expressed surprisingly moderate views. But moderation could not guarantee a warm reception by embittered white Southerners. The freed blacks would need all the friends—and the power—they could find in Washington.

The Freedmen's Bureau

Abolitionists had long preached that slavery was a degrading institution. Now the emancipators had to face the brutal truth that the former slaves were in many ways indeed degraded. The freedmen were overwhelmingly unskilled, unlettered, without property or money, and with scant knowledge of how to survive as free persons. To cope with this problem throughout the conquered South, Congress created the Freedmen's Bureau in 1865.

On paper at least, the bureau was intended to be a kind of primitive welfare agency. It was to provide food, clothing, and education both to freedmen and to white refugees. It was also authorized to distribute up to forty acres of abandoned or confiscated land to black settlers. The bureau achieved its greatest successes in education. It

taught an estimated 200,000 blacks to read. Many former slaves had a passion for learning, partly because they wanted to close the gap between themselves and the whites and partly because they longed to read the Word of God.

But in other areas the Bureau's accomplishments were meager—or even mischievous. It distributed virtually no land. Its local administrators often collaborated with planters in expelling blacks from towns and cajoling them into signing labor contracts to work for their former masters. Yet the white South resented the bureau as a meddlesome federal interloper that threatened to upset white racial dominance. President Andrew Johnson, who shared the white-supremacist views of most white Southerners, repeatedly tried to kill it, and it expired in 1872.

Johnson: The Tailor President

Few Presidents have ever been faced with a more perplexing sea of troubles than that confronting Andrew Johnson. What manner of man was this medium-built, dark-eyed, black-haired Tennessean, now chief executive by virtue of the bullet that killed Lincoln?

No citizen, not even Lincoln, has ever reached the White House from humbler beginnings. Born to impoverished parents in North Carolina and early orphaned, Johnson never attended school but was apprenticed to a tailor at age ten. Ambitious to get ahead, he taught himself to read, and later his wife taught him to write and do simple arithmetic. Like many another self-made man, he was inclined to overpraise his maker.

Johnson early became identified with politics in Tennessee, to which he had moved when seventeen years old. He shone as an impassioned champion of the poor whites against the planter aristocrats and excelled as a two-fisted stump speaker before angry and heckling crowds. Elected to Congress, he refused to secede with his state, and was then appointed war governor after Tennessee was partially "redeemed" by Union armies.

Destiny next thrust Johnson into the vice-presidency. Lincoln's Union party in 1864 needed to attract support from the War Democrats and other pro-Southern elements, and Johnson, a Democrat, seemed to be the ideal man.

"Old Andy" Johnson was no doubt a man of parts—unpolished parts. He was intelligent, able, forceful, and steadfastly devoted to duty and the Constitution. Yet the man who had raised himself from the tailor's bench to the president's chair was a misfit. A Southerner who did not understand the North, a Tennessean who had earned the distrust of the South, a Democrat who had never been accepted by the Republicans, a president who had never been elected to the office, he was not at home in a Republican White House. Hotheaded, contentious, and stubborn, he was the wrong man in the wrong place at the wrong time. A Reconstruction policy devised by the angels might well have failed in his tactless hands.

Presidential Reconstruction

Even before the shooting war had ended, the political war over Reconstruction had begun. Abraham Lincoln believed that the Southern states had never legally withdrawn from the Union. Their formal restoration to the Union would therefore be relatively simple. Accordingly, Lincoln in 1863 proclaimed his "10 per cent" Reconstruction plan. It decreed that a state could be reintegrated into the Union when 10 percent of its voters in the presidential election of 1860 had taken an oath of allegiance to the United States and pledged to abide by emancipation. The next step would be formal erection of a state government. Lincoln would then recognize the purified regime.

Lincoln's proclamation provoked a sharp reaction in Congress, where Republicans feared the restoration of the planter aristocracy to power and the possible re-enslavement of the blacks. Republicans therefore rammed through Congress in 1864 the Wade-Davis Bill, which required that 50 percent of a state's voters take an oath of allegiance and demanded stronger safeguards for emancipation than Lincoln's as the price of readmission. Republicans were outraged when Lincoln "pocketvetoed" this bill by refusing to sign it after Congress had adjourned.

The controversy surrounding the Wade-Davis Bill had revealed deep differences between the president and Congress. Unlike Lincoln, many in Congress insisted that the seceders had indeed left the Union—had "committed suicide" as republican states—and had therefore forfeited all their rights. They could be readmitted only as "conquered provinces" on such conditions as Congress should decree.

The episode further revealed differences among two emerging Republican factions, moderates and radicals. The majority moderate group tended to agree with Lincoln that the seceded states should be restored to the Union as simply and swiftly as reasonable—though on Congress's terms, not the president's. The minority radical group believed that before the South could be restored its social structure should be uprooted, the haughty planters punished, and the helpless blacks protected by federal power.

Some radicals hoped that spiteful "Andy" Johnson, who shared their hatred for the planter aristocracy, would also share their desire to reconstruct the South with a rod of iron. But Johnson soon disillusioned them. He quickly recognized several of Lincoln's 10 percent governments, and on May 29, 1865, he issued his own Reconstruction proclamation. It disfranchised certain leading Confederates, though they might petition him for personal pardons, and called for special state conventions, which were required to repeal secession, repudiate all Confederate debts, and ratify the slave-freeing Thirteenth Amendment.

Johnson, savoring his dominance over the high-toned aristocrats who now begged his favor, granted pardons in abundance. Bolstered by the political resurrection of the planter elite, the recently rebellious states moved rapidly in the second half of 1865 to organize governments. But as the pattern of the new governments became clear, Republicans of all stripes grew furious.

The Baleful Black Codes

Among the first acts of the new Southern regimes sanctioned by Johnson was the passage of the iron-toothed Black Codes. These laws were designed to regulate the affairs of the emancipated blacks, much as the slave statutes had done in pre–Civil War days. The Black Codes aimed, first of all, to ensure a stable labor supply. Severe penalties were therefore imposed on blacks who "jumped" their labor contracts, which usually committed them to work for the same employer for one year, and generally at pittance wages.

The codes also sought to restore as nearly as possible the pre-emancipation system of race relations. Freedom was legally recognized, as were some other privileges, such as the right to marry. But all the codes forbade blacks to serve on juries or vote, and some even barred them from renting or leasing land.

These oppressive laws mocked the ideal of freedom, so recently purchased by buckets of blood. The Black Codes imposed terrible burdens on the blacks, struggling against ignorance and poverty to make their way as free persons. Thousands of impoverished former slaves, as well as many landless whites, slipped into virtual peonage as indebted sharecrop farmers.

The Black Codes made an ugly impression in the North. If the former slaves were being re-enslaved, people asked one another, had not the Boys in Blue spilled their blood in vain? Had the North really won the war?

Congressional Reconstruction

These questions grew more insistent when the congressional delegations from the newly reconstituted Southern states presented themselves in the Capitol in December 1865. To the shock and disgust of the Republicans, many former Confederate leaders were on hand to claim their seats.

The appearance of these ex-rebels was a natural but costly blunder. Voters of the South, seeking able representatives, had turned instinctively to their experienced statesmen. But most of the Southern leaders were tainted by active association with the "lost cause." Among them were four former Confederate generals, five colonels, and various members of the Richmond cabinet and Congress. Worst of all, there was the shrimpy but brainy Alexander Stephens, ex-vice-president of the Confederacy, still under indictment for treason.

The presence of these "whitewashed rebels" infuriated the Republicans in Congress. The war had been fought to restore the Union, but not on these kinds of terms. Many Republicans balked at giving up the political advantage they had enjoyed while the South had been "out" from 1861 to 1865. On the first day of the congressional session, December 4, 1865, they banged shut the door in the face of the newly elected Southern delegations.

Looking to the future, Republicans had good reason to fear that a restored South would be stronger than ever in national politics. Before the war a black slave had counted as three-fifths of a person in apportioning Congressional representation, but now, owing to full counting of free blacks, the eleven rebel states were entitled to twelve more votes in Congress, and twelve more electoral votes, than they had previously enjoyed. Again, angry voices in the North raised the cry: Who won the war, anyway?

Republicans had good reason to fear that ultimately they might be elbowed aside. Southerners might join hands with Democrats in the North and win control of Congress or maybe even the White House. If this happened, they could perpetuate the Black Codes, perhaps even formally re-enslave the blacks. They could dismantle the economic program of the Republican party, and possibly repudiate the national debt. President

Principal Reconstruction Proposals and Plans

Year	Proposal or Plan
1864–1865	Lincoln's 10 percent proposal
1865–1866	Johnson's version of Lincoln's proposal
1866–1867	Congressional plan: 10 percent plan with Fourteenth Amendment
1867–1877	Congressional plan of military Reconstruction: Fourteenth Amendment plus black suffrage, later established nationwide by Fifteenth Amendment

Johnson thus deeply provoked the congressional Republicans when he announced on December 6, 1865, that the recently rebellious states had satisfied his conditions and that in his view the Union was now restored.

Johnson Clashes With Congress

A clash between president and Congress was now inevitable. It exploded into the open in February 1866, when the president vetoed a bill (later repassed) extending the life of the controversial Freedmen's Bureau.

Aroused, the Republicans swiftly struck back. In March 1866 they passed the Civil Rights Bill, which conferred on the blacks the privileges of American citizenship and struck at the Black Codes. President Johnson resolutely vetoed this forward-looking measure, but in April congressmen steamrollered it over his veto—something they repeatedly did henceforth. The hapless president, dubbed "Sir Veto" and "Andy Veto," had his presidential wings clipped short, as Congress assumed the dominant role in running the government.

The Republicans now undertook to rivet the principles of the Civil Rights Bill into the Constitution as the Fourteenth Amendment. The proposed amendment, as approved by Congress and sent to the states in June 1866, was sweeping. It (1) conferred civil rights, including citizenship but excluding the franchise, on the freedmen; (2) reduced proportionately the representation of a state in Congress and in the Electoral College if it denied the blacks the ballot; (3) disqualified from federal and state office former Confederates who as federal officeholders had once sworn to "support the Constitution of the United States"; and (4) guaranteed the federal debt, while repudiating all Confederate debts. (See text of Fourteenth Amendment in the Appendix.)

The radical faction was disappointed that the Fourteenth Amendment did not grant the right to vote, but all Republicans agreed that no state should be welcomed back into the Union fold without first ratifying the Fourteenth Amendment. Yet

An Inflexible President. *This Republican cartoon shows Johnson knocking blacks out of the Freedmen's Bureau by his veto. (Thomas Nast,* Harper's Weekly, *1866)*

President Johnson advised the Southern states to reject it, and all of the "sinful eleven," except Tennessee, defiantly spurned the amendment.

Swinging 'Round the Circle with Johnson

As 1866 lengthened, the battle grew between the Congress and the president. Now the issue was whether Reconstruction was to be carried on with or without the drastic Fourteenth Amendment. The Republicans would settle for nothing less.

The crucial congressional elections of 1866— more crucial than some presidential elections—

were fast approaching. President Johnson was naturally eager to escape from the clutch of Congress by securing a majority favorable to his soft-on-the-South policy. Invited to dedicate a Chicago monument to Stephen A. Douglas, he undertook to speak at various cities en route in support of his views.

Johnson's famous "swing around the circle," beginning in the late summer of 1866, was a seriocomedy of errors. The president delivered a series of "give 'em hell" speeches, in which he accused the radicals in Congress of having planned large-scale antiblack riots and murder in the South. As he spoke, hecklers hurled insults at him. Reverting to his stump-speaking days in Tennessee, he shouted back angry retorts, amid cries of "You be damned" and "Don't get mad, Andy." The dignity of his high office sank to a new low.

As a vote-getter, Johnson was highly successful—for the opposition. His inept speechmaking heightened the cry "Stand by Congress" against the "Tailor of the Potomac." When the ballots were counted, the Republicans had rolled up more than a two-thirds majority in both Houses of Congress.

Republican Reconstruction

The Republicans now had a veto-proof Congress and virtually unlimited control of Reconstruction policy. But moderates and radicals still disagreed over the best course to pursue in the South.

The radicals were led in the Senate by courtly and principled Charles Sumner, and in the House by crusty and vindictive Thaddeus Stevens, both devoted not only to black freedom but to racial equality. Still opposed to rapid restoration of the Southern states, the radicals wanted to keep them out as long as possible, and apply federal power to bring about a drastic social and economic transformation in the South.

Moderate Republicans, more attuned to time-honored Republican principles of states' rights and self-government, preferred policies that restrained the states from abridging citizens' rights, rather than policies that directly involved the federal government in individual lives. The actual policies adopted by Congress showed the influence of both

these schools of thought, though the moderates, as the majority faction, had the upper hand. And one thing both groups agreed on by 1867 was the necessity to enfranchise black voters, even if it took federal troops to do it.

Against a backdrop of vicious and bloody race riots that had erupted in several Southern cities, Congress passed the Military Reconstruction Act of March 2, 1867. This drastic legislation divided the South into five military districts, each commanded by a Union general and policed by blue-clad soldiers, about twenty thousand all told.

Congress additionally laid down stringent requirements for the readmission of the seceded states. The wayward sisters were required to ratify the Fourteenth Amendment, giving the former slaves their rights as citizens, and to guarantee in their state constitutions full suffrage for their former adult male slaves. Yet the act, reflecting moderate sentiment, stopped short of giving the freedmen land or education at federal expense. The overriding purpose of the moderates was to create an electorate in Southern states that would vote those states back into the Union on acceptable terms and thus free the federal government from direct responsibility for the protection of black rights. As later events would demonstrate, this approach proved woefully inadequate to the cause of justice for the blacks.

Radical Republicans, still worried that unrepentent states, once readmitted, would amend their constitutions to withdraw the ballot from the blacks, sought the ironclad safeguard of incorporating black suffrage in the federal Constitution. This goal was finally achieved by the Fifteenth Amendment passed by Congress in 1869 and ratified by the required number of states in 1870. (For text, see the Appendix.)

Military Reconstruction of the South not only usurped certain functions of the president as commander in chief but set up a martial regime of dubious legality. The Supreme Court had already ruled, in the case *Ex parte Milligan* (1866), that military tribunals could not try civilians, even during wartime, in areas where the civil courts were open. Peacetime military rule seemed starkly con-

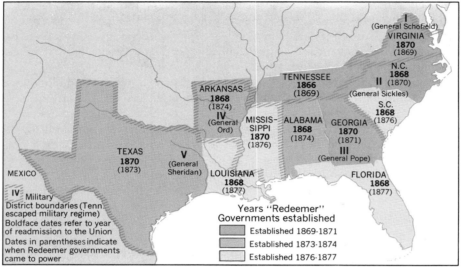

Military Reconstruction, 1867 (five districts and commanding generals). *For many white Southerners, military Reconstruction amounted to turning the knife in the wound of defeat. An often-repeated story of later years had a Southerner remark, "I was sixteen years old before I discovered that damnyankee was two words."*

Presidential Electoral Vote by Party.

trary to the spirit of the Constitution, but for the time being the Supreme Court avoided giving offense to the Republican Congress.

Prodded into line by federal bayonets, the Southern states got on with the task of constitution making. By 1870 all of them had reorganized their governments and had been accorded full rights. The hated "bluebellies" were withdrawn from police work only when the new regimes—usually called "radical" regimes—seemed to be firmly entrenched. Finally, in 1877, the last federal muskets were removed from state politics.

The Realities of Radical Reconstruction in the South

The blacks now had freedom, of a sort. By 1867 Republican hesitation over black voting had given way to a hard determination to enfranchise the former slaves wholesale and immediately, while thousands of white Southerners were being denied the right to vote. By glaring contrast most of the

Northern states, before ratification of the Fifteenth Amendment in 1870, withheld the ballot from their tiny black minorities. White Southerners naturally concluded that the Republicans were being hypocritical in insisting that blacks in the South be allowed to vote.

How well did the radical regimes rule? Black voters made up a majority of the electorate in five states, but only in South Carolina did blacks predominate in the lower house of the legislature. Many of the newly elected black legislators were literate and able; more than a few came from the ranks of the prewar free blacks who had acquired considerable education. More than a dozen black congressmen and two black United States senators, Hiram Revels and Blanche K. Bruce, both of Mississippi, did creditable work in the national capital.

Yet in many Southern capitals, former slaves held offices, to the bitter resentment of their one-time masters. Some untutored blacks fell under the control of white "scalawags" (Southerners who collaborated in creating the new regimes) and "carpetbaggers" (Northerners who had come South at war's end to seek their fortune).

In many radical regimes, graft did run rampant. This was especially true in South Carolina and Louisiana, where conscienceless promoters and other pocket-padders used politically inexperienced blacks as cat's-paws. The worst "black-and-white" legislatures purchased, as "legislative supplies," such "stationery" as hams, perfumes, suspenders, bonnets, corsets, champagne, and a coffin. Yet this sort of corruption was no worse than the scams and felonies being perpetrated in the North at the same time, especially in Boss Tweed's New York.

The radical legislatures also passed many desirable reforms. For the first time in Southern history, steps were taken toward establishing adequate public schools. Tax systems were streamlined; public works were launched; and property rights were guaranteed to women. Many of these reforms were so welcome that they were retained by the all-white "redeemer" governments that later returned to power.

Knights of the White Sheet

Deeply embittered, some Southern whites resorted to savage measures against "Radical" rule. Many whites resented the success and ability of black legislators as much as they resented alleged "corruption." A number of secret organizations mushroomed forth, the most notorious of which was the "Invisible Empire of the South," or Ku Klux Klan, founded in Tennessee in 1866. Besheeted night riders, their horses' hoofs muffled, would approach the cabin of an "upstart" black and hammer on the door. In ghoulish tones one thirsty horseman would demand a bucket of water. Then, under pretense of drinking, he would pour it into a rubber attachment concealed beneath his mask and gown, smack his lips, and declare that this was the first water he had tasted since he was killed at the Battle of Shiloh. If fright did not produce the desired effect, force was employed.

Such tomfoolery and terror proved partially effective. Many ex-bondsmen and white "carpet-

Persons in United States Lynched [by race], 1882–1970*

Year	Whites	Blacks	Total
1882	64	49	113
1885	110	74	184
1890	11	85	96
1895	66	113	179
1900	9	106	115
1905	5	57	62
1910	9	67	76
1915	13	56	69
1920	8	53	61
1925	0	17	17
1930	1	20	21
1935	2	18	20
1940	1	4	5
1945	0	1	1
1950	1	1	2
1965	0	0	0

* There were no lynchings in 1965–1970. In every year from 1882 (when records were first kept) to 1964, the number of lynchings corresponded roughly to the figures here given. The worst year was 1892, when 161 blacks and 69 whites were lynched (total 230); the next worst was 1884, when 160 whites and 51 blacks were lynched (total 211).

baggers," quick to take a hint, shunned the polls. But those stubborn souls who persisted in their "upstart" ways were flogged, mutilated, or even murdered.

Congress, outraged by this night-riding lawlessness, passed the harsh Force Acts of 1870 and 1871. Federal troops were able to stamp out much of the "lash law," but by this time the "Invisible Empire" had already done its work of intimidation.

Attempts to empower the blacks politically failed miserably. The white South, for many decades, openly flouted the Fourteenth and Fifteenth Amendments. Wholesale disfranchisement of the blacks, starting conspicuously about 1890, was achieved by intimidation, fraud, and trickery. Among various underhanded schemes were the literacy tests, unfairly administered by whites to the advantage of illiterate whites. In the eyes of white

Southerners, the goal of white supremacy fully justified dishonorable devices.

Johnson Walks the Impeachment Plank

Radicals meanwhile had been sharpening their hatchets for President Johnson. Not content with curbing his authority, they decided to remove him altogether by constitutional processes.*

As an initial step, Congress in 1867 passed the Tenure of Office Act—as usual over Johnson's veto. Contrary to precedent, the new law required the President to secure the consent of the Senate before he could remove his appointees, once they had been approved by that body. One purpose was to freeze into the Cabinet the secretary of war, Edwin M. Stanton, a holdover from the Lincoln administration. Though outwardly loyal to Johnson, he was secretly serving as a spy and informer for the Republicans in Congress. Another purpose was to goad Johnson into breaking the law, and thus establish grounds for his impeachment. An aroused Johnson, eager to get a test case before the Supreme Court, abruptly dismissed the two-faced Stanton early in 1868.

A radical-influenced House of Representatives struck back swiftly. By a count of 126 to 47, it voted to impeach Andrew Johnson for "high crimes and misdemeanors," as called for by the Constitution. Most of the specific accusations grew out of the president's so-called violation of the Tenure of Office Act, which Johnson considered unconstitutional. Two additional articles related to Johnson's verbal assaults on the Congress, involving "disgrace, ridicule, hatred, contempt, and reproach."

A Not-Guilty Verdict for Johnson

With evident zeal, the Senate now sat as a court to try Johnson on the dubious impeachment charges. The House conducted the prosecution. The trial aroused intense public interest and, with 1,000 tickets printed, proved to be the biggest show of

1868. Johnson kept his dignity and sobriety, and maintained a discreet silence. His battery of attorneys was extremely able, while the House prosecutors, including oily-tongued Benjamin F. Butler and embittered Thaddeus Stevens, bungled their case.

On May 16, 1868, the day for the first voting in the Senate, the tension was electric, and heavy breathing was heard in the galleries. By a margin of only one vote, the radicals failed to muster the two-thirds majority for Johnson's removal.

The radicals were infuriated. "The country is going to the Devil!" cried the crippled Stevens as he was carried from the hall. The nation, though violently aroused, accepted the verdict with a good temper that did credit to its political maturity. In a less stable republic, an armed uprising might have erupted against the President.

The nation thus narrowly avoided a bad precedent that would have gravely weakened one of the three branches of the federal government. Johnson was clearly guilty of bad speeches, bad judgment, and bad temper, but not of "high crimes and misdemeanors." From the standpoint of the radicals, his greatest crime had been to stand inflexibly in their path.

The Purchase of Alaska

Johnson's administration, though largely reduced to a figurehead, achieved its most enduring success in the field of foreign relations.

The Russians by 1867 were in a mood to sell the vast and chilly expanse now known as Alaska. The region had been ruthlessly "furred out" and was a growing economic liability. The Russians were therefore eager to unload their "frozen asset" on the Americans, primarily because they wanted to strengthen further the republic as a barrier against their ancient enemy, Britain.

In 1867 Secretary of State Seward, an ardent expansionist, signed a treaty with Russia which transferred Alaska to the United States for the bargain price of $7.2 million. But Seward's enthusiasm for these frigid wastes was not shared by his ignorant or uninformed countrymen, who jeered at "Seward's Folly," "Seward's Icebox," "Frigidia,"

---

*For impeachment, see Art. I, Sec. II, para. 5; Art. I, Sec. II, paras. 6, 7; Art. II, Sec. IV, in Appendix.

and "Walrussia." The American people, still preoccupied with Reconstruction and other internal vexations, were extremely economy-minded and anti-expansionist.

Then why did Congress and the American public sanction the purchase? For one thing Russia, alone among the powers, had been conspicuously friendly to the North during the recent Civil War. Americans did not feel that they could offend their great and good friend, the czar, by hurling his walrus-covered icebergs back into his face. Besides, the territory was rumored to be teeming with furs, fish, and gold, and it could "pan out" profitably—as it did, with natural resources, including oil and gas.

The Heritage of Reconstruction

Many white Southerners regarded Reconstruction as a more grievous wound than the war itself. It left an angry scar that would take generations to heal. They resented the upending of their social and racial system, the humiliation of being ruled by blacks, and the insult of federal intervention in their local affairs. Yet given the explosiveness of the issues that had caused the war, and the bitterness of the fighting, the wonder is that Reconstruction was not far harsher than it was. Most policymakers had

no clear picture of what federal policy toward the South should be, and were influenced as much by Southern responses to defeat and emancipation as by any specific plans of their own.

The Republicans acted from a mixture of idealism and political expediency. They wanted both to protect the freed slaves and to promote the fortunes of the Republican party. In the end, their efforts backfired badly. Republican Reconstruction conferred only fleeting benefits on the blacks, envenomed the whites, and virtually extinguished the Republican party in the South for nearly one hundred years.

In the light of hindsight, the Republican Reconstruction program seems too narrowly conceived. Moderate Republicans in particular never appreciated the efforts necessary to make the freed slaves completely independent citizens, nor the lengths to which Southern whites would go to preserve their system of racial dominance. Had the radicals' program of drastic economic reforms and heftier protection of political rights been enacted, things might have been different. But ingrained American resistance to tampering with property rights and violating the principle of local self-government, combined with spreading indifference in the North to the plight of the blacks, formed too formidable an obstacle.

VARYING VIEWPOINTS

Few topics have triggered as much intellectual warfare as the "dark and bloody ground" of Reconstruction. The period provoked questions—sectional, racial, and constitutional—about which people felt deeply and remain deeply divided even today. Scholarly argument goes back to the early years of the twentieth century, when historian William A. Dunning and his students wrote about Reconstruction as a kind of national disgrace, foisted upon a prostrate South by vindictive, self-seeking radical Republican politicians. Influenced by the spirit

of sectional reconciliation as well as by current theories about black racial inferiority, these writers sympathized with the white South. Except for black historian W. E. B. DuBois's *Black Reconstruction* (1935), the "Dunning school" held almost total sway on the topic until World War II.

After the Second World War, the spread of more egalitarian racial attitudes and the conviction that ideals counted in the controversy led to a new examination of the Dunning approach. Historians now showed much more interest in the real problems of the black freedmen, more admiration for the "helpful" radical Republicans as genuine idealists rather than as self-seeking politicians, and less sympathy for the beaten and defiant white South. Kenneth Stampp's *Era of Reconstruction* (1965) probably best summarizes these newer views.

Recent trends in Reconstruction scholarship have reinforced this "revisionist" view.

First, historians have concentrated on the earliest stages of Reconstruction, concluding that Lincoln was more sympathetic to the radicals than was Johnson and would probably have pursued a vigorous policy. Second, economic analyses have lent credence to the radicals' claim that only a drastic transformation of Southern society could secure fair treatment for the freedmen.

SELECT READINGS

Primary Source Documents

Booker T. Washington's classic autobiography *Up from Slavery** (1901) records one freedman's experiences. Contemporary comments on the process of Reconstruction include the laments of editor Edwin L. Godkin, *The Nation* (December 7, 1871, p. 364),* and Frederick Douglass, *The Life and Times of Frederick Douglass** (1882), as well as the debates in the *Congressional Globe* (1867–1868)* between radicals like Thaddeus Stevens and moderates like Lyman Trumbull.

Secondary Sources

Overall accounts may be found in James G. Randall and David Donald, *The Civil War and Reconstruction* (rev. ed., 1969) and James McPherson, *Ordeal By Fire: The Civil War and Reconstruction* (1981), perhaps the best brief introduction. Lincoln's early efforts at Reconstruction are handled in Peyton McCrary, *Abraham Lincoln and Reconstruction* (1978). Dan Carter, *When the War Was Over: The Failure of Self-Reconstruction in the South, 1865–1867* (1985) charts the first years of the period. Following up the story of national politics is Eric L. McKitrick, *Andrew Johnson and Reconstruction: Principle and Prejudice, 1865–1866* (1963). Sympathethic to the radical Republicans are James M. McPherson, *The Struggle for Equality* (1964) and Hans L. Trefousse, *The Radical Republicans* (1969). Conditions in the South are analyzed in W. E. B. DuBois' controversial classic *Black Reconstruction* (1935) and in Leon F. Litwack's brilliantly evocative *Been in the Storm So Long* (1979), a revealing study of the initial responses, by both whites and blacks, to emancipation. Race relations is the subject of Joel Williamson, *The Crucible of Race* (1984). C. Vann Woodward's *The Strange Career of Jim Crow* (rev. ed., 1974) is a classic study of the origins of segregation. New scholarship is presented in Kenneth M. Stampp and Leon Litwack, eds., *Reconstruction: An Anthology of Revisionist Writings* (1969) and Robert P. Swierenga, *Beyond the Civil War Synthesis* (1975). Eric Foner looks at emancipation in a comparative perspective in *Nothing but Freedom* (1983). A comprehensive study of the climax of this troubled period is William Gillette, *Retreat from Reconstruction, 1869–1879* (1979).

Appendix

DECLARATION OF INDEPENDENCE
In Congress, July 4, 1776

The Unanimous Declaration of the Thirteen United States of America

[Bracketed material in color has been inserted by the authors. For adoption background, see p. 67.]

When, in the course of human events, it becomes necessary for one people to dissolve the political bands which have connected them with another, and to assume, among the powers of the earth, the separate and equal station to which the laws of nature and of nature's God entitle them, a decent respect to the opinions of mankind requires that they should declare the causes which impel them to the separation.

We hold these truths to be self-evident: That all men are created equal; that they are endowed by their Creator with certain unalienable rights; that among these are life, liberty, and the pursuit of happiness; that, to secure these rights, governments are instituted among men, deriving their just powers from the consent of the governed; that whenever any form of government becomes destructive of these ends, it is the right of the people to alter or to abolish it, and to institute new government, laying its foundation on such principles, and organizing its powers in such form, as to them shall seem most likely to effect their safety and happiness. Prudence, indeed, will dictate that governments long established should not be changed for light and transient causes; and accordingly all experience hath shown that mankind are more disposed to suffer, while evils are sufferable, than to right themselves by abolishing the forms to which they are accustomed. But when a long train of abuses and usurpations, pursuing invariably the same object, envinces a design to reduce them under absolute despotism, it is their right, it is their duty, to throw off such government, and to provide new guards for their future security. Such has been the patient sufferance of these colonies; and such is now the necessity which constrains them to alter their former systems of government. The history of the present King of Great Britain is a history of repeated injuries and usurpations, all having in direct object the establishment of an absolute tyranny over these states. To prove this, let facts be submitted to a candid world.

He has refused his assent to laws, the most wholesome and necessary for the public good. [See royal veto, p. 54.]

He has forbidden his governors to pass laws of immediate and pressing importance, unless suspended in their operation till his assent should be obtained; and, when so suspended, he has utterly neglected to attend to them.

He has refused to pass other laws for the accommodation of large districts of people [by establishing new counties], unless those people would relinquish the right of representation in the legislature, a right inestimable to them, and formidable to tyrants only.

He has called together legislative bodies at places unusual, uncomfortable, and distant from the depository of their public records, for the sole purpose of fatiguing them into compliance with his measures [e.g., removal of Massachusetts Assembly to Salem, 1774].

He has dissolved representative houses repeatedly, for opposing, with manly firmness, his invasions on the rights of the people [e.g., Virginia Assembly, 1765].

He has refused for a long time, after such dissolutions, to cause others to be elected; whereby the legislative powers, incapable of annihilation, have returned to the people at large for their exercise; the state remaining, in the mean time, exposed to all the dangers of invasions from without and convulsions within.

He has endeavored to prevent the population [populating] of these states; for that purpose obstructing the laws for naturalization of foreigners; refusing to pass others to encourage their migration hither, and raising the conditions of new appropriations of lands. [e.g., Proclamation of 1763, pp. 49–50].

He has obstructed the administration of justice, by refusing his assent to laws for establishing judiciary powers.

He has made judges dependent on his will alone, for the tenure of their offices, and the amount and payment of their salaries. [See Townshend Acts, p. 57.]

He has erected a multitude of new offices, and sent hither swarms of officers to harass our people and eat out their substance. [See enforcement of Navigation Laws, pp. 53–54.]

He has kept among us, in times of peace, standing armies, without the consent of our legislatures. [See p. 55.]

He has affected to render the military independent of, and superior to, the civil power.

He has combined with others to subject us to a jurisdiction foreign to our constitution, and unacknowledged by our laws, giving his assent to their acts of pretended legislation:

For quartering large bodies of armed troops among us [see Boston Massacre, p. 57];

For protecting them, by a mock trial, from punishment for any murders which they should commit on the inhabitants of these states [see 1774 Act, p. 59];

For cutting off our trade with all parts of the world [see Boston Port Act, p. 59];

For imposing taxes on us without our consent [see Stamp Act, p. 55];

For depriving us, in many cases, of the benefits of trial by jury;

For transporting us beyond seas, to be tried for pretended offenses;

For abolishing the free system of English laws in a neighboring province [Quebec], establishing therein an arbitrary government, and enlarging its boundaries, so as to render it at once an example and fit instrument for introducing the same absolute rule into these colonies [Quebec Act, p. 59];

For taking away our charters, abolishing our most valuable laws, and altering fundamentally the forms of our governments [e.g., in Massachusetts, p. 59];

For suspending our own legislatures, and declaring themselves invested with power to legislate for us in all cases whatsoever [see Stamp Act repeal, pp. 56–57].

He has abdicated government here, by declaring us out of his protection and waging war against us [Proclamation, p. 65].

He has plundered our seas, ravaged our coasts, burned our towns, and destroyed the lives of our people [e.g., the burning of Falmouth (Portland), p. 65].

He is at this time transporting large armies of foreign mercenaries [Hessians, p. 65] to complete the works of death, desolation, and tyranny already begun with circumstances of cruelty and perfidy scarcely paralleled in the most barbarous ages, and totally unworthy the head of a civilized nation.

He has constrained our fellow-citizens, taken captive on the high seas [by impressment], to bear arms against their country, to become the executioners of their friends and brethren, or to fall themselves by their hands.

He has excited domestic insurrection among us [i.e., among slaves], and has endeavored to bring on the inhabitants of our frontiers the merciless Indian savages, whose known rule of warfare is an undistinguished destruction of all ages, sexes, and conditions.

In every stage of these oppressions we have petitioned for redress in the most humble terms; our repeated petitions have been answered only by repeated injury [e.g., pp. 64–65]. A prince, whose character is thus marked by every act which may define a tyrant, is unfit to be the ruler of a free people.

Nor have we been wanting in our attentions to our British brethren. We have warned them, from time to time, of attempts by their legislature to extend an unwarrantable jurisdiction over us. We have reminded them of the circumstances of our emigration and settlement here. We have appealed to their native justice and magnanimity; and we have conjured them, by the ties of our common kindred, to disavow these usurpations, which would inevitably interrupt our connections and correspondence. They, too, have been deaf to the voice of justice and of consanguinity [blood relationship]. We must, therefore, acquiesce in the necessity which denounces [announces] our separation, and hold them, as we hold the rest of mankind, enemies in war, in peace friends.

We, therefore, the representatives of the United States of America, in General Congress assembled, appealing to the Supreme Judge of the world for the rectitude of our intentions, do, in the name and by the authority of the good people of these colonies, solemnly publish and declare, That these United Colonies are, and of right ought to be, FREE AND INDEPENDENT STATES; that they are absolved from all allegiance to the British crown, and that all political connection between them and the state of Great Britain is, and ought to be, totally dissolved; and that, as free and independent states, they have full power to levy war, conclude peace, contract alliances, establish commerce, and do all other acts and things which independent states may of right do. And for the support of this declaration, with a firm reliance on the protection of Divine Providence, we mutually pledge to each other our lives, our fortunes, and our sacred honor.

[Signed by]   JOHN HANCOCK [President]
                                                               [and fifty-five others]

CONSTITUTION OF
THE UNITED STATES OF AMERICA

[Boldface headings and bracketed explanatory matter and marginal comments (both in color) have been inserted for the reader's convenience. Passages that are no longer operative are printed in italic type.]

PREAMBLE

On "We the people," see p. 153n.

We the people of the United States, in order to form a more perfect union, establish justice, insure domestic tranquillity, provide for the common defense, promote the general welfare, and secure the blessings of liberty to ourselves and our posterity, do ordain and establish this CONSTITUTION for the United States of America.

Article I. Legislative Department

Section I. Congress

Legislative power vested in a two-House Congress. All legislative powers herein granted shall be vested in a Congress of the United States, which shall consist of a Senate and a House of Representatives.

Section II. House of Representatives

1. The people elect representatives biennially. The House of Representatives shall be composed of members chosen every second year by the people of the several States, and the electors [voters] in each State shall have the qualifications requisite for electors of the most numerous branch of the State Legislature.

2. Who may be representatives. No person shall be a Representative who shall not have attained to the age of twenty-five years, and been seven years a citizen of the United States, and who shall not, when elected, be an inhabitant of that State in which he shall be chosen.

See 1787 compromise, pp. 83–84.

See 1787 compromise p. 84.

3. Representation in the House based on population; census. Representatives and direct taxes[1] shall be apportioned among the several States which may be included within this Union, according to their respective numbers, *which shall be determined by adding to the whole number of free persons, including those bound to service for a term of years* [apprentices and indentured servants], *and excluding Indians not taxed, three-fifths of all other persons* [slaves].[2] The actual enumeration [census] shall be made within three years after the first meeting of the Congress of the United States, and within every subsequent term of ten years, in such manner as they shall by law direct. The number of Representatives shall not exceed one for every thirty thousand, but each State shall have at least one Representative; *and until such enumeration shall be made, the State of New Hampshire shall be entitled to choose three, Massachusetts eight, Rhode Island and Providence Plantations one, Connecticut five, New York six, New Jersey four, Pennsylvania eight, Delaware one, Maryland six, Virginia ten, North Carolina five, South Carolina five, and Georgia three.*

4. Vacancies in the House are filled by election. When vacancies happen in the representation from any State, the Executive authority [governor] thereof shall issue writs of election [call a special election] to fill such vacancies.

See Johnson trial, p. 282; Nixon trial preliminaries, pp. 514–515.

5. The House selects its Speaker; has sole power to vote impeachment charges (i.e., indictments). The House of Representatives shall choose their Speaker and other officers; and shall have the sole power of impeachment.

---

[1] Modified in 1913 by the 16th Amendment re income taxes.

[2] The word *slave* appears nowhere in the Constitution; *slavery* appears in the 13th Amendment. The three-fifths rule ceased to be in force when the 13th Amendment was adopted in 1865 (see p. 256 and text of Amendments following).

Section III.   *Senate*

1. Senators represent the states. The Senate of the United States shall be composed of two Senators from each State, *chosen by the legislature thereof,* [1] for six years; and each Senator shall have one vote.

2. One-third of Senators chosen every two years; vacancies. *Immediately after they shall be assembled in consequence of the first election, they shall be divided as equally as may be into three classes. The seats of the Senators of the first class shall be vacated at the expiration of the second year, of the second class at the expiration of the fourth year, and of the third class at the expiration of the sixth year,* so that one-third may be chosen every second year; *and if vacancies happen by resignation or otherwise, during the recess of the legislature of any State, the Executive* [governor] *thereof may make temporary appointments until the next meeting of the legislature, which shall fill such vacancies.* [2]

3. Who may be Senators. No person shall be a Senator who shall not have attained to the age of thirty years, and been nine years a citizen of the United States, and who shall not, when elected, be an inhabitant of that State for which he shall be chosen.

4. The Vice-President presides over the Senate. The Vice-President of the United States shall be President of the Senate, but shall have no vote, unless they be equally divided [tied].

5. The Senate chooses its other officers. The Senate shall choose their other officers, and also a President *pro tempore,* in the absence of the Vice-President, or when he shall exercise the office of President of the United States.

See Johnson trial, p. 282.

6. The Senate has sole power to try impeachments. The Senate shall have the sole power to try all impeachments. When sitting for that purpose, they shall be on oath or affirmation. When the President of the United States is tried, the Chief Justice shall preside:[3] and no person shall be convicted without the concurrence of two-thirds of the members present.

7. Penalties for impeachment conviction. Judgment in cases of impeachment shall not extend further than to removal from office, and disqualification to hold and enjoy any office of honor, trust or profit under the United States: but the party convicted shall nevertheless be liable and subject to indictment, trial, judgment and punishment, according to law.

Section IV.   Election and Meetings of Congress

1. Regulation of elections. The times, places and manner of holding elections for Senators and Representatives shall be prescribed in each State by the legislature thereof; but the Congress may at any time by law make or alter such regulations, except as to the places of choosing Senators.

2. Congress must meet once a year. The Congress shall assemble at least once in every year, and such meeting *shall be on the first Monday in December, unless they shall by law appoint a different day.* [4]

Section V.   Organization and Rules of the Houses

1. Each house may reject members; quorums. Each house shall be the judge of the elections, returns and qualifications of its own members, and a majority of each shall constitute a quorum to do business; but a smaller number may adjourn from day to day, and may be authorized to compel the attendance of absent members, in such manner, and under such penalties, as each house may provide.

---

[1] Repealed in favor of popular election in 1913 by the 17th Amendment.
[2] Changed in 1913 by the 17th Amendment.
[3] The Vice-President, as next in line, would be an interested party.
[4] Changed in 1933 to January 3 by the 20th Amendment (see p. 442 and text of Amendments).

*See "Bully"
Brooks case,
pp. 237–238.*

2. Each House makes its own rules. Each house may determine the rules of its proceedings, punish its members for disorderly behavior, and with the concurrence of two-thirds, expel a member.

3. Each House must keep and publish a record of its proceedings. Each house shall keep a journal of its proceedings, and from time to time publish the same, excepting such parts as may in their judgment require secrecy; and the yeas and nays of the members of either house on any question shall, at the desire of one-fifth of those present, be entered on the journal.

4. Both Houses must agree on adjournment. Neither house, during the session of congress, shall, without the consent of the other, adjourn for more than three days, nor to any other place than that in which the two houses shall be sitting.

Section VI.   Privileges of and Prohibitions upon Congressmen

1. Congressional salaries; immunities. The Senators and Representatives shall receive a compensation for their services, to be ascertained by law and paid out of the treasury of the United States. They shall in all cases except treason, felony and breach of the peace, be privileged from arrest during their attendance at the session of their respective houses, and in going to and returning from the same; and for any speech or debate in either house, they shall not be questioned in any other place [i.e., they shall be immune from libel suits].

2. A Congressman may not hold any other federal civil office. No Senator or Representative shall, during the time for which he was elected, be appointed to any civil office under the authority of the United States, which shall have been created, or the emoluments whereof shall have been increased, during such time; and no person holding any office under the United States shall be a member of either house during his continuance in office.

Section VII.   Method of Making Laws

*See 1787
compromise,
p. 84.*

1. Money bills must originate in the House. All bills for raising revenue shall originate in the House of Representatives; but the Senate may propose or concur with amendments as on other bills.

President Nixon, more than any predecessors, "impounded" billions of dollars voted by Congress for specific purposes, because he disapproved of them. The courts generally failed to sustain him, and his impeachment foes regarded wholesale impoundment as a violation of his oath to "faithfully execute" the laws.

2. The President's veto power; Congress may override. Every bill which shall have passed the House of Representatives and the Senate, shall, before it become a law, be presented to the President of the United States; if he approve he shall sign it, but if not he shall return it with his objections to that house in which it shall have originated, who shall enter the objections at large on their journal, and proceed to reconsider it. If after such reconsideration two-thirds of that house shall agree to pass the bill, it shall be sent, together with the objections, to the other house, by which it shall likewise be reconsidered, and if, approved by two-thirds of that house, it shall become a law. But in all such cases the votes of both houses shall be determined by yeas and nays, and the names of the persons voting for and against the bill shall be entered on the journal of each house respectively. If any bill shall not be returned by the President within ten days (Sundays excepted) after it shall have been presented to him, the same shall be a law, in like manner as if he had signed it, unless the Congress by their adjournment prevent its return, in which case it shall not be a law [this is the so-called pocket veto].

3. All measures requiring the agreement of both Houses go to President for approval. Every order, resolution, or vote to which the concurrence of the Senate and House of Representatives may be necessary (except on a question of adjournment) shall be presented to the President of the United States; and before the same shall take effect, shall be approved by him, or being disapproved by him, shall be repassed by two-thirds of the Senate and House of Representatives, according to the rules and limitations prescribed in the case of a bill.

Section VIII.   Powers Granted to Congress

Congress has certain enumerated powers:

1. It may lay and collect taxes. The Congress shall have power to lay and collect taxes, duties, imposts, and excises, to pay the debts and provide for the common defense and general welfare of the United States; but all duties, imposts and excises shall be uniform throughout the United States;

2. It may borrow money. To borrow money on the credit of the United States;

3. It may regulate foreign and interstate trade. To regulate commerce with foreign nations, and among the several States, and with the Indian tribes;

For 1798 naturalization, see p. 105.

4. It may pass naturalization and bankruptcy laws. To establish an uniform rule of naturalization, and uniform laws on the subject of bankruptcies throughout the United States;

5. It may coin money. To coin money, regulate the value thereof, and of foreign coin, and fix the standard of weights and measures;

6. It may punish counterfeiters. To provide for the punishment of counterfeiting the securities and current coin of the United States;

7. It may establish a postal service. To establish post offices and post roads;

8. It may issue patents and copyrights. To promote the progress of science and useful arts by securing for limited times to authors and inventors the exclusive right to their respective writings and discoveries;

See Judiciary Act of 1789, p. 93.

9. It may establish inferior courts. To constitute tribunals inferior to the Supreme Court;

10. It may punish crimes committed on the high seas. To define and punish piracies and felonies committed on the high seas [i.e., outside the three-mile limit] and offenses against the law of nations [international law];

11. It may declare war; authorize privateers. To declare war,[1] grant letters of marque and reprisal,[2] and make rules concerning captures on land and water;

12. It may maintain an army. To raise and support armies, but no appropriation of money to that use shall be for a longer term than two years;[3]

13. It may maintain a navy. To provide and maintain a navy;

14. It may regulate the army and navy. To make rules for the government and regulation of the land and naval forces;

See Whiskey Rebellion, p. 96.

15. It may call out the state militia. To provide for calling forth the militia to execute the laws of the union, suppress insurrections, and repel invasions;

16. It shares with the states control of militia. To provide for organizing, arming, and disciplining the militia, and for governing such part of them as may be employed in the service of the United States, reserving to the States respectively the appointment of the officers, and the authority of training the militia according to the discipline prescribed by Congress;

17. It makes laws for the District of Columbia and other federal areas. To exercise exclusive legislation in all cases whatsoever, over such district (not exceeding ten miles square) as may, by cession of particular States, and the acceptance of Congress, become the seat of government of the United States,[4] and to exercise like authority over all places purchased by the consent of the legislature of the State, in which the same shall be, for the erection of forts, magazines, arsenals, dock-yards, and other needful buildings;—and

---

[1] Note that the President, though he can provoke war (see the case of Polk, pp. 172–174) or wage it after it is declared, cannot declare it.
[2] Papers issued private citizens in wartime authorizing them to capture enemy ships.
[3] A reflection of fear of standing armies earlier expressed in the Declaration of Independence.
[4] The District of Columbia, 10 miles square, was established in 1791 with a cession from Virginia (see p. 94).

Congress has certain implied powers:

This is the famous "Elastic Clause"; see pp. 95–96.

18. It may make laws necessary for carrying out the enumerated powers. To make all laws which shall be necessary and proper for carrying into execution the foregoing powers, and all others powers vested by this Constitution in the government of the United States, or in any department or officer thereof.

Section IX.   Powers Denied to the Federal Government

1. Congressional control of slave trade postponed until 1808. *The migration or importation of such persons as any of the States now existing shall think proper to admit shall not be prohibited by the Congress prior to the year 1808; but a tax or duty may be imposed on such importation, not exceeding $10 for each person.*

See 1787 slave compromise, pp. 83–84.

2. The writ of habeas corpus[1] **may be suspended only in case of rebellion or invasion.** The privilege of the writ of habeas corpus shall not be suspended, unless when in cases of rebellion or invasion the public safety may require it.

See Lincoln's unlawful suspension, p. 266.

3. Attainders[2] **and ex post facto laws**[3] **forbidden.** No bill of attainder or ex post facto law shall be passed.

4. Direct taxes must be apportioned according to population. No capitation [head or poll tax], or other direct, tax shall be laid, unless in proportion to the census or enumeration herein before directed to be taken.[4]

5. Export taxes forbidden. No tax or duty shall be laid on articles exported from any State.

6. Congress must not discriminate among states in regulating commerce. No preference shall be given by any regulation of commerce or revenue to the ports of one State over those of another; nor shall vessels bound to, or from, one State, be obliged to enter, clear, or pay duties in another.

7. Public money may not be spent without congressional appropriation; accounting. No money shall be drawn from the treasury, but in consequence of appropriations made by law; and a regular statement and account of the receipts and expenditures of all public money shall be published from time to time.

8. Titles of nobility prohibited; foreign gifts. No title of nobility shall be granted by the United States: and no person holding any office of profit or trust under them, shall, without the consent of the Congress, accept of any present, emolument, office, or title, of any kind whatever, from any king, prince, or foreign state.

Section X.   Powers Denied to the States

Absolute prohibitions on the states:

1. The states are forbidden to do certain things. No State shall enter into any treaty, alliance, or confederation; grant letters of marque and reprisal [i.e., authorize privateers]; coin money; emit bills of credit [issue paper money]; make anything but gold and silver coin a [legal] tender in payment of debts; pass any bill of attainder, ex post facto,[5] or law impairing the obligation of contracts, or grant any title of nobility.

On contracts, see Fletcher v. Peck, p. 139.

---

[1] A writ of habeas corpus is a document that enables a person under arrest to obtain an immediate examination in court to ascertain whether he is being legally held.

[2] A bill of attainder is a special legislative act condemning and punishing an individual without a judicial trial.

[3] An ex post facto law is one that fixes punishments for acts committed before the law was passed.

[4] Modified in 1913 by the 16th Amendment (see text of following Amendments).

[5] For definitions, see footnotes 3 and 4.

Conditional prohibitions on the states:

2. The states may not levy duties without the consent of Congress. No State shall, without the consent of the Congress, lay any imposts or duties on imports or exports, except what may be absolutely necessary for executing its inspection laws: and the net produce of all duties and imposts, laid by any State on imports or exports, shall be for the use of the treasury of the United States; and all such laws shall be subject to the revision and control of the Congress.

Cf. Confederation chaos, p. 80.

3. Certain other federal powers are forbidden the states except with the consent of Congress. No State shall, without the consent of Congress, lay any duty of tonnage [i.e., duty on ship tonnage], keep [non-militia] troops or ships of war in time of peace, enter into any agreement or compact with another State, or with a foreign power, or engage in war, unless actually invaded, or in such imminent danger as will not admit of delay.

Article II. Executive Department

Section I. President and Vice-President

1. The President the chief executive; his term. The executive power shall be vested in a President of the United States of America. He shall hold his office during the term of four years,[1] and, together with the Vice-President, chosen for the same term, be elected as follows:

See 1787 compromise, pp. 83–84.

2. The President is chosen by electors. Each State shall appoint, in such manner as the legislature thereof may direct, a number of electors, equal to the whole number of Senators and Representatives to which the State may be entitled in the Congress; but no Senator or Representative, or person holding an office of trust or profit under the United States, shall be appointed an elector.

A majority of the electoral votes needed to elect a President. *The electors shall meet in their respective States, and vote by ballot for two persons, of whom one at least shall not be an inhabitant of the same State with themselves. And they shall make a list of all the persons voted for, and of the number of votes for each; which list they shall sign and certify, and transmit sealed to the seat of government of the United States, directed to the President of the Senate. The President of the Senate shall, in the presence of the Senate and House of Representatives, open all certificates, and the votes shall then be counted. The person having the greatest number of votes shall be the President, if such number be a majority of the whole number of electors appointed; and if there be more than one who have such majority, and have an equal number of votes, then the House of Representatives shall immediately choose by ballot one of them for President; and if no person have a majority, then from the five highest on the list the said house shall in like manner choose the President. But in choosing the President the votes shall be taken by States, the representation from each State having one vote; a quorum for this purpose shall consist of a member or members from two-thirds of the States, and a majority of all the States shall be necessary to a choice. In every case, after the choice of the President, the person having the greatest number of votes of the electors shall be the Vice-President. But if there should remain two or more who have equal votes, the Senate shall choose from them by ballot the Vice-President.*[2]

See Burr-Jefferson disputed election of 1800, pp. 106–108.

See Jefferson as Vice-President in 1796, p. 103.

3. Congress decides time of meeting of Electoral College. The Congress may determine the time of choosing the electors and the day on which they shall give their votes; which day shall be the same throughout the United States.

---

[1] No reference to re-election; for anti-third term 22d Amendment, see text of Amendments following.
[2] Repealed in 1804 by the 12th Amendment (see text of Amendments following).

To provide for foreign-born like Alexander Hamilton, born in the British West Indies.

4. Who may be President. No person except a natural-born citizen, *or a citizen of the United States at the time of the adoption of this Constitution,* shall be eligible to the office of President; neither shall any person be eligible to that office who shall not have attained to the age of thirty-five years, and been fourteen years a resident within the United States [i.e., a legal resident]

Modified by Amendments XX and XXV.

5. Replacements for President. In case of the removal of the President from office or of his death, resignation, or inability to discharge the powers and duties of the said office, the same shall devolve on the Vice-President, and the Congress may by law provide for the case of removal, death, resignation, or inability, both of the President and Vice-President, declaring what officer shall then act as President, and such officer shall act accordingly, until the disability be removed, or a President shall be elected.

6. The President's salary. The President shall, at stated times, receive for his services a compensation, which shall neither be increased nor diminished during the period for which he shall have been elected, and he shall not receive within that period any other emolument from the United States, or any of them.

7. The President's oath of office. Before he enter on the execution of his office, he shall take the following oath or affirmation;—"I do solemnly swear (or affirm) that I will faithfully execute the office of the President of the United States, and will to the best of my ability preserve, protect and defend the Constitution of the United States."

Section II.   Powers of the President

1. The President has important military and civil powers. The President shall be commander in chief of the army and navy of the United States, and of the militia of the several States, when called into the actual service of the United States; he may require the opinion, in writing, of the principal officer in each of the executive departments, upon any subject relating to the duties of their respective offices, and he shall have power to grant reprieves and pardon for offenses against the United States, except in cases of impeachment.[1]

See Cabinet evolution, p. 92.

2. The President may negotiate treaties and nominate federal officials. He shall have power, by and with the advice and consent of the Senate, to make treaties, provided two-thirds of the Senators present concur; and he shall nominate, and by and with the advice and consent of the Senate, shall appoint ambassadors, other public ministers and consuls, judges of the Supreme Court, and all other officers of the United States, whose appointments are not herein otherwise provided for, and which shall be established by law: but the Congress may by law vest the appointment of such inferior officers, as they think proper, in the President alone, in the courts of law, or in the heads of departments.

For President's removal power, see p. 282.

3. The President may fill vacancies during Senate recess. The president shall have power to fill up all vacancies that may happen during the recess of the Senate, by granting commissions which shall expire at the end of their next session.

Section III.   Other Powers and Duties of the President

For President's personal appearances, see p. 341.

Messages; extra sessions; receiving ambassadors: execution of the laws. He shall from time to time give to the Congress information of the state of the Union, and recommend to their consideration such measures as he shall judge necessary and expedient; he may, on extraordinary occasions, convene both houses, or either of them, and in case of disagreement between them, with respect to the time of adjournment, he may adjourn them to such time as he shall think proper; he shall receive ambassadors and other public ministers; he shall take care that the laws be faithfully executed, and shall commission all the officers of the United States.

---

[1] To prevent the President's pardoning himself or his close associates, as was feared in the case of Richard Nixon. See pp. 514–515.

See Johnson's acquittal, p. 282; also Nixon's near impeachment, pp. 514–515.

Section IV.　Impeachment

Civil officers may be removed by impeachment. The President, Vice-President and all civil officers[1] of the United States shall be removed from office on impeachment for, and on conviction of, treason, bribery, or other high crimes and misdemeanors.

Article III.　Judicial Department

Section I.　The Federal Courts

See Judiciary Act of 1789, p. 93.

The judicial power belongs to the federal courts. The judicial power of the United States shall be vested in one Supreme Court, and in such inferior courts as the Congress may from time to time ordain and establish. The judges, both of the Supreme and inferior courts, shall hold their offices during good behavior, and shall, at stated times, receive for their services a compensation which shall not be diminished[2] during their continuance in office.

Section II.　Jursidiction of Federal Courts

1. Kinds of cases that may be heard. The judicial power shall extend to all cases, in law and equity, arising under this Constitution, the laws of the United States, and treaties made, or which shall be made, under their authority;—to all cases affecting ambassadors, other public ministers and consuls;—to all cases of admiralty and maritime jurisdiction;—to controversies to which the United States shall be a party;—to controversies between two or more States;—*between a State and citizens of another State*,[3]—between citizens of different States;—between citizens of the same State claiming lands under grants of different States, and between a State, or the citizens thereof, and foreign states, citizens or subjects.

2. Jurisdiction of the Supreme Court. In all cases affecting ambassadors, other public ministers and consuls, and those in which a State shall be party, the Supreme Court shall have original jurisdiction.[4] In all the other cases before mentioned, the Supreme Court shall have appellate jurisdiction,[5] both as to law and fact, with such exceptions, and under such regulations, as the Congress shall make.

3. Trial for federal crime is by jury. The trial of all crimes, except in cases of impeachment, shall be by jury; and such trial shall be held in the State where the said crimes shall have been committed; but when not committed within any State, the trial shall be at such place or places as the Congress may by law have directed.

Section III.　Treason

See Burr trial, pp. 115–116.

1. Treason defined. Treason against the United States shall consist only in levying war against them, or in adhering to their enemies, giving them aid and comfort. No person shall be convicted of treason unless on the testimony of two witnesses to the same overt act, or on confession in open court.

2. Congress fixes punishment for treason. The Congress shall have power to declare the punishment of treason, but no attainder of treason shall work corruption of blood, or forfeiture except during the life of the person attainted.[6]

---

[1] I.e., all federal executive and judicial officers, but not members of Congress or military personnel.
[2] In 1978, in a case involving federal judges, the Supreme Court ruled that diminution of salaries by inflation was irrelevant.
[3] The 11th Amendment (see text of Amendments following) restricts this to suits by a state against citizens of another state.
[4] I.e., such cases must originate in the Supreme Court.
[5] I.e., it hears other cases only when they are appealed to it from a lower federal court or a state court.
[6] I.e., punishment only for the offender; none for his heirs.

Article IV.   Relations of the States to One Another

Section I.   Credit to Acts, Records and Court Proceedings

Each state must respect the public acts of the others. Full faith and credit shall be given in each State to the public acts, records, and judicial proceedings of every other State.[1] And the Congress may by general laws prescribe the manner in which such acts, records, and proceedings shall be proved [attested], and the effect thereof.

Section II.   Duties of States to States

1. Citizenship in one state is valid in all. The citizens of each State shall be entitled to all privileges and immunities of citizens in the several States.

This stipulation is sometimes openly flouted. In 1978 Governor Jerry Brown of California, acting on humanitarian grounds, refused to surrender to South Dakota an American Indian, Dennis Banks, who was charged with murder in an armed uprising.

2. Fugitives from justice must be surrendered by the state to which they have fled. A person charged in any State with treason, felony, or other crime, who shall flee from justice, and be found in another State, shall on demand of the executive authority [governor] of the State from which he fled, be delivered up, to be removed to the State having jurisdiction of the crime.

Basis of fugitive slave laws; see pp. 225–227.

3. Slaves and apprentices must be returned. *No person held to service or labor in one State, under the laws thereof, escaping into another, shall, in consequence of any law or regulation therein, be discharged from such service or labor, but shall be delivered up on claim of the party to whom such service or labor may be due.*[2]

Section III.   New States and Territories

E.g., Maine (1820); see p. 137.

1. Congress may admit new states. New States may be admitted by the Congress into this Union; but no new State shall be formed or erected within the jurisdiction of any other State; nor any State be formed by the junction of two or more States, or parts of States, without the consent of the legislatures of the States concerned as well as of the Congress.[3]

2. Congress regulates federal territory and property. The Congress shall have power to dispose of and make all needful rules and regulations respecting the territory or other property belonging to the United States; and nothing in this Constitution shall be so construed as to prejudice any claims of the United States, or of any particular State.

Section IV.   Protection to the States

United States guarantees to states representative government and protection against invasion and rebellion. The United States shall guarantee to every State in this Union a republican form of government, and shall protect each of them against invasion; and on application of the legislature, or of the executive [governor] (when the legislature cannot be convened), against domestic violence.

See Cleveland and the Pullman strike, pp. 343–344.

Article V.   The Process of Amendment

The Constitution may be amended in four ways. The Congress, whenever two-thirds of both houses shall deem it necessary, shall propose amendments to this Constitution, or, on the

---

[1] E.g., a marriage valid in one is valid in all.

[2] Invalidated in 1865 by the 13 Amendment (see text of Amendments following).

[3] Loyal West Virginia was formed by Lincoln in 1862 from seceded Virginia. This act was of dubious constitutionality and was justified in part by the wartime powers of the President. See pp. 249–250.

application of the legislatures of two-thirds of the several States, shall call a convention for proposing amendments, which, in either case, shall be valid to all intents and purposes, as part of this Constitution, when ratified by the legislatures of three-fourths of the several States, or by conventions in three-fourths thereof, as the one or the other mode of ratification may be proposed by the Congress; provided *that no amendments which may be made prior to the year one thousand eight hundred and eight shall in any manner affect the first and fourth clauses in the ninth section of the first article,* [1] and that no State, without its consent, shall be deprived of its equal suffrage in the Senate.

Article VI.   General Provisions

This pledge honored by Hamilton, pp. 93–94.

1. The debts of the Confederation are taken over. All debts contracted and engagements entered into, before the adoption of this Constitution, shall be as valid against the United States under this Constitution, as under the Confederation.

2. The Constitution, federal laws, and treaties are the supreme law of the land. This Constitution, and the laws of the United States which shall be made in pursuance thereof; and all treaties made, or which shall be made, under the authority of the United States, shall be the supreme law of the land; and the judges in every State shall be bound thereby, anything in the Constitution or laws of any State to the contrary notwithstanding.

3. Federal and state officers bound by oath to support the Constitution. The Senators and Representatives before mentioned, and the members of the several State legislatures, and all executive and judicial officers, both of the United States and of the several States, shall be bound by oath or affirmation to support this Constitution; but no religious test shall ever be required as a qualification to any office or public trust under the United States.

Article VII.   Ratification of the Constitution

See 1787 irregularity, p. 85.

The Constitution effective when ratified by conventions in nine states. The ratification of the conventions of nine States shall be sufficient for the establishment of this Constitution between the States so ratifying the same.

Done in Convention by the unanimous consent of the States present, the seventeenth day of September in the year of our Lord one thousand seven hundred and eighty-seven and of the Independence of the United States of America the twelfth. In witness whereof we have hereunto subscribed our names.

[Signed by]

G° WASHINGTON
Presidt and Deputy from Virginia
[and thirty-eight others]

AMENDMENTS TO THE CONSTITUTION

Amendment I.   Religious and Political Freedom

For background of Bill of Rights, see p. 92.

Congress must not interfere with freedom of religion, speech or press, assembly, and petition. Congress shall make no law respecting an establishment of religion,[2] or prohibiting the free exercise thereof; or abridging the freedom of speech, or of the press; or the right of the people peaceably to assemble, and to petition the government for a redress of grievances.

---

[1] This clause, re slave trade and direct taxes, became inoperative in 1808.
[2] In 1787 "an establishment of religion" referred to an "established church," or one supported by all taxpayers, whether members or not. But the courts have often acted under this article to keep religion, including prayers, out of the public schools.

Amendment II.   ## Right to Bear Arms

The people may bear arms. A well-regulated militia being necessary to the security of a free State, the right of the people to keep and bear arms [i.e., for military purposes] shall not be infringed.[1]

Amendment III.   ## Quartering of Troops

See Declaration of Independence and British quartering above.

Soldiers may not be arbitrarily quartered on the people. No soldier shall, in time of peace, be quartered in any house without the consent of the owner, nor in time of war, but in a manner to be prescribed by law.

Amendment IV.   ## Searches and Seizures

A reflection of colonial grievances against Crown.

Unreasonable searches are forbidden. The right of the people to be secure in their persons, houses, papers, and effects, against unreasonable searches and seizures, shall not be violated, and no [search] warrants shall issue but upon probable cause, supported by oath or affirmation, and particularly describing the place to be searched, and the persons or things to be seized.

Amendment V.   ## Right to Life, Liberty, and Property

When witnesses refuse to answer questions in court, they routinely "take the Fifth Amendment."

The individual is guaranteed certain rights when on trial and the right to life, liberty, and property. No person shall be held to answer for a capital, or otherwise infamous crime, unless on a presentment [formal charge] or indictment of a grand jury, except in cases arising in the land or naval forces, or in the militia, when in actual service in time of war or public danger; nor shall any person be subject for the same offense to be twice put in jeopardy of life or limb; nor shall be compelled in any criminal case to be a witness against himself, nor be deprived of life, liberty, or property, without due process of law; nor shall private property be taken for public use [i.e., by eminent domain] without just compensation.

Amendment VI.   ## Protection in Criminal Trials

See Declaration of Independence above.

An accused person has important rights. In all criminal prosecutions, the accused shall enjoy the right to a speedy and public trial, by an impartial jury of the State and district wherein the crime shall have been committed, which district shall have been previously ascertained by law, and to be informed of the nature and cause of the accusation; to be confronted with the witnesses against him; to have compulsory process [subpoena] for obtaining witnesses in his favor, and to have the assistance of counsel for his defense.

Amendment VII.   ## Suits at Common Law

The rules of common law are recognized. In suits at common law, where the value in controversy shall exceed twenty dollars, the right of trial by jury shall be preserved, and no fact tried by a jury shall be otherwise re-examined in any court of the United States, than according to the rules of the common law.

Amendment VIII.   ## Bail and Punishments

Excessive fines and unusual punishments are forbidden. Excessive bail shall not be required, nor excessive fines imposed, nor cruel and unusual punishments inflicted.

---

[1] The courts, with "militia" in mind, have consistently held that the "right" to bear arms is a limited one.

Amendment IX.

Amendments IX and X were bulwarks of Southern states' rights before the Civil War.

Concerning Rights Not Enumerated

The people retain rights not here enumerated. The enumeration in the Constitution, of certain rights, shall not be construed to deny or disparage others retained by the people.

Amendment X.

A concession to states' rights, pp. 95–96.

Powers Reserved to the States and to the People

Powers not delegated to the federal government are reserved to the states and the people. The powers not delegated to the United States by the Constitution, nor prohibited by it to the States, are reserved to the States respectively, or to the people.

Amendment XI.

Suits against a State

The federal courts have no authority in suits by citizens against a state. The judicial power of the United States shall not be construed to extend to any suit in law or equity, commenced or prosecuted against one of the United States by citizens of another state, or by citizens or subjects of any foreign state. [Adopted 1798.]

Amendment XII.

Election of President and Vice-President

1. Changes in manner of electing President and Vice-President; procedure when no presidential candidate receives electoral majority. The electors shall meet in their respective States, and vote by ballot for President and Vice-President, one of whom, at least, shall not be an inhabitant of the same State with themselves; they shall name in their ballots the person voted for as President, and in distinct ballots the person voted for as Vice-President, and they shall make distinct lists of all persons voted for as President, and of all persons voted for as Vice-President, and of the number of votes for each, which lists they shall sign and certify, and transmit sealed to the seat of government of the United States, directed to the President of the Senate;—the President of the Senate shall, in the presence of the Senate and House of Representatives, open all the certificates and the votes shall then be counted;—the person having the greatest number of votes for President shall be the President, if such number be a majority of the whole number of electors appointed; and if no person have such majority, then from the persons having the highest numbers not exceeding three on the list of those voted for as President, the House of Representatives shall choose immediately, by ballot, the President. But in choosing the President, the votes shall be taken by States, the representation from each State having one vote; a quorum for this purpose shall consist of a member or members from two-thirds of the States, and a majority of all the States shall be necessary to a choice. And if the House of Representatives shall not choose a President whenever the right of choice shall devolve upon them, before *the fourth day of March*[1] next following, then the Vice-President shall act as President, as in the case of death or other constitutional disability of the President.

Forestalls repetition of 1800 electoral dispute, pp. 106–107.

See 1876 disputed election, pp. 289–290.

See 1824 election, pp. 146–147.

2. Procedure when no vice-presidential candidate receives electoral majority. The person having the greatest number of votes as Vice-President shall be the Vice-President, if such number be a majority of the whole number of electors appointed; and if no person have a majority, then from the two highest numbers on the list the Senate shall choose the Vice-President; a quorum for the purpose shall consist of two-thirds of the whole number of Senators, and a majority of the whole number shall be necessary to a choice. But no person constitutionally ineligible to the office of President shall be eligible to that of Vice-President of the United States. [Adopted 1804.]

---

[1] Changed to January 20 by the 20th Amendment (see text of Amendment following).

Amendment XIII.   Slavery Prohibited

For background, see pp. 255–256.

Slavery forbidden. 1. Neither slavery[1] nor involuntary servitude, except as a punishment for crime whereof the party shall have been duly convicted, shall exist within the United States, or any place subject to their jurisdiction.

2. Congress shall have power to enforce this article by appropriate legislation. [Adopted 1865.]

Amendment XIV.   Civil Rights for Ex-slaves,[2] etc.

For background, see pp. 274–278.

For corporations as "persons," see p. 309.

Abolishes three-fifths rule for slaves, Art.I, Sec. II, para. 3.

1. Ex-slaves made citizens; U.S. citizenship primary. All persons born or naturalized in the United States, and subject to the jurisdiction thereof, are citizens of the United States and of the State wherein they reside. No State shall make or enforce any law which shall abridge the privileges or immunities of citizens of the United States; nor shall any State deprive any person of life, liberty, or property, without due process of law; nor deny to any person within its jurisdiction the equal protection of the laws.

2. When a state denies citizens the vote, its representation shall be reduced. Representatives shall be apportioned among the several States according to their respective numbers, counting the whole number of persons in each State, excluding Indians not taxed. But when the right to vote at any election for the choice of Electors for President and Vice-President of the United States, Representatives in Congress, the executive and judicial officers of a State, or the members of the legislature thereof, is denied to any of the male inhabitants of such State, being twenty-one years of age and citizens of the United States, or in any way abridged, except for participation in rebellion, or other crime, the basis of representation therein shall be reduced in the proportion which the number of such male citizens shall bear to the whole number of male citizens twenty-one years of age in such State.

Leading ex-Confederates denied office. See p. 278.

3. Certain persons who have been in rebellion are ineligible for federal and state office. No person shall be a Senator or Representative in Congress, or Elector of President and Vice-President, or hold any office, civil or military, under the United States, or under any State, who, having previously taken an oath, as a member of Congress, or as an officer of the United States, or as a member of any State legislature, or as an executive or judicial officer of any State, to support the Constitution of the United States, shall have engaged in insurrection or rebellion against the same, or given aid or comfort to the enemies thereof. But Congress may, by a vote of two-thirds of each house, remove such disability.

The ex-Confederates were thus forced to repudiate their debts and pay pensions to their own veterans, plus taxes for the pensions of Union veterans, their conquerors.

4. Debts incurred in aid of rebellion are void. The validity of the public debt of the United States, authorized by law, including debts incurred for payment of pensions and bounties for services in suppressing insurrection or rebellion, shall not be questioned. But neither the United States nor any State shall assume or pay any debt or obligation incurred in aid of insurrection or rebellion against the United States, or any claim for the loss or emancipation of any slave; but all such debts, obligations, and claims shall be held illegal and void.

5. Enforcement. The Congress shall have power to enforce, by appropriate legislation, the provisions of this article. [Adopted 1868.]

Amendment XV.   Suffrage for Blacks

For background, see pp. 274–278.

Black males are made voters. 1. The right of citizens of the United States to vote shall not be denied or abridged by the United States or by any State on account of race, color, or previous condition of servitude.

---

[1] The only explicit mention of slavery in the Constitution.
[2] Occasionally an offender is prosecuted under the 13th Amendment for keeping an employee or other person under conditions approximating slavery.

2. The Congress shall have power to enforce this article by appropriate legislation. [Adopted 1870.]

Amendment XVI.   Income Taxes

Congress has power to lay and collect income taxes. The Congress shall have power to lay and collect taxes on incomes, from whatever source derived, without apportionment among the several States, and without regard to any census or enumeration. [Adopted 1913.]

Amendment XVII.   Direct Election of Senators

Senators shall be elected by popular vote. 1. The Senate of the United States shall be composed of two Senators from each State, elected by the people thereof, for six years; and each Senator shall have one vote. The electors in each State shall have the qualifications requisite for electors of [votors for] the most numerous branch of the State legislatures.

2. When vacancies happen in the representation of any State in the Senate, the executive authority of such State shall issue writs of election to fill such vacancies: Provided, that the Legislature of any State may empower the executive thereof to make temporary appointments until the people fill the vacancies by election as the Legislature may direct.

3. This amendment shall not be so construed as to affect the election or term of any Senator chosen before it becomes valid as part of the Constitution. [Adopted 1913.]

Amendment XVIII.   National Prohibition

For background, see p. 406.

The sale or manufacture of intoxicating liquors is forbidden. 1. *After one year from the ratification of this article the manufacture, sale, or transportation of intoxicating liquors within, the importation thereof into, or the exportation thereof from the United States and all territory subject to the jurisdiction thereof, for beverage purposes, is hereby prohibited.*

2. *The Congress and the several States shall have concurrent power to enforce this article by appropriate legislation.*

3. *This article shall be inoperative unless it shall have been ratified as an amendment to the Constitution by the legislatures of the several States, as provided by the Constitution, within seven years from the date of the submission thereof to the States by the Congress.* [Adopted 1919; repealed 1933 by 21st Amendment.]

Amendment XIX.   Woman Suffrage

For background, see pp. 207, 328–329, 369, 392.

Women guaranteed the right to vote. 1. The right of citizens of the United States to vote shall not be denied or abridged by the United States or by any State on account of sex.

2. The Congress shall have power to enforce this article by appropriate legislation. [Adopted 1920.]

Amendment XX.   Presidential and Congressional Terms

Shortens lame-duck periods by modifying Art. I, Sec. IV, para. 2.

1. Presidential, vice-presidential, and congressional terms of office begin in January. The terms of the President and Vice-President shall end at noon on the 20th day of January, and the terms of Senators and Representatives at noon on the 3d day of January, of the years in which such terms would have ended if this article had not been ratified; and the terms of their successors shall then begin.

2. New meeting date for Congress. The Congress shall assemble at least once in every year, and such meeting shall begin at noon on the 3d day of January, unless they shall by law appoint a different day.

3. Emergency presidential and vice-presidential succession. If, at the time fixed for the beginning of the term of the President, the President-elect shall have died, the Vice-President elect shall become President. If a President shall not have been chosen before the time fixed for the beginning of his term, or if the President-elect shall have failed to qualify, then the Vice-President-elect shall act as President until a President shall have qualified; and the Congress may by law provide for the case wherein neither a President-elect nor a Vice-President-elect shall have qualified, declaring who shall then act as President, or the manner in which one who is to act shall be selected, and such persons shall act accordingly until a President or Vice-President shall have qualified.

4. The Congress may by law provide for the case of the death of any of the persons from whom the House of Representatives may choose a President whenever the right of choice shall have devolved upon them, and for the case of the death of any of the persons from whom the Senate may choose a Vice-President whenever the right of choice shall have devolved upon them.

5. Sections 1 and 2 shall take effect on the 15th day of October following the ratification of this article.

6. This article shall be inoperative unless it shall have been ratified as an amendment to the Constitution by the Legislatures of three-fourths of the several States within seven years from the date of its submission. [Adopted 1933.]

Amendment XXI.   Prohibition Repealed

For background, see p. 436.

1. 18th Amendment repealed. The eighteenth article of amendment to the Constitution of the United States is hereby repealed.

2. Local laws honored. The transportation or importation into any State, Territory, or Possession of the United States for delivery or use therein of intoxicating liquors, in violation of the laws thereof, is hereby prohibited.

3. This article shall be inoperative unless it shall have been ratified as an amendment to the Constitution by conventions in the several States, as provided in the Constitution, within seven years from the date of the submission thereof to the States by the Congress. [Adopted 1933.]

Amendment XXII.   Anti-Third Term Amendment

Sometimes referred to as the anti-Franklin Roosevelt amendment.

Presidential term is limited. 1. No person shall be elected to the office of President more than twice, and no person who has held the office of President, or acted as president, for more than two years of a term to which some other person was elected President shall be elected to the office of President more than once. But this article shall not apply to any person holding the office of President when this article was proposed by the Congress [i.e., Truman], and shall not prevent any person who may be holding the office of President, or acting as President, during the term within which this article becomes operative [i.e., Truman] from holding the office of President or acting as President during the remainder of such term.

2. This article shall be inoperative unless it shall have been ratified as an amendment to the Constitution by the legislatures of three-fourths of the several States within seven years from the date of its submission to the States by the congress. [Adopted 1951.]

Amendment XXIII.   District of Columbia Vote

Designed to give the District of Columbia three electoral votes and to quiet the century-old cry of "No taxation without

1. Presidential Electors for the District of Columbia. The District constituting the seat of Government of the United States shall appoint in such manner as the Congress may direct:

A number of electors of President and Vice-President equal to the whole number of Senators and Representatives in Congress to which the District would be entitled if it were a State, but in no event more than the least populous State; they shall be in addition to those appointed by *representation." Yet the District of Columbia still has only one non-voting member of Congress.*

the States, but they shall be considered for the purposes of the election of President and Vice-President, to be electors appointed by a State; and they shall meet in the District and perform such duties as provided by the twelfth article of amendment.

2. Enforcement. The Congress shall have the power to enforce this article by appropriate legislation. [Adopted 1961.]

Amendment XXIV. Poll Tax

Designed to end discrimination against blacks and other poor folk. An aspect of the civil rights crusade under President Lyndon Johnson.
See p. 501.

1. Payment of poll tax or other taxes not to be prerequisite for voting in federal elections. The right of citizens of the United States to vote in any primary or other election for President or Vice-President, for electors for President or Vice-President, or for Senator or Representative in Congress, shall not be denied or abridged by the United States or any State by reason of failure to pay any poll tax or other tax.

2. Enforcement. The Congress shall have the power to enforce this article by appropriate legislation. [Adopted 1964.]

Amendment XXV. Presidential Succession and Disability[1] (1967)

1. Vice-President to become President. In case of the removal of the President from office or of his death or resignation, the Vice-President shall become President.[2]

2. Successor to Vice-President provided. Whenever there is a vacancy in the office of the Vice-President, the President shall nominate a Vice-President who shall take office upon confirmation by a majority vote of both Houses of Congress.

Gerald Ford was the first "appointed President."
See pp. 512, 515.

3. Vice-president to serve for disabled President. Whenever the President transmits to the President pro tempore of the Senate and the Speaker of the House of Representatives his written declaration that he is unable to discharge the powers and duties of his office, and until he transmits to them a written declaration to the contrary, such powers and duties shall be discharged by the Vice-President as Acting President.

4. Procedure for disqualifying or requalifying President. Whenever the Vice-President and a majority of either the principal officers of the executive departments or of such other body as Congress may by law provide, transmit to the President pro tempore of the Senate and the Speaker of the House of Representatives their written declaration that the President is unable to discharge the powers and duties of his office, the Vice-President shall immediately assume the powers and duties of the office as Acting President.

Thereafter, when the President transmits to the President pro tempore of the Senate and the Speaker of the House of Representatives his written declaration that no inability exists, he shall resume the powers and duties of his office unless the Vice-President and a majority of either the principal officers of the executive department [s]or of such other body as Congress may by law provide, transmit within four days to the President pro tempore of the Senate and the Speaker of the House of Representatives their written declaration that the President is unable to discharge the powers and duties of his office. Thereupon Congress shall decide the issue, assembling within forty-eight hours for that purpose if not in session. If the Congress, within twenty-one days after receipt of the latter written declaration, or, if Congress is not in session, within twenty-one days after Congress is required to assemble, determines by two-thirds vote

---

[1] Passed by a two-thirds vote of both Houses of Congress in July 1965; ratified by the requisite three-fourths of the state legislatures, February 1967, or well within the seven-year limit.

[2] The original Constitution (Art. II, Sec. I, para. 5) was vague on this point, stipulating that "the powers and duties" of the President, but not necessarily the title, should "devolve" on the Vice-President. President Tyler, the first "accidental President," assumed not only the powers and duties but the title as well.

of both Houses that the President is unable to discharge the powers and duties of his office, the Vice-President shall continue to discharge the same as Acting President; otherwise, the President shall resume the powers and duties of his office.

Amendment XXVI.   Lowering Voting Age (1971)

A response to the current revolt of youth; see p. 509.

1. Ballot for eighteen-year-olds. The right of citizens of the United States, who are eighteen years of age or older, to vote shall not be denied or abridged by the United States or by any State on account of age.

2. Enforcement. The Congress shall have power to enforce this article by appropriate legislation.

An American Profile:
The United States and Its People

Growth of U.S. Population and Area

Census	Population of United States	Increase over the Preceding Census		Land Area (Sq. Mi.)	Pop. per Sq. Mi.
		Number	Percent		
1790	3,929,214			867,980	4.5
1800	5,308,483	1,379,269	35.1	867,980	6.1
1810	7,239,881	1,931,398	36.4	1,685,865	4.3
1820	9,638,453	2,398,472	33.1	1,753,588	5.5
1830	12,866,020	3,227,567	33.5	1,753,588	7.3
1840	17,069,453	4,203,433	32.7	1,753,588	9.7
1850	23,191,876	6,122,423	35.9	2,944,337	7.9
1860	31,433,321	8,251,445	35.6	2,973,965	10.6
1870	39,818,449	8,375,128	26.6	2,973,965	13.4
1880	50,155,783	10,337,334	26.0	2,973,965	16.9
1890	62,947,714	12,791,931	25.5	2,973,965	21.2
1900	75,994,575	13,046,861	20.7	2,974,159	25.6
1910	91,972,266	15,997,691	21.0	2,973,890	30.9
1920	105,710,620	13,738,354	14.9	2,973,776	35.5
1930	122,775,046	17,064,426	16.1	2,977,128	41.2
1940	131,669,275	8,894,229	7.2	2,977,128	44.2
1950	150,697,361	19,028,086	14.5	2,974,726*	50.7
1960†	179,323,175	28,625,814	19.0	3,540,911	50.6
1970	203,235,298	23,912,123	13.3	3,536,855	57.5
1980	226,504,825	23,269,527	11.4	3,536,855	64.0
1985	239,000,000 (est.)				

*As remeasured in 1940; shrinkage offset by increase in water area.
†First year for which figures include Alaska and Hawaii.
Source: Census Bureau, *Historical Statistics of the United States,* updated by relevant *Statistical Abstract of the United States.*

Characteristics of the U.S. Population

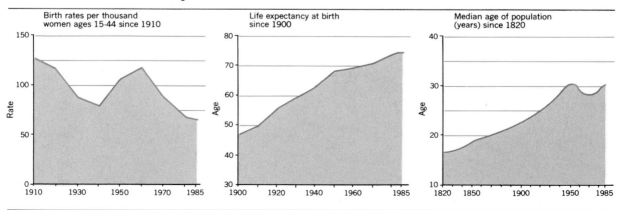

Sources: *Historical Statistics of the United States* and *Statistical Abstract of the United States,* relevant years. Department of Health and Human Services, *Health, United States, 1985.*

Changing Lifestyles in the Twentieth Century

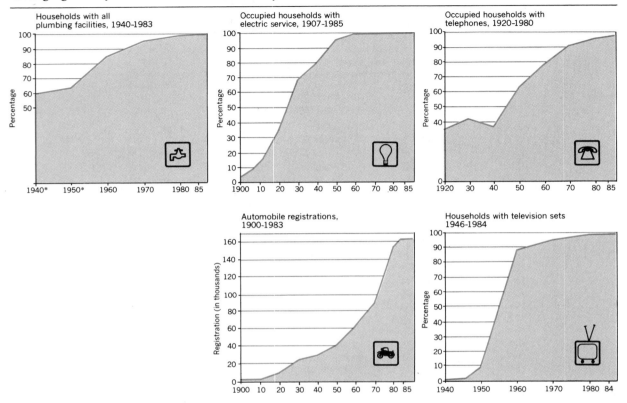

*Except for 1940 and 1950, figures are for "all plumbing facilities" (not defined in source). For 1940, figure is for flush toilet, inside structure, private use (64.7 percent had flush toilet, and private and/or shared inside structure, and 60.9 percent had installed bath or shower). For 1950, figure designates units with private toilet and bath, and hot running water (flush toilet, private or shared inside structure is 74.3 percent; installed bathtub or shower, 72.9 percent).
Sources: *Historical Statistics of the United States* and *Statistical Abstract of the United States,* relevant years.

Characteristics of the U.S. Labor Force

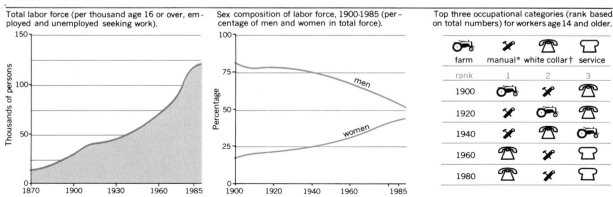

*Manual workers = operators, fabricators, and laborers plus precision production, craft, and repair.
†White collar workers = managerial and professional plus technical, sales, and administrative support.
Sources: *Historical Statistics of the United States* and *Statistical Abstract of the United States,* relevant years, and Department of Labor Statistics, *Handbook of Labor Statistics,* relevant years.

Leading Economic Sectors (Various Years)

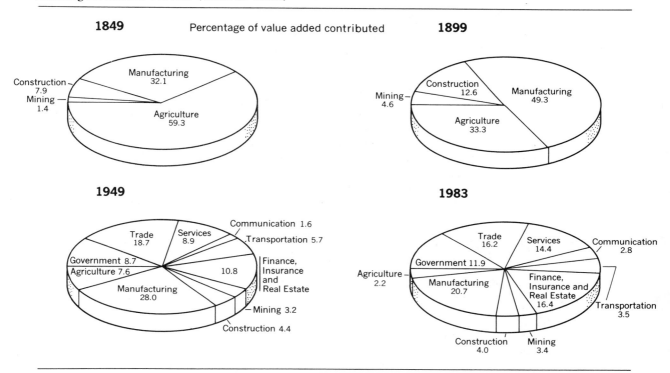

1849 Percentage of value added contributed **1899**

Construction 7.9
Mining 1.4
Manufacturing 32.1
Agriculture 59.3

Construction 12.6
Mining 4.6
Manufacturing 49.3
Agriculture 33.3

1949 **1983**

Communication 1.6
Trade 18.7
Services 8.9
Transportation 5.7
Government 8.7
Agriculture 7.6
Manufacturing 28.0
10.8
Finance, Insurance and Real Estate
Mining 3.2
Construction 4.4

Trade 16.2
Services 14.4
Communication 2.8
Government 11.9
Agriculture 2.2
Manufacturing 20.7
Finance, Insurance and Real Estate 16.4
Transportation 3.5
Construction 4.0
Mining 3.4

Sources: *Historical Statistics of the United States* and *Statistical Abstract of the United States,* relevant years.

Per-Capita Disposable Personal Income in Constant (1982) Dollars, 1929–1985

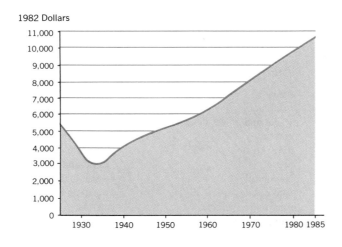

Sources: *Historical Statistics of the United States* and *Statistical Abstract of the United States.*

Value of Imports by Place of Origin (Millions of Dollars)

YEAR	WESTERN HEMISPHERE TOTAL	CANADA	EUROPE TOTAL	U.K.	ASIA TOTAL	JAPAN	AUSTRALIA AND OCEANIA	AFRICA
1900	224	39	441	160	146	33	29	11
1910	503	95	806	271	210	66	20	17
1920	2,424	612	1,228	514	1,397	415	80	150
1930	1,195	402	911	210	854	279	33	68
1940	1,089	424	390	155	981	158	35	131
1950	5,063	1,960	1,449	335	1,638	182	208	494
1960	6,864	2,901	4,268	993	2,721	1,149	266	534
1970	16,928	11,092	11,395	2,194	9,621	5,875	871	1,113
1980	78.687	41,459	48,039	9,842	80,299	30,714	3,392	34,410
1985	115,916	69,006	81,692	14,937	131,884	67,783	3,819	11,964

Value of U.S. Exports by Destination

YEAR	WESTERN HEMISPHERE TOTAL	CANADA	EUROPE TOTAL	U.K.	ASIA TOTAL	JAPAN	AUSTRALIA AND OCEANIA	AFRICA
1900	227	95	1,040	534	68	29	41	19
1910	479	216	1,136	506	78	22	34	19
1920	2,553	972	4,466	1,825	872	378	172	166
1930	1,357	659	1,838	678	448	165	108	92
1940	1,501	713	1,645	1,011	619	227	94	161
1950	4,902	2,039	3,306	548	1,539	418	151	376
1960	7,684	3,810	7,398	1,487	4,186	1,447	514	793
1970	15,612	9,079	14,817	2,536	10,027	4,652	1,189	1,580
1980	74,114	35,395	71,372	12,694	60,168	20,792	4,876	9,060
1985	78,271	47,251	59,978	11,273	60,745	22,631	6,399	7,388

Principal Exports, 1900–1985 (Leading Three Exports by Value in Dollars)

YEAR	FIRST	SECOND	THIRD
1900	cotton	wheat and wheat flour	meat products
1910	cotton	machinery	petroleum and products
1920	cotton	wheat and wheat flour	petroleum and products
1930	machinery	cotton	petroleum and products
1940	machinery	iron and steel mill products	petroleum and products
1950	machinery	cotton	automobiles*
1960	machinery	automobiles*	wheat and wheat flour
1970	machinery	automobiles*	wheat and wheat flour
1980	machinery	road motor vehicles*	metals and manufactures
1985	office machinery/automatic data processing	aircraft/space parts	electrical equipment

*includes parts

U.S. Foreign Trade, Ratio of Raw Materials to Manufactured Goods

YEAR	U.S. DOMESTIC EXPORTS		U.S. GENERAL IMPORTS	
	PERCENTAGE OF RAW MATERIALS	PERCENTAGE OF MANUFACTURED GOODS	PERCENTAGE OF RAW MATERIALS	PERCENTAGE OF MANUFACTURED GOODS
1900	41.3	58.7	44.7	55.3
1910	40.0	60.0	46.4	53.6
1920	34.7	65.3	44.8	55.2
1930	26.7	73.3	45.8	54.2
1940	13.7	86.3	51.0	49.0
1950	26.8	73.2	47.7	52.3
1960	21.8	78.2	31.4	68.6
1970	17.2	82.8	16.8	83.2
1980	28.3	71.7	44.8†	55.2
1983	27.4	72.6	32.3	67.7
1985‡	17.3	82.7	34.1	65.9

†includes manufactured food
‡petroleum accounts for 70.7 percent of raw material imports and 31.7 percent of total imports

Value of Exports and Imports and Status of the Balance of Trade

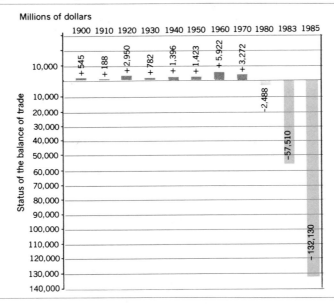

Sources for tables and graph: *Historical Statistics of the United States* and *Statistical Abstract of the United States,* relevant years.

Tariff Levies on Dutiable Imports, 1821–1985 (Ratio of Duties to Value of Dutiable Imports)

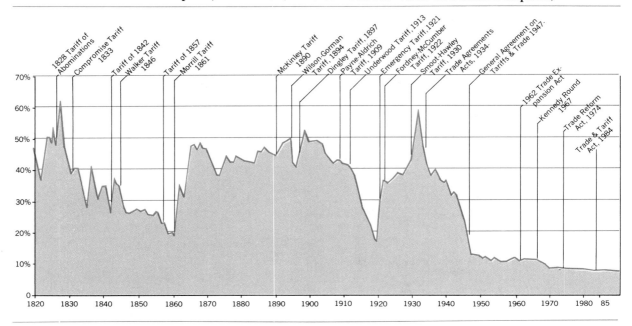

Sources: *Historical Statistics of the United States* and *Statistical Abstract of the United States,* relevant years.

Gross National Product in Current and Constant (1972) Dollars, 1900–1985

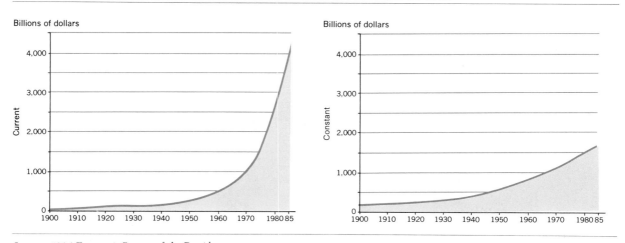

Source: *1986 Economic Report of the President.*

Presidential Elections*

Election	Candidates	Parties	Popular Vote	Electoral Vote
1789	GEORGE WASHINGTON	No party designations		69
	John Adams			34
	Minor Candidates			35
1792	GEORGE WASHINGTON	No party designations		132
	John Adams			77
	George Clinton			50
	Minor Candidates			5
1796	JOHN ADAMS	Federalist		71
	Thomas Jefferson	Democratic-Republican		68
	Thomas Pinckney	Federalist		59
	Aaron Burr	Democratic-Republican		30
	Minor Candidates			48
1800	THOMAS JEFFERSON	Democratic-Republican		73
	Aaron Burr	Democratic-Republican		73
	John Adams	Federalist		65
	Charles C. Pinckney	Federalist		64
	John Jay	Federalist		1
1804	THOMAS JEFFERSON	Democratic-Republican		162
	Charles C. Pinckney	Federalist		14
1808	JAMES MADISON	Democratic-Republican		122
	Charles C. Pinckney	Federalist		47
	George Clinton	Democratic-Republican		6
1812	JAMES MADISON	Democratic-Republican		128
	DeWitt Clinton	Federalist		89
1816	JAMES MONROE	Democratic-Republican		183
	Rufus King	Federalist		34
1820	JAMES MONROE	Democratic-Republican		231
	John Q. Adams	Independent Republican		1
1824	JOHN Q. ADAMS (Min.)[†]	Democratic-Republican	108,740	84
	Andrew Jackson	Democratic-Republican	153,544	99
	William H. Crawford	Democratic-Republican	46,618	41
	Henry Clay	Democratic-Republican	47,136	37
1828	ANDREW JACKSON	Democratic	647,286	178
	John Q. Adams	National Republican	508,064	83
1832	ANDREW JACKSON	Democratic	687,502	219
	Henry Clay	National Republican	530,189	49
	William Wirt	Anti-Masonic ⎱	33,108	7
	John Floyd	National Republican ⎰		11
1836	MARTIN VAN BUREN	Democrat	762,678	170
	William H. Harrison	Whig ⎫		73
	Hugh L. White	Whig ⎬	736,656	26
	Daniel Webster	Whig ⎪		14
	W. P. Mangum	Whig ⎭		11

*Candidates receiving less than 1 percent of the popular vote are omitted. Before the 12th Amendment (1804), the Electoral College voted for two presidential candidates, and the runner-up became Vice-President. Basic figures are taken primarily from *Historical Statistics of the United States, 1789–1945* (1949), pp. 288–290; *Historical Statistics of the United States, Colonial Times to 1957* (1960), pp. 682–683; and *Statistical Abstract of the United States, 1969* (1969), pp. 355–357.

[†] "Min." indicates minority President—one receiving less than 50 percent of all popular votes.

Presidential Elections* (Continued)

Election	Candidates	Parties	Popular Vote	Electoral Vote
1840	WILLIAM H. HARRISON	Whig	1,275,016	234
	Martin Van Buren	Democratic	1,129,102	60
1844	JAMES K. POLK (Min.)†	Democratic	1,337,243	170
	Henry Clay	Whig	1,299,062	105
	James G. Birney	Liberty	62,300	
1848	ZACHARY TAYLOR	Whig	1,360,099	163
	Lewis Cass	Democratic	1,220,544	127
	Martin Van Buren	Free Soil	291,263	
1852	FRANKLIN PIERCE	Democratic	1,601,274	254
	Winfield Scott	Whig	1,386,580	42
	John P. Hale	Free Soil	155,825	
1856	JAMES BUCHANAN (Min.)*	Democratic	1,838,169	174
	John C. Fremont	Republican	1,341,264	114
	Millard Fillmore	American	874,534	8
1860	ABRAHAM LINCOLN (Min.)*	Republican	1,867,198	180
	Stephen A. Douglas	Democratic	1,379,434	12
	John C. Breckinridge	Democratic	854,248	72
	John Bell	Constitutional Union	591,658	39
1864	ABRAHAM LINCOLN	Union	2,213,665	212
	George B. McClellan	Democratic	1,802,237	21
1868	ULYSSES S. GRANT	Republican	3,012,833	214
	Horatio Seymour	Democratic	2,703,249	80
1872	ULYSSES S. GRANT	Republican	3,597,132	286
	Horace Greeley	Democratic and Liberal Republican	2,834,125	66
1876	RUTHERFORD B. HAYES (Min.)*	Republican	4,036,298	185
	Samuel J. Tilden	Democratic	4,300,590	184
1880	JAMES A. GARFIELD (Min.)*	Republican	4,454,416	214
	Winfield S. Hancock	Democratic	4,444,952	155
	James B. Weaver	Greenback-Labor	308,578	
1884	GROVER CLEVELAND (Min.)*	Democratic	4,874,986	219
	James G. Blaine	Republican	4,851,981	182
	Benjamin F. Butler	Greenback-Labor	175,370	
	John P. St. John	Prohibition	150,369	
1888	BENJAMIN HARRISON (Min.)*	Republican	5,439,853	233
	Grover Cleveland	Democratic	5,540,309	168
	Clinton B. Fisk	Prohibition	249.506	
	Anson J. Streeter	Union Labor	146,935	
1892	GROVER CLEVELAND (Min.)*	Democratic	5,556,918	277
	Benjamin Harrison	Republican	5,176,108	145
	James B. Weaver	People's	1,041,028	22
	John Bidwell	Prohibition	264,133	
1896	WILLIAM MC KINLEY	Republican	7,104,779	271
	William J. Bryan	Democratic	6,502,925	176
1900	WILLIAM MC KINLEY	Republican	7,207,923	292
	William J. Bryan	Democratic; Populist	6,358,133	155
	John C. Woolley	Prohibition	208,914	

*"Min." indicates minority President—one receiving less than 50 percent of all popular votes.

Presidential Elections* (Continued)

Election	Candidates	Parties	Popular Vote	Electoral Vote
1904	THEODORE ROOSEVELT	Republican	7,623,486	336
	Alton B. Parker	Democratic	5,077,911	140
	Eugene V. Debs	Socialist	402,283	
	Silas C. Swallow	Prohibition	258,536	
1908	WILLIAM H. TAFT	Republican	7,678,908	321
	William J. Bryan	Democratic	6,409,104	162
	Eugene V. Debs	Socialist	420,793	
	Eugene W. Chafin	Prohibition	253,840	
1912	WOODROW WILSON (Min.)*	Democratic	6,293,454	435
	Theodore Roosevelt	Progressive	4,119,538	88
	William H. Taft	Republican	3,484,980	8
	Eugene V. Debs	Socialist	900,672	
	Eugene W. Chafin	Prohibition	206,275	
1916	WOODROW WILSON (Min.)*	Democratic	9,129,606	277
	Charles E. Hughes	Republican	8,538,221	254
	A. L. Benson	Socialist	585,113	
	J. F. Hanley	Prohibition	220,506	
1920	WARREN G. HARDING	Republican	16,152,200	404
	James M. Cox	Democratic	9,147,353	127
	Eugene V. Debs	Socialist	919,799	
	P. P. Christensen	Farmer-Labor	265,411	
1924	CALVIN COOLIDGE	Republican	15,725,016	382
	John W. Davis	Democratic	8,386,503	136
	Robert M. La Follette	Progressive	4,822,856	13
1928	HERBERT C. HOOVER	Republican	21,391,381	444
	Alfred E. Smith	Democratic	15,016,443	87
1932	FRANKLIN D. ROOSEVELT	Democratic	22,821,857	472
	Herbert C. Hoover	Republican	15,761,841	59
	Norman Thomas	Socialist	881,951	
1936	FRANKLIN D. ROOSEVELT	Democratic	27,751,597	523
	Alfred M. Landon	Republican	16,679,583	8
	William Lemke	Union, etc.	882,479	
1940	FRANKLIN D. ROOSEVELT	Democratic	27,244,160	449
	Wendell L. Willkie	Republican	22,305,198	82
1944	FRANKLIN D. ROOSEVELT	Democratic	25,602,504	432
	Thomas E. Dewey	Republican	22,006,285	99
1948	HARRY S TRUMAN (Min.)*	Democratic	24,105,812	303
	Thomas E. Dewey	Republican	21,970,065	189
	J. Strom Thurmond	States' Rights Democratic	1,169,063	39
	Henry A. Wallace	Progressive	1,157,172	
1952	DWIGHT D. EISENHOWER	Republican	33,936,234	442
	Adlai E. Stevenson	Democratic	27,314,992	89
1956	DWIGHT D. EISENHOWER	Republican	35,590,472	457
	Adlai E. Stevenson	Democratic	26,022,752	73
1960	JOHN F. KENNEDY (Min.)*	Democratic	34,226,731	303
	Richard M. Nixon	Republican	34,108,157	219

* "Min." indicates minority President—one receiving less than 50 percent of all popular votes.

Presidential Elections* (Continued)

Election	Candidates	Parties	Popular Vote	Electoral Vote
1964	LYNDON B. JOHNSON	Democratic	43,129,484	486
	Barry M. Goldwater	Republican	27,178,188	52
1968	RICHARD M. NIXON (Min.)*	Republican	31,785,480	301
	Hubert H. Humphrey, Jr.	Democratic	31,275,166	191
	George C. Wallace	American Independent	9,906,473	46
1972	RICHARD M. NIXON	Republican	45,767,218	520
	George S. McGovern	Democratic	28,357,688	17
1976	JIMMY CARTER	Democratic	40,828,657	297
	Gerald R. Ford	Republican	39,145,520	240
1980	RONALD W. REAGAN	Republican	43,201,220	489
	Jimmy Carter	Democratic	34,913,332	49
	John B. Anderson	Independent	5,581,379	0
1984	RONALD W. REAGAN	Republican	52,609,797	525
	Walter Mondale	Democratic	36,450,613	13

*"Min." indicates minority President—one receiving less than 50 percent of all popular votes.

Presidents and Elected Vice-Presidents

Term	President	Vice-President
1789–1793	George Washington	John Adams
1793–1797	George Washington	John Adams
1797–1801	John Adams	Thomas Jefferson
1801–1805	Thomas Jefferson	Aaron Burr
1805–1809	Thomas Jefferson	George Clinton
1809–1813	James Madison	George Clinton (d. 1812)
1813–1817	James Madison	Elbridge Gerry (d. 1814)
1817–1821	James Monroe	Daniel D. Tompkins
1821–1825	James Monroe	Daniel D. Tompkins
1825–1829	John Quincy Adams	John C. Calhoun
1829–1833	Andrew Jackson	John C. Calhoun (resigned 1832)
1833–1837	Andrew Jackson	Martin Van Buren
1837–1841	Martin Van Buren	Richard M. Johnson
1841–1845	William H. Harrison (d. 1841) John Tyler	John Tyler
1845–1849	James K. Polk	George M. Dallas
1849–1853	Zachary Taylor (d. 1850) Millard Fillmore	Millard Fillmore
1853–1857	Franklin Pierce	William R. D. King (d. 1853)
1857–1861	James Buchanan	John C. Breckinridge
1861–1865	Abraham Lincoln	Hannibal Hamlin
1865–1869	Abraham Lincoln (d. 1865) Andrew Johnson	Andrew Johnson

Presidents and Elected Vice-Presidents

Term	President	Vice-President
1869–1873	Ulysses S. Grant	Schuyler Colfax
1873–1877	Ulysses S. Grant	Henry Wilson (d. 1875)
1877–1881	Rutherford B. Hayes	William A. Wheeler
1881–1885	James A. Garfield (d. 1881) Chester A. Arthur	Chester A. Arthur
1885–1889	Grover Cleveland	Thomas A. Hendricks (d. 1885)
1889–1893	Benjamin Harrison	Levi P. Morton
1893–1897	Grover Cleveland	Adlai E. Stevenson
1897–1901	William McKinley	Garret A. Hobart (d. 1899)
1901–1905	William McKinley (d. 1901) Theodore Roosevelt	Theodore Roosevelt
1905–1909	Theodore Roosevelt	Charles W. Fairbanks
1909–1913	William H. Taft	James S. Sherman (d. 1912)
1913–1917	Woodrow Wilson	Thomas R. Marshall
1917–1921	Woodrow Wilson	Thomas R. Marshall
1921–1925	Warren G. Harding (d. 1923) Calvin Coolidge	Calvin Coolidge
1925–1929	Calvin Coolidge	Charles G. Dawes
1929–1933	Herbert C. Hoover	Charles Curtis
1933–1937	Franklin D. Roosevelt	John N. Garner
1937–1941	Franklin D. Roosevelt	John N. Garner
1941–1945	Franklin D. Roosevelt	Henry A. Wallace
1945–1949	Franklin D. Roosevelt (d. 1945) Harry S Truman	Harry S Truman
1949–1953	Harry S Truman	Alben W. Barkley
1953–1957	Dwight D. Eisenhower	Richard M. Nixon
1957–1961	Dwight D. Eisenhower	Richard M. Nixon
1961–1965	John F. Kennedy (d. 1963) Lyndon B. Johnson	Lyndon B. Johnson
1965–1969	Lyndon B. Johnson	Hubert H. Humphrey, Jr.
1969–1973	Richard M. Nixon	Spiro T. Agnew
1973–1977	Richard M. Nixon (resigned 1974) Gerald R. Ford	Spiro T. Agnew; Gerald R. Ford Nelson Rockefeller
1977–1981	Jimmy Carter	Walter F. Mondale
1981–1985	Ronald Reagan	George Bush
1985–1989	Ronald Reagan	George Bush

Ratification of the Constitution   Admission of States to the Union

State	Date	Order of Admission	State	Date of Admission	Order of Admission	State	Date of Admission
1. Delaware	Dec. 7, 1787	14	Vermont	March 4, 1791	33	Oregon	Feb. 14, 1859
2. Pennsylvania	Dec. 12, 1787	15	Kentucky	June 1, 1792	34	Kansas	Jan. 29, 1861
3. New Jersey	Dec. 18, 1787	16	Tennessee	June 1, 1796	35	West Virginia	June 20, 1863
4. Georgia	Jan. 2, 1788	17	Ohio	March 1, 1803	36	Nevada	Oct. 31, 1864
5. Connecticut	Jan. 9, 1788	18	Louisiana	April 30, 1812	37	Nebraska	March 1, 1867
6. Massachusetts	Feb. 7, 1788	19	Indiana	Dec. 11, 1816	38	Colorado	Aug. 1, 1876
(incl. Maine)		20	Mississippi	Dec. 10, 1817	39	North Dakota	Nov. 2, 1889
7. Maryland	Apr. 28, 1788	21	Illinois	Dec. 3, 1818	40	South Dakota	Nov. 2, 1889
8. South Carolina	May 23, 1788	22	Alabama	Dec. 14, 1819	41	Montana	Nov. 8, 1889
9. New Hampshire	June 21, 1788	23	Maine	March 15, 1820	42	Washington	Nov. 11, 1889
10. Virginia	June 26, 1788	24	Missouri	Aug. 10, 1821	43	Idaho	July 3, 1890
11. New York	July 26, 1788	25	Arkansas	June 15, 1836	44	Wyoming	July 10, 1890
12. North Carolina	Nov. 21, 1789	26	Michigan	Jan. 26, 1837	45	Utah	Jan. 4, 1896
13. Rhode Island	May 29, 1790	27	Florida	March 3, 1845	46	Oklahoma	Nov. 16, 1907
		28	Texas	Dec. 29, 1845	47	New Mexico	Jan. 6, 1912
		29	Iowa	Dec. 28, 1846	48	Arizona	Feb. 14, 1912
		30	Wisconsin	May 29, 1848	49	Alaska	Jan. 3, 1959
		31	California	Sept. 9, 1850	50	Hawaii	Aug. 21, 1959
		32	Minnesota	May 11, 1858			

Estimates of Total Costs and Number of Battle Deaths of Major U.S. Wars*

	TOTAL COSTS	ORIGINAL COSTS	NUMBER OF BATTLE DEATHS
	(MILLIONS OF DOLLARS)		
Vietnam Conflict	352,000	140,600	47,318†
Korean Conflict	164,000	54,000	33,629
World War II	664,000	288,000	291,557
World War I	112,000	26,000	53,402
Spanish-American War	6,460	400	385
Civil War { Union only	12,952	3,200	140,414
Civil War { Confederacy (est.)	N.A.	1,000	94,000
Mexican War	147	73	1,733
War of 1812	158	93	2,260
American Revolution	190	100	6,824

*Deaths from disease and other causes are not shown. In earlier wars especially, owing to poor medical and sanitary practices, non-battle deaths substantially exceeded combat casualties.
†1959–1983
Sources: *Historical Statistics of the United States, Statistical Abstract of the United States,* relevant years, and *The World Almanac and Book of Facts, 1986.*

INDEX